Leonardo on Art and the Artist

Leonardo da Vinci

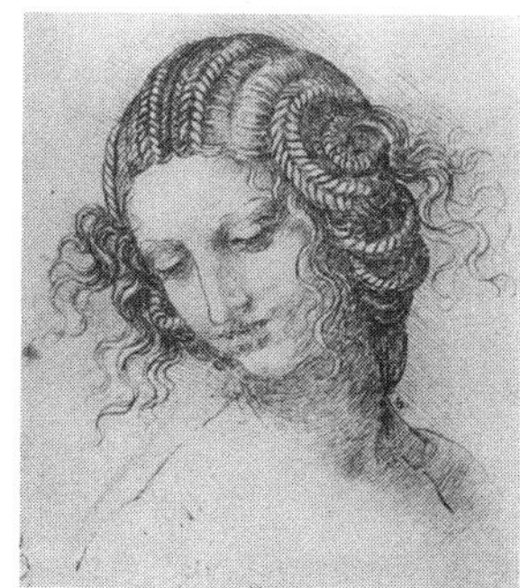

DOVER PUBLICATIONS, INC.
Mineola, New York

Bibliographical Note

This Dover edition, first published in 2002, is an unabridged republication of the text and illustrations from the work originally published in English translation in 1961 by The Orion Press, Inc., New York, under the title *The Genius of Leonardo da Vinci*. The original publication of the work in French was under the title *Traité de la peinture, Leonard de Vinci,* by Club des Libraires de France, Paris, in 1960. The material was assembled, edited, and introduced by André Chastel. For the 1961 Orion Press edition, the text was translated from the French by Ellen Callmann. Plates that appeared in color in the earlier editions are reproduced in black and white in the 2002 edition.

Library of Congress Cataloging-in-Publication Data

Leonardo, da Vinci, 1452–1519.
[Trattato della pittura. English]
Leonardo on art and the artist / Leonardo da Vinci.
p. cm.
Translated from French version of Trattato della pittura.
Originally published as: The genius of Leonardo da Vinci. New York : Orion Press, 1961.
Includes bibliographical references.
ISBN 0-486-42166-X (pbk.)
1. Painting—Technique—Early works to 1800. 2. Drawing—Technique—Early works to 1800. I. Title.

ND1471 .L4613 2002b
709'.2—dc21

2002019776

Manufactured in the United States of America
Dover Publications, Inc., 31 East 2nd Street, Mineola, N.Y. 11501

Contents

Introduction

Leonardo da Vinci and his writings on painting

Leonardo stands preeminent, and in more than one respect. Different pictures emerge when we consider what is known of him as a person, what has been preserved of his writings, and what remains of his work. It is this diversity that prompts us to search for the underlying unity of his activities, and this search has given rise to the myth that now surrounds the name of Leonardo. This myth, with its overtones of mystery and its Freudian implications, is perhaps, or has been until now, nothing but a desperate attempt to give an all too subtle and elusive artist and man the coherence and consistency usually found only in the heroes of fiction. As a rule we are not obliged to go to such lengths with Renaissance men. They stand out sharply and unequivocally against their background. Leonardo's contemporaries, Mantegna, Botticelli, Giovanni Bellini, to mention the most outstanding, or even Francesco di Giorgio and Bramante, are well-defined personalities, each one, cut, as it were, out of a single piece of cloth. Not one of them gives us the ambiguous impression that Leonardo does — and, it seems, already did to some of his contemporaries — as soon as one tries to pinpoint fundamental questions, eluding all attempts at classification.

It is surprising how few pictures he painted, particularly after his fortieth year, and this has been remarked on ever since the sixteenth century. Equally surprising is how soon and how assiduously his works were copied, so that one has the feeling that whatever he did produce was observed and made use of with disturbing persistence. The naïveté of the myth, which made him a high priest who was something of a necromancer, a sage who could satisfy every expectation, and a technician who could perform any feat, whether it was in hydraulics or military machines, is actually less remarkable than the servility and veneration which obviously surrounded him and which assured his every whim as well as his major discoveries the same applause nowadays accorded to the least act of Matisse or Picasso. And that, too, is unusual.

One would think that artists of a reflective turn of mind, aware of the problems of art, would not approach Leonardo with impunity. In Florence itself, he had two imitators or, to put it less crudely, two disciples who battened on his motifs, ideas, and suggestions : Lorenzo di Credi, the devotee of glossy, slick forms, always anxious to achieve a high finish, whom Leonardo was one day to repudiate, and Piero di Cosimo, who took from Leonardo a freedom in his activities that he pushed to the point of eccentricity, a taste for the fantastic in nature, and the idea of "inventive vision." Like Rubens and El Greco, Leonardo left his mark in that later painters took up new problems and discovered new facets of their craft. But that was not all. He initiated new deviations, pretenses, fixations, which leads one to think that, like Gauguin or even André Masson, he influenced through tension, disquiet, questioning, and criticism, in short, through intellectual and nervous stimulation as much as through his work. It was no doubt for this reason that, when he came to Rome in 1513, at the ripe age of sixty, to reap the fruits of fame, it became impossible for him to remain in a city ruled by Leo X and dominated by men more willing to please or more impressive : the heroes of the hour, Raphael, Bramante, and Michelangelo.

The individual, the theorizer, and the painter are so close one to another that they almost merge, particularly if one takes into consideration how much of what Leonardo has left us consists of literary works ; these give the impression of an immense circle within which this agile and demanding mind seemed to feel he had to enclose his art. In other words, the "hero" and his activities become intelligible if one thinks in terms of equating painting and philosophy, and regards this equation as an advance, not the equivalent or substitute of, or, worse, the conclusion of the philosophical system in its traditional sense. If we can also relate this painting-philosophy to the modern concept of painting-poetry, Leonardo will probably lose some of the false grandeur and mystery that until now have surrounded him. This work attempts to clarify several, in themselves simple aspects of this relationship by tracing it from the artist's behavior to the idea of "objective" painting, and by connecting its spell to a specific attitude toward nature and culture.

What one generally admires and instinctively respects in Leonardo is an unusual quality of independence in his actions. Within the framework of patronage conditioning the lives of the artists of the period, Leonardo chose his patrons on the basis of the opportunities they afforded him to develop his own ideas. His very presence brought out demands which, in turn, created tasks he could consider more or less interesting — decorations for feasts, costumes, the arrangements of gardens and pavillions, etc. — and which satisfied his needs. Having protected himself from the demands of clients by keeping them awed with new and original ideas, he kept to himself and, as may be seen from the notebooks, had his own way of seeing things.

His behavior was both self-assured and original. Cardinal Pietro Bembo, the advisor of Isabella d'Este, who was to order a painting for her, noted in 1501 that Leonardo lived from day to day. His behavior was unpredictable. Surely there was merit in achieving this state of freedom and forcing princes and leading men to accept it at a time when the standing of the painter was no better than that of any other craftsman. Obedience to orders and subservience to custom rather than an aloof and independent attitude were the order of the day. Hardly anyone but Leonardo could have rid himself politely of an "abusive" patron like Isabella d'Este. Giovanni Bellini could only get out of it by being ill, Perugino, Costa, and others remained under her thumb and produced their poorest works on this occasion. Nonetheless, the fifteenth century was a time when strong personalities counted. They had some freedom of movement and Leonardo merely carried to an extreme a proud and at times insolent manner that other Florentine artists also manifested.

What is unique in Leonardo is his way of perceiving and of expanding the artist's scope as if being an artist demanded a special way of life. Delacroix defended himself by distance and disdain, Cézanne by retreat and solitude; Leonardo's method is at once more tortuous and more picturesque. Like the retiarius with his net, Leonardo overwhelms and beguiles; he beats his opponent at his own game. To the snobs and the worldly he gives his elegance, his fine manners, the games he invents, and the beautiful young men who surround him; to the intellectuals, the doctrines he discusses, and the omnipresent challenge of his superior intellect; to soldiers, his "secrets" of the art of warfare; to churchmen, his "philosophy" of the world and his analysis of customs; and to the world at large, the wonder of his paintings. Indeed, he surrounds painting with much peripheral activity, and this is what gives him his fascination. His independent behavior may appeal to us because it makes him seem a rebel, but is this really the basis of his actions? His independent behavior aims sooner at creating an atmosphere that has much in common with feasts and pageantry, for the great game of painting — far from being the result of cold and morbid preoccupation — is the culmination of a constant need for spectacle, for brilliance, and for the marvelous.

Significant in this respect are the riddles that were meant to confuse the mind through twisting terms ; they were no doubt intended as an evening's entertainment of the court or of salons. Leonardo wrote down a whole collection of them, as for instance, "One may see the bones of the dead, by their quick movement, decide the fates of those who move them." What is meant? The throw of dice. One's first reaction is that such games are a waste of time or, at best, relaxation. However, one should ask oneself whether it is not a mental exercise that actually points up a whole way of life. This constant intrusion of jests and of disconcerting twists, even of farce in daily life, brings Leonardo closer than one would at first think to Picasso or even to Marcel Duchamp.

It has thus been shown that Leonardo was able to relate art to a certain way of life, and it matters little whether he could do so because of favorable circumstances at his disposal or despite others not available to him. Or better yet, he conceived of artistic creation as an act so complete, so diversified, so delightful, and one in which so many unexpected aspects of human experience participate that it cannot be isolated. All kinds of feelings, from the most bizarre to the most sensuous — fear, disgust, love, the sight of monsters, the thrill of danger — all are essential elements of this all-encompassing activity and not things that detract from it. Leonardo was so imbued with the idea that through concentration he could achieve an investigation that came close to being psychoanalytical. In his Treatise on Painting *there are lyrical passages, imaginative to the point of mythomania, in which the intimate connections between life and art are stated in the most intense terms. One of these is the famous passage dealing with the ambivalence of inner feelings when the artist, standing at the entrance of a dark cave and unable to see into it, peers and is torn by two emotions : fear and desire, fear of the dark and menacing cave, desire to see if it may not contain some extraordinary marvel.*

One of Leonardo's superiorities over his age, and in a way over ours, may be seen in the ease with which he conducted the "psychoanalysis" of the painter, exposing at various times hypocrisy, facileness, lazy shortcuts, passivity, and meanness. His most incisive notation can be considered the one in which he discusses the greatest fault of the painter, that of repeating the same type over and over again, which, as he says, stems from the unconscious' subjective attachment to the body it inhabits, that is, a narcissistic tendency. These subjective "screens" through which the painter views the world and which are without interest, must be removed as well as everything else that makes the perception rigid and causes inertia in art. The removal of these impediments, which are triteness itself, is a fundamental operation. The Treatise is full of suggestions of this type, dealing with everyting from asceticism to hygiene. The originality of Leonardo's position, in which painting is conceived as a total art, results in a new objectivity achieved by the interaction of speculation and experience ; this raises the work of art to a level freed of foolish encumbrances. Through this constant internal debate (and we will have to come back to its consequences later), the artist gradually is able to heighten his sensibilities, not in order to become effusive, which is always vulgar, but to express basic and significant truths vividly. Leonardo most certainly avoided effusiveness and, like other restrained artists from Poussin to Matisse, thought of it as the offscourings of subjective mediocrity. Thus, the internal debate, bound to the practice of painting, may and even should assume unprecedented scope. However, it is possible that the excessive intellectualizing called for by Leonardo's theory of painting resulted in concerns which seem to have little to do with painting and which, in the end, may hold back the painter and even paralyze him completely.

Unfortunately, Leonardo, having discovered all these ideas, did not have at his disposal any philosophical framework within which to use them and thus found himself in an even more exposed and unsupported position than did Van Gogh or Cézanne. For most of his life Leonardo found himself caught in a dilemma : Painting requires as much thought as though it were a purely intellectual activity, but this thought must culminate in an act that axiomatically is more significant than the thoughts that preceded it. Inversely, the act of painting, that long, contemplative operation, takes its meaning from the thought that gives it direction and informs it. Leonardo states this basic situation, this constitutional paradox, in the most modern terms : "The science of painting resides in the mind that conceived it, from which is born the execution that is much more noble than the said theory or science." Naturally, Leonardo included under this heading, reflection, science, and theory, a whole list of specific disciplines and not the vague musings of the artist. He probably did not assign the "pure act of painting" the value it is given today. But in the long run it is as if through the breadth of his vision Leonardo had given us at least in general terms a definition that is not far from modern concepts.

Of as great interest to us today is Leonardo's concept of the "visible," through which he makes of the visual arts, especially painting, the best tools for exploring and apprehending the universe. It has been stated elsewhere — and the commentaries to the various sections of this book will go into greater detail — what the circumstances were that made it possible during the Renaissance to formulate this fundamental concept of vision which is at times something like the optics of universal reality. It is as far removed from the conceptual and architectonic universe of medieval scholasticism as it is from the universe of classical science deduced from mathematical postulates. Leonardo was not the first to have this idea ; it was central to the thought of the times, although fraught with contradictions and difficulties, but he applied it in a way current philosophical thought did not anticipate. Because he was preeminently a man of what one might call the life of the workshops, Leonardo was the only one who at this time could give concrete meaning to speculative themes. In this way he destroyed its balance and finally the whole system. Everything appears to be different when one takes literally the whole complex of metaphors, definitions, and concepts contained in contemporary philosophy, filled as it was with images whose implications were not perceived. Whenever the key notion of light enters into the discussion, Leonardo is able to develop a whole phenomenology : because his approach is that of a painter, he can absorb the most contradictory ideas. In comparison, the theologian seems to do little more than to manipulate words and the physicist to measure things that the painter experiences in all their effects — recording them, as well — with the advantage of being able to grasp all the parts, top and bottom, beginning and end, simultaneously.

Light is at the same time the object of vision and the means by which we see : it constitutes the object of vision because it intervenes in the structure and outer appearances of things and transmits them. It fills empty space and brings the object to the eye. It elaborates the object. It is as indispensible to the container as to the thing contained. It is the exterior and the interior. As such it is to the philosopher the definition of the mind and to Leonardo that of painting, for Leonardo, pushing the metaphoric definition of the mental act as far as possible, probably identifies " plastic realization" with intellectual perception. However, he also remembered that the luminous principle of space and things acts in two ways which philosophers had paid little attention to : according to the invisible structure of space, revealed by mathematics, but also revealed by the painted representation, and according to the unlimited conflicts of the negative principle of shadow and the expansion of light which is left to painting to investigate and perhaps to magnify.

Here we are at the core of the difficulties inherent in Renaissance thought and art. But thanks to Leonardo's insights the tangle of preoccupations that in the twentieth century were basic to at least the two divergent schools of Cubism and Surrealism can easily be perceived. The full development of the former had to take into account one of Leonardo's leading intuitions, one that is expressed in the Treatise. The universe of phenomena is arranged in facets, in extremely mobile and elusive elements that circulate at mad speeds in networks of luminous rays forming pyramids with innumerable intersections. According to the text of the first statement of doctrine in a manuscript of 1490 (our entry no. 105), " Any opaque body will fill the surrounding air with an infinite number of images representing it completely everywhere and at each point by virtue of the infinite numbers of pyramids filling this air. Each pyramid, formed by long rays, encloses an infinite number of pyramids and each one contains all of them in its power and all each . . ." Hence, we can see how a mind practiced in paradox — such as the definition of the throw of the dice — can apply this mental agility to the vision of a most active and most "diabolically possessed" space. This luminous spatial merry-go-round is regulated by the fact that the image detached from the object obeys a mathematical rule over which the painter has managed to get control. He finds himself in the position of control at the precise moment at which the intuition of spatial interaction would become untenable. In the work of art all these relations will be given concrete form by the lines formed by the intersection of two surfaces and the reflections inside the perspective network ; the painting is the totality of these roving images that are so numerous and entangled that all these much too rapid movements in the end result in a trembling but relatively stable image. Hence, when read today by someone whose concept of the universe is organized along altogether different lines, Leonardo's texts suggest a prismatic projection of these rays. And it was after having read the Treatise (in the poor translation published by Péladan in 1910) that Jacques Villon formed his concept of an articulated painting in refraction and disseminated it among the younger generation of artists.

It is no less remarkable that the work by Gleizes and Metzinger (Du Cubisme, *1912*), *meant to promote the seriousness and poetic dignity of Cubism, should base itself, at the decisive moment, on Leonardo's observation of the "totalizing" nature of vision : "The painting, only yielding itself slowly, always waits to be questioned as if it held back an infinity of answers for an infinity of questions. On this subject we shall let Leonardo da Vinci defend Cubism : '. . . we know well', says Leonardo, 'that sight, through rapid observation, discovers in one glance an infinity of forms ; nonetheless, it can only take in one thing at a time.' "*

One might interpret this agreement as one of those curious coincidences that are possible in different periods, no matter how far apart, through the play of cultural forces if there were not a second, equally explicit and equally significant example in quite another sphere : Max Ernst's remarks on Leonardo's statements on the value of stains on walls and the practice of daydreaming as a stimulus for setting in motion inspiration, the use of "frottages," and the rapid superposition of images of a highly emotional content :

"On August 10, 1925, an unbearable visual obsession made me discover the technical means that made possible a very broad application of this lesson of Leonardo's . . . It is a question of using uneven surfaces that have irresistibly attracted and held the painter's attention. In the same way my curiosity, was awakened and startled, and I came to examine indiscriminately all kinds of materials which happened to fall within my field of vision ; leaves and their veins, the unraveled edges of a piece of sacking, the brush work in a modern *painting, thread unwound from a bobbin, etc. My eyes then saw human heads, various animals, a battle that ended in a kiss, rocks, the sea and rain, earthquakes, the sphinx in her lair . . ." (Max Ernst, "Au-delà de la peinture,"* Cahiers d'Art, *1937).*

A wealth of new and fantastic motifs were thus added to the "inventions" listed by Leonardo with whose fantasies of battles, landscapes, and monstrous figures they agreed well. It should be shown in what context and at what point in his personal development Leonardo found the intervention of these "visions before natural stains" useful and the conclusions he drew from them — in a sense close to the superpositions of the surrealists — in the practice of the componimento inculto, *the informed sketch, to which they are directly related. Furthermore, this recipe appears where Leonardo's psychology and cosmology meet. The forms seem to palpitate according to subtle movements of light and shadow that respond to the disturbance and the inner throbbing of the soul as to the vitality intrinsic in nature.*

It is not only because he was toying with cultural effects that Max Ernst gave full recognition to Leonardo's role as intercessor. There is an interesting similarity between the two painters, not only in the exposition of the motifs and the analysis of the central processes in which one can see what Ernst owes to Leonardo, but also in the effects. The hallucinatory backgrounds of the Mona Lisa *and the* Virgin and Child with St. Anne, *the lunar ice fields that reach as far as the uninhabited plains have always been irresistible to poets. Indeed, one of the painters who derived directly from Leonardo, Piero di Cosimo, became the model of eccentric behavior and also displayed a fierce attachment to the fantastic both in his works and in what we know of him. Better yet, to give a contemporary example, a Jacques Villon, stimulated by the mathematical view of the cosmos, and a Max Ernst, by the imaginative suggestions, combined, suggest an intriguing result : Marcel Duchamp. His famous denunciations of Mona Lisa's smile and of esthetic convention appear as the counterpart of an attitude — more ambivalent than has been realized — toward the surprising chess game that is Leonardo's giant undertaking and an ability he had to catch the indefinite that modern artists may well envy.*

It may seem strange to find this "Orphic painting" and these surrealist "frottages" within the main line of development marked out by such classic artists as Correggio and Prud'hon. But even on the level of later periods, it must be noted that within an academic application that had become less and less serious, Leonardo's example was given sincere thought between 1880 and 1890 by two diametrically opposed and antagonistic groups : one was scientific, like Seurat to whom a definition of painting as cosa mentale *was the password to systematic research and led him to separate from painting the facts of a problem to be solved (according to Charles Henry, the relevant problem was the mathematics of sensations). The other group was comprised of symbolists, like Gustave Moreau who explored the "melting," the merging of distant views, the uncertain expressions, and the strange suggestiveness of Leonardo's work.*

There is, then, both in Leonardo's work and

in his Treatise, plenty of food for thought for contemporary, independent artists : thoughts that lend painting a more and more elevated intellectual flavor and that attempt to turn it into a bit of magic, a crystal ball or an elixir. But on the whole these two ideas are opposed to each other ; one can ask if it is not through a trick of perspective or by an agreement whose mechanics we cannot see (and therefore in a sense have little interest in and which may be almost accidental), that they are united in Leonardo. This is a serious suspicion and makes us fear, all things considered, that the favorable moments are likely to cancel each other out. In this respect it will be useful to read the Treatise on Painting *with an open mind and even more so, to read it in the reconstruction of its arrangement given here. A reasonably extensive perusal of Leonardo's themes will show how these two tendencies, the scientific and the irrational, coexist, imbuing and fortifying each other. The two concepts work in his mind like two equally necessary sides of the marvelous. This is explained by the relation of painting conceived in this way with nature (that is, its purpose with regard to the cosmos) and its relation with the culture (that is, its human values).*

Painting is the mirror of the universe. Leonardo went to considerable lengths to establish that painting alone is the adequate speculative interpreter of the universe that surrounds us, and there are traces of this in the Treatise. As has been summarily shown, the universe is both a structure and a mass of energy. The nature of its elements is such that the well-ordered image exactly catches the harmony of this structure and the pulsation of this energy. Hence the advent of a second nature — or a nature in the second stage — which completes the first. A painting is the only means of obtaining the basic collaboration of forms and to extract from them the final harmony. Painting reproduces the image of the world less than it "completes" the energies through a strict and systematic interception.

At what price this is possible to achieve is shown in detail in those sections of the Treatise that deal with the elements of cosmology, psychology, perspective, the science of colors, and, finally, the fabric of a vast apparatus for tracking down the phenomena and the senses through which they are perceived. But contrary to what Leonardo seems to hope, what at times he even states, the pictorial realization — composition, values, etc. — cannot be deduced purely from principles. The most moving passages, at least those most able to touch the modern mind familiar with these difficulties through recent crises in philosophy, are precisely those in which Leonardo, after having pushed the relativism which imposes itself on the analysis of phenomena as far as possible, no longer applies it. In these he decides to act as though there were a real color, a real shadow, in short, absolute forms — and painting is exactly the way to represent them.

On the other hand, Leonardo considered subject matter that was part of the common iconography, that is to say narrative scenes, landscapes, and portraits. It is advantageous to investigate them thoroughly in order to isolate in each the aspects of general value and, one might say, the suggestive connotations. In effect, the problem is to maintain against commonplace conventions and unconscious habits, the harmonious respiration through which the painting, as an entity, is in true union with the world. Here Leonardo proclaims significant contrasts, strict analysis of movements, and especially the relationship of the figure to the landscape as the elements that give greater resonance to the theme. Beginning with the Madonna of the Rocks, *the figures are inscribed in a pyramid and the universe radiates from it. The Treatise does not include all of Leonardo's working notes ; but it goes beyond such a catalogue. For example, the descriptions of natural catastrophes are written in a manner that is developed far beyond the needs of any definite project. But, as my commentaries emphasize, there are remarkable similarities between Leonardo's increasing pessimism, the evolution of his cosmology, the way his doctrines become flexible, the discovery of the informed sketch, the practice of the "unfinished," and the drawings of his last years ; to the same type belongs the withdrawal — and stalemate — in which his career ended, for it is supplementary and decisive proof of the close tie between form and the vision of the world.*

There can be no doubt that Leonardo found himself increasingly in a position of general controversy in regard to contemporary ideas ; this does not, however, mean, as has been assumed a little hastily, that he anticipated modern science, and even less that he preserved rare fragments of a lost knowledge : that of the Middle Ages. On the contrary, he is a man of his time : all his activities aim at preserving the way of life of the workshops, that is, the accumulation of knowledge from which the artist profited and which was his monopoly. However, he goes to the trouble of articulating these attitudes and does so by means of ideas generally borrowed from contemporary speculation which he changed to fit his own purposes when necessary. Out of this develops a point of view that is both observant and skeptical, that of an "inner emigré." It is not unreasonable to relate it to the one the independent painters of the nineteenth century had toward industrialization and positivism (though admittedly the positions are reversed) : an inability to adhere wholly to ideals which are necessary to one's position but which one changes to fit each occasion.

In fact, Leonardo made no effort to establish the painter's place within his culture and his time. He simply remains silent on all subjects that do not concern him directly, and it has been difficult to identify his references since he does not cite sources as he goes along. In practice, his "philosophy" is made up of two distinct traits : recourse to experience and affirmation of the principle of mathematics. These two complementary demands correspond to a need to find a tie between the ex-

treme concreteness that attracts the painter and the instrumental abstraction that he cannot do without, all the more so as the dignity of the visual arts was founded, during the Renaissance, on their ability to measure — the gift of Hermes according to Marsilio Ficino. But these two principles of Leonardo's contain a more precise value that distinguished them from the way the humanists used them even when dealing with the arts. The rule of mathematics is postulated as a means of systematizing the plethora of assumptions and of insuring universally measured calculations. It should be understood in a broad enough sense to permit one to treat as mathematical proofs observations of the flight of birds and laying of ghosts. As for experience, actually it is observation suitable to graphic statement. *To Leonardo, whoever does not draw, does not observe ; concept becomes scheme. The Treatise is filled with illustrations, as are all theoretical works of this type nowadays, but this is the first time it was done. Moreover, Leonardo did not rework a large number of his "discoveries" in the field of natural science. They consist of quick drawings which by their mere existence go beyond the nomenclature of the scholastics and sharpen observation. Leonardo actually stated this about anatomy, and whole pages of the manuscripts are filled with notes, scribbles, and quick sketches. They are "graphic thoughts" that are meant to make everything plain and only become confused when they overlap each other.*

None of this was in agreement with contemporary teaching and practice. One can only say that he simply thought he had rediscovered a method known in antiquity but lost through neglect and ignorance. He neither praised nor condemned the Ancients. Nor did he vaunt himself for being ignorant of their contributions and it is a mistake to think that Leonardo was proud of being thought a boor. What he was proud of was the construction of a viable organism capable of solving practical problems and assimilating useful assumptions from other fields if they related to painting : "The beauties simultaneously joined (by this) *give me so much pleasure by their divine proportions that I cannot see that there is any human work on earth that can give me more."*

Evidently, it was around 1490, when Leonardo was not yet forty years, that he determined to write the Treatise on Painting *he outlined in a manuscript in the Institut de France, Paris (BN 2038). From then on he never stopped collecting notes and observations and working out ideas that might have a place in the new work. Moreover, he knew the time was ripe for publishing this vast accumulation of texts and drawings and in his manuscripts stated his intention of doing so in the near future. It was never published, however, and soon it was too late ; Leonardo could no more overcome material difficulties than he could his own inner resistance. Nothing was published during his lifetime and in his last years he was as much plagued by unfinished work as ever.*

All of Leonardo's writings were inherited by Francesco Melzi (1491-1570), a Milanese gentleman who had become Leonardo's intimate during his second sojourn in Milan (1506-1513) and later accompanied him to Amboise. Melzi took all the notebooks and loose sheets to the family villa at Vaprio d'Adda near Milan where they could be freely consulted and copied. He must have meant to publish the most important parts himself for he had two scribes compile the body of material that later went under the title of Trattato della pittura. *Why this work, which was never completely finished, came into the hands of a Milanese painter, mentioned but not identified by Vasari, is not known. Nor is it known how it later came into the library of the Dukes of Urbino, from which it passed into the Vatican when the Duchy of Urbino was annexed by the Papal States in 1626, and where it is today (Codex Urbinas latinus 1270).*

*Melzi's death was a serious blow to the preservation of Leonardo's written works. His son Orazio began the dispersal of the papers, and the curious or learned could easily acquire them. The innumerable dealings are reported in detail by a Milanese, Ambrogio Mazzenta, in his memoirs published in 1631. Pompeo Leoni was one of the most shameless and active among those profiting from this situation and in 1590 owned as many as ten Leonardo manuscripts. Since Leonardo's drawings had acquired a market value, he cleverly constituted two collections and sold them. One, scientific, consisted of the largest sheets available, assembled without any order. This is the Codex Atlanticus which Arconati acquired about 1622 and presented to the Ambrosian Library in 1636 (see illustrations, page 28). The other consists of drawings of artistic interest and is made up of fragments cut out from the leaves of the Codex Atlanticus and mounted on new sheets of paper. This manuscript was once in the possession of the Earl of Arundel and is now in the collection at Windsor Castle. * Other portfolios were stolen, recovered, and lost again. The present strange dispersal of Leonardo's writings in English, French, and Italian collections is the result of more than half a century's negligence and cupidity following the death of Melzi. Until the nineteenth century the high level of Leonardo's scientific writings was forgotten except by a few astute individuals who had some contact, either direct or indirect, with the manuscripts.*

All knowledge of his ideas on painting, however, was not lost since the Treatise had come to light during the seventeenth century and had been published by Raphael Du Fresne in 1651 (in an edition based on manuscripts derived from the Codex Urbinas). The importance of the Treatise is twofold. Previous to the systematic publication of all known manuscripts at the end of the nineteenth century, it represented the only compilation of Leonardo's writings, as well as a remarkable selection. The Treatise also preserves a large number of passages that would otherwise have been lost since they do not appear in any of the manuscripts in Leonardo's own hand that have come down to us.

The Treatise's place in the corpus vincianum *must be examined with care.* As it is presented in the Codex Urbinas, it is incomplete in its compilation and mediocre in plan. That the arrangement was not final is amply proven by the number of blank pages, temporary notations, words scratched out, and rubrics inserted between paragraphs by the scribe but not followed in the classification of the material. The work had not advanced far enough for publication when Melzi died and his heirs dropped the project. This unsatisfactory stage is evident in every detail. Those reflections and notations that are in some way related to each other or deal with broadly similar subjects are grouped together. Nonetheless, the final groupings remain arbitrary and awkward, and merely present an unorganized mass of statements placed one after the other. To say the least, they vary considerably in their effectiveness and in the interest they arouse. The Treatise's greatest weakness lies in the fact that it gives no clear idea of the contents of the chapters and of the special books Leonardo had either intended to write or had actually drawn up. The following references indicate that he had had a systematic arrangement in mind : a notation on foam (McMahon, no. 525) refers to the fourth proposition ; another, on misty landscapes (McMahon, no. 966) to the thirty-second proposition of his book on perspective ; a note on shadows (McMahon, no. 109) refers to a third proposition but it is not known to which treatise it should be assigned. However, the compilers either could not find or were not able to keep to the author's system.* Indeed, at times, a note of despair escapes the discouraged scribe : to wit, in the margin of a passage on the expressiveness of hands and arms (McMahon, no. 396), he emphasizes that Leonardo often refers to themes which, in fact, he has not actually discussed. Another drawback of Melzi's Treatise is that passages are often placed side by side which were composed at very different periods of Leonardo's career. Thus Book III, which is on the movements of the human body, takes up questions of color and perspective in its later sections. Moreover, it includes fragments that can be dated between 1490 and 1500 by comparisons with extant original writings, as well as others dating 1502, 1505, and even 1513-1517. As a result passages are indiscriminately grouped together that are not on the same level and, being separated by many years, may revise or add to earlier formulations. There is no, and indeed could not be any internal chronology so that there is no chronological perspective and this is a serious fault since Leonardo's internal dialogue has been lost.**

As it stands, the plan of the Treatise is extremely awkward. It begins with the Paragone *or comparison of the arts ; he then studies the painter (II), considering his dominant qualities, questions on light, and rules of anatomy ; next come the books on movements (III) and on drapery (IV), followed by those on light and shadow (V), trees (VI), clouds (VII), and the horizon (VIII), that is, the landscape elements. As a result, the work's true orientation, its immediate aim, and its underlying goals are not clear.*

Understandably, many critics have hesitated in their judgment of the work. The Milanese theoretician, G. P. Lomazzo, who had a personal knowledge of a number of Leonardo's manuscripts, made good use of them in his Trattato dell' arte della pittura *(Milan, 1584). On the other hand, Federico Zuccari, who had had the use of a manuscript copy of the Codex Urbinas, expressed doubts on Leonardo's speculative investigations in his* Idea de' pittori, scultori e architetti *(Turin, 1607). He says that the work is "of little interest and mediocre substance, written backwards and illustrated, by a man of talent but too much of a sophist. His purely mathematical propositions deal with the movements and bending of figures as shown by perpendiculars, squares, and compasses. All this is very ingenious but pure fantasy and without profit or substance..." Actually this criticism is directed chiefly at Book III which deals with the* Trattato del moto actionale *(known from the Huygens Ms. in the Pierpont Morgan Library, New York, compiled about 1570). But the evident skepticism corresponds to an attitude already widespread by this time. Cassiano del Pozzo's fervent defense of the Codex Urbinas encountered severe objections. Félibien* (Entretiens, *vol. II, Paris, 1696) had written that Poussin (who had been entrusted with the illustrations for Cassiano del Pozzo's project), "did not think that one should publish this treatise by Leonardo, which, to tell the truth, is neither in order or well enough worked through."*

The Codex Urbinas, then, does not deserve respect either in its selections or in its arrangement, and at times not even in the actual passages. All its editors have felt a need to modify the order of the passages but on the whole they have preferred to retain the overall framework. This, however, is so vague that it can hardly introduce the reader to Leonardo's thought processes or to a knowledge of painting. Ludwig H. Heydenreich has recently presented a reconstruction of the ideal plan of the Treatise which is plausible and appropriate. Leonardo himself could only have considered it a considerable improvement over all earlier versions. Heydenreich suggests that the introductory book, or Paragone, *which was to establish the intellectual position of painting and its superiority over the other arts, would be followed by three main books : one on theory and two with practical advice. The theoretical book would have two parts : one on perspective in its three aspects, and the other on light and shadow. One of the books of practical advice would contain the chapters on drawing and on color, as well as the studies of the human figure. The other would be devoted to the representation of nature. Finally, in conclusion, one might assume a collection of personal and moral advice, the* Precetti, *which are among the more original of Leonardo's ideas. A study of this outline points up the weaknesses and gaps in Melzi's compi-*

lation. While the Paragone *is well represented, the principles of perspective are not ; the passages on drawing are inadequate and those on the human figure fragmentary.* On *the other hand, those on movement and on landscape are copious, as are the aphorisms of the* Precetti. *In trying to ascertain the scope and depth of Leonardo's undertaking one should not overlook Melzi's Treatise but one must not be bound by its structure or its selections.*

A systematic collation has shown that about a third of the passages in the Treatise appear in extant manuscripts by Leonardo. Their transcription is precise enough to permit a general acceptance of the passages collected in the Codex Urbinas, allowing of course for distortions and misunderstandings. * *How the Treatise is to be used is a problem. The situation is similar to the one confronting an editor of Pascal's Pensées.* * *He must take into consideration an old version with later changes and a separate plan for a large part of the entries. He cannot follow this anthology but he cannot ignore it either.*

In choosing the passages for this book it has been necessary to take a stand. The useful pages of Melzi's Treatise and all the fragments from the manuscripts, by now fully published, should be brought together. It is then possible to see the development, at times the reversals, and in any case the differences in Leonardo's ideas. The direct relationship between the text and drawings should be maintained ; this principle is often indicated in the Treatise, and without it the work is not intelligible, though editors have rarely followed it. * *Indeed, it is one of Leonardo's most original contributions. No attempt should be made to hide the fragmentary and interrupted state of the writings.*

It is still necessary to give the work a basic plan for that is as important as the material itself. The one that emerges is as follows :

1. *The* Paragone *: the position of painting in relation to other intellectual activities.*
2. *The Universal Program : the painter and reality.*
3. *The Problems of the Painter : theory and practice.*
4. *The Painter's Studio : rules and recipes.*
5. *The Painter's Activities : his life and personal dignity.*

This classification can be justified on two counts. The sections appear in an order that corresponds to the intellectual and emotional development of painting and at the same time constitutes an encyclopedia of tenets and specific points of interest to the painter. From the outset the painter is presented as the person who occupies the highest position in the intellectual life of his society. The possibilities inherent in the art and the resources of the craft are then analyzed in a manner that confirms this premise. The painter must be something of an ideal man who is the model of human dignity and is capable of the ethics and the sacrifices that are called for. Painting is complete knowledge, the exciting process of creation, and an exalted way of life.

In a book based on these ideas it is not neces-

sary to reproduce the whole of Melzi's Treatise and all the passages from the manuscripts that relate more or less closely to painting. Such an extensive publication would have to be the joint enterprise of historians and philologists working on a complete and critical edition of all the extant writings of Leonardo. We have not reached this point yet. * *This book is limited to the central theme of painting which is revealed in its full significance once unclear or misplaced passages no longer encumber it. Each fragment included is meant to correspond to a more or less important point that actively contributes to this great undertaking, an undertaking whose internal order and complex ramifications it has been our aim to restore. As a result it has become as interesting to note the precise position of each detail as to follow the more weighty development of the whole. Once again it must be emphasized how seriously Leonardo's theories have suffered through the loss of a number of sections, such as the chapter on composition that he announced several times, or the passages touching on the vital question of style. As far as possible, this gap has been filled by assembling related texts though in themselves they are obviously quite different from anything that would have been included in an actual Treatise. Nonetheless, they seemed indispensable to a full understanding of Leonardo. The chapter and section headings are meant to indicate the passages' positions within the whole. It has been my aim to substitute for the propounder of doctrines Leonardo never succeeded in becoming, the artist struggling with disproportionate ambitions, working his way through problems that his incredible intelligence gave rise to at each step.*

In closing, it should be said that the translation cannot hope to be perfect and, for reasons that would be easy but tedious to explain, is not always literal. Leonardo writes beautifully, alternately nervous and sinuous, direct and complex, cold and enthusiastic. Every effort has been made to preserve the alternating cadences, but the rhythms of Renaissance Italian are rich in paratactic phrases that could rarely be rendered. * *Leonardo's vocabulary is extensive and its sources varied. The elements taken from popular speech can only be fully grasped by a skilled philologist and the nuances are often lost in translation. Moreover the concepts themselves — and it is tempting to modernize them though great caution must be exercized — by their very unfamiliarity often give the style a flavor that thoroughly resists translation.*

André Chastel

Below is Leonardo's alphabet as established by Richter according to the letters and digits in the original manuscripts.

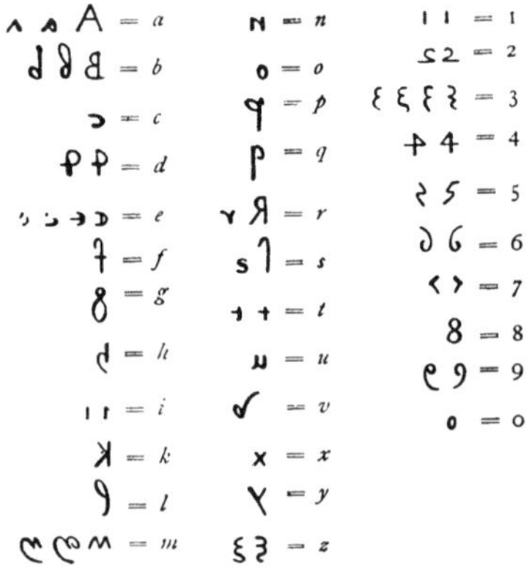

= *a*
= *b*
= *c*
= *d*
= *e*
= *f*
= *g*
= *h*
= *i*
= *k*
= *l*
= *m*

= *n*
= *o*
= *p*
= *q*
= *r*
= *s*
= *t*
= *u*
= *v*
= *x*
= *y*
= *z*

= 1
= 2
= 3
= 4
= 5
= 6
= 7
= 8
= 9
= 0

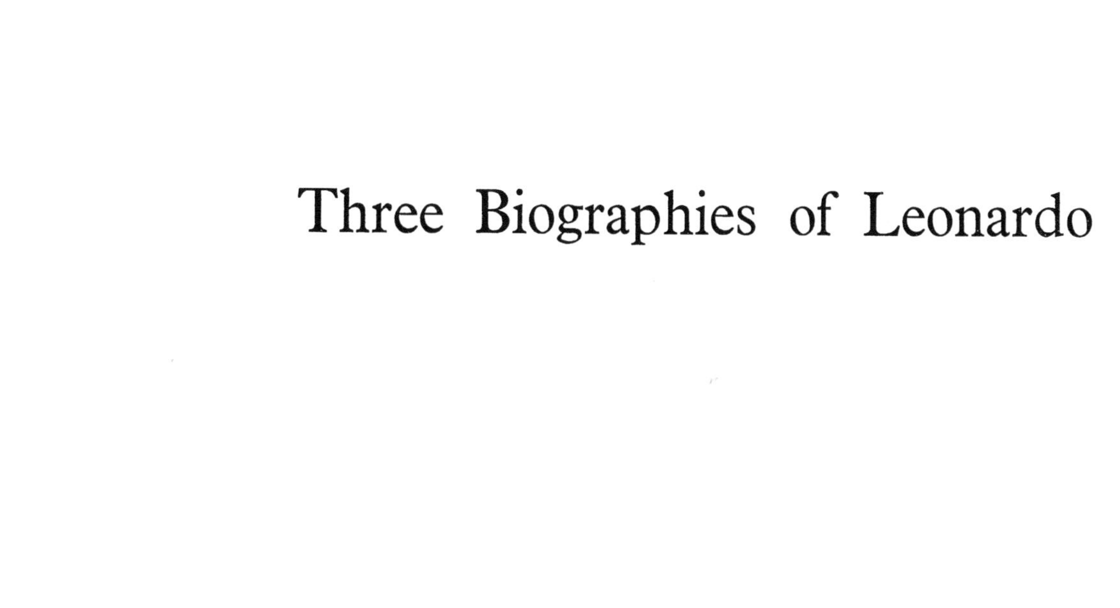

Three Biographies of Leonardo

Vasari's Life *of Leonardo da Vinci is one of that famous Florentine historian's finest biographies. First published in 1550 (the second edition of 1568 has important corrections and variations), it has by now achieved a position of authority and contrasts favorably with the innumerable romanticized biographies Leonardo's personality inspired during the last one hundred years. Nonetheless, it is worthwhile to consider two shorter texts in conjunction with it. One was written about 1527 by the humanist Paolo Giovio (1483-1552). The other is included in the lives of illustrious men compiled by the* so-called *Anonimo Gaddiano, an unidentified Tuscan who, despite some errors and a particularly confused chronology, does supply valuable additions to Leonardo's oeuvre. These three works, at times inexact and even contradictory, constitute the early record of the artist and as such it is well to keep them in mind.*

THE LIFE OF LEONARDO DA VINCI BY PAOLO GIOVIO*

Leonardo, born in the little Tuscan village of Vinci, added greatly to the glory of the art of painting for he established that this art could only be practiced successfully by those conversant with the sciences and the higher disciplines, which he considered its indispensable aids. He placed modeling before brush work as the order to follow in the development of a painting. According to him, nothing is of greater importance than the rules of optics for they permit him to distribute light and to utilize the laws of shade

Self-portrait detail. ▶

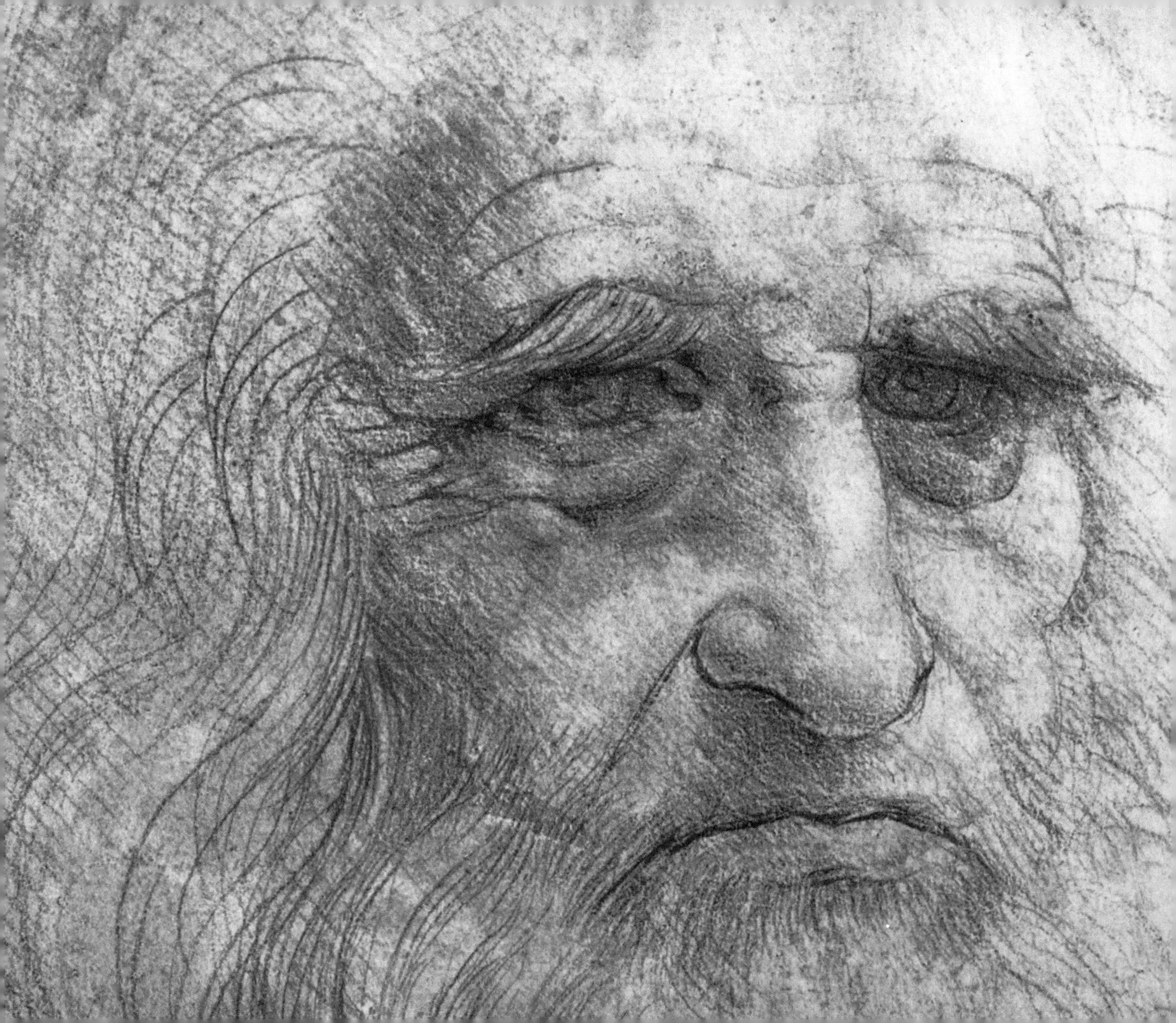

with great care down to the smallest detail. Furthermore, he learned to dissect the corpses of criminals in the schools of medicine, despite the inhuman and disgusting nature of this work, in order to paint the bending and stretching of the different members according to the action of the muscles and the natural articulation of the joints. That is why, with admirable care, he recorded the shapes of all the elements down to the smallest vein and the insides of the bones on metal so that by means of prints the product of many years' work should become known through innumerable copies for the benefit of art.

But while he spent his time in exploring the obscure regions of his art, his versatile mind and erratic temperament always held him back from final execution and he completed very few works.

However, in Milan there is an admirable fresco of the Last Supper of Christ and the Apostles. It is said that King Louis * so ardently desired to possess this work when he saw it that he pressed his entourage with questions asking whether it would not be possible to remove it by cutting the wall though this would destroy the famous refectory. There also exists a painting of the Christ Child playing with the Virgin Mother and Saint Anne bought by King Francis of France and placed in his chapel. Besides, in the Council Chamber of the Palazzo della Signoria in Florence one can also see a battle and victory over the Pisans. * It is of supreme excellence but unfortunately unfinished and because of a defective base resistant to colors prepared with walnut oil. One might say that the sorrow this unexpected damage quite naturally causes us adds to the attraction of this unfinished work. He also made a colossal horse in clay for Lodovico Sforza as a model for a bronze monument of his father, the illustrious *condottiere* Francesco. The horse's snorting and violent rearing are proof of his profound knowledge of both sculpture and the natural sciences.

His mind was of a delightful, brilliant, and generous cast, his face outstandingly pleasing ; since he was a marvelous inventor and judge of all sorts of amusements and distinguished pastimes, especially of pageants, as well as an expert singer who accompanied himself on the lyre, he was a favorite of the princes of his time. He departed this life in his sixty-seventh year, in France, mourned by his friends whose sorrow was increased by the fact that among the host of young men who brought such renown to his workshop, there was not one of true greatness.

LEONARDO DA VINCI BY THE ANONIMO GADDIANO *

Leonardo da Vinci, a citizen of Florence, the natural son of Ser Piero da Vinci, was of noble origins on his mother's side. He was so exceptional and so many-sided that one might say that nature produced a miracle in his birth. Not only did she endow him abundantly in the beauty of his person but also bestowed on him innumerable gifts that place him beyond compare. He had great ability in mathematics and perspective, practiced sculpture, and by far surpassed all others in drawing. He made many fine inventions but, because he was never satisfied with his own work, paintings in color by him are rare. He spoke most eloquently ; he played the lyre exceptionally well and taught this art to Atalante Migliorotti. He took great interest and pleasure in botany, he was gifted in matters of artillery, hydraulics, and other strange inventions ; nor did his mind ever rest but created new inventions with great ingenuity.

In his youth he was employed by Lorenzo de' Medici the Magnificent for whom he worked on the gardens of the square of San Marco in Florence. When he was thirty years of age, Lorenzo de' Medici the Magnificent sent him to present a lyre *(lira da braccio)* to the Duke of Milan, together with Atlante Migliorotti, because he played it exceptionally well. He then returned to Florence where he remained for a long time, but later, either from vexation or for some other reason, he left while working in the Council Chamber and returned to Milan where he remained for several years in the service of the Duke. He then entered the service of the Duke of Valentino* and finally went to several places in France. Back again in Milan, a revolutionary outbreak there while he was engaged in casting the equestrian statue forced him to return to Florence where he stayed for six months with the sculptor Francesco Rustici in the via de' Martelli. * Once again he went to Milan and then to France in the service of the king, François I, taking with him many drawings but leaving others in Florence at the Hospital of Santa Maria Nuova together with other things, also the greater part of the cartoon for the Council Chamber, of which the design of the group of horsemen that one can still see today remained in the Palace. He died at Amboise, in France, at the age of seventy-two, in a place called Cloux where he had settled. In his testament he left to Messer Francesco da Melzio, a Milanese nobleman, all his money, clothing, books and writings, drawings, instruments and projects useful for painting, and all his art and activities just as they were left and made him the executor of his will.

He left to Battista Villani, his servant, half his garden outside of Milan, and the other half to his pupil Salai. To his brothers he left four hundred ducats which he had on deposit at the Hospital of Santa Maria Nuova, but after his death only three hundred ducats were found.

He had several pupils while he was working in the Hall of the Palazzo della Signoria, among them Salai of Milan, Zoroastro of Peretola, Riccio Fiorentino, and the Spaniard, Ferrando.

He painted Ginevra d'Amerigho Benci from life and was so successful that it seemed not merely a portrait but Ginevra herself.

He made a panel of Our Lady that was altogether remarkable.

He also painted a St. John.

And also a water color of Adam and Eve, today in the house of Ottaviano de' Medici.

He painted Piero Francesco del Giocondo from life.

At . . . he painted a head of Medusa with astounding and bizarre knots of serpents, today in the chamber of the most Illustrious and Excellent Duke Cosimo.

For the fresco in the Council Chamber of the Palazzo in Florence he made the cartoon of the Florentines' victory at Anghiari over Niccolò Piccinino, captain of Duke Filippo of Milan. He began its execution at that place, where one may still see it today ; he used varnishes.

In the same palace he began work on a panel which was later finished according to his design by Filippino, the son of Fra Filippo.

He painted an altarpiece for the lord of Milan,Lodovico ; the connoisseurs who have seen it consider it one of the most beautiful and exceptional things ever painted. The aforementioned lord sent it to the Emperor of Germany.

He also painted a Last Supper at Milan, a most excellent work.

At Milan he also made an enormous horse, with the Duke Francesco Sforza on it ; a very beautiful work meant to be cast in bronze ; but every one considered this an impossibility, especially as he thought he could cast it in one piece. The work was never executed.

He made an infinite number of drawings, truly marvelous, among them a Madonna and St. Anne that was taken to France and plates of anatomical drawings in the Hospital of Santa Maria Nuova in Florence.

THE LIFE OF LEONARDO DA VINCI BY GIORGIO VASARI*

The greatest gifts are often seen, rained on human creatures by influences that seem celestial rather than natural ; and sometimes beauty, grace, and talent are united beyond measure in

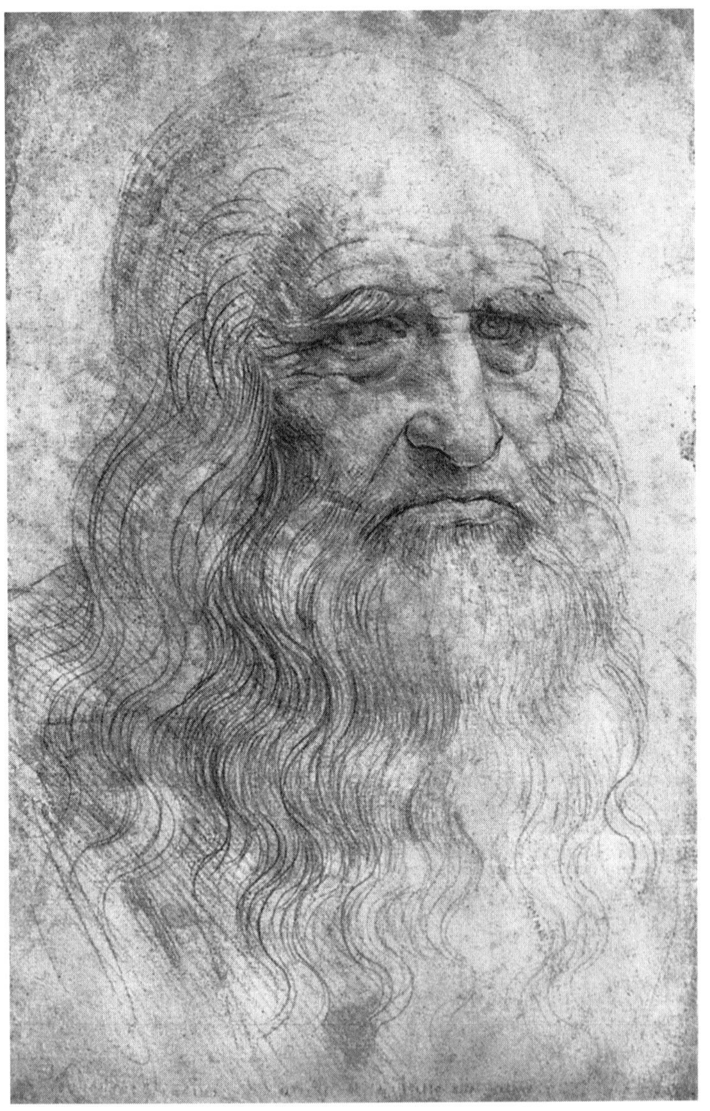

a single person, in such a manner that to whatever he turns his attention, his every action is so divine, that, surpassing all other men, it makes itself clearly known as a thing divine and not acquired by human endeavor. This was seen by all in Leonardo da Vinci. His beauty of body was beyond praise, he had infinite grace in all his actions, and so great and all-inclusive a talent, that to whatever difficulties he turned his mind, he solved them with ease. His great bodily strength was joined to dexterity, his spirit and courage ever princely and magnanimous. His fame so increased, that not only in his lifetime was he held in high esteem, but his reputation became even greater after his death.

Truly marvelous and celestial was Leonardo, the son of Ser Piero da Vinci ; and in learning and the study of letters he would have gone far if he had not been so variable and unstable, for he set himself to learn many things and, having once begun them, abandoned them. Thus, he studied arithmetic for a few months and made such progress that he often confounded the master who was teaching him by raising problems and difficulties. He also spent some time on music and quickly resolved to learn to play the lyre. By nature a lofty and refined spirit, he sang divinely while improvising. Despite such a variety of pursuits, he never ceased to draw and work in relief, for these appealed to his fancy more than anything else.

Having observed this, and having considered the loftiness of his son's intellect, Ser Piero one day took some of his drawings and carried them to Andrea del Verrocchio, who was much his friend, and besought him straightaway to tell him whether it would be worth Leonardo's while to devote himself to drawing. Andrea was astonished to see these extraordinary beginnings and urged Ser Piero to make Leonardo study.

◀ *Self-portrait.*

Ser Piero arranged with Leonardo that he should enter the workshop of Andrea, which Leonardo did with great willingness, practicing not one branch of art only, but all those in which drawing plays a part ; and having a divine and marvelous intellect and great ability as a geometrician, he not only worked in sculpture, making in his youth, some heads of smiling women and likewise heads of boys which seem to be from the hand of a master, but in architecture, also, he made many drawings both of architectural plans and elevations, and when still a youth, was the first to suggest that the waters of the Arno be used for a canal from Pisa to Florence. He made designs for flour mills, fulling machines, and engines which might be driven by the force of water. But his true vocation was painting. He practiced much in working from nature and at times made clay models over which he draped wet pieces of cloth dipped in clay, and then set himself patiently to drawing them on a certain kind of very fine Reims cloth or on squares of prepared linen. He achieved marvelous effects in black and white with the point of his brush, as certain drawings in my collection still bear witness. Besides, he drew on paper with such care and perfection that no one could ever in any way improve on these subtle works. I have one of these, a head drawn with silver point in chiaroscuro, of divine quality.

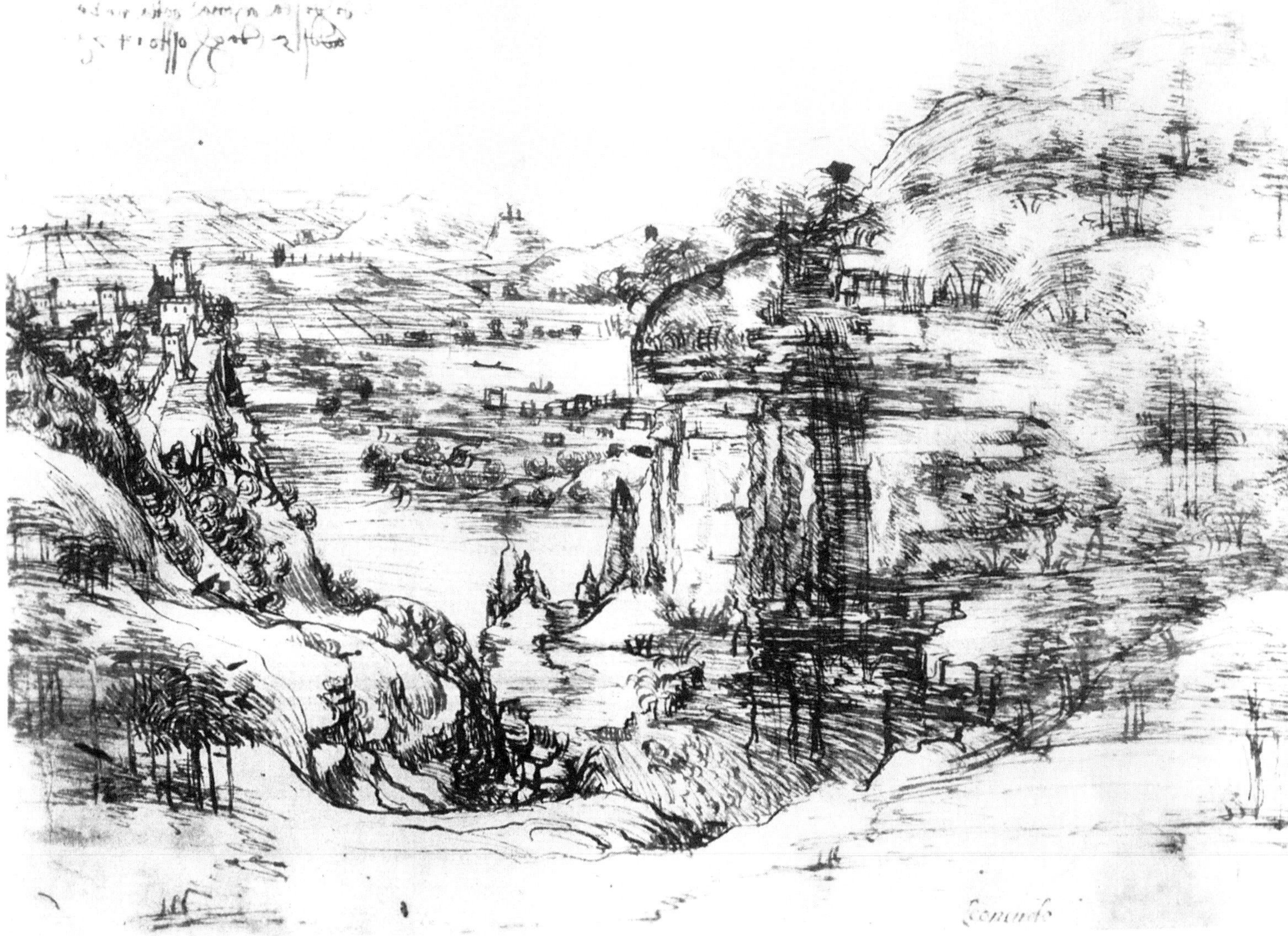

◀ *View of the Arno Valley,* Leonardo's first dated work, August 5, 1473.

And that mind, adorned by God with such graces, possessed such imperious powers of precise reasoning, served by intelligence and memory, that by means of drawing, his hands could render his thoughts, so that he vanquished with his discourse, and confuted with his reasoning the most capable minds. He was continually making models and designs to remove mountains with ease, to bore a passage through them in order to pass from one plain to another, to raise great weights by means of levers, windlasses, and screws, together with methods for emptying harbors, and pumps to bring up water. His brain never ceased from devising subtle ideas and labors ; and of these many drawings may be seen dispersed among those who practice our art, and I myself have seen not a few. He even went so far as to waste his time in drawing knots of cords, methodically made so that one can follow them from one end to the other, the whole forming a circle. One of these, a most complicated and beautiful one, is to be seen in a print with the inscription : *Leonardus Vinci Academia.** Among these models and designs, there was one by which he demonstrated to the citizens, men of spirit who were then governing Florence, how he proposed to raise the Baptistry of San Giovanni, and place steps beneath it without damaging it. And with such convincing reasons did he urge this, that it appeared possible, although each man, after he had departed, would recognize for himself the impossiblity of such an undertaking.

His conversation was so pleasing that he attracted the hearts of men to himself. Although

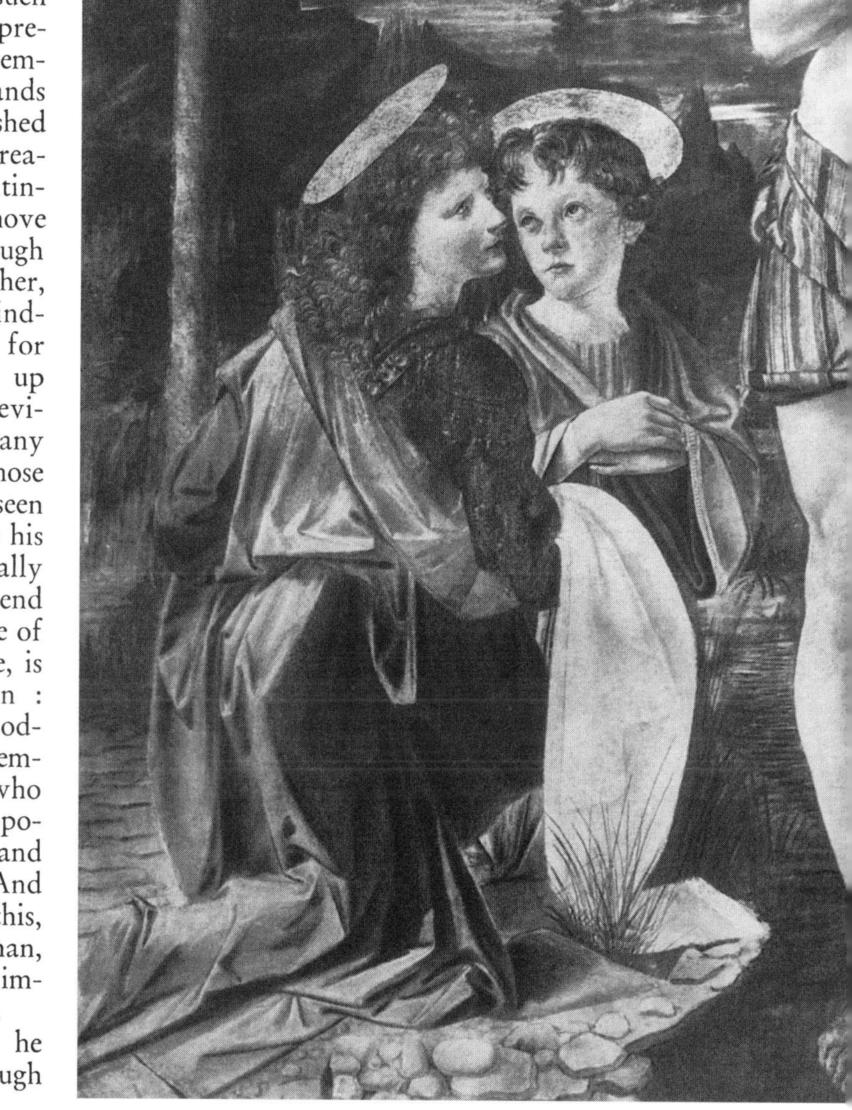

Verrocchio, *The Baptism of Christ.* Detail. The angel on the left is by Leonardo. ▶

more or less without wealth and working very irregularly, he always kept servants and horses, in which he took much delight, and all sorts of animals which he managed with immense interest and patience. It is told that when passing the market where birds were sold, he would take them out of their cages, having paid the price that was asked, and let them fly away in order to restore to them their lost liberty. Nature so showered favors on him that wherever he turned his thoughts, brain and mind, he had something so divine and manifested such dexterity, vivacity, goodness, beauty, and grace that he was without equal. But it is clear that this comprehension of art made him begin many things, and he never finished one of them because it seemed to him that the hand could not attain the perfection he had imagined ; he conceived in idea difficulties so subtle and so marvelous, that they could never be expressed by the hands, be they ever so skillful. The caprices of his investigations led him to natural philosophy, to the study of the properties of plants, to the assiduous observation of the motions of the heavenly bodies, the path of the moon, and the course of the sun. [And in his mind he formed so heretical a doctrine that he no longer depended on any religion, preferring, perhaps, to be a philosopher rather than a Christian.] *

At the instance of Ser Piero, as has been said, having been placed in his boyhood to learn art with Andrea del Verrocchio, when the latter made a Baptism of Christ, Leonardo painted an angel holding some garments. Although he was very young, Leonardo executed it in such a manner that his angel was much better than the figures of Andrea, and that was the reason why Andrea would never again touch color, humiliated to see a child know more than he.

Leonardo was commissioned to make a cartoon for a door-hanging that was to be woven in Flanders in gold and silk, for the King of Portugal, showing Adam and Eve at the moment of their sin, in Paradise. He made in chiaroscuro, highlighted with lead-white, a meadow filled with herbs and some animals, and, in truth, it may be said that for diligence and fidelity to nature, not even a divinely inspired genius could have equaled him. The fig tree is shown, with the foreshortening of the leaves and the varying aspects of the branches, wrought with such care that the brain reels at the mere thought of a man having such patience. There is also a palm tree which has the radiating crown of the palm executed with such great and marvelous art that nothing save the patience and intellect of Leonardo could avail to do it. The work was never executed. The cartoon is now at Florence, in the blessed house of the illustrious Ottaviano de' Medici, presented to him not long ago by Leonardo's uncle.

It is said that Ser Piero, being at his country house, one day was visited by one of his peasants who had made a shield with his own hands out of a fig tree he had cut down on his land, and asked him to have it painted for him in Florence. He consented most willingly for the peasant was very skillful at catching birds and fish and in these respects was very useful to

Ser Piero. The latter had it taken to Florence, and asked Leonardo to paint something on it without telling him where it had come from. Leonardo, having one day taken the shield in his hands and, seeing it twisted, badly made, and clumsy, straightened it with the aid of fire and, having given it to a turner, from the rude and clumsy thing that it was, caused it to be made smooth and even. He gave it a coat of gesso and prepared it in his own way, and began to think what he might paint on it that would terrify the enemy as did the head of Medusa in ancient times. For this purpose, Leonardo carried to a room into which no one entered save himself alone, lizards, newts, crickets, serpents, butterflies, grasshoppers, bats and other strange animals ; out of these, variously put together, he formed an ugly monster, horrible and terrifying, which emitted a poisonous breath and turned the air to flame ; he made it emerge from a dark and jagged rock, belching forth venom from its open throat, fire from its eyes, and smoke from its nostrils and it had the appearance of a strange and horrible monster.

The whole time that he was engaged in this work, he had to suffer the terrible stench of the dead animals, but so great was his love for his art that he did not notice it. When it was finished neither the peasant nor his father any longer asked for it. Leonardo asked the latter to send at his convenience for the completed shield. Ser Piero therefore one morning went to the room and knocked at the door ; Leonardo opened to him and asked him to wait a little. Having gone back into the room, he exposed the shield on the easel, opened the window so that a bright light fell on it, and then bade his father come in to see it. Taken by surprise, Ser Piero received a great shock, not realizing that it was the shield or even a painted form that he beheld, and falling back a step, Leonardo checked him, saying, " This work serves the end for which it was made ; take it, then, and carry it away, since this is the effect it was meant to have. " This thing appeared to Ser Piero nothing short of a miracle and he praised very greatly the singular ingenuity of Leonardo. Privately he bought another shield decorated with a heart transfixed by an arrow, and gave it to the peasant, who remained obliged to him for it as long as he lived. He then secretly sold Leonardo's shield to certain merchants in Florence for a hundred ducats who soon resold it to the Duke of Milan for three hundred.

Leonardo then made a picture of Our Lady, a most excellent work, which afterwards was in the possession of Pope Clement VII ; among other things painted therein, he counterfeited a glass vase full of water holding some flowers, admirable in its lively tones, with the dewdrops still on the flowers so that it seemed more real than the reality. For Antonio Segni, his close friend, he executed with great care on a sheet of paper a Neptune that seemed wholly alive. In it one saw the ocean troubled, and Neptune's car drawn by sea horses with fantastic creatures, orcs, winds, and some very beautiful heads of sea gods. This drawing was presented by Fabio, the son of Antonio, to Giovanni Gaddi, with this epigram :

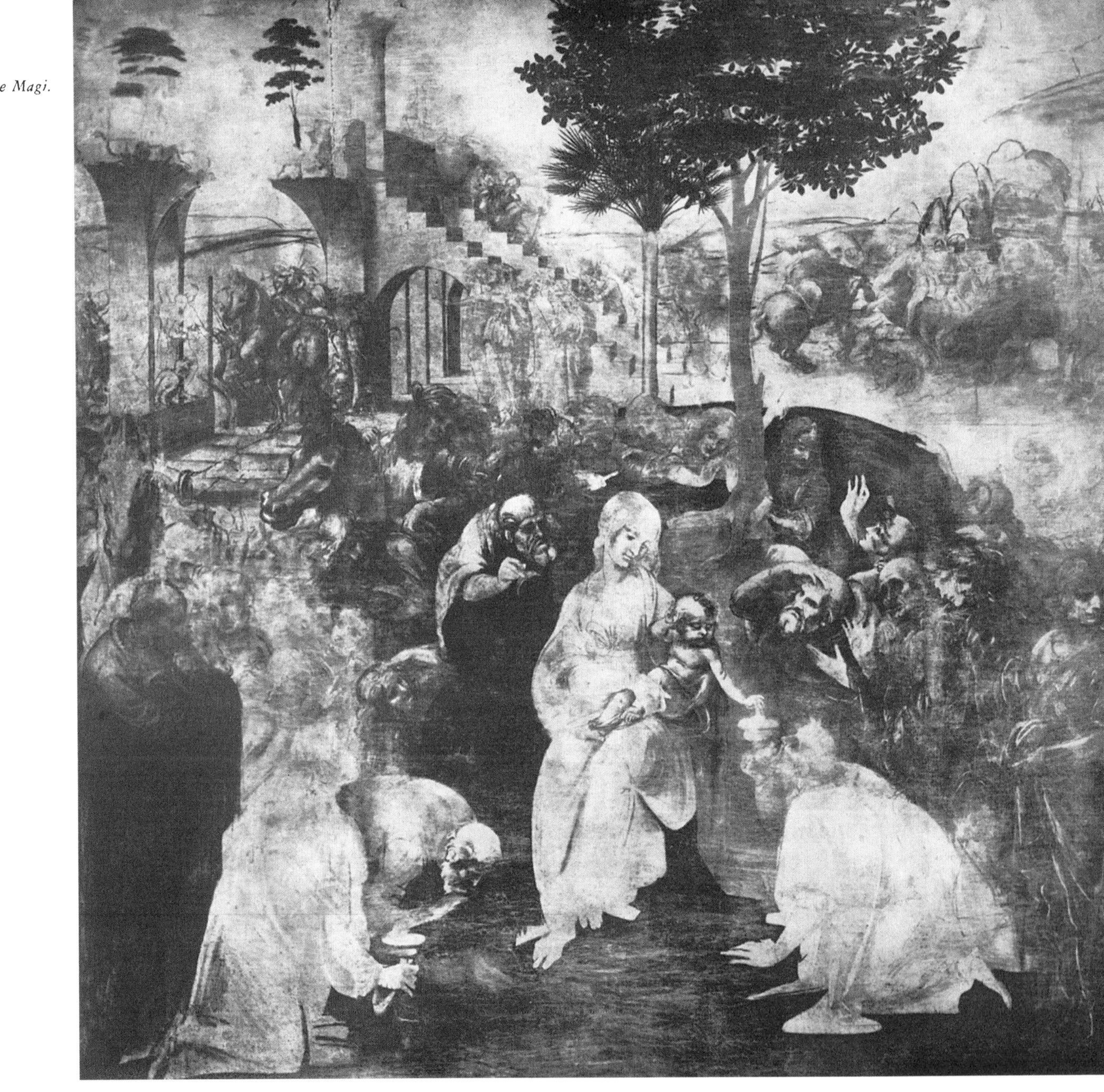

The Adoration of the Magi.

Virgil and Homer could paint Neptune
Leading the horses over the seaway of waves
The poets have seen him in their mind's eye
But da Vinci *saw him with his own eyes*
and so vanquished them. *

It took his fancy to paint in oils the head of a Medusa, intertwined snakes attiring the head, the most bizarre and unique invention that could be made ; but being a work that took time, it remained unfinished, as happened with almost all his things. This painting is among the choice works in the collection of Duke Cosimo, together with the bust of an angel, who raises one arm, foreshortened from the shoulder to the elbow in the air, while the other is folded across the chest. It is an extraordinary thing how that genius, in his desire to give the highest relief to the objects he represented, sought out the darkest back-grounds with the deepest shadows, wanting blacks which might make deeper shadows and be darker than other blacks, so that his ligths might seem brighter. In the end this method turned out so dark that no light remained any-where, and the forms of the objects seemed to evoke night rather than the clarity of day. But all this came from seeking to give greater relief, and to achieve the final perfection of art.

He delighted so much in seeing certain strange heads, with the beard or hair growing wildly, that he would follow about anyone that pleased him for a whole day, so fixing him in his mind that at home he could draw him as if he had him before his eyes. Of this kind, many heads are to be seen, both of men and of women ; and I have

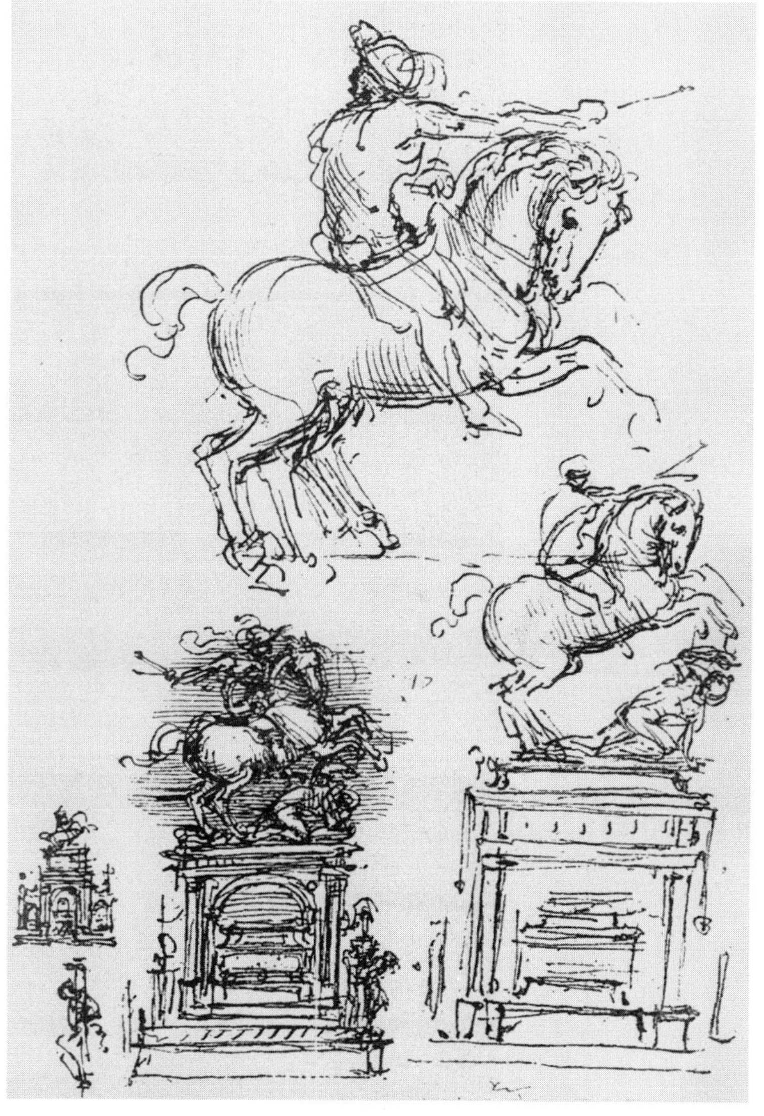

tudies for the *Trivulzio Monument.* ▶

several of them, drawn in pen, in my collection, which I have mentioned several times, particularly that of Amerigo Vespucci, which is a magnificent head of an old man, done in charcoal, and that of Scaramuccia, captain of the gypsies, which formerly belonged to Messer Donato Valdambrini of Arezzo, canon of St. Lorenzo, who had it from Giambullari.

He began a picture of the Adoration of the Magi, containing many beautiful things, particularly in the heads. It was in the house of Amerigo Benci, opposite the Loggia de' Peruzzi, and this also remained unfinished, like so many of his other works.

It came to pass that Giovan Galeazzo, Duke of Milan, being dead, and Lodovico Sforza having succeeded him in 1494, Leonardo, having great repute, was brought to Milan * to play the lyre before the Duke who took much delight in this instrument. Leonardo took with him an instrument he had made himself, in silver in the form of a horse's skull so that by this bizarre and new design he might obtain a more powerful harmony, more sonorous in tone, and he surpassed all the musicians who had come together there to play. Besides this, he was the best improviser in verse of his day. The Duke, hearing the marvelous presentation of Leonardo, became so enamored of his genius, that it was a thing incredible. He had him paint an altarpiece of the Nativity which he sent to the Emperor.

He also painted in Milan, for the Dominican monks of Santa Maria delle Grazie, a Last Supper of admirable beauty. To the heads of the Apostles he gave such majestic beauty that he left the head of Christ unfinished, not believing that he could give it that divine air befitting an image of Christ. The work, thus considered finished, has ever been held in great veneration by the Milanese and by foreigners as well. For Leonardo conceived and succeeded in expressing the apprehension that seized the Apostles in wishing to know who would betray their Master. In their faces may be read love, fear, anger, or grief at not being able to understand the meaning of Christ ; nor does one distinguish with any less a sense of marvel, the obstinacy, hatred, and treachery of Judas. The least part of the work displays unbelievable care ; even the texture of the tablecloth is painted in such a manner that the linen itself could not seem more real.

It is said that the prior of the monastery kept pressing Leonardo, in a most importunate manner, to finish the work. It seemed strange to him to see Leonardo sometimes stand half a day at a time lost in contemplation, and he would have preferred it if, like the laborers hoeing in his garden, he had worked without ever stopping his brush. That was not all. He complained to the Duke so insistently that the latter was constrained to send for Leonardo ; he delicately urged Leonardo to finish the work, nevertheless contriving to show him that the prior's importunity obliged him to do so. Leonardo, aware of the discernment and tact of the prince, wished to explain the matter thoroughly, a thing he would never have done with the prior. He reasoned about art and showed how men of lofty genius sometimes accomplish the most when they work the least, seeking out inventions with the mind, and forming those perfect ideas which the hands afterwards express and reproduce from the images. He added that only two heads remained to be done ; the head of Christ which he had given up hope of finding on earth and thought it impossible to conceive in the imagination with the beauty and divine grace befitting God incarnate. Next there was also wanting that of Judas, which was troubling him, for he could not imagine a face capable of expressing the lowness and cruelty of one who, after so many benefits received, had a soul so ignoble as to betray his Lord, the Creator of the world. However, he would search for one, and if he could not find a better one, he would always be able to take the one of the importunate and tactless prior. This thing moved the Duke to laugh mightily, and he said Leonardo was a thousand times right. And so the poor prior, in confusion, confined himself to his garden, leaving Leonardo in peace, while the artist indeed finished the head of Judas, the very embodiment of treachery and ignominity. But that of Christ, as has been said, remained unfinished. The nobility of this painting, both in its composition and in the incredible care taken in its execution, awoke a desire in the King of France * to take it into his kingdom. He tried by all possible means to discover whether there were architects to make it secure enough to transport safely. He had no consideration for any expense that might have been involved, so much did he desire it ; but the painting adhered to its wall and his Majesty retained his desire and the Milanese their picture. In the same refectory, where he made the Last

Anatomical Study. Leonardo tends to make his anatomical drawings diagrammatical so they will be clearer. ▶

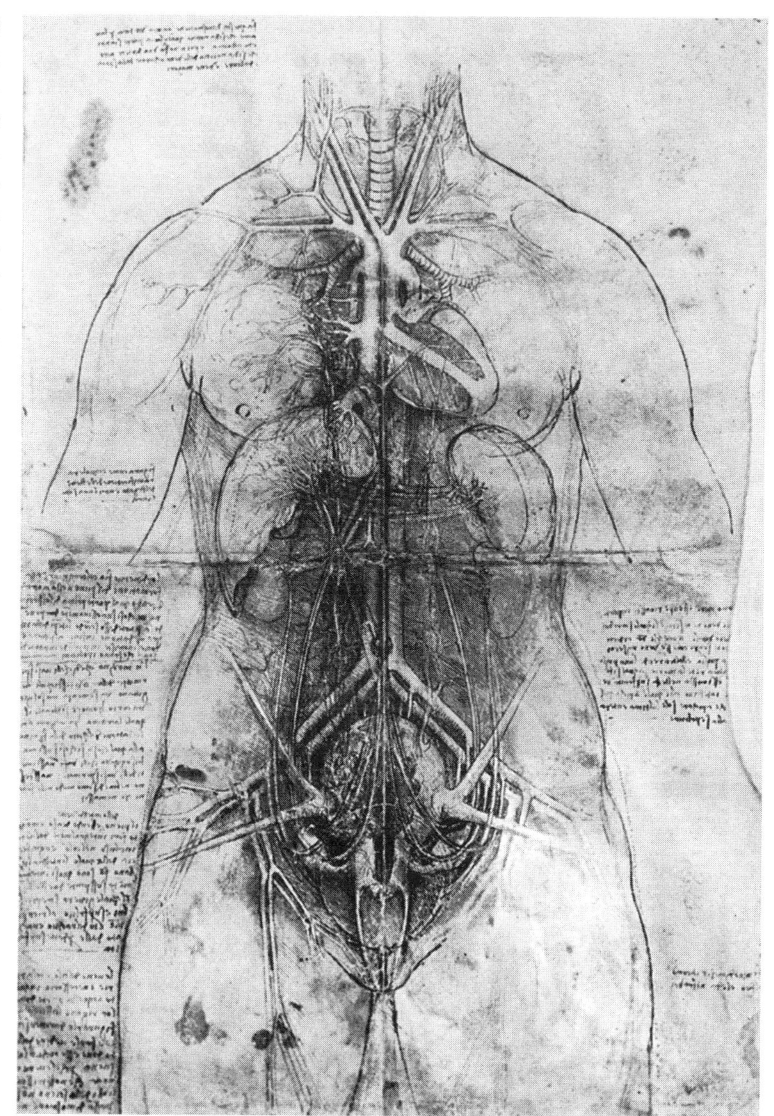

Supper, at the end where there is a Passion in the old style, Leonardo painted Lodovico with Massimiliano, his eldest son, and on the other side, the Duchess Beatrice, with Francesco, their second son ; both afterwards became Dukes of Milan ; and all are portrayed marvelously well.

While he was engaged on this work, he proposed to the Duke to make a horse in bronze of extraordinary size, as a memorial to the Duke. * And on so vast a scale did he begin it, that it could never be completed. It has been said — the judgments of men being various and often malign out of envy — that, like so many other works, Leonardo began it with no intention of finishing it, because, being of so great a size, it would be incredibly difficult to cast in one piece. This opinion may have been formed on the fact that so many of his works have remained unfinished. But in truth, his soul was so great and elevated, that he was paralyzed by his overly high ambition. The true reason was that he wished ever to go from excellence to excellence, from perfection to perfection and that, as Petrarch said, the work was retarded by the desire. * Indeed, those who saw the great model that Leonardo made in clay vow that they have never seen a more beautiful thing, or a more superb one ; this model was preserved until the French came to Milan, with King Louis XII, and broke it all to pieces. Lost, also, is a little model of it in wax, which was held to be perfect, together with a treatise on the anatomy of the horse, which he had made by way of study.

He next applied himself, with even greater earnestness, to the anatomy of man, assisted by and in turn assisting in this research Messer Marc' Antonio della Torre, an excellent philosopher, who was then lecturing at Pavia and concerned himself with these matters. And I have been told that he was one of the first to explain the problems of medicine according to Galen, and to throw true light on anatomy, which up to that time had been wrapped in the thick darkness of ignorance. And in this he found great aid in the brain, work, and hand of Leonardo, who made a book with drawings in red chalk, enhanced by strokes of the pen, of the human figure beneath the skin, dissected by his own hand, and drawn with the greatest care. Herein he showed the bones first, then, in their order, the nerves, and covered them with muscles ; the first attached to the bone, the second that hold firm the joints, and the third that give movement ; and step by step he commentated on them, in an irregular script, written with the left hand, backwards, and whoever is not practiced at deciphering it can only unterstand it with the aid of a mirror. Of these papers on the anatomy of man, a great part is in the hands of Messer Francesco da Melzo, a gentleman of Milan, who in the time of Leonardo was a very beautiful boy and much beloved by the master, and now is a beautiful and noble old man ; and he keeps these papers together as precious, much as one would relics, along with a portrait of Leonardo of happy memory. All who read these writings, will be astonished at the excellence with which that divine spirit should have discoursed on art, anatomy, the muscles, nerves and veins, and all with such care. There are also in the hands of a Milanese painter certain writings of Leonardo, likewise written backwards with the left hand, which treat of painting, and of the rules of drawing and of coloring. Not long ago, he came to Florence to see me, with the aim of having this work printed, and he took it to Rome, to have it published, but I do not know what may afterwards have become of it.

To come back to the works of Leonardo : being asked to devise something original for the king of France's visit to Milan, Leonardo made a lion which walked several steps, whose chest then opened, disclosing it full of lilies. In Milan he took for his assistant the Milanese Salai, who was delightfully graceful and beautiful, with a wealth of curls, and whom Leonardo loved greatly. He taught him many things of art, and certain works at Milan, which are said to be by Salai, were retouched by Leonardo.

He returned to Florence. * The Servite Friars had entrusted to Filippino the painting for the high altar of the Annunziata ; Leonardo said that he would willingly have done such a work and Filippino, having heard this, courteously retired from the undertaking. The Friars, to make it possible for Leonardo to paint it, took him into their house, meeting the expenses both of himself and of all his household. He kept them in suspense for a long time, without beginning anything. In the end, he made a cartoon showing Our Lady, St. Anne, and the Christ Child ; it not only caused all the artists to marvel, but after it was finished it was displayed in the room, and for two days men and women, young and old, flocked there as to a solemn festival to gaze at the marvels of Leonardo, which caused all to be amazed. In the face of the Madonna could be seen all the simplicity and beauty that confer grace on the Mother of God, as well as that modesty and humility of the Virgin supremely content at seeing the beauty of her Son, tenderly held to her breast, while at the same time with modestly bent eyes she looked down at the little St. John playing with a lamb, while St. Anne smiled, overflowing with joy at the sight of her earthly progeny become divine — ideas truly worthy of the mind and genius of Leonardo. This cartoon, as will be seen, afterwards went to France.

Leonardo made the portrait of Ginevra d'Amerigo Benci, a most beautiful work for the sake of which he abandoned the work for the Friars, who once more gave it to Filippino, but he, being overtaken by death, was not able to finish it. For Francesco del Giocondo, Leonardo undertook to portray his wife, Mona Lisa, and after working at it for four years, left it unfinished. The work is now in the collection of King Francis of France at Fontainebleau. Whoever wished to see how closely art may imitate nature, could grasp it with ease in this face, for in it are counterfeited the least details with all the subtlety permitted to painting. The eyes had that luster and humidity always seen in life, and around them all those rosy and pearly tints, as well as the eyelashes, rendered with the greatest delicacy. The eyebrows, having shown the manner in which the hairs spring from the flesh, here more close and there more scanty, and curved according to the direction

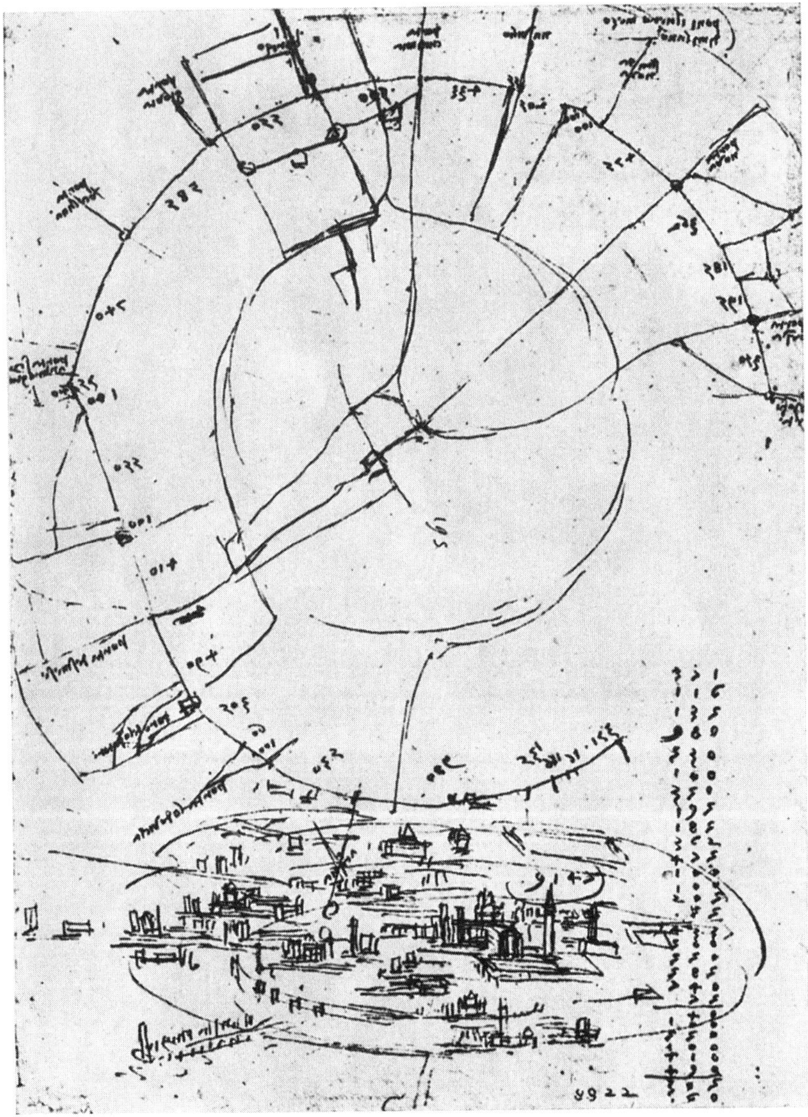

Plan and bird's-eye view of Milan.

of the pores, could not be more natural. The nose, with its beautiful nostrils, rosy and delicate, appeared to be alive. The mouth, with its slight opening, and the transition imperceptibly melting from the red of the lips into the carnation of the face, seemed to be not painted colors but true flesh. In the pit of the throat, if one

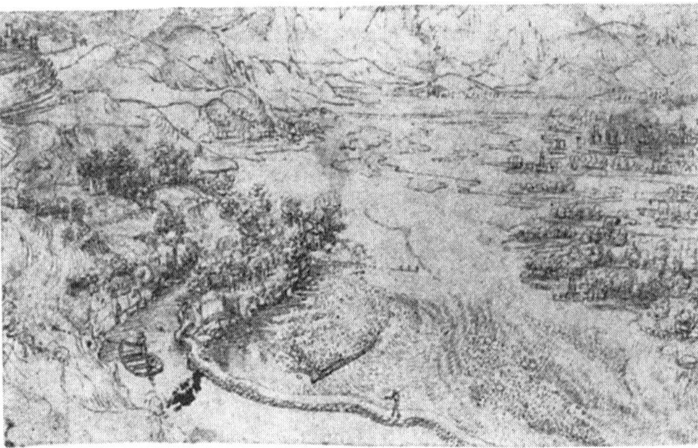

Alpine Valley.

gazed upon it intently, could be seen the beating of the pulse. It must be avowed that the painting was such as to make the most valiant artist, be he who he may, tremble and lose heart. He made use, also, of this device : Mona Lisa being very beautiful, he always employed musicians to play or sing, and jesters, who might keep her in a gay mood, in order to eliminate that melancholy cast that the painter often gives to his sitter. And in this portrait, there was a smile so pleasing, that it was a thing more divine than human to behold, and it was held to be a marvel, in that it was quite equal to life itself.

The excellence of the works of this most di-

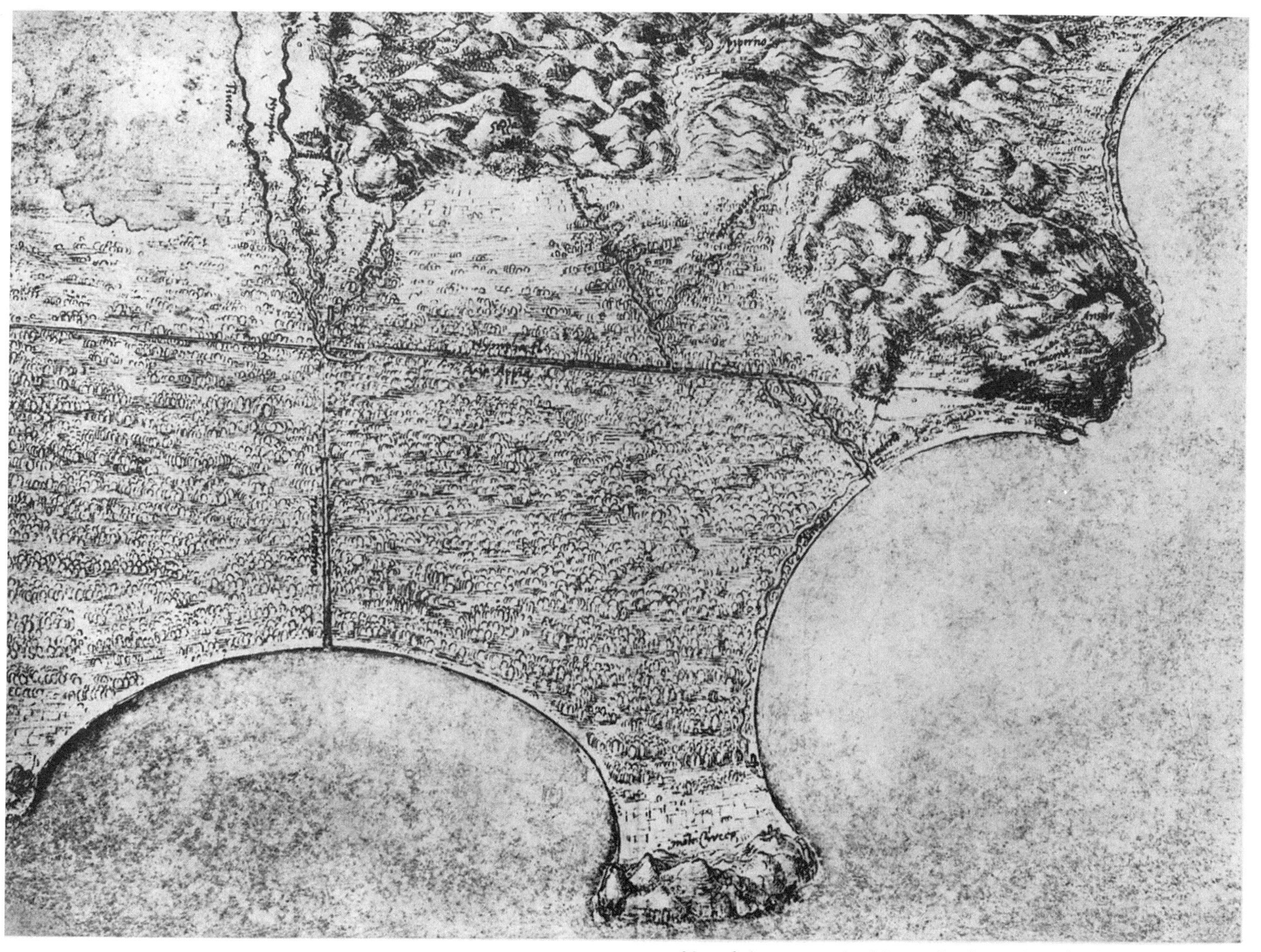

Map of the coast south of Rome, showing projects for draining the marshes.

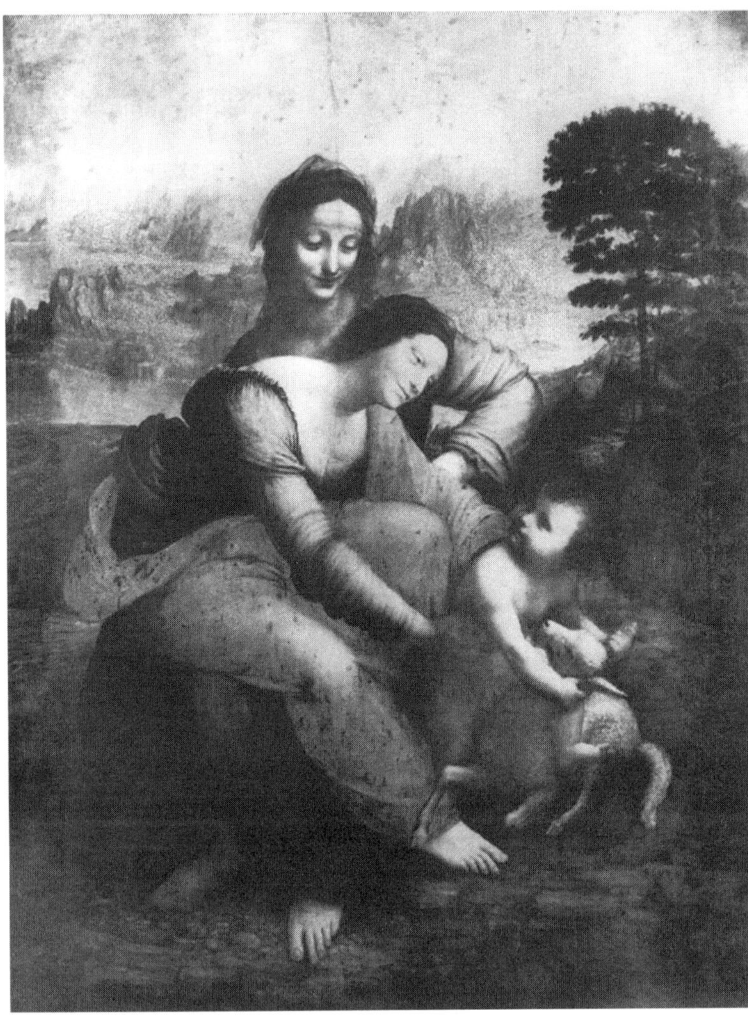

The Virgin and Child with St. Anne.

vine artist so increased his fame that all persons who took delight in art, indeed the entire city, desired that he should leave them some memorial; everyone, therefore, endeavored to have him execute some great and noble work so that the city would be adorned and honored by the genius, grace, and judgment that was known to be Leonardo's. The Gonfalonier and the leading citizens concluded that, the Great Council Chamber having been recently rebuilt and its architecture decided on with the help of his advice and that of Giuliano da San Gallo, Michelangelo Buonarroti, and Baccio d'Agnolo (as will be related in greater detail in the chapters devoted to them) and after it had been finished with great speed, it was ordained by public decree that Leonardo should be commissioned to paint a beautiful work. And so Piero Soderini, the Gonfalonier of Justice, allotted this hall to him. Thereupon Leonardo, determined to execute this work, began his cartoon in the Sala del Papa, in Santa Maria Novella, with an episode concerning Niccolò Piccinino, Captain of Duke Filippo of Milan, in which a group of horsemen fight for a standard, a great master's magnificent creation by reason of the marvelous ideas he introduced into this battle. Rage, fury, revenge are no less perceptible in the horses than in the men, and two of the horses, their forelegs interlocked, are fighting with their teeth as fiercely as the men around the standard. A soldier, grasping the staff with his hands and thrusting with his shoulder to wrest the staff from the hands of four others who surround it, urges his horse to flight. Of the four, two hold it with one hand while they raise their swords in the other in an attempt to sever the staff; an old soldier in a red cap, yelling, grips the staff with

Rubens, cop[y] after the lo[st] cartoon of *The Battle o[f] Anghiari.* ▶

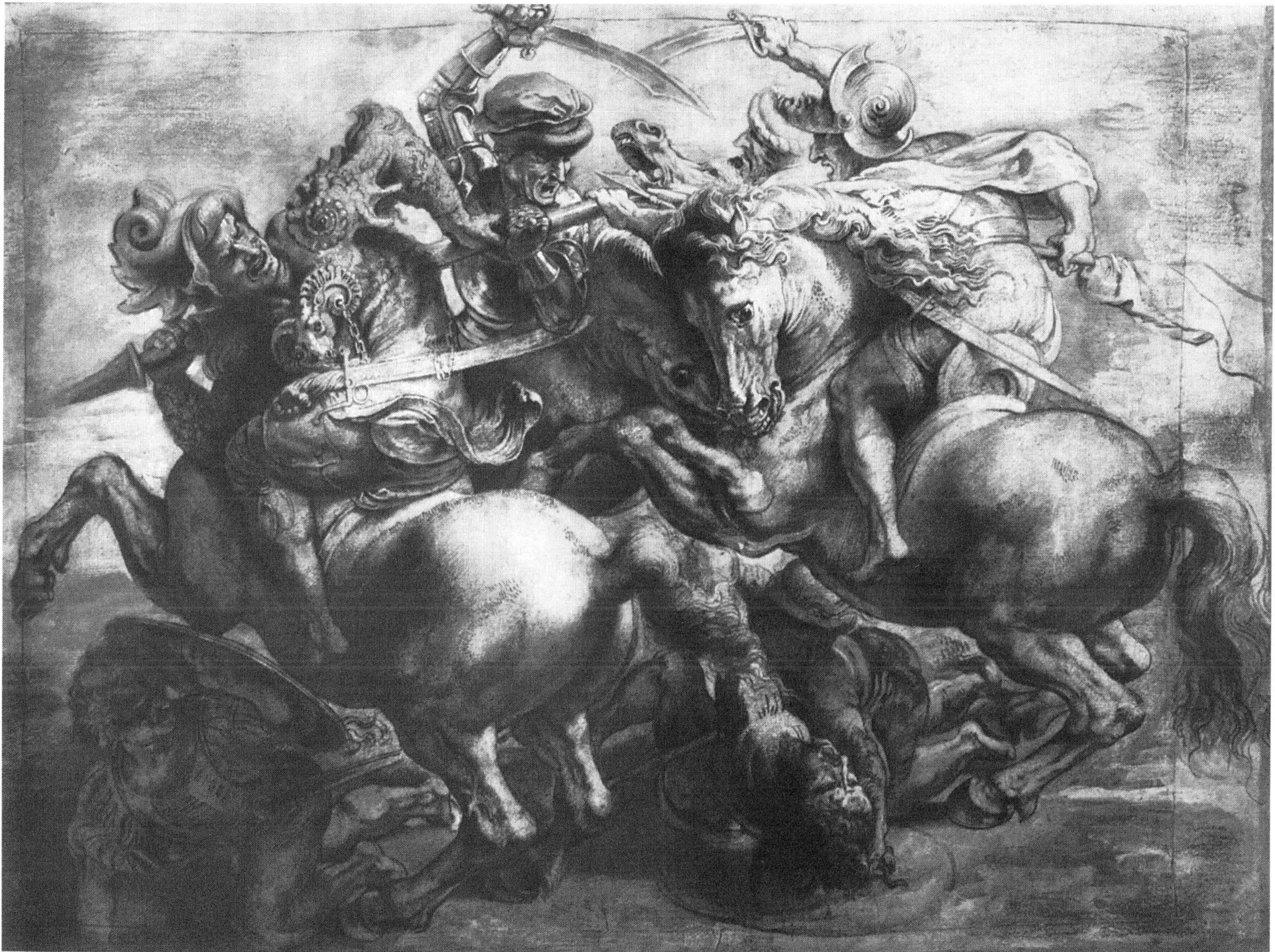

Studies for the dome of the Cathedral of Milan. ▶

one hand and raising a sabre, aims a furious blow to cut off the hands of the two who, gnashing their teeth, struggle with utmost fierceness to defend their banner. Furthermore, on the ground, between the legs of the horses, two figures, seen foreshortened, fight together ; one, on the ground, is beneath a soldier who is raising his arm so that he may plunge the dagger that is to kill his adversary into his throat with all his might, and the victim struggles with his arms and legs to avoid death. It is not possible to describe the invention that Leonardo showed in the design of the garments of the soldiers, in the helmets, and in the ornaments, much less the incredible mastery that he displayed in the form and lineaments of the horses, whose muscles and graceful beauty he rendered with greater dexterity than any other master. It is said that, in order to draw the cartoon, he had a most elaborate scaffold built, which could be raised by being pulled together and lowered by being let out. Having taken it into his head to paint in oil on the wall, he prepared so thick a mixture for the binder that it began to run during the execution of the painting, and in a short time he gave it up, seeing it was spoiled.

Leonardo was very high minded and most generous in all his actions. It is said that, having gone to the bank for the stipend he received every month from Piero Soderini, the cashier wanted to give him packets of pennies ; he refused them saying, " I am not a penny-painter. " Suspected of having cheated Piero Soderini, there began to be murmurings against him ; but Leonardo did not rest until with his friends he had brought together the sum and taken it to Piero, but Piero would not accept it.

He went to Rome with Duke Giuliano de'

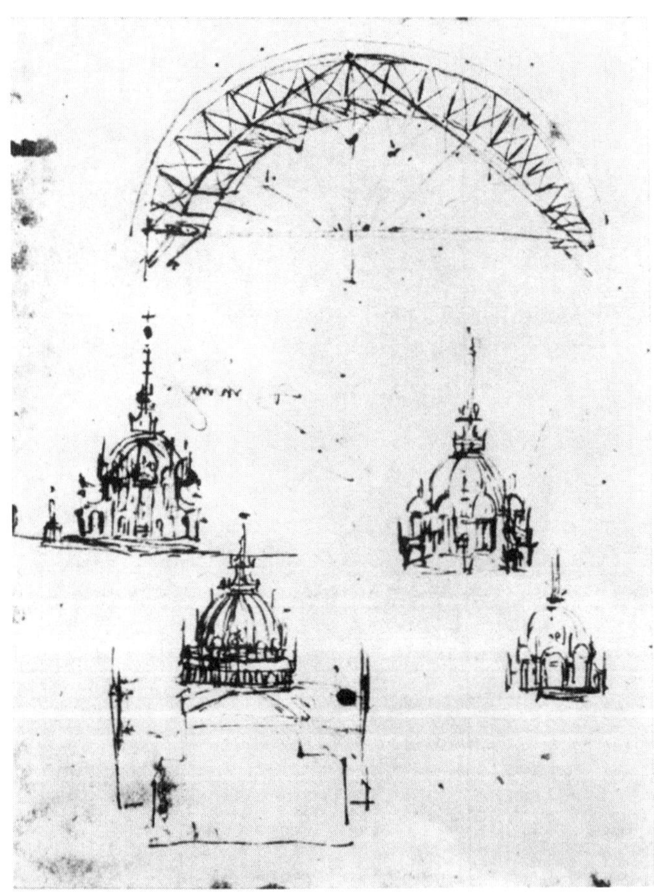

Medici (after the election of Pope Leo) who was very interested in the sciences and most of all in alchemy. During the trip, Leonardo made light, hollow animals out of a wax paste, and by blowing them up he could make them fly through the air, but when the air ceased they fell to the ground. On the back of a most strange lizard, found by a vinedresser of the Belvedere, Leonardo attached wings made of scales taken from other lizards, held by quicksilver, which, as the lizard moved, quivered with the motion. He then made it eyes, a horn, and a beard, tamed it and, keeping it in a box, he showed it to his friends to make them flee for fear. It also pleased him to have the guts of a sheep completely freed of fat and cleaned so that they became so small they could be held in the palm of the hand ; and having placed a pair of blacksmith's bellows in another room, to which he fixed one end of the guts, he could, by blowing into them, extend them to such a size that they filled the room, although it was very large, and the assistants would be forced to retreat into a corner. These transparent objects full of wind, which had taken up so little space in the beginning and so much at the end, he likened to virtue. He gave himself up to all kinds of follies of this sort, concerned himself with mirrors, and experimented with the strangest methods to discover oils with which to paint and varnishes to preserve the finished work.

He then made for Messer Baldassare Turini da Pescia, datary to Pope Leo X, a small picture of the Madonna and Child with infinite art and care but either through the fault of the person who primed it or because of his strange mixtures of binding materials and colors, it is now greatly ruined. In another picture, he painted a most marvelously beautiful and graceful little boy. These two works are in Pescia in the possession of Messer Giulio Turini. It is said that the Pope having commissioned a work by him, he began to distill oils and herbs for the varnish. And the Pope exclaimed, " Alas this man will never do anything, for he thinks of the end of the work before beginning it. "

There was great enmity between Michelangelo Buonarroti and him. Michelangelo departed from Florence, with the permission of Duke Giuliano, having been summoned by the Pope who wished to consult him about the façade of San Lorenzo. Hearing of this, Leonardo departed for France where the king, who knew his work, bore him great affection and desired him to paint a cartoon of St. Anne, but Leonardo for a long time diverted him with fine words.

Finally, having grown old, he was ill for many months and, feeling himself near death, [wished to inform himself diligently of Catholic practices and of the good and holy Christian religion, and then, with many tears, confessed and repented.] * And, though he could no longer support himself on his feet, he had himself supported by his friends and servants so that he might piously receive the holy sacrament out of his bed. The King, who was in the habit of often paying him affectionate visits, then came. Out of deference Leonardo raised himself up on his bed, explaining his illness and his symptoms, and reiterating how much he had offended God and mankind in not working at his art as he ought to have done. Thereupon he was seized by a spasm, the messenger of death.

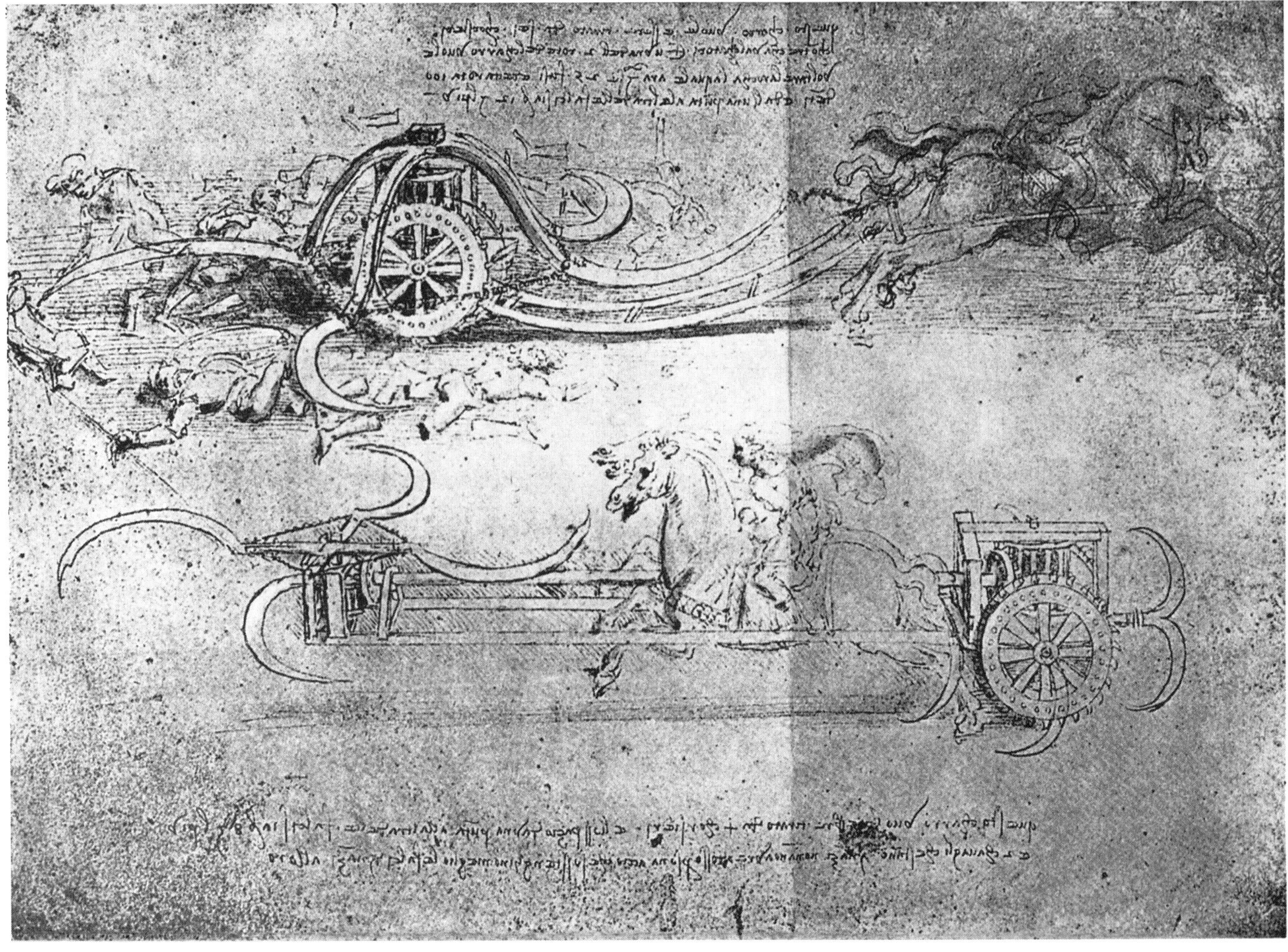

War machines.

The King, having risen, held his head to help him and to show his tenderness by alleviating his suffering. And, his marvelous spirit, knowing that it could not have greater honor, expired in the arms of the King, at the age of sixty-five. *

The loss of Leonardo was felt beyond measure by all who had known him, for never was there an artist who did painting greater honor. The splendor of his aspect was so marvelous that he made every sad spirit serene and he could do whatever he wished even with the most obstinate wills. With his strength he could restrain even the most violent rages. With his hand he could twist the handle of a bell or a horseshoe, as if they were lead. With his liberality he made welcome and supported his every friend, rich or poor, who was talented and worthy. His actions were an honor and an ornament to the humblest or most despised abode. Thus the birth of Leonardo was a great gift for Florence and his death an incalculable loss. In painting, he added to the manner of using oils a certain obscurity whereby the moderns can give great force and relief to their figures. And in sculpture he proved his worth in the three bronze figures that are over the door on the north side of the Baptistry of San Giovanni, executed by Giovan Francesco Rustici under Leonardo's supervision ; they are the most beautiful pieces of casting, the best designed, and the most perfect that have yet been seen in modern days. There has come down to us Leonardo's treatise on the anatomy of the horse and another, more complete one, on the anatomy of man. Before so many and so divine aspects,

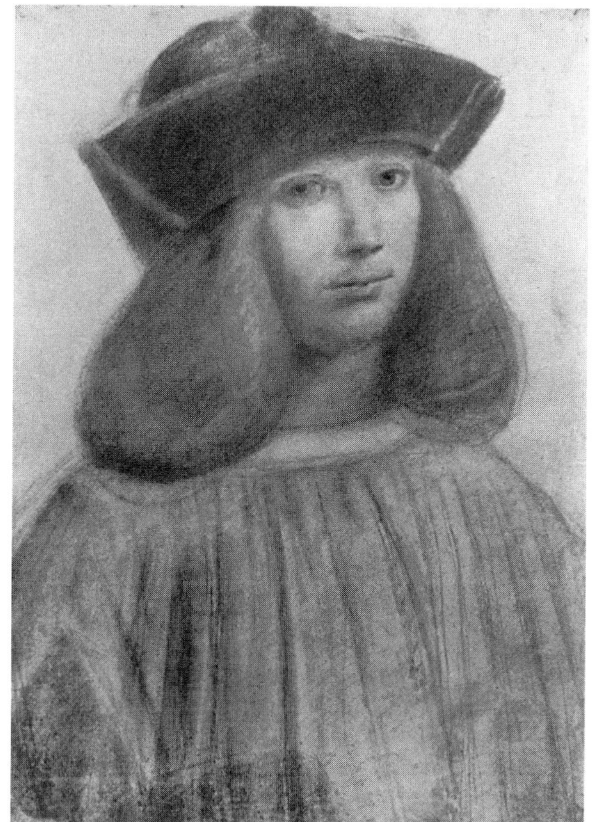
Boltraffio, *Portrait of Francesco Melzi.*

although he spent more time speaking than creating, the fame of his name can never be extinguished. Wherefore it was thus said in his praise by Messer Giovan Battista Strozzi :

He all alone inVINCIble
Conquers all others; he surpasses Phidias, Apelles
And all their conquering legion. *

The Projects

Leonardo frequently made specific references to the books that were to comprise his new opus : Perspective (and optics), Mechanics, Anatomy. However, it is difficult to tell whether these were already written or only contemplated, nor do we have a clear idea of how he saw the relation between these separate parts. In any case, in the Treatise on Painting *he must have planned a comprehensive collection if one is to believe a notation made soon after 1500, "Study the rainbow in the last book of the* Treatise on Painting." * *Initially the Treatise may have included geology and human anatomy as subsections, but eventually he accumulated so much material that he probably planned to publish them as separate works. Entries from his notebooks, given below, show that from time to time he thought about the problems of arranging and publishing the material.*

Following these entries, we give the well-known attack on "abbreviators" and the replies to anticipated criticism, since he expounds attitudes toward knowledge and methods of study in these passages that guided him throughout his life. These pages are written with a liveliness and clarity that suggest Leonardo was conscious of the originality of his undertaking and took considerable pains in preparing these introductory remarks. They also show the independence of his position, which was analogous to that claimed by the most gifted of the humanist poets, such as Poliziano, as opposed to compilers and popularizers. Throughout there runs a disquieting note of life slipping by, of work not being accomplished, and of the message that must be delivered. *

NOTATIONS CONCERNING THE TREATISES

1. On the 2nd of April, 1489, book entitled "Of the Human Figure."

2. On the 23rd of April, 1490, I have commenced this book and recommenced the horse.

3. On the 1st of August, 1499, I have here written on movement and weight.

4. Begun by me, Leonardo da Vinci, on the 12th of July, 1505: the book on the transformation of one body into another without diminution or increase of material.

5. Begun, in Florence, in the house of Piero di Braccio Martelli, on the 22nd of March, 1508. This is to be a collection without order, made up of many loose sheets which I have copied out in the hope of putting them in their proper order later, each placed according to its subject. But I am afraid that before I come to do this, I will have to repeat the same things several times. Do not blame me, O reader, for the subjects are many and memory cannot retain all and say: This I have written, I will not write it again. To avoid falling into such error and not to repeat myself, I would have to reread all I have written each time I record something, and all the more so since long periods of time elapse between writing.

6. This winter of 1510, I hope to finish all this anatomy.

7. The "Treatise on Mechanics" should precede the "Treatise on Useful Machines." Have the books on anatomy bound.

My "Treatise on Voice" is in the hands of Messer Battista dell'Aquila, steward in waiting to the Pope. 8.

Completed, the 7th of July, 1514, at eleven o'clock at night, at the Belvedere, in the studio the Magnificent procured for me. 9.

It seems to me that it must be my destiny to write about the kite for one of my earliest memories is that I dreamt, that lying in my cradle, a kite came and opened my mouth with its tail and beat against the insides of my lips several times. 10.

AGAINST ABBREVIATORS

To criticize the supreme certainty of mathematics is to sow confusion and to deprive oneself of the possibility of reducing the contradictions of the sophistical sciences, which forever give forth nothing but noise. 11.

The authors of abridgments do harm to knowledge and to love, for love is ever the offspring of knowledge, being the more fervent in proportion as knowledge is more certain, and this certainty derives from the thorough knowledge of all the elements that make up the thing that is loved.

What use is it, under pretext of giving a condensation of all the elements composing the complete body of knowledge, actually to omit the greater part of the whole?

It is true that impatience, the mother of folly, praises abridgments, as if people did not have

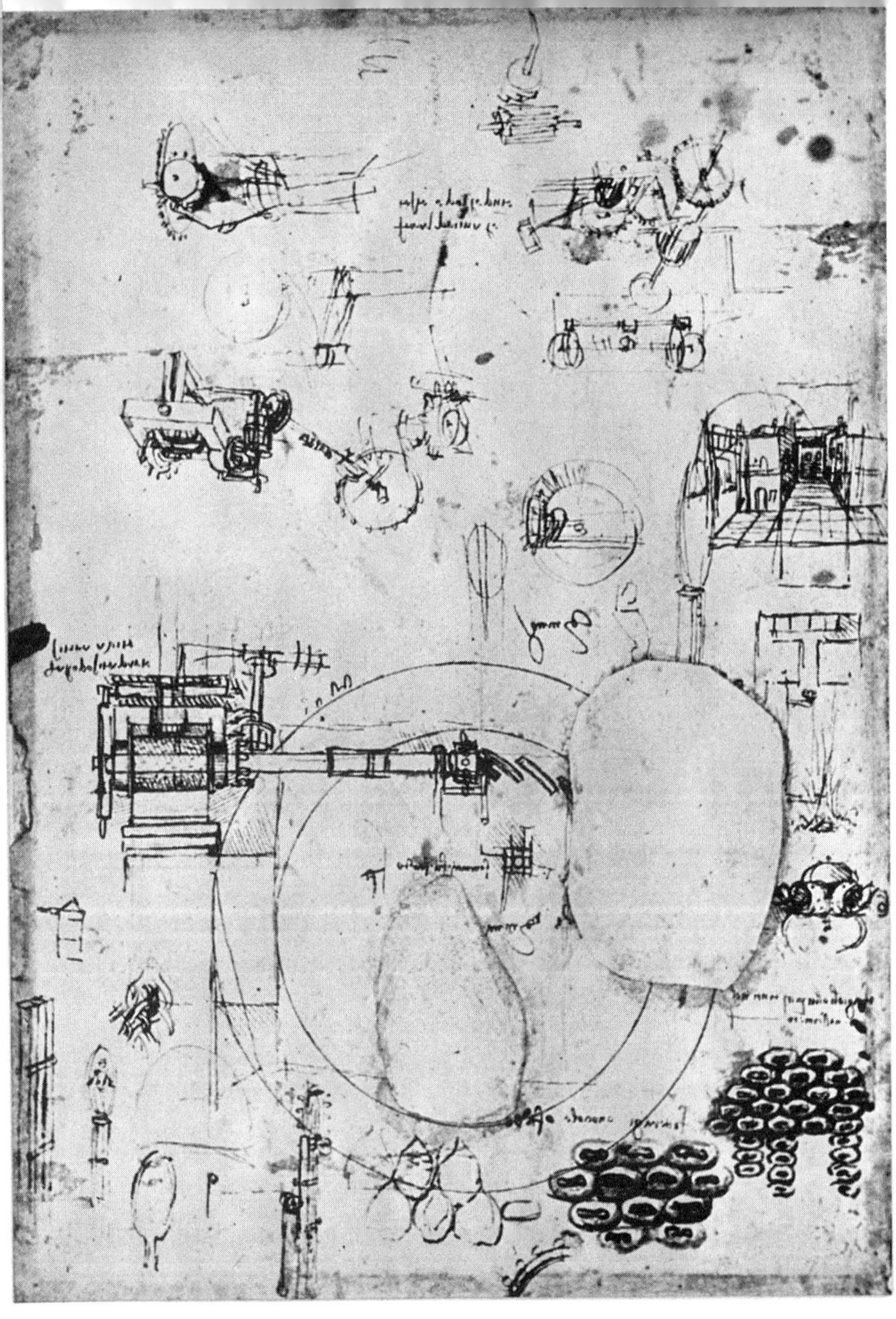

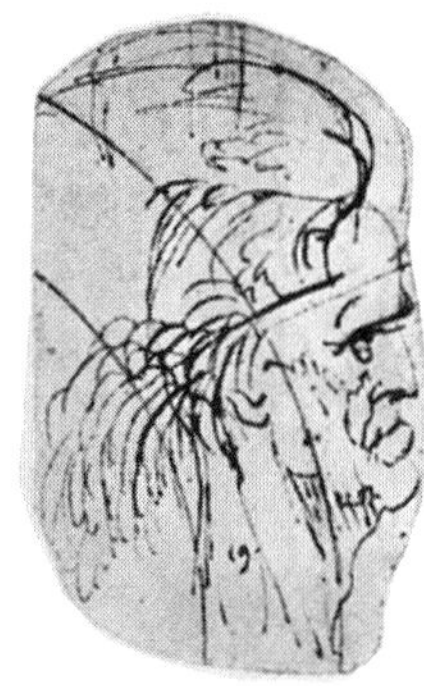

A sheet of technical designs and two sketches cut out of it during the sixteenth century (see p. XIX).

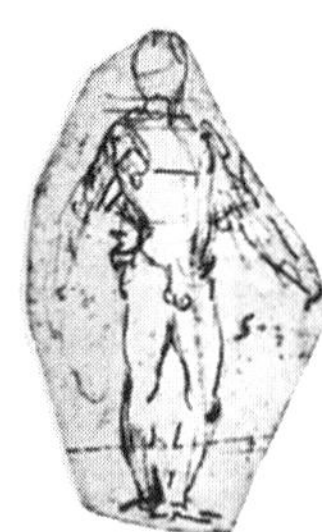

time enough in a lifetime to acquire complete knowledge of one single subject such as the human body. And then they think to encompass the spirit of God, which embraces the whole universe, by weighing it and reducing it to little pieces as though to dissect it.

O human folly ! Do you not perceive that you have spent your whole life with yourself and yet are not aware of that which is most visible, of your own folly ? And, together with the crowd of sophists, do you wish to deceive yourselves and others by despising mathematics, which contains the truth about the things within its province. And you would range among miracles and enlighten on subjects the knowledge of which is foreign to the human mind, and not demonstrable by any examples from nature. And you think that you have performed a miracle when you have spoiled the work of an ingenious mind ; and you do not realize that your error is to strip trees of their ornament, of their branches covered with leaves and sprinkled with fragrant flowers and fruit, but seem to think that you must make bare planks of them.

This was done by Justin, author of the abridged version of the history by Trogus Pompeius, who wrote in an elaborate style of the great deeds of his ancestors, which are much to be admired, but composed a flat work, good only for those who are so impatient that they think they waste their time when they spend it in studying the works of nature and the acts of human beings. Let them keep company with beasts, let them have an entourage of dogs and other beasts of prey, and live with them. They may pursue that which flees before them, hunt innocent animals whom hunger has driven toward the house during the season of snow to beg for alms as one might from a protector.

Studies for interlace ornaments. A favorite activity of Leonardo's.

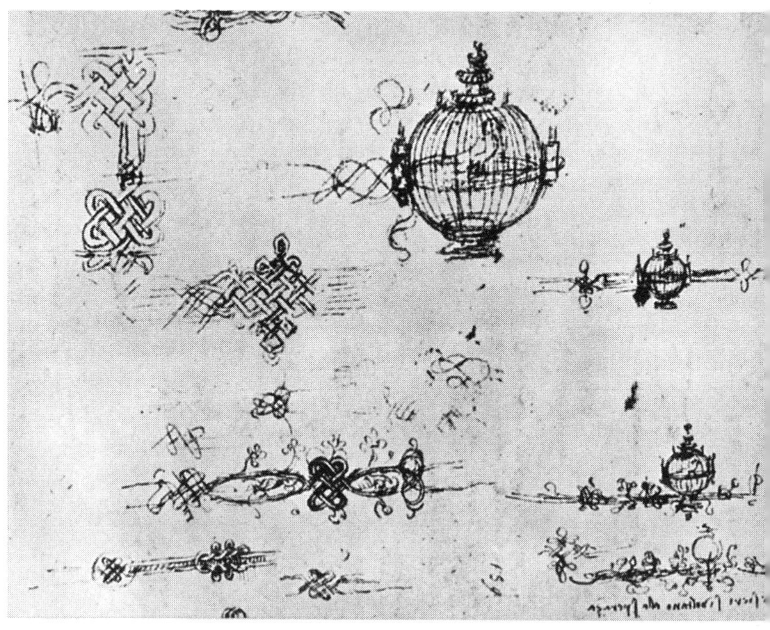

REPLIES MADE TO FORESTALL CRITICS

If I do not quote from authors, as they do, it is surely more worthy of the reader for me to quote from experience, the instructress of their masters. They strut about puffed up and pompous, adorned and clothed not in their own labors but in those of others, and will not allow me my own. But if they scorn me for being an inventor, how much harsher a judgment do not they 12.

deserve who are not inventors but trumpeters who can only recite the works of others ?

The inventors, who interpret between Nature and Man, should be judged and thought of, in comparison to trumpeters who recite the works of others, as the object placed before the mirror is in comparison to its image seen in the mirror ; the one is something in itself, the other nothing ; there are persons who owe nothing to the gifts of nature but only to an artificial guise without which they would belong with the herds of animals.

13. Many believe they have the right to censure me on the grounds that my proofs contradict the authority of certain authors whom they hold in great reverence due to the inexperience of their own judgment, without seeing that my inquiries are based on pure and simple experience, the true mistress.

These rules enable you to distinguish the true from the false; this helps men to apply themselves only to that which is possible and moderate, and hinders them in hiding themselves in a cloak of ignorance, for the road of failure leads, by way of despair, to melancholy.

Seeing that I cannot find a subject that is particularly useful or pleasant, since the men who have preceded me have taken all the useful and necessary themes for themselves, I shall be like the poor man who is the last to arrive at the fair and can only provide for himself by taking what the others have seen and not chosen, but left, because it was of little value. These despised and rejected wares, rejected by many buyers, will make up my modest supply, and I will go and distribute them, not throughout the great cities but in the little towns, taking the rewards that befit the things I offer.

The desire for knowledge is natural to good men.

I know that many will consider this work useless, and they will be those of whom Demetrius said that he paid no more attention to the wind produced by the words in their mouths than the wind that came out of their posteriors. I speak of men moved only by the desire for material riches, who are entirely destitute of the desire for wisdom, the sustenance and true wealth of the soul. The riches of the soul are as much above those of the body as the soul is more worthy than the body. Often, when I see one of these men take this work in hand, I wonder whether he will not put it to his nose like an ape and ask himself whether it is something edible.

Since I am not a man of letters, I know that certain presumptuous persons will feel justified in censuring me, alleging that I am ignorant of all learning in matters of writing. Fools ! They do not know that I might reply, as did Marius to the Roman patricians, " They who treat themselves to the labors of others will not grant me my own. " * They maintain that because of my lack of literary learning, I cannot properly express the subjects I wish to treat. They do not realize that my subjects do not require the words of others for their expression but only experience, the mistress of whoever wishes to write well. I have taken her as my mistress and will not cease to state it. *

The Paragone or Comparison of the Arts

The Paragone *is one of the most interesting as well as one of the most complete sections of the Codex Urbinas. The theme is only sketched out in the Ashburnham manuscript (now Paris, Institut de France, Ms. BN. 2038) and seems to have been written mainly between 1495 and 1499 while Leonardo was at the court of Lodovico Il Moro. In the discussions of the learned and the literary, mentioned by Luca Pacioli, the traditional debate on the preeminence among the arts, that is, the profane disciplines, medicine, law, etc., was also adapted to the fine arts. They thus developed a canon that was to be continued in the age of the academies in exhaustive and precious debates between sculpture and painting; the theme was already exploited by Baldassare Castiglione in his* Il Cortegiano *(1528), and it also gave rise to the investigations and discourse by the academician Benedetto Varchi (1546).*

These often empty and scholastic discussions on the standing of one or another of the visual arts or on their relative merit in comparison to music and poetry are the outcome of an aesthetic peculiar to the Renaissance. To Leonardo da Vinci they were fundamental, for they formed the basis on which his " new science " rested. It was a matter of putting painting at the head of all the activities in which man's mind could be engaged. Before defining the means by which this superior goal is to be achieved (which is the aim of the section on the Problems of the Painter, p. 73) and before setting forth for the artist the conditions prerequisite to an attitude worthy of this aspiration (which is the object of the precepts for the painter, pp. 161 ff.), he establishes the superiority of art in terms of the principles of learning and the laws of knowledge. This is the strictly theoretical section of the work, and the Paragone *is the logical result.*

This concept has led to numerous misunderstandings. It is much more original than nineteenth-century historians have believed, for they saw in Leonardo's observations only simple affirmations of the hard and fast rules of modern science, as if these were the only foundations of knowledge. Instead, one must follow the development of the concept to its logical conclusion along the general lines laid down by Leonardo, who denies that art can be separated from science or science from art, and one must see it within its evolutionary context, that is, as a part of the contemporary cultural crisis to which he hoped to find a solution.

The new organum *is developed in three stages:*

As opposed to theological knowledge, it turns to the idea of experience, which is given a specific meaning (and in practice is realized chiefly through a graphic representation or a mechanical model). It is not ı factual science in the modern sense, as opposed to the speculations of the schoolmen, but rather a type of knowledge in which the whole man is involved and which ultimately finds its fulfillment in the two areas in which the artist reigns : engineering and painting. This first stage requires an awareness that Necessity rules nature and an application of mathematical proofs ; these ideas and methods, however, are not enough to show us the essentials of the visible world.

In the second stage the argument changes. For Leonardo it is a question of subordinating the achievements of poetry — and, more generally, all literature — to those of the visual arts, mainly of painting. Once these premises are accepted they assure painting a dominance over verbal activity. This latter develops over a period of time and is not adapted to creating the total image that the visual arts can present. The same argument applies to music, though its value is not underestimated. Indeed, musical harmony furnishes the idea of a more general harmony adapted to the spatial arts. But ultimately these take a higher position than the temporal arts. This distinction was not new and was to be maintained for a long time thereafter. It is the principle of classification used by Lessing in his Laocoön, *which opposes the arts that exist in time because of the succession of their symbols (poetry, music) to those that exist in space because of the simultaneity of their symbols (painting, sculpture). According to Leonardo, the latter carry greater weight ; in appearance they preserve the* proportionalità *(harmonious proportion) operating equally in the work of art and in the mind of the spectator. At this point a discussion and even eulogy of architecture would have been appropriate, but as Leonardo does not consider it purely an art of composition of simultaneous forms, he excludes it, as he does engineering, from his argument.*

At the next stage, painting and sculpture, the two representational arts that consolidate all the power of the visible compete with each other. But the sculptor does not have at his disposal either light or the diversity of effects that the painter has, so that the painting has a unique range of illusion. Through the development of this principle, painting ceases once and for all to be classed with mechanics and minor activities ; indeed, the Quattrocento artists and their spokesmen, the humanists, clarified this situation and prepared the way for the visual arts' acceptance among the " liberal arts. " More significantly, painting is placed on the highest branch of the tree of knowledge and is its finest fruit. Painting includes all that learning has to offer and constitutes the complete synthesis of thought and reality.

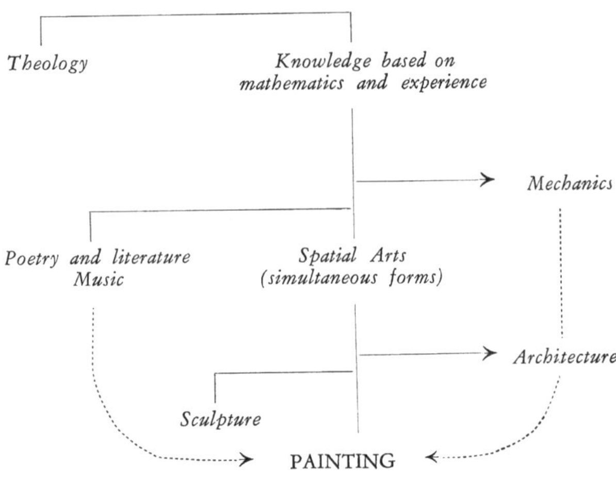

Any agreement between this complex " demonstration " and modern ideas is only sporadic and illusionary, for today art is clearly separated from science, and pure science is based on premises which Leonardo would have unequivocally rejected. Nor is his terminology always as simple as it seems. For instance, the meaning of " phenomenon " alternates between " cause " and " manifestation " ; " experience " does not imply participation in action but lucid observation. In this sense experience is indispensable to constructive thought. Though it may require serious attention and even considerable research, Leonardo at no time seems to be concerned with a body of knowledge for its own sake or with the defining of things except as this relates to their being represented and their use in art.

By choosing isolated sentences, or certain fragmentary or temporary formulations, one may elicit surprisingly progressive statements. Leonardo had an intellectual awareness that is without equal, but he used it exclusively to further his dream of " synthesis " which, despite his rejection of the theological position and his disdain for the " mendacious " sciences, is closer to the neo-Platonism of the humanists than to the modern idea of science.

Leonardo's curiosity and his desire for precision surely took him further afield than he had intended, but one might suggest that he examined the sciences with such care for the sole purpose of enhancing the position of painting within the intellectual hierarchy. This he did by showing that it absorbs, correlates, and completes all the activities of the mind. In so doing, he has repeatedly occasion to state the two propositions which, amongst the complexities and lifelong tergiversations of his recorded thought, seem to constitute his final statement : the mathematical sciences " are not concerned with anything but

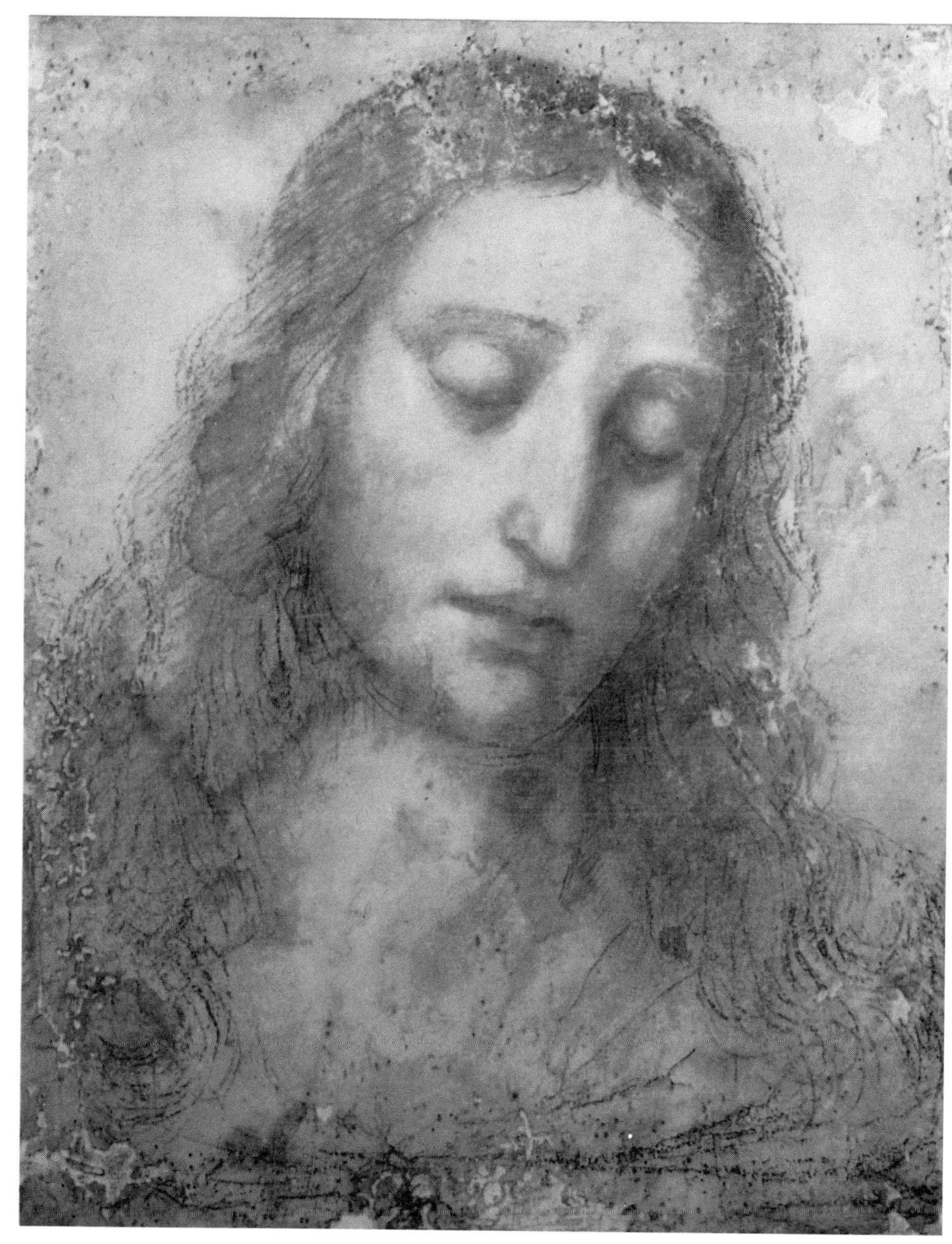

Head of Christ, Study for *The Last Supper.*

the knowledge of continuous and discontinuous quantity and are not concerned with quality, which is the beauty of nature's creations and the grace of the world." (See no. 18.) And above the sciences, at the very wellspring of painting, is vision, the infinite expanse of the visible world, the great realm of the eye. (See no. 20.)

I. PAINTING AND SCIENCE

14. *Which science is mechanical and which is not.* One calls mechanical that discipline that derives from experience, scientific that which has its origin and its conclusion in the mind, and semi-mechanical that which originates in a theory but ends in a manual activity. But to me all sciences seem vain and full of error that are not born of experience, mother of all certainty, and do not terminate in an actual experience ; or to put it another way, those of which neither the beginning, nor the middle, nor yet the end is made known to one of the five senses. And if we doubt the certainty of what is submitted to the senses, how much more should we doubt that which cannot be tested by the senses, such as the essence of God, and of the soul, and such matters about which discussions and arguments never cease. In fact, whenever reason is lacking, loud protest makes up for it, something that does not occur when things are certain. Therefore, we say that whenever voices are raised true sciences are absent, for truth brooks no argument, and once it is demonstrated controversy ends forever ; and if it is reopened, the science is confused and lying, and not certain. *

But the true sciences are those which become known to us through our senses by experience, and silence the tongues of the sententious. They do not feed those who study them with dreams but proceed step by step to their conclusion from the first known, true principles by means of proper deductions. This is evident in the elementary principles of mathematics, that is, numbers and measures, or, to put it another way, arithmetic and geometry, which treat discontinuous and continuous quantities with perfect truth . . .

And if you say to me that these true and exact sciences belong to the mechanical sciences because it is impossible to carry them to their conclusion without manual operations, * I say as much of the arts which require the services of a scribe ; writing is equal to drawing, which is a part of painting. And, astronomy and other disciplines proceed by means of manual activities after having been intellectual ones. In the same way, paintings are first in the mind of him who conceives them and cannot achieve perfection without the manual activity. The true and scientific first principles of painting establish what is the opaque body, primitive and derivative shadow, what is lighting, that is, darkness, light, color, volume, the placing of figures, distance, proximity, movement or repose. * All these take place in the mind without any manual activity. This constitutes the science of painting, which is in the mind of the theorist who conceives it ; from it issues the execution, which is much more noble than the theory or science just mentioned.

15. *That painting is "mental"*

If you say to me that the non-mechanical sciences are mental, I would reply that painting is mental and that, like music and geometry, which deal with the proportions of continuous quantities, and arithmetic, with those of discontinuous quantities, painting deals with all the continuous quantities, with the qualities of proportions of shades to light and, through perspective, with distance. *

16. *Definition of science*

Whether or not painting is a science. One calls science that reasoning which emanate from first principles, beyond which there is nothing in nature that could be the object of the said science. Thus, in continuous quantity (or the science of geometry) one begins with the surface of the object, and one finds that this surface has its origin in the line, which delimits it. But this is not yet satisfactory, for we know that the line has its origin in the point and the point is that which excludes anything smaller. The point, therefore, is the first principle of geometry ; nothing else could exist, either in nature or in the mind, which could be the origin of the point . . .

No human investigation can be called truly scientific if it is not capable of mathematical demonstration . . . *

17. *Drawing, the basic principle of all arts*

. . . But the divine science of painting treats of the works of man and of God according to the limits of its surfaces, that is, of the contours that determine the volume. This is what makes possible the perfection of the sculptor's statues. By her basic principle, which is design, she teaches the architect, so that he can make his buildings agreeable to the eye. And the same is true for potters of all kinds, for goldsmiths, weavers, embroiderers ; she invented letters to express the different languages, she gave the mathematicians numbers, taught the geometricians to draw figures, and taught those concerned with optics, * astronomers, designers of machines, and engineers.

18. *Painting as "mathematics" of quality*

How the science of astronomy stems from the eye, being born of the eye. There is nothing in astronomy that is not the result of visual lines and of perspective, daughter of painting ; for it is the painter who, for the requirements of his art, created perspective and cannot practice it without lines which enclose all the different shapes of bodies created by nature. Without them the art of geometry would be blind ; since the geometer reduces all surfaces surrounded by lines to the figure of the square and all volume to the cube * and since the mathematician proceeds in the same way with his cubic and square roots, these two sciences are not concerned with anything but the knowledge of continuous and discontinuous quantity and are not concerned with quality, which is the beauty of nature's creations and the grace of the world.

19. *Painting as "philosophy" of surfaces*

That painting encompasses the surfaces, shapes, and colors of natural bodies, but philo-

sophy only their natural properties. Painting is concerned with the surfaces, colors, and shapes of everything created by nature, and philosophy penetrates these things by considering the properties inherent in them ; but philosophy is not rewarded by that truth which the painter, who embraces the primary truth, achieves ; for the eye is deceived less.

II. PAINTING, MUSIC, AND POETRY

20. *Conclusion of the dispute between the poet and the painter.* Since we have concluded that in principle poetry speaks to the intelligence of the blind and painting to that of the deaf, we accord proportionately a greater value to painting than to poetry, as painting serves a better and more noble sense. Its nobility is three times as great, because the loss of hearing, taste, and touch have been preferred to the loss of sight.

To lose one's sight means to be deprived of the beauty of the universe and is as if a living man were shut into a tomb in which he can exist and move. Do you not see that the eye embraces the beauties of the whole world ? It is the master of astronomy, the author of cosmography, the advisor and corrector of all the human arts ; it carries men to different parts of the world ; it is the prince of mathematics ; its sciences are quite certain ; it has determined the altitudes and dimensions of the stars, and discovered the elements and their levels ; * it has made it possible to predict future events from the course of stars ; it has brought forth architecture, perspective, and divine painting — most excellent of all God's creations ! What praise is there worthy of your nobility ? What peoples, what tongues truly can describe your scope ?

It is the window of the human body through which the soul observes the beauties of the world and rejoices in them and therefore accepts the prison of the body, which would otherwise be a place of torment. Through it, human enterprise could discover fire, which has given back to the eye what darkness had first taken from it. It has adorned nature with agriculture and with pleasant gardens.

But what need is there for me to carry my discourse to such heights and length ? What is there that is not accomplished by the eye ? It moves men from east to west, it invented navigation and surpasses nature, whose works are defined, for what the hands can produce, when commanded by the eye, is infinite, as the painter shows by representing the infinite numbers of forms of animals, herbs, plants, and places * he has imagined. *(Scribe's note : End of the debate between the painter and the poet.)*

Of the eye . . . Surely there is no person who 21.
would not prefer to lose the sense of hearing, as well as of smell, rather than lose his sight. For though the loss of hearing means the loss of all the disciplines that use words, * one would accept this, if only not to be deprived of the beauty of the world, which is attached to the forms

of all things, both natural and man-made, which are reflected in the human eye.

22. *Differences and similarities between painting and poetry* . . . It is a sin against nature to tell the ear what should be told to the eye. One must assign it the function of music and not the science of painting, the only imitator of natural forms and all things. *

23. Painting is mute poetry and poetry is blind painting. The aim of each is to imitate nature with the means at its disposal, and each can express moral attitudes, just as Apelles did in his *Calumny.* *

24. *Vision and imagination*

Comparison between painting and poetry. The imagination does not see as perfectly as the eye receives the images or likenesses of objects and makes them available to the perceptions, from which they are transmitted to the community of the senses, where they are judged. * The imagined image cannot go beyond the community of senses except to be committed to the memory, and there it stops and dies, if the thing imagined is of no great value. It is in this way that poetry exists in the mind or imagination of the poet, who conjures up the same things as the painter and for this reason considers himself the painter's equal, but in fact is far from it, as we have shown.

Hence, we may say with good reason that in the domain of the fictitious, the same difference exists between painting and poetry as between a body and the shadow derived from it ; or perhaps even a greater one, for at least the mind perceived the shadow of a body by means of the eye, whereas the imagined form is not transmitted by it, but exists in the interior eye. What a difference there is between imagining a light and actually seeing it outside this interior darkness ! *

25. *Limitations of the poet's means*

The only function particular to the poet is to invent the words of people who speak, and those are the only things he can present to the sense of hearing in their natural state, for they are by nature the creation of the human voice ; and in all other matters the painter surpasses him.

The scope of painting is incomparably greater than that of words, for the painter creates an infinite number of things which speech cannot even name because it lacks the appropriate words. Do you not see that when the painter wants to invent animals, or even demons in hell, what wealth of imaginary forms is available to him ? *

26. *Conclusion of the dispute about the poet, painter, and musican.* There is the same difference between the representation of bodily things by the painter and by the poet as between bodies that have been dismembered and bodies that are whole. The poet describing the beauty or ugliness of a body describes it member by member, one after another ; the painter makes it all visible at once. The poet cannot give you in words the true shape of the parts of which the whole is composed, as can the painter who pla-

ces it before you with the truthfulness of nature. *

The same thing happens to the poet as does to the musician who, by himself, sings a song composed for four voices by singing first the soprano part, then the tenor, continuing with the contralto, and finally the bass. It excludes the grace of harmonious relations that results from the chords. This is what the poet does when

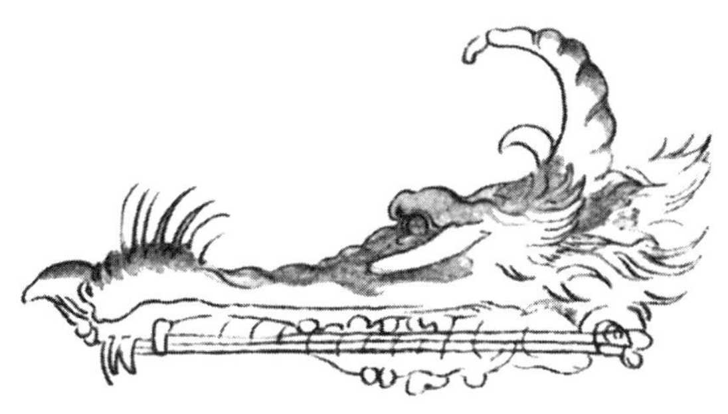

Musical instrument in the shape of a fantastic animal.

he describes a beautiful face feature by feature. This method does not present its beauty to you in a satisfactory manner, because that depends on the divine proportion of all these features together. It is only by their union at one and the same time that they give rise to a harmony that can enslave him who beholds it.

Music, with its harmonious accords, also produces smooth melodies composed of various voices. Poetry is deprived of the efficacy of harmony ; although, like music, it reaches the seat of judgment through the sense of hearing, poetry cannot render the harmony of music, since it does not have the power to say different things at one and the same time as does the harmonious proportion of painting. For the latter is composed of different parts at one time and its sweet accord is at the same time judged both as a whole and in its parts : as a whole from the point of view of the composition, in the details with respect to the intent of the parts which compose the whole.

Hence, the poet remains far behind the painter in the representation of bodily things, and far behind the musician in the representation of invisible things. But, if he borrows from the other disciplines, he can appear at the fair like a merchant bringing various things made by many inventors. He acts in this manner when he borrows from the sciences of the orator, the philosopher, the astronomer, the cosmographer, and others, all sciences wholly separate from that of the poet. Thus, he is like an agent who gathers together several people in order to conclude a sale. If you wish to define the true function of a poet, you will find that he is nothing but a collector of goods stolen from other disciplines of which he makes a lying composition, or, if you would express it more politely, a fictitious composition. And it is this freedom of imagination that has permitted a comparison between the poet and the painter, * though this is the weakest aspect of painting.

Reply of King Matthias to a poet who competed with a painter. On the birthday of King Matthias a poet brought him a work written in honor of the day on which the world was bene- 27. *Harmony of simultaneous expression*

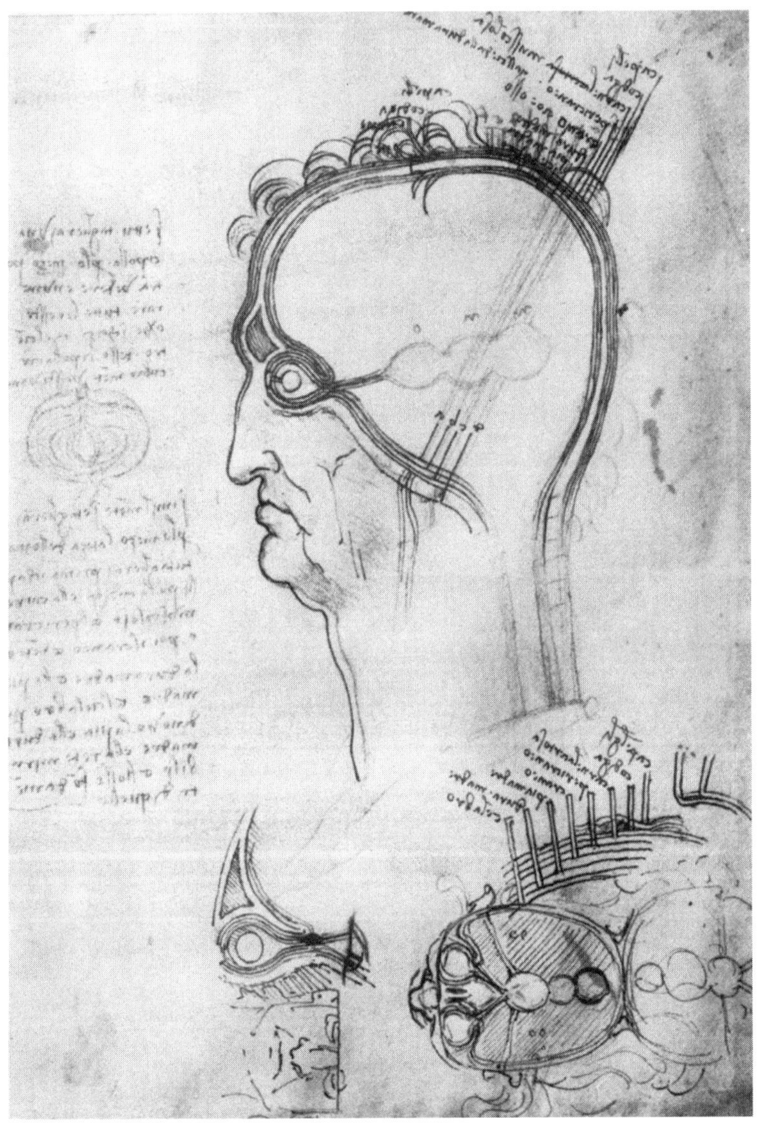

fited by his birth. And a painter presented him with a portrait of his beloved. The King immediately closed the book, turned to the painting, and fixed his gaze upon it with great admiration. The poet, much vexed, then said to him : "Read, read, O King, you will find much weightier things here than in a mute painting."

The King, hearing himself reproached for looking at mute objects, said : " Poet, be still, for you do not know what you are saying. This painting serves a higher sense than does your work, which is for blind men. Give me something I can see and touch, and not only hear ; and do not reproach me my choice, because I have put your work under my elbow and hold the painter's with both my hands, offering it to my eyes. For my hands have taken it of their own accord to serve a sense which is more noble than hearing. For my part, I consider that there is the same relation between the science of the painter and that of the poet that there is between the senses to which they appeal.

"Do you not know that our souls are composed of harmony and that harmony is only engendered in moments when we see or hear the proportion of things ? Do you not see that in your discipline there is no harmony of the parts, but that they follow each other, one born of another, and that none appears until the preceding one has died away ? That is why I consider your production to be much inferior to that of the painter. By the sole fact that it does not produce a harmonious accord, it does not satisfy the mind of the spectator or listener as does the

◄ The coverings of the brain compared to an onion. Diagram of the three ventricles in which the community of the senses, imagination, and memory reside ; see no. 24

harmony of the very beautiful features composing the divine beauties of this face before me ; all brought together at the same time, they give me so much pleasure by their divine harmony that I cannot see that there might be another thing on this earth made by man that could please me more. " *

28. *Lasting harmony*

The musican speaks with the painter. The musician says that his discipline is comparable to that of the painter because it consists of a body of elements, of which the listener may contemplate all the graces in as many harmonious measures as there are measures in which the music is born and dies, and by these measures it delights the soul residing in the body of him who listens to it. But the painter replies that the body, which is composed of human limbs, does not give pleasure by means of measures of harmony wherein its beauty must change and take on a different form. Nor does it have to be born and die thusly, for the painting permits the pleasure to last for many years. It has the excellent quality of preserving the finely proportioned harmony of the elements when nature, with all its strength, is no longer capable of doing so. How many paintings have preserved the likeness of a divine beauty where time or death had soon destroyed the natural model, so that the work of the painter has become of greater value than that of nature, his teacher.

29. *Music as inferior*

How music should be called a younger sister of painting. Music can only be termed the younger sister of painting, for it is subject to the

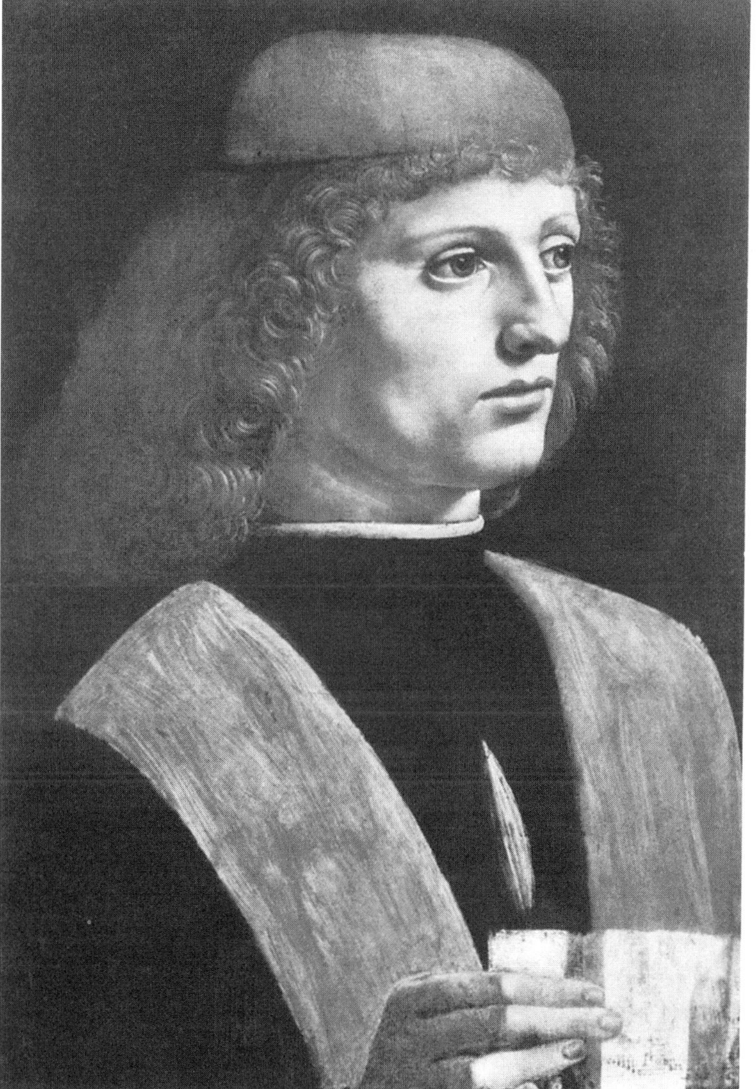

Portrait of a Musician.

sense of hearing, a sense inferior to sight. It composes harmony by the union of proportioned parts, produced together and obliged to be born and to die in one or in a number of harmonic chords. These chords enclose the relation of elements out of which the harmony is created, a harmony no different from the line surrounding the forms which make up human beauty.

But painting prevails over music and dominates it, because it does not die as soon as it is created, as does unfortunate music. Thus it remains in being and shows you as alive what is in fact only a surface. O marvelous science ! You preserve the ephemeral beauties of mortals and give them a greater permanence than have the works of nature, which continually undergo change until they reach their expected old age. Such a science stands in the same relation to divine nature as its works do to the works of nature ; therefore is it adored.

III. PAINTING AND SCULPTURE

30. *Difference between painting and sculpture.* I do not find any difference between painting and sculpture except this : the sculptor pursues his work with greater physical effort, and the painter pursues his with greater mental effort. This may be proved, for the sculptor in producing his work makes a manual effort in striking the marble or stone, whichever it is, to remove what is superfluous and extends beyond the figure shut in it. This demands a wholly mechanical exercise that is often accompanied by much sweat and this combines with the dust and turns into a crust of dirt. His face is covered with this paste and powdered with marble dust, like a baker, and he is covered with tiny chips as if it had snowed on him. His lodgings are dirty and filled with stone splinters and dust.

In the case of the painter (and we are speaking of the best among painters as among sculptors), just the opposite occurs. He sits at great ease in front of his work, well dressed, moving a light brush with agreeable colors ; he is adorned with such garments as he pleases, and his dwelling is clean and filled with beautiful paintings. He often has himself accompanied with music or the sound of different, beautiful works being read, which he may hear with great pleasure, undisturbed by the pounding of hammers or other noises. *

That the sculptor's work is less intellectual than the painter's and that many wonderful aspects of nature escape him. Practicing myself 31.
sculpture as well as painting and doing both the one and the other with the same skill, it seems to me that without suspicion of bias I can judge which of the two is the more intellectual, the more difficult, and the more perfect. *

In the first place, sculpture is dependent on certain lights, namely from above, while painting carries its own light and shadow with it. Light and shadow are therefore of importance to sculpture, and the artist is assisted by nature, that is, by the relief which, of its own, furnishes it. * The painter creates them by his art in the places where nature would logically place them.

The sculptor cannot create variety by using the different kinds of colors of things; but painting is not deprived of anything. The lines of perspective of the sculptor do not seem true in any way ; * the space of the painter may seem to extend for hundreds of miles beyond the work itself. Aerial perspective is outside the scope of the sculptor's work, and he cannot represent transparent or luminous bodies, or the reflection of rays, or shining things such as mirrors or other objects that reflect light, or mists or overcast weather, or innumerable other things which I will not mention in order not to be boring.

The one advantage of sculpture is that ordinarily it resists time better ; yet painting is more lasting than sculpture when done upon copper covered with white enamel, painted with enamel colors, and placed in a fire and fused.

The sculptor may say that if he makes a mistake, he cannot easily correct it. But it is a weak argument to try to magnify the work because an oversight is irremediable. I would say that it is more difficult to correct the mind of the master who makes such mistakes than to correct the work . . . for he who takes away too much understands too little and is not a master. If he has control of the measurements he will not remove what he should not take off. Hence, we assert that the fault is in the master and not in his material.

Painting is a marvelous art, based on the most subtle reflections of which sculpture, in its summary presentation, is incapable.

The painter and the sculptor. The sculptor says that his art is more noble than painting because it is more enduring, having less to fear from humidity, fire, heat, and cold. One must reply to him, that this does not confer nobility on sculpture, because the capacity to last comes from the material and not from the artist. The same quality may be found in painting when it is done in vitreous colors on metals or terra cotta, which are then fused in a furnace and treated with various instruments producing a polished and lustrous surface, as may be seen nowadays in several places in France and Italy, and especially in Florence in the della Robbia family, who have discovered a way of painting with vitreous glazes covering the terra cotta, in any kind of work, no matter what its scope. It is true that these works are subject to being broken and cracked, as is also sculpture in marble, but they cannot be melted like figures in bronze. In their ability to last they equal sculpture and surpass it in beauty, since they combined the two perspectives, while sculpture in the round can have only that found in nature. * In making a figure in the round, the sculptor makes only two forms, and not an infinite number corresponding to the countless points of view from which it can be seen ; one of these forms is a view from the front, the other is from the back. This can be proven to be so, for if you make a figure in bas-relief, seen from the front, you would never claim to have shown more than the painter shows in a figure seen from the same angle ; and the same is true for a figure seen from the back. *

32. *Limitations of sculpture.*

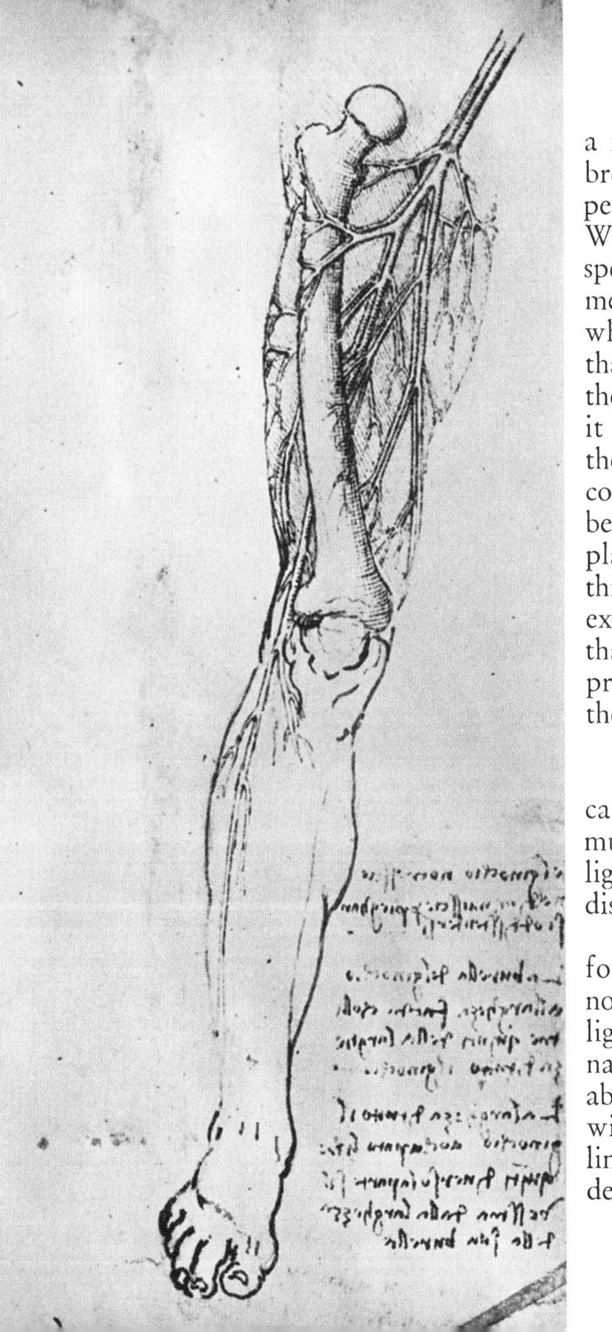

Study of the veins of the leg.

But there is incomparably greater subtlety in a relief than in sculpture in the round ; in the breadth of its theory and in its contact with perspective it somewhat approaches painting. Work in the round is not concerned with perspective, because it takes over the measurements it finds in the living model. And that is why the painter learns sculpture more readily than the sculptor painting. But to come back to the aims of the relief just mentioned, I say that it requires less physical effort than sculpture in the round, but more study, because it requires consideration of the proportion of the distances between the bodies of the first and the second planes, * between those of the second and the third, and so forth. If you, master in perspective, examine these you will find that there is no relief that is not full of errors in the greater or lesser projection of the planes of bodies nearer or further from the eye. . . . *

33. *Conclusion*

Difference between painting and sculpture. In carrying his work to completion, the painter must consider ten different subjects, that is : light, shadow, colors, volume, form, placement, distance, proximity, movement, and rest.

The sculptor need only consider volume, form, placement, movement, and rest. He does not need to be concerned about darkness and light, because in sculpture they are produced by nature herself, nor is there any concern at all about color. He concerns himself moderately with distance and proximity. He makes use of linear perspective but not of color perspective, despite the great variations that colors and the

The human heart; see no. 34. ▶

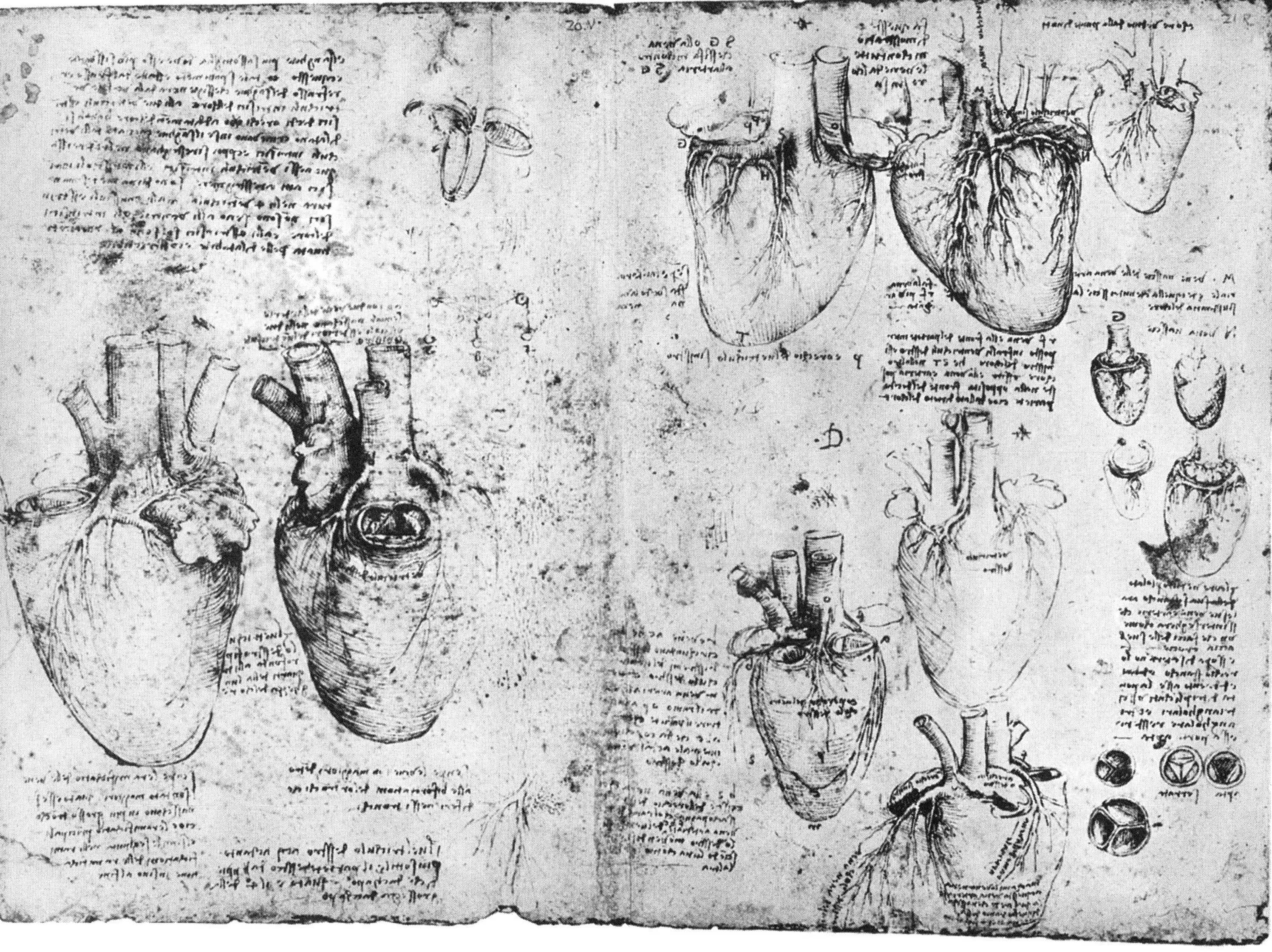

clarity of outlines of forms undergo at different distances from the eye.

Therefore, sculpture is of a simpler cast and makes fewer demands on the mind than painting. *

IV. EXPERIENCE AND DRAWING

34. Writer, with what words can your descriptions equal the complete image here rendered by the drawing ? For you give only a confused description and a weak idea of the true form of objects. You delude yourself if you believe you can fully satisfy the listener when it is a question of evoking solid forms enclosed by a surface.

I ask you not to encumber yourself with words unless you are speaking to blind men ; if you wish to speak to men's ears with words and not to their eyes, speak of such kinds of things as are of substance or of nature. * Do not encumber yourself with what concerns the eyes in order to transmit it through the ears. You will remain far from surpassing the painter.

With what words would you describe the heart that is shown here, without filling a book ? The more lengthily you go into details, the more confusion will you sow in the mind of the listener. You will always need commentaries or references to experience, but for you the latter is short and deals with few things concerning the subject of which you desire full knowledge. *

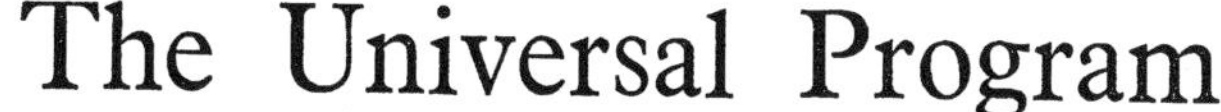

The Universal Program

1. The Principles

An awareness of the close relation between scientifically organized knowledge and painting is at the core of Leonardo's thought. He cannot paint an object without seeing it in its context ; he cannot observe without questioning : the forms of nature cannot be known if their origins are not understood. Though he often comes close to a narrow naturalism, Leonardo manages to avoid it by concerning himself with the essence of whatever he is studying. In his basic pronouncements the necessity to adhere to the actual appearance of things alternates with the equal necessity of searching out the laws that govern them. It is as if extreme abstraction (as of mathematics) had to go hand in hand with extreme concreteness of presentation. Another characteristic contradiction results : the painter must be a mirror, but he must also be a thinking mirror. Though the juxtaposition of passivity and receptivity to selective action seems paradoxical, it is, for Leonardo, the source of all the joy and magic of painting. He exalts himself by attributing to his art the superhuman dignity of that universal light that fills the world according to the rhythm of necessity.

He is willing to attempt the impossible and even gets some sort of satisfaction out of trying to bring all that is within the scope of the universe into one painting. In this he is influenced by a tendency to make lists that is characteristic of medieval and Renaissance poets, including Poliziano and Ariosto. Instinctively he tends to substitute some sort of order for this interminable cataloguing, even if it is only one of contrast : for example, it may be between delightful and frightful scenes — a rapid transition from sweetness to horror is typical of Leonardo — or he may present phenomena in terms of the four elements and their properties — here he is the metaphysician considering Aristotelian causes. The most fascinating, and the least obvious organization is the one that results from the artist's unique ability to discern the universal kinship of forms existing between even the most disparate aspects of reality, a relationship he alone can express and mold as he desires.

Quick changes in the sensibilities, evidence of powerful forces, secret motives of universal life, these are the major subjects of the investigations which endow paintings with the wealth and opacity of reality. Without setting up a systematically constructed presentation, Leonardo has given the main idea in a number of telling "fantasies." These are not only descriptions for paintings, but they as much present irresistible situations taken from the life of the imagination and, as such, have a direct connection with the intellectual formulation of principles.

THE PAINTER QUESTIONS NATURE

35. *O marvelous necessity !* Seeing that images of objects are all spread throughout the air surrounding them and are at every point within it, the images of our hemisphere necessarily enter and pass, together with those of all the heavenly bodies, through the natural point in which they merge and become united by mutually penetrating and intersecting each other ; the image of the moon in the east and the image of the sun in the west become united at this point and fuse with our hemisphere.

O marvelous necessity, that brings about the union and merging of the east and the west at this natural point within our hemisphere.

O marvelous necessity, with precise reasoning you constrain all effects to be the direct result of their causes ; by an irrevocable and exacting law, every natural action obeys you by the shortest possible process.

Who would believe that such a limited space could contain all the images of the universe ? O mighty process ! What talent could penetrate your nature ? What tongue could expound such wonders ? None, surely. This is what makes human discourse turn to the contemplation of the divine. *

That he who disparages painting loves neither 36.
knowledge nor nature. If you disparage painting, which alone can imitate all the visible works of nature, you surely disparage a most subtle device which, by its philosophical and formidable reasoning, examines all manner of forms : the seas, places on land, plants, animals, grass, flowers, all bathed in shadow and light. Certainly, this science is the true daughter of nature, for it is nature that has brought it forth ; but for the sake of accuracy, we shall call it the grandchild of nature, for nature has brought forth all visible things and painting is born of these. Hence, we may rightly call painting the grandchild of nature and related to God. *

37. *To paint is to judge* *Of the painter's judgment of his own work and of that of others.* When the work of a painter equals his judgment, that is a bad sign for the judgment; and when his work surpasses his judgment, that is worse, as happens when a painter is amazed at having done so well. But when the judgment surpasses the work, that is good. With this attitude, if the painter is young, he will surely become an excellent master. He will produce few works, but these will be of a kind to make people stop to marvel at their perfection. *

38. The painter contends with and rivals nature.

39. Let no one read my principles who is not a mathematician. *

40. *That principles are everything* There is no result in nature without a cause; understand the cause and you will have no need for experiments.

41. Nature is full of infinite reasons which were never set forth in experiments.

42. Nature is bound by the processes of her own law which she has herself created.

THE SOVEREIGN SPIRIT: ATTENTION AND IMAGINATION

43. *The joy of seeing* *Of the difference and similarity of painting and poetry . . .* What moves you, O man, to abandon your home in town and to leave your relatives and friends to go to the country, over mountains and through valleys, if not the natural beauty of the world, which, if you consider well, you can enjoy only through the sense of sight? *

44. *Be a conscious mirror* *Painting.* The mind of the painter should liken itself to a mirror which always takes on the color of the thing it reflects and is filled by as many images as there are objects before it. O Painter, know that to excel you must have the universal power to represent all the varieties of forms nature produces, and this you will not know how to do without seeing and retaining them in your mind.

Therefore, when in the country, give your attention to the various objects, looking carefully first at one thing and then at another, and make up your sheaf of carefully selected things from which the least good have been winnowed out.

Do not imitate the painters who, when tired by imaginative work, lay aside their task and take a walk to find relaxation, but retain such a weariness of mind that it keeps them from paying attention to what they see. They often meet relatives or friends who greet them; they see them and hear them, but recognize them as little as if they were air. *

45. The painter who works from habit and by guessing, without reasoning about things, is like the mirror that reproduces within itself all that appears before it, without taking any notice of it. *

46. *How the painter is master of all sorts of people*

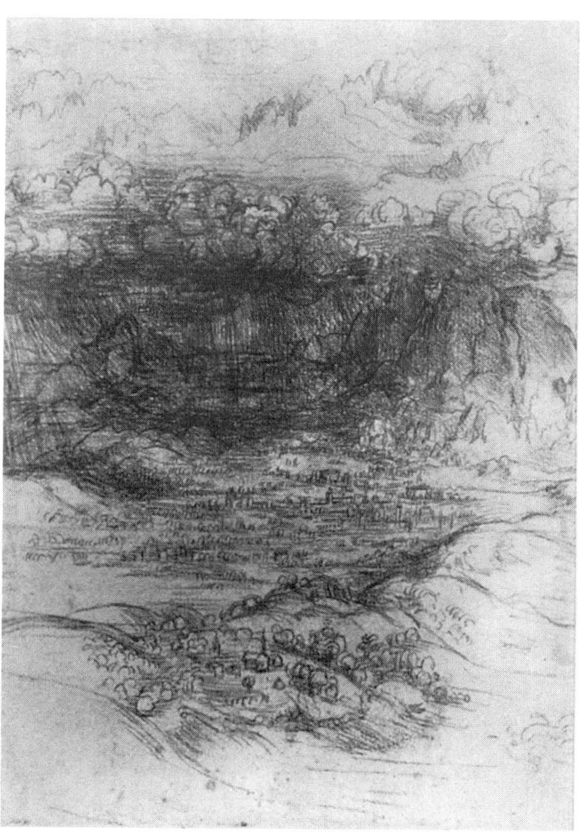

Storm over an Alpine Valley.

and of all things. If the painter wishes to see beauties capable of inspiring love, he has the ability of creating them, and if he wishes to see monstrous things that frighten, or jests that cause laughter, or things that inspire piety, he is their lord and master. If he wishes to create landscapes, or deserts, or fresh and shady places in warm weather, he depicts them ; so also warm places in bad weather. If he wishes valleys, if he wishes to disclose great sweeps of land from the high peaks of mountains, and if he then wishes to see the horizon of the sea, he has the power to do so. If from the depths of the valleys he wishes to see high mountains, or from the high mountains the low valleys or the shore, and all that exists in the universe through essence, real or imaginary, * he has it first in his mind and then in his hands. And these are of such excellence that at a given moment they create a proportioned harmony taken in by the eye as the reality itself.

Of the pleasure of the painter. The divinity 47.
inherent in painting transmutes the painter's mind into a resemblance of the spirit of God, for with free forcefulness it gives itself to the creation of diverse things : animals of all kinds, plants, fruits, landscapes, fields, landslides in the mountains, frightful and appalling places that terrify those who see them, or instead, delightful places, soft and pleasant with meadows of many-colored flowers, swayed by soft waves of breezes, watching the winds flee, rivers that descend from the high mountains with the force of great floods, dragging along uprooted trees wildly mixed with stones, roots, earth, and foam, pushing away

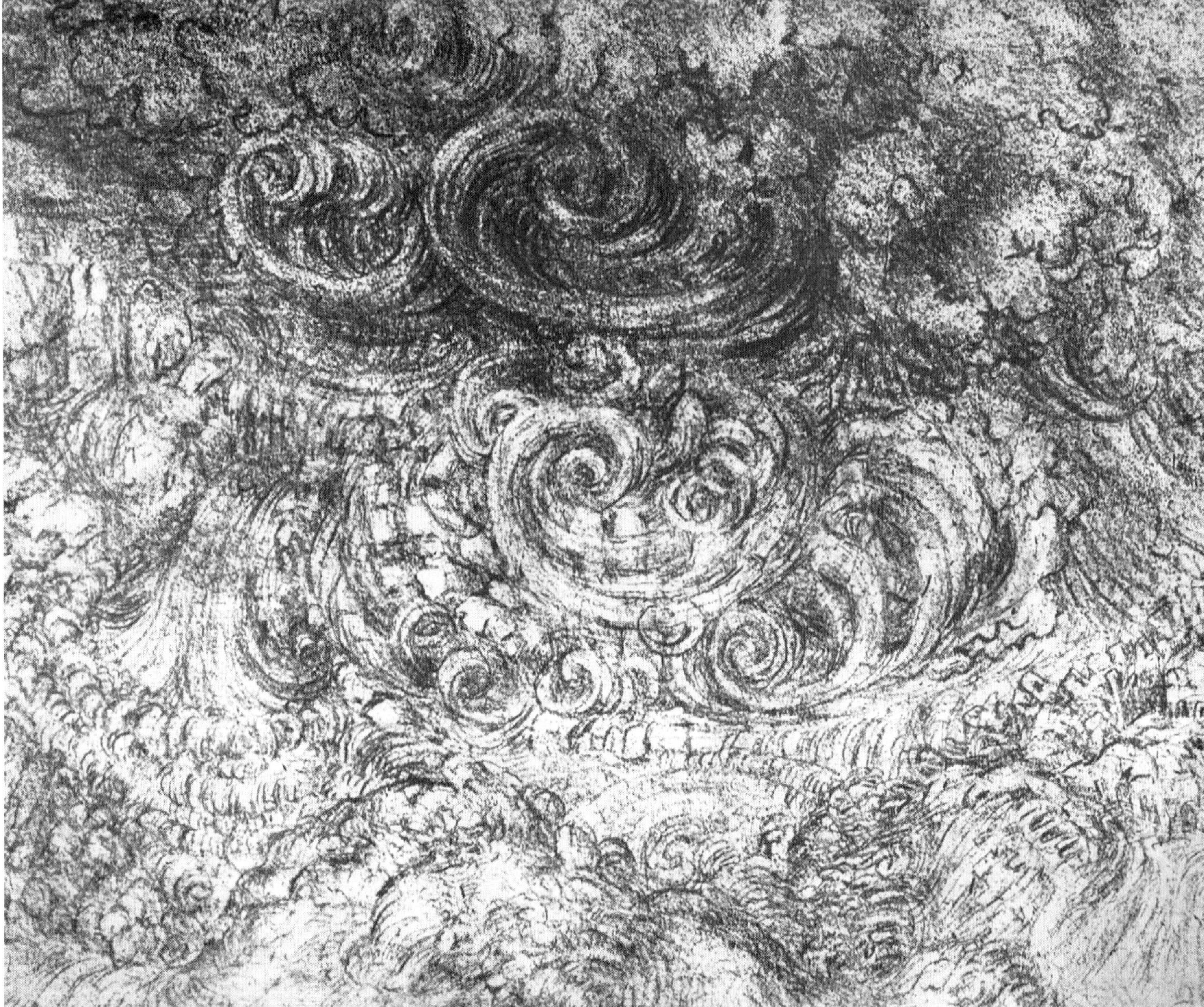

◀ *The Flood.* One of a series of drawings of *The End of the World* from Leonardo's last years, illustrating fantasies that are both geological and apocalyptical.

everything that opposes its flow ; and the sea with its tempest that battles and rages against opposing winds, and raising itself in proud waves, it falls, destroying the wind that beats against the base of the waves, enclosing and imprisoning it, beating and breaking it into a mixture of troubled foam. Then the fury of the sea is stilled. At times, overcome by the winds, the water leaves the sea and plunges over the high banks of neighboring promontories and, reaching over the summits of mountains, it descends into the valleys beyond. A part dissolves into spray, torn away by the wind, a part escapes by falling back into the sea as rain, and a part descends from the high promontories, spreading ruin and pushing away all that hinders its course. Often, meeting a wave coming at it, it crashes against it and raises itself heavenward, filling the air with a confused and clouded foam, which, thrown by the winds into the innermost recesses of the promontories, forms dark clouds that are the prey of the conquering wind. *

THE INFINITE SCOPE OF THE TASK

48. *Take the place of nature* — *Comparison of painting and sculpture . . .* Necessity compels the mind of the painter to transform itself into the very mind of nature and to become an interpreter between nature and art. It resorts to nature to show the reasons for its course, manifestations that are subjected to its own laws . . . *

49. *That everywhere there is something to learn.*

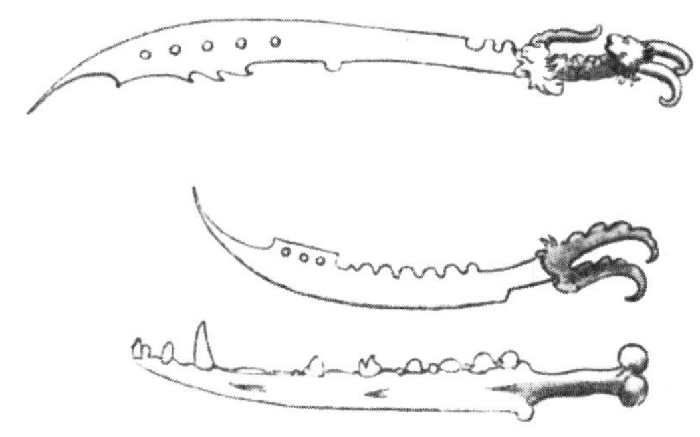

Knives derived from animal forms.

Beneficent nature has provided that you may find something to imitate everywhere.

That the painter is not praiseworthy unless he is versatile. Let us refute unhesitatingly those who call that painter a good master who succeeds only in painting well one type of head or one 50.

Mask and imaginary animal.

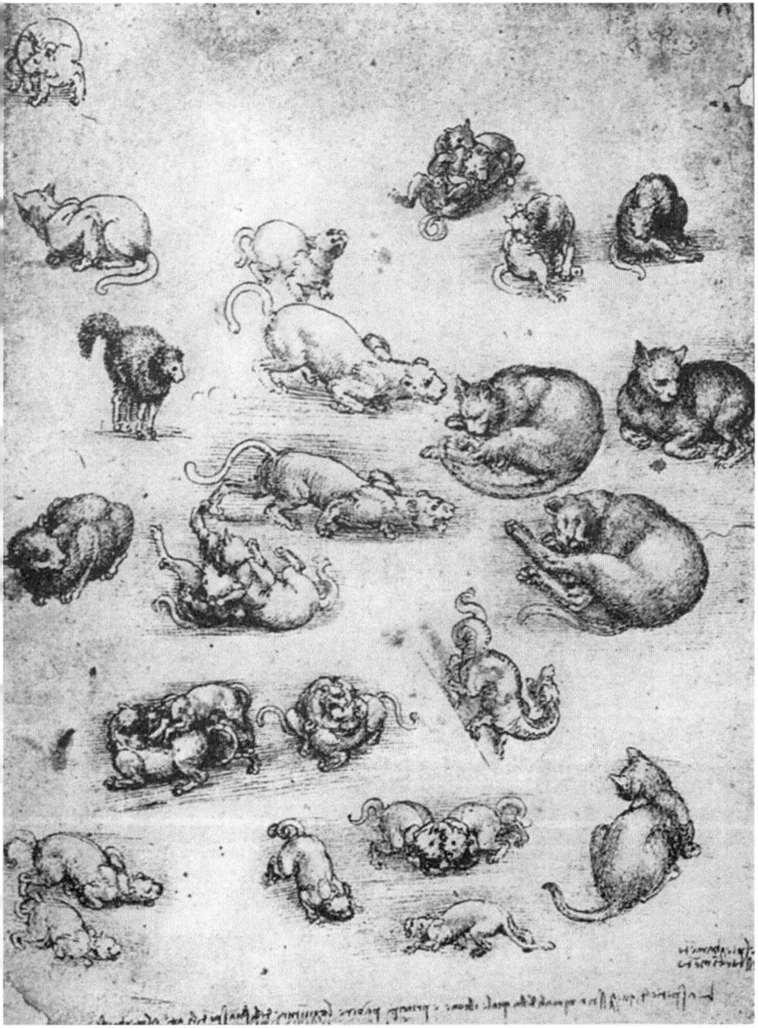

Studies of cats and a dragon.

figure. Surely it is not a great feat that he who studies only one single thing throughout his lifetime should reach some degree of perfection. But since we know that painting embraces all the things that nature produces and all those things which the activities of man have added to it, in short, all that is visible, he seems to me a poor master who can execute but one figure well.

Now, do you not see how many and how varied the acts of one man are? Do you not see how many different animals there are, and how many trees, plants, flowers, and how great is the variety of mountainous places and of plains, springs, rivers, cities, public and private edifices, instruments meet for human usage, and of different kinds of dress, ornaments, and crafts? All these things must be executed with skill and excellently well when depicted by one who deserves to be called master.

Of the variety of figures . . . for a man may be well proportioned or be fat and short, tall and thin, or average. And he who takes no account of these differences, makes his figures as if they had been turned out by a stamp, so that they all seem brothers—which merits great reproof. 51.

Of the manner of representing the four seasons or things having to do with them . . . Do not, as some do, paint all kinds of trees, even when at the same distance, * in the same shade of green. Whether it is a matter of fields, or plants, or other types of ground, or rocks and tree trunks, you must always vary them, for nature is infinitely variable, and not only in regard to species; 52.

The infinite variety within a species

different colors are found in the same trees, the leaves being more beautiful and larger on some branches than on others. Nature is so delightful and rich in her variations that among trees of the same kind there would not be found one that closely resembles another ; and not only among whole plants, but also among the branches, the leaves, and the fruit, not one will be found that is precisely like another. You must remember this and give as much variety as you can.

53. *Variety among the people in narrative paintings.* The persons in narrative paintings ought to differ in complexion, age, flesh tints, attitudes, fatness, leanness, such as heavy, slender, large, small, fat, great, proud, courteous, old, young, strong and muscular, weak and with few muscles, cheerful, melancholy ; with curly or straight, short or long hair ; with brisk or common movements ; with variety in clothing and colors, and whatever else is required in narrative painting. It is an extreme vice in a painter to portray the faces so that they look like one another, and even the repetition of gestures is a grave defect. *

54. *Ways of becoming versatile.* It is an easy thing for a man to become versatile, for all terrestrial animals have a certain similarity in their parts, that is, muscles, sinews, and bones, and these do not vary except in length or in breadth, as will be shown in the book on anatomy. Then there are the marine animals, which are of great variety, and concerning which I will not encourage the painter to make any rule, since they are of almost infinite variety, as are the insects. *

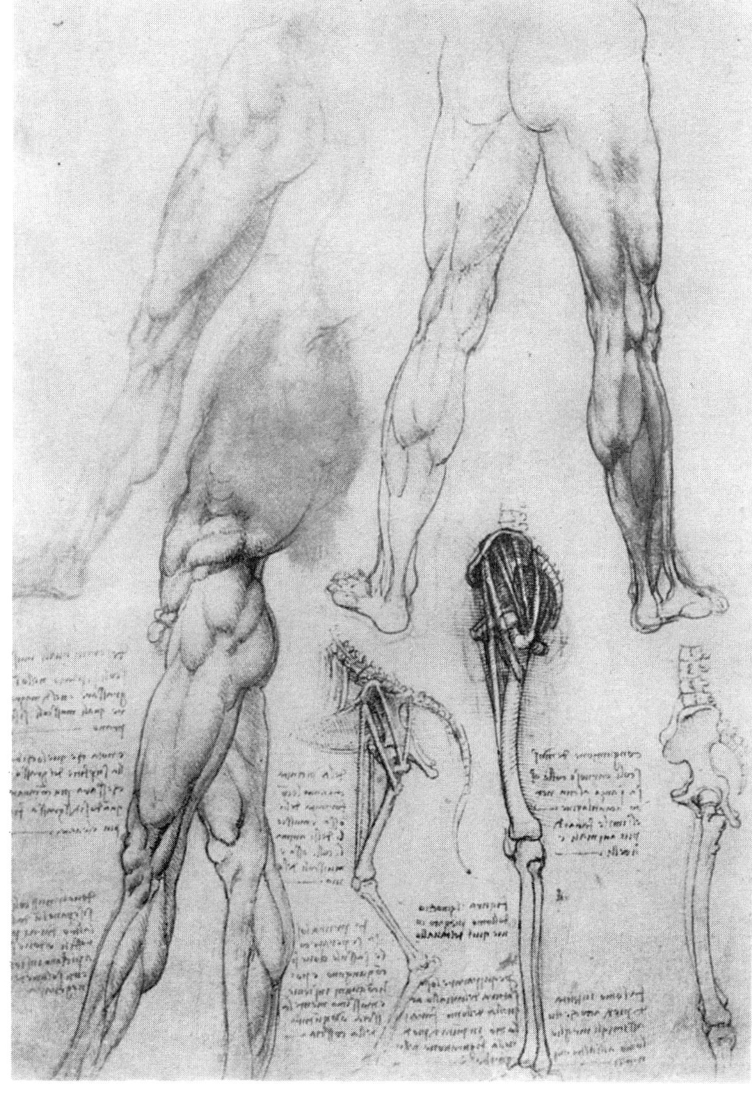

Studies in comparative anatomy showing the differences between the human leg and those of quadrupeds that result from the erect position. ▸

2. The Great Themes: Man and Nature

If painting alone can reveal the wonders of nature, it must be allowed to fulfill its destiny of revealing the whole universe. However, between this distant goal and the commissioned works there stretches a vast territory where dream paintings mingle with usable ideas and motifs actually applied effectively. Here, too, are those grand lyric themes which alone can encompass the complex and moving aspects of man and the physical universe which alone can fire the painter's imagination and set in motion his activity. These great themes, these arrangements of forms and images, make up the true raw material, the pure spectacle which the painter assembles and arranges in the numberless variations that express his interior vision. For Leonardo these themes were a favorite subject of contemplation, and they became increasingly important to him with the years. Their origin is probably to be sought in a need to state in general terms the actual problems met with in connection with actual works. But their relation to specific paintings, either religious or secular, became looser with time. Beginning with the Virgin of the Rocks *(ca. 1482), Leonardo's paintings compromise between the well-defined requirements of each subject and that greater aspiration toward total painting that can never be realized fully. It is therefore not surprising that, besides innumerable drawings enriching the material expression of these great themes that could not be executed, Leonardo attempted to assure their validity and to maintain interest in them by means of literary descriptions. Though their purpose is not always clear, these visions have a character that is direct, nar-*

rative, and personal and are informed by an imagination capable of creating a convincing illusion. One might easily believe them to be stories, travelogues, or accounts of explorations. They should, however, be interpreted as exercices indispensable to keeping a certain kind of visual imagination fresh or, perhaps, as descriptions of imaginary paintings, paintings too complex to be realized that can, however, be explored in a makeshift but convenient fashion by writing about them. It seems ironic, however, that someone who so consistently praised painting at the expense of literature should feel the need to supplement his art with writing. *

TALES *

55. *The frightful giant of Libya*

Dear Benedetto Dei,

To give you news of things from the East, know that in June there appeared a giant who came from the Libyan desert. This giant was born on Mount Atlas, and was black, and he had fought against Artaxerxes with the Egyptians, and the Arabs, the Medes, and the Persians. He lived in the sea upon whales, great leviathans, and ships.

When the bold giant fell on the ground, which was covered with blood and mire, one would have thought a mountain had collapsed ; the country shook as though from an earthquake so that Pluto in Hell felt terror, and Mars, fearing for his life, took refuge under the bed of Jupiter.

From the violence of the shock, he lay prostrate on the ground. Right away, the people, believing that he had been killed by a thunderbolt, gathered in a crowd about him, like ants rushing about on the trunk of an oak that has been cut down. And they hurried over his huge limbs and pricked them with many wounds, like ants spreading furiously over the oak cut down by the sturdy peasant's axe.

At this the giant, having come to himself, perceived himself to be almost covered by the crowd and suddenly felt himself smarting from their stabs ; he uttered a roar which resounded like terrifying thunder, set his hands on the ground and raised up his terrible force. Putting one of his hands to his head, he found it covered with men sticking to his hair like the insects that live there. He raised his head and the men were thrown into the air like hail carried by a gust of wind. As they clung to the hairs and strove to hide among them, they resembled sailors in a storm climbing the rigging to lower the sails in order to lessen the force of the wind. A large number of those who had climbed on him were found dead. Then, standing up, he trampled them under his feet.

The black face at first seems most horrible and 56.
terrifying to look upon, especially the swollen and bloodshot eyes set beneath awful, lowering eyebrows, which cause the sky to be overcast and the earth to tremble.

Believe me, there is no man so proud that, when the flaming eyes turned on him, he would not have willingly taken wings to escape. The face of infernal Lucifer would seem angelic by contrast with this. The nose was turned up and had wide nostrils out of which stuck large bristles, the mouth had thick, up-turned lips and, at the extremities, hairs like those of a cat, and the teeth were yellow. His instep was higher than men on horseback.

Tired of lying down and annoyed by . . . his rage turned to frenzy, and he began, with all the fury that possessed his mighty limbs, to enter in among the crowd with his feet ; and with his heels he tossed men into the air, so that they fell down again upon the rest like a thick hailstorm. And many, in dying, dealt out death. This horror continued until he had raised so much dust with his great feet that it compelled his infernal fury to abate.

How many attacks were made on this fiendish monster against whom all was in vain ! Wretched men, your impregnable fortresses, the high walls of your cities, your great hosts, your houses, and palaces, none will avail you. Like crabs or crickets or other such little creatures, all that remains for you are the small cavities, the subterranean caves. There seek refuge and safety.

How many mothers and fathers had the misfortune of losing their children ; how many unhappy women were deprived of their companions ! No, no, my dear Benedetto, I do not believe that since the world was created has there been seen such lamentation and wailing of people, accompanied by so much terror.

Indeed, human beings in such a plight may envy all other species. While the eagle has greater strength than all other birds, these can still resort to the swiftness of their flight, and so the swallows escape the rapaciousness of the falcon by their swiftness, and the dolphins avoid the voracious whales and great leviathans by their speed.

But for us wretched mortals flight is of no avail, for the monster's slowest step by far outstrips the swiftest runner.

I know not what to say or do. I seem to find myself swimming, head bent, within the mighty throat, and dead, I will be swallowed up, indistinguishably, in the huge belly.

To the Defterdar of Syria, lieutenant of the sacred Sultan of Babylon : 57.

The journey to the East

The new catastrophes that occurred in the northern region of the province will, I am certain, seem terrifying to the whole universe, as they will also to you. I shall reveal them to you in due order, showing first the effect, then the cause . . .

I found myself in this part of Armenia in order to discharge with zeal and devotion the task that you had confided to me ; in order to commence in a place that seemed most suitable, I had entered the city of Calindra, which is near the frontiers. This city is situated in the lowlands of the Taurus Mountains where they are separated from the Euphrates and look westward to the peaks of the great mountain. These peaks are so high that they seem to touch the sky ; there is no place on earth higher than the summit, and this is always struck by the rays of the sun for four hours before day. The stone is so white that it shines brilliantly and performs for the Armenians of these parts the same role as would the

Description of Mount Taurus. ▶

beautiful light of the moon amidst darkness. Its great altitude reaches above the highest level of the clouds for four miles in a straight vertical line. Many regions to its west see this summit illuminated by the sun after its setting for as long as a third of the night, and it is this which among you in calm weather has formerly been thought to be a comet. In the darkness of the night, it seems to us to assume various shapes, sometimes dividing into two or three parts, sometimes long, sometimes short. This proceeds from the fact that the clouds on the horizon intervene between part of this mountain and the sun and, by intercepting the rays of the sun, the light of the mountain is broken by various spaces of clouds and the brightness takes on changing forms.

58. *The Divisions of the Book :*

Preaching and conversion.

The sudden inundation, until its end.

The destruction of the city.

The death and despair of the people.

The pursuit of the preacher, his liberation, and his benevolence.

Description of the cause of the fall of the mountain.

The havoc that it made.

The destruction by avalanche.

The finding of the prophet.

His prophecy.

The inundation of the lower parts of western Armenia, the course of which was determined by the piercing of Mount Taurus.

How the new prophet showed that this destruction occurred as he had foretold it.

Description of Mount Taurus and the River Euphrates.

Why the mountain shines at its summit for a half or a third of the night and seems after sundown like a comet to the inhabitants of the West, and, before sunrise, to those of the East. Why this comet seems variable in shape — round, or long, divided into two or three parts, or united, invisible or again visible.

The shape of Mount Taurus. I am not rightly accused of idleness, O Defterdar, as your reproaches seem to intimate, but unbounded affection, born of your great benefits, has constrained me to search with the greatest diligence and to investigate with care the cause of so momentous and so surprising an occurrence. This took some time to accomplish. And to explain to you fully the reasons for this great occurrence, it is necessary that I shall describe the nature of the place before proceeding to the event, which, I believe, will satisfy you. 59.

Do not be angry, O Defterdar, that I have been slow in replying to your urgent request, for the matters about which you have asked me are of a kind that cannot well be expressed without taking time ; especially, in explaining the cause of so great an effect, it is necessary to give an exact description of the nature of the place, from which you will easily be able to see the abovementioned request satisfied.

I will not delay by describing the general aspect of Asia Minor or what seas or lands encompass its expanse, for I know the diligence and care of your studies will not have left you without this knowledge. I turn, therefore, to describing the true form of Mount Taurus, which is the cause of so surprising and disastrous an event ; this may serve to advance our purpose.

Many persons consider this Mount Taurus the ridge of the Caucasus. For my own information, I wished to speak with some of the inhabitants on the shores of the Caspian Sea ; according to what they said, their mountains bear the same name but these are higher. They confirmed that this is the true Caucasus, since in Scythian Caucasus means highest summit. And, in fact, nothing is known either to the east or to the west of any mountain that is as high, and the proof of it is that the inhabitants of the countries to the west see the rays of the sun illuminate part of its summit for a fourth part of the longest night, and the same is true in the countries to the east.

60. *Structure and dimensions of Mount Taurus.* The shadow of this ridge of Taurus is so high that in the middle of June, when the sun is at the meridian, it reaches to the borders of Sarmatia, which are twelve days away, and in the middle of December, it extends all the way to the Hyperborean Moutains, which are a month's journey to the north. And the side that faces the winds is covered with clouds and mists, for the wind, which is divided in two on encountering the rock and comes together again behind, carries with it the clouds from all parts and lets go of them only at the moment of impact. It is therefore always full of thunder because of all the clouds that accumulate there, and the rock is full of fissures and huge débris.

The base around the mountain is inhabited by very prosperous peoples, is rich in magnificent springs and rivers, and fertile and abundant in all kinds of good things, especially on the side facing south. After an ascent of about three miles, begin the forests of great firs, pines, beeches, and other trees ; three miles further on are meadows and vast pastures, and all the rest, as far as the beginning of the mountains, is eternal snow which never goes away and extends to a height of fourteen miles in all.

From this point, where the peak of Taurus begins to the height of one mile, no cloud ever passes, so that there are fifteen miles, that is, about five miles in a straight vertical line, and at again as great a distance, or almost as great, we find the summit of Taurus. About half way up one finds the air grow hot, and there is not the least breath of wind, and nothing can live there very long. Nothing is brought forth there except some birds of prey, which nest in the high crevices of Taurus and descend below the clouds to seek their prey along the upper reaches of the pastures. Above the clouds all is bare rock, and the rock is dazzling white, but it is impossible to reach the lofty summit because of the great difficulties and dangers of the ascent.

In my letters I have often rejoiced with you in your good fortunes, and I know that today, like a true friend, you will share my sorrow at the miserable condition to which I am reduced. It is as follows : during the past days I, together with the unfortunate inhabitants of the country, have known so many troubles, fears, dangers, and ills, that we have come to envy the dead. Surely, since the elements were divided and brought an end to chaos, they have never joined forces and raged to do so much evil to man as we have now seen and suffered, so that I cannot imagine any misfortune that could still be added to these.

First we were assailed and buffeted by the mighty rage of the winds. This was followed by avalanches from the snow-covered mountains, which filled the valley and crushed a great part of our city. And, as if that were not enough, the storm submerged the lower part of the city in a sudden flood ; to this was added a sudden burst of rain, or rather, a raging torrent of water, sand, mud, and stones all mingled together with roots, branches, and stems of various trees ; and all came hurtling through the air and descended on us. Finally a great fire broke out ; one would have thought that it was not the wind but thirty thousand devils who brought it. It burned up and destroyed the whole country and has not yet died down. The few survivors are in such a state of prostration and terror, and so dazed, we hardly have the courage to speak one with another. Having given up all our usual occupations, we huddle together in the ruins of some of the churches, men and women, young and old, all together like a herd of goats. (The neighboring people, who had been our enemy before, took pity on us and brought us aid and food) and if there had been no one to succor us, we would all have died of hunger.

Now you see the state we are in ; and yet all these evils are nothing in comparison to those which we expect soon.

I know that you as a friend will be saddened by my misfortunes, just as in my letters I have shown myself glad at your good fortunes . . . .

SCENES AND VISIONS

You shall make* stairs on all four sides which 61. *The Island of Venus*
give access to a natural plateau at the top of the rock ; it should be hollowed out ; give it a façade with pillars, and beneath open it up by a great portico, where water will pour into basins of granite, porphyry, and serpentine amidst semi-circular niches, and flow out around the portico : on the north let there be a lake with a small island in the center and in the middle of it a thick and somber grove. Let the water pour down from the top of the pillars into the vases placed at their bases from which will run little rivulets.

From the coast of Cilicia, facing toward the south, one discovers the beauties of the isle of Cyprus.

From the southern coast of Cilicia one sees to the south the beautiful isle of Cyprus, formerly the realm of the goddess Venus. Many, drawn there by her beauty, have wrecked their ships and riggings on the reefs amid the turbulent waters. Here the beauty of gentle hills invites the wandering mariner to rest among flowering meadows where roving breezes fill the island and the surrounding sea with fragrant odors. How many ships have foundered here ! How many vessels have been wrecked upon these reefs! Here one can see ships without number, some broken in pieces, some half-buried in the sands ; of one the poop is visible, of another the prow, here a keel, there a rib. One might think it a day of judgment on which dead ships are raised, so many of them are on the northern shore. Here blows the north wind with various strange sounds.

62. *Fossil of a sea-monster*

O powerful and once living instrument of creative Nature, your great strength was of no use to you and you had to give up your tranquil life to obey the laws that God and time imposed on procreative Nature.

The powerful fins with which, when pursuing your prey, you clove your way through the water and opened up a path for yourself with your chest, tearing through the tempestuous, briny waves.

How many times could one see the frightened shoals of dolphins and great tunny flee before your mad fury, and you, beating your swift fins and forked tail like lightning, raised a sudden tempest in the sea and a great uproar and shipwrecks. With mighty waves you have filled the bare shores with frightened and distracted fish. And having escaped you, they were left high and dry when the sea pulled back, the plenteous spoil of nearby peoples.

O Time, you who consumes all things and takes them back into herself, you give to the lives you take a new and different existence.

O Time, you who quickly despoil all created things, how many kings, how many peoples have you brought to nought . . . how many revolutions and occurrences have succeeded each other since the wondrous form of this fish died here! In the crevices of this winding recess . . . Now, broken up by Time, you are peacefully embedded in this enclosed space. Your bones, without their flesh and other matter, now serve as armature supporting the mountain which rises above you.

How many times have you been seen amid the waves of the vast and swelling ocean with your black back bristling, like a mountain, stately and superb in appearance . . . *

How to represent a battle. * First paint the smoke of the artillery, mixed in the air with the 63.
dust raised by the movement of the horses and the combatants ; and you should produce the following mixture : the dust, being an earthly matter and heavy, though easily raised because of its fineness and easily dispersed, nevertheless tends to settle down again ; it is its finest part that rises the highest, so that this upper part is the least visible and seems almost to be the color of air. The smoke that mingles with the dusty air seems more like a dark cloud the higher it rises, and in the upper regions one sees the smoke more clearly than the dust. The dust will seem slightly bluish, the smoke will tend to remain close to its natural color. * This mixture of air, smoke, and dust will be much lighter on the side from which the light comes than on the opposite one. As for the combatants, the further they plunge into the fray the less will one be able to distinguish them, and the slighter will be the difference between

the sides that are lighted and those that are in shadow. Their faces and bodies and appearance and firearms, as well as those around them, will be reddish. * This reddish cast lessens as the distance from its origin increases. And the figures between you and the light, if they are far away, seem dark against a light background, and their legs will be less visible closer to the ground, because there the dust is denser and heavier. And if you paint horses fleeing from the fray, paint little swirls of dust, one as far from the next as the horse's stride is long, and the one farthest from the horse should be the least visible but also the highest, the most spread out, and the thinnest, while the closest one should be the most visible as well as the smallest, and the thickest. The air should be full of arrows flying in different directions, one rising, another descending, and others moving in a straight line ; and a little smoke should follow the balls of the firearms in their course. And you will paint the figures in the foreground with dust on their hair, their eyebrows, and other surfaces to which it might stick. You will show the winners running, with their hair and all that is light streaming in the wind, and their eyebrows drawn down ; they will advance with opposite members, that is, if one advances the right foot, he will also bring his left arm forward. If you depict the fall of a combatant, you should also show the trace of where his foot dragged through the dust turned to bloody mud; and in the viscous earth around him, show the footprints of the men and horses that have passed there. You will show a horse dragging his dead rider and leaving behind him in

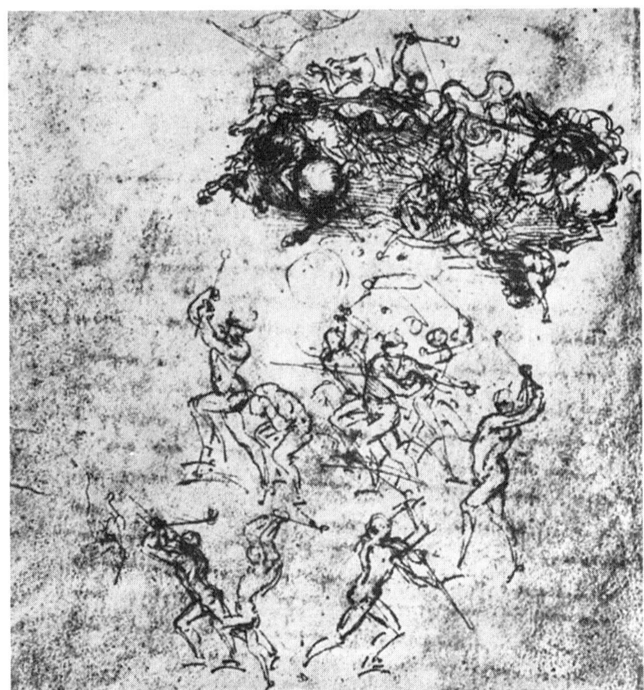

Studies for battle scenes.

the dust and mud the trace of the dragged body. You will show the conquered and beaten pale, with their eyebrows raised and coming together, and the skin above them creased with pain ; and at the sides of the nose they should have wrinkles rising in an arc from the nostrils to the corners of the eyes, the nostrils flaring — which causes these creases — the lips arched to show the upper teeth, the jaw opening for a cry of pain. One hand should shield the frightened eyes, with the palm turned out to the enemy, while the other is on the ground to support the raised upper body. You will paint others screaming, their mouths open, and fleeing. You will show various kinds of arms among the feet of the combatants, such as split shields, lances, broken swords, etc. You will portray the dead, some half, some entirely covered by dust. Dust mixed with blood becomes a red mud, and by its color one can recognize the twisted course of the blood flowing from the corpse through the dust. Others, dying, grind their teeth, roll their eyes, press their fists against their bodies, and contort their legs. A man, disarmed and beaten by his enemy, may be seen taking cruel and bitter vengeance with his teeth and nails. A swift horse, his mane blowing in the air, may be seen running against the enemy and doing much damage with his hoofs. You may see a wounded man falling on the ground and covering himself with his shield, and his enemy, bending over him, tries to kill him. Several men may be seen fallen in a group on top of a dead horse. You would see several of the victors leaving the fight and going away from the fray, with both hands wiping from their eyes and cheeks the mud formed by the tears that the dust had brought to their eyes. You would see the reserves waiting, full of hope and ready to act, shading their drawn brows with their hands, peering into the thick and dark fray, and attentive to the command of the captain. And likewise, the captain, his baton raised, running toward the reserves to show them the place where they are needed. And a river with running horses filling the water around them with troubled waves of a mixture of foam and water, which splashes into the air between the legs and bodies of the horses. And do not leave any open surface without blood filling the footprints.

Description of the Flood. * First there should 64.
be the summit of a steep mountain with some valleys around its base, and on its sides a layer of soil with small roots of bushes should be seen slipping and leaving a great part of the surrounding rock bare. Coming down these precipices and spreading ruin, in their wild course, they strike and lay bare the twisted and gnarled roots of the great trees and overturn them head downwards ; and the mountains, becoming bare, should begin to reveal the deep fissures made by earlier earthquakes ; and the bases of the mountains should be covered and concealed in great part by the débris and shrubs precipitated from the slopes of the peaks, and this should be mingled with mud, roots, branches, and diverse foliage mixed into this mud, earth, and rocks. The débris from some of the mountains has fallen down into the bottom of some of the valleys and formed dams for the swollen rivers ; but these

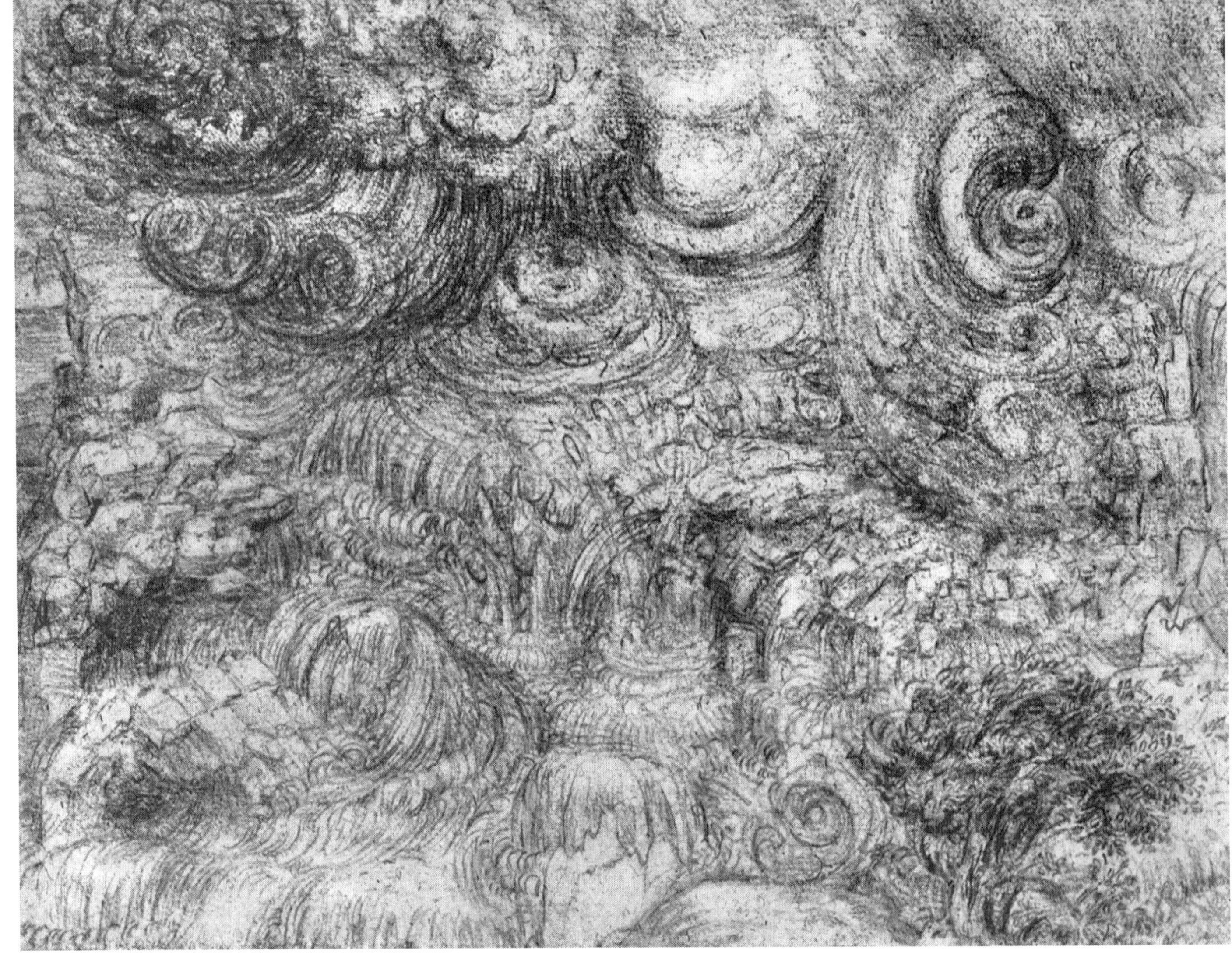

dams are already broken and are being carried away by the huge waves, the highest of which beat against and break down the walls of the towns and farms of the valley. And the fall of the great buildings of these towns raises great quantities of dust which mount upward with the appearance of smoke or wreathed clouds fighting against the rain that is falling.

But the swollen waters should be whirling around in the lake confining them and throw up wild breakers against various objects, thrown into the air with turbid foam, then falling back, so that the water they strike is thrown into the air. And the circles of waves which emanate from the place of impact are impelled by their impetus to cross the path of other circles of waves coming from another direction, and their impact raises them into the air, but without their becoming detached from the main body of water. And toward the outlet of this lake, the spent waves may be seen flowing toward it, at the bottom of which, falling or descending through the air, the water acquires weight and impetus ; thereafter, penetrating the water that receives it, it tears it apart, hurling itself furiously to strike against the bottom, which repulses it, so that it rises again to the surface of this *(lower)* pool, together with the air it had pulled down with it and which then remains in the foam mixed with pieces of wood and other things that are lighter than the water ; here arise the circular waves ; their movement increases with the diameter, but the movement makes the waves lower as their base becomes wider, and that is why the last ones are almost imperceptible ; but if these waves strike any kind of object, they are thrown back against the waves following them while continuing to increase in the curve of the circle, as if their initial movement had never been interrupted.

Drawing from the series on *The End of the World.*

But the rain falling from the clouds is the same color as these clouds — that is on the side in the shade * — unless the rays of the sun penetrate that far, for in that case the rain is less dark than the cloud. And if the great weight of the masses of débris from the high mountains or from other proud edifices, in their fall, strike the great masses of water, then a huge quantity of water will be thrown into the air, and its movement will be in the opposite direction of the substance that had struck it, that is, the angle of reflection will be equal to the angle of incidence.

Among the objects carried away by the current of the water, those which are heaviest or bulkiest will be furthest away from the two banks. The movement of the waters constituting a whirlpool is swiftest the closer it is to its center. * The crests of the waves of the sea, falling forward to their bases, strike and scrape the particles *(foam)* of the surface ; and this friction pulverizes the water so that it falls in tiny particles which are changed into a thick mist ; this mingles with the currents of the winds, like wreathing smoke or swirling clouds, and at last is lifted up into the air and transformed into clouds. But the rain which falls through the air, because it is driven and beaten by the current of the winds, becomes finer or thicker according to the fineness or density of these winds, so that a fine veil of humidity is formed that is caused by the fall of rain near the eye that perceives it. The waves of the sea that beat against the slopes of the nearby mountains cause foam to spout up quickly on the ridges of these hills and, in falling back, to meet the succeeding wave and, after a loud impact, flooding everything, they return to the sea from which they came. A great many beings, men and various animals, may be seen driven toward the peaks of the mountains near these waters by the rising flood.

65. *The Flood and its representation in painting. . . .* You may think you have good reason to reproach me for having represented the course the wind takes through the air because the wind itself cannot be seen in the air. To this I reply that what is visible in the air is not the movement of the wind itself, but that of the things carried by it.

Divisions :

Darkness, wind, tempest at sea, flood of water, forest fires, rain, lightning in the sky, earthquakes, the fall of mountains, the leveling of cities.

Whirlwinds which carry water, branches of trees, and men through the air.

Branches torn loose by the wind, carried along the current of the wind with people on them.

Trees broken and laden with people.

Ships broken in pieces, hurled onto reefs.

Herds, hail, lightning, cyclones.

People on trees unable to hold on. Trees and rocks, towers, hills crowded with people, boats, tables, troughs, and other means for floating.

Studies for *The Last Supper.* ▶

Hills covered with men and women and animals, and lightning from the clouds which illuminates everything.

NOTES ON HIS OWN PAINTINGS

One who was drinking has put down the glass and turned to the speaker. 66. *The Last Supper*

Another, twisting the fingers of his hand, turns with frowning brow to his companion. Another, with open hands showing the palms, raises his shoulders as high as his ears and expresses surprise with his mouth. Another speaks into the ear of his neighbor, and the other who listens to him has turned to him, giving him his ear and holding a knife in one hand and in the other the half-cut piece of bread. Another, holding a knife in his hand, turns around and knocks over a glass on the table. Another, his hand resting on the table, watches. Another breathes heavily with his mouth full, another leans forward to see who is speaking and shades his eyes with his hands. Another leans back behind the one bent forward and, between him and the wall, looks at the speaker. *

Christ : Count Giovanni, who belongs to the household of the Cardinal of Mortaro.

Alessandro Carissimo of Parma for the hand of Christ.

*(Lead)*ers of the Florentines : 67. *The Anghiari Battle*

Neri di Gino Capponi
Bernardetto de' Medici
Niccolò da Pisa
Count Francesco

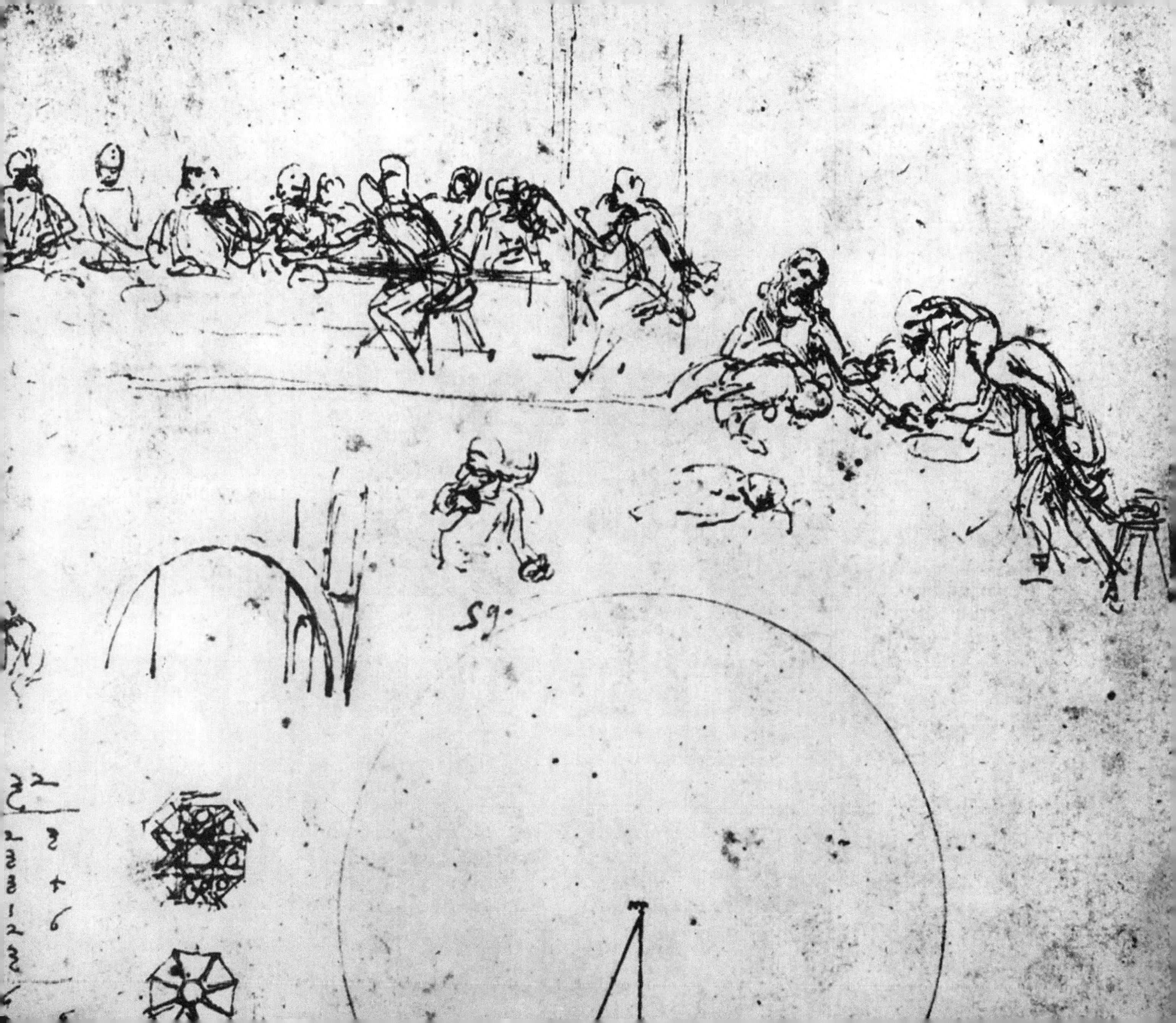

Micheletto
Pietro Gian Paolo
Guelfo Orsino
Messer Rinaldo degli Albizzi. *

Begin with Niccolò Piccinino's speech to the soldiers and exiled Florentines among whom were Messer Rinaldo degli Albizzi and others. Then show how he was the first to mount his horse, and how the whole army followed him.

Forty squadrons of cavalry.

Two thousand foot soldiers went with him, among them three hundred who guarded the standard of the wyvern. *

At an early hour of the morning the Patriarch climbed a hill in order to reconnoiter the country, that is, the hills, fields, and valleys watered by a river, and he saw Niccolò Piccinino approaching from Borgo San Sepolcro with his men, raising much dust, and, having seen him, he returned to the station of the leader of his men and spoke to them. Having spoken, he prayed to God with hands joined, and he saw a cloud from which St. Peter appeared and spoke to the Patriarch.

The Patriarch had sent five hundred cavalrymen to stop and break the momentum, etc.

In the foremost troop Francesco, the son of Niccolò Piccinino, was the first to attack the bridge which was guarded by *(the people)* and the Florentines.

He sent foot soldiers beyond the bridge, to the left, to divert our men who beat them off. Their leader was Micheletto, to whom the troops happened to have been assigned.

Here there was a great battle for the bridge, our troops * were victorious, the enemy was routed.

Here Guido and his brother Astorre, Lord of Faenza, and many men reformed their ranks, took up the fight again, and so violently assailed the Florentine forces that they regained possession of the bridge and advanced as far as the tents. Simonetto moved against them with six hundred horsemen, to strike the enemy, and he routed them a second time from the spot and reconquered the bridge. And behind him there came others with two thousand horses, and so the battle continued for a long time with changing success. Then the Patriarch, to throw the ranks into confusion, sent Niccolò da Pisa and Napoleone Orsino, a beardless youth, and behind them a great many men. And here was another great deed of arms accomplished. And during this time, Niccolò Piccinino had the reinforcements of his army advance, which made our troops fall back once more ; and if the Patriarch had not interposed himself and sustained the captains by word and deed, our troops * would have fled. And the Patriarch had certain pieces of artillery set up on a hill with which he broke up the infantry of the enemy, and the route was so great that Niccolò called his son and all the other men to him and they fled towards Borgo *(San Sepolcro)*. And at this spot there occurred a great massacre of men, and only those escaped who had been the first to flee and hide themselves. The passage of arms continued until sunset ; and the Patriarch took great care to recall his men and to bury the dead, and then he had a trophy * set up, etc.

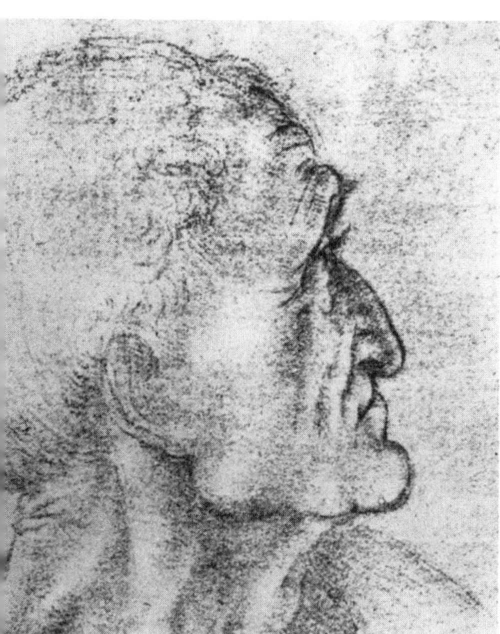

Studies for *The Last Supper* : Head of Judas.

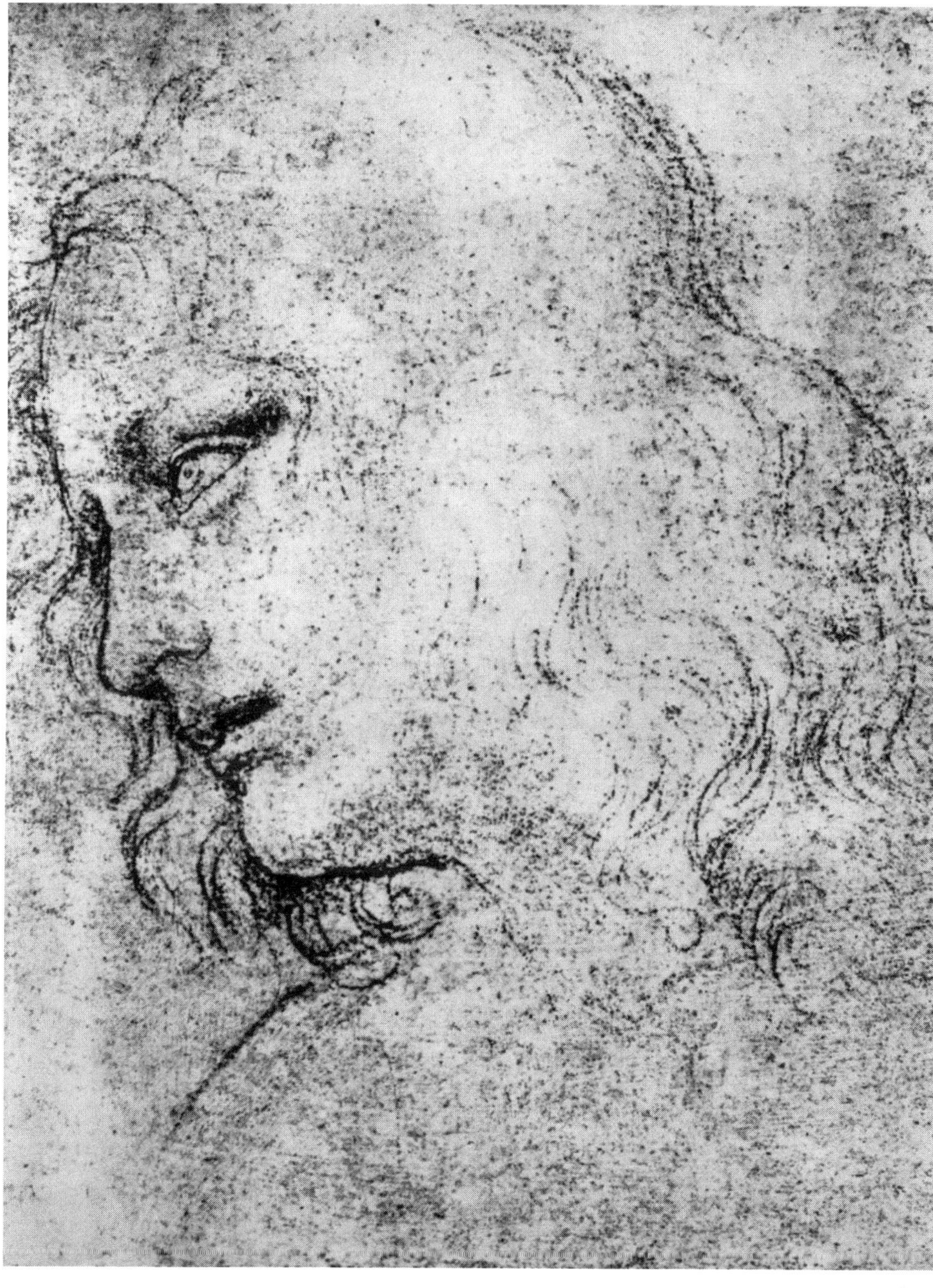

Head of St. Philip.

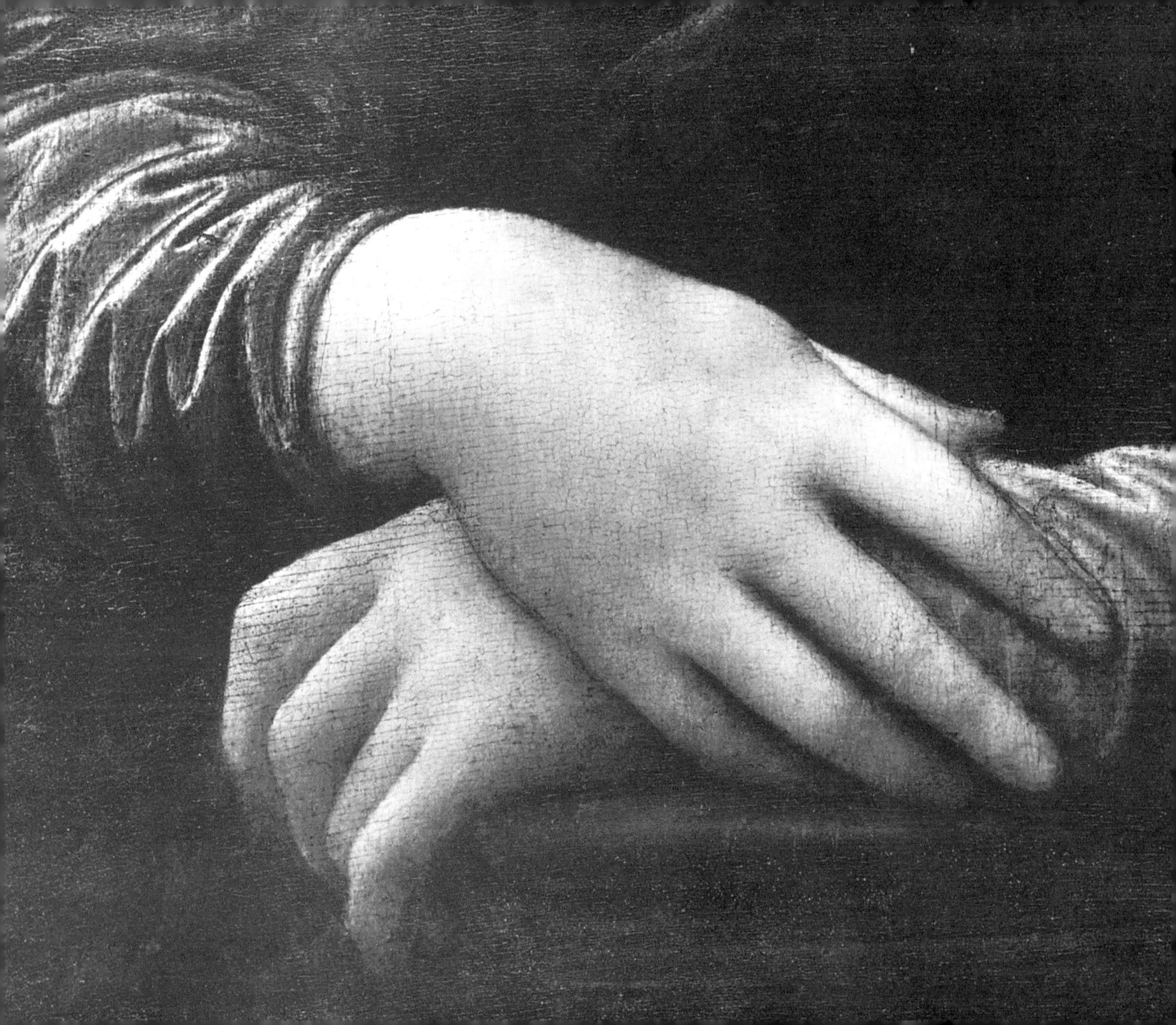

The Problems of the Painter

Mona Lisa. Detail, the hands.

Leonardo as critic

" First study science, then follow the practice born of that science " is one of Leonardo's most insistently expressed injunctions. It was as valid for him as for others and was the reason he undertook to write the* Treatise on Painting. *The discovery of this principle brought about Leonardo's complete reversal and reconstruction of the order of learning and as a result " knowledge-experience " of the visible, that is, painting, was placed at its summit. Naturally, the rules deduced from this principle had to include a detailed discussion of the great gifts of vision ; such discussions are indeed to be found in the notebooks, and the fragments below are meant to give an idea of them.*

There is, however, more to what Leonardo called the theory of art than a methodical classification of the solutions to all the problems of the painter. His theoretical works include : 1. A general analysis of the elements of vision and a thorough exploration of its special domains. 2. Notes aiming to formulate and to justify a specific style or organization of the pictorial data. 3. Specific information helpful in the actual practice of painting and study.

Consequently it will be useful to look at Leonardo's criticism first. He was an extremely severe critic who frequently expressed contempt for facile and superficial works. In these strict judgments and clear insights he usually has someone definite in mind, and, as a rule, it is easy to identify the victims. However, the most interesting aspect of his thesis, here as in his philosophical discussions, is the way in which impersonal, scientific needs are reconciled to an irrational, subjective point of view. In fact, in certain instances a reluctance to draw a conclusion is evident beneath his facility in stating theoretical positions, and in others he postpones making a final statement by thoroughly examining both sides of the question. At times, however, he seems to toss out his conclusions impatiently at his imaginary audience — an opponent who is actually his critical self. As a result, the precepts of the Treatise are backed up by airtight reasoning.

Painting's fundamental aims are twofold : to celebrate the beauty of space modulated by light, and to glorify the characteristic manifestations of life, or, to put it another way, form as the outgrowth of physical reality and as the expression of the vital energy of the universe. Clearly, these two classes do not belong to the same order since one is concerned with " pure " observation and the other with psychological perception. The terms " pure space " and " pure expression" are equally important to the creative act. Each is analyzed at length ; the former is discussed in relation to perspective and the dialectics of light and shadow, and the latter in relation to movement and its meaningful expression. Unlike modern artists, Leonardo is not disturbed by the problem that the painter should consider the changes of expression (a smile or frown) first as plastic realities — lines, folds, the play of light — and that this formal interpretation is only possible if emotional content is neglected. Indeed, Leonardo is very willing, even eager, to study expression in terms of plastic realities. However, such a concern would remove emotional content only if the arrangement of pure forms were reduced to a kind of non-expressive geometry. This is not the case. The space is animated, the play of light and shadow on the " outgrowths of physical realities" is always endowed with emotional content. In short, far from weakening the expressiveness of the human figure, Leonardo extends its force to all of nature.

Since it is rewarding to follow the steps of this development in its subtle changes, this section begins with passages in which Leonardo, while stating his dialectical position, defines, weighs the pros and cons, and selects. Then follow passages showing the two major directions he takes in his attempt to grasp the problems of painting conceived of as the mirror of space and of life. He lends them the greatest exactness and objectivity, either by a mathematical (or pseudo-mathematical) definition of form, or simply by unprecedented clarity of statement ; but at the same time, by means of a significant phrase, metaphor, or exclamation he emphasizes the effect on the sensibilities which, according to him, cannot give rise to any conceptual metaphysics or theology outside of art : the presence of fascinating evidence in the concrete organization of the universe. This is the aim of intellectual art : emotion in terms of objective expression.

Two salient points gradually emerge as Leonardo's ideas unfold. One is the use of shadow to alter and modulate the light, and it becomes more and more important because of his stress on chiaroscuro. The other is the use of subtle variations of expression to display emotions — such as Mona Lisa's smile. The first creates an ambiguity in the perception of space, the second in the perception of emotions. The one blurs the neat outlines in the drawing and in place of sharp definition produces an impression of inchoate diffuseness. The latter replaces all lively and obvious gestures with subtle and almost secret motions. As a result, the most interesting effects in his absolute painting are in direct opposition to his statements on the precise and scientific basis of the painter's craft. The coming together of these special effects mark the moment of beauty. It therefore seems appropriate to follow the sections on Space and Light, and Man and the Emotions with the fragmentary but powerful passages that relate either directly or indirectly to the execution of this superior work.

HOW TO JUDGE PAINTING

68. *The application of rules*

These rules are useful only in testing the figures, for all of us make mistakes in the first drafts, and whoever does not know the rules cannot correct them. Hence, knowing your errors, you will correct your works, and wherever you find errors, rectify them and take care not to fall into them again. But if you were to apply all these rules while making your first composition, you would never finish it and would cause confusion in your work.

With the aid of these rules, your judgment is free and sure, because good judgment is born of good understanding, and good understanding is born of reasons elicited from good rules, and good rules are the offspring of good experience, the common mother of all the sciences and all the arts. Therefore, if you remember what my rules prescribe, you will be able, because of your sound judgment, to estimate and recognize all disproportions in the work, whether in the perspective, or in the figures, or in anything else.

69. *Criteria*

Of the judgment that you should make upon a painter's work. Firstly, you should consider the figures, whether they have the relief required by the location and by the light that strikes them. Shadows should not be the same at the edges of a group as in its center, for it is one thing to be encircled by shadows and another to have the shadows at one side only . . . .

Secondly, there is the distribution and division of the figures ; this should be made according to the needs of the story you intend to represent.

Thirdly, the figures should be decisive in their action. *

70. *All styles should be used*

To avoid the reproaches resulting from the different preferences of painters. If you wish to avoid the master painters' criticisms of all those who do not agree with them on the various points of art, it is necessary to practice the art in several manners in order to conform to some extent with the judgment of each who passes on

The Annunciatio[n] Detail, landscape. ▶

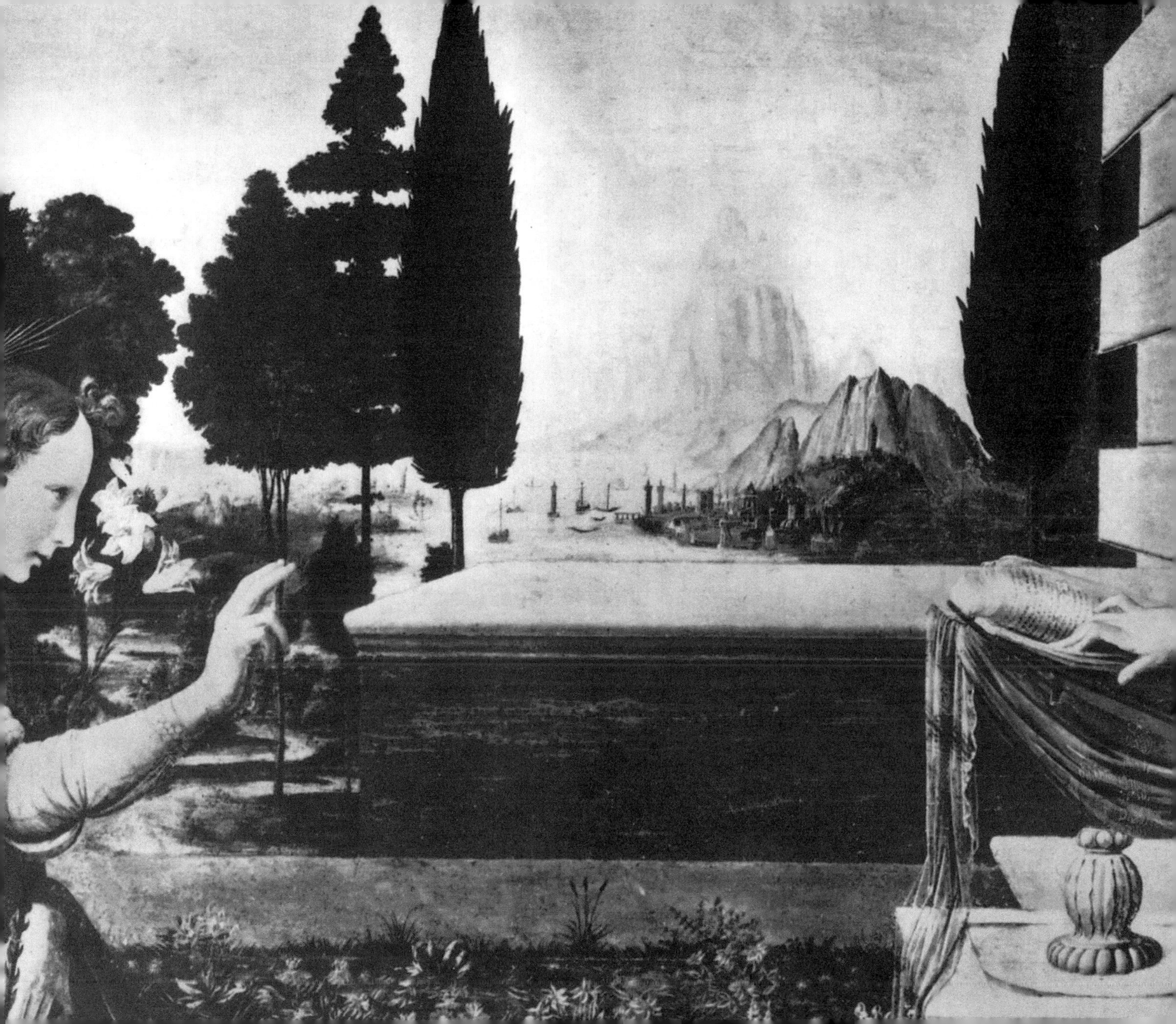

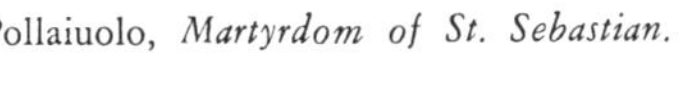

Pollaiuolo, *Martyrdom of St. Sebastian.*

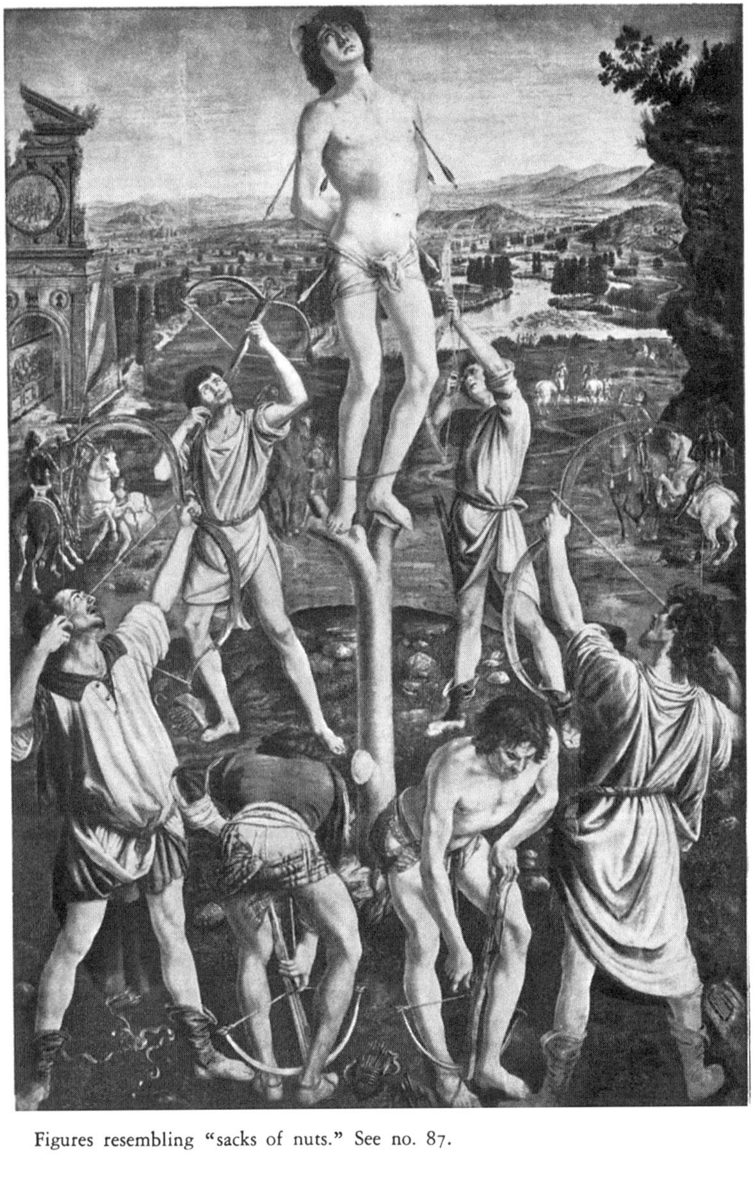

Figures resembling "sacks of nuts." See no. 87.

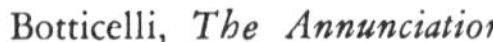

Botticelli, *The Annunciation.*

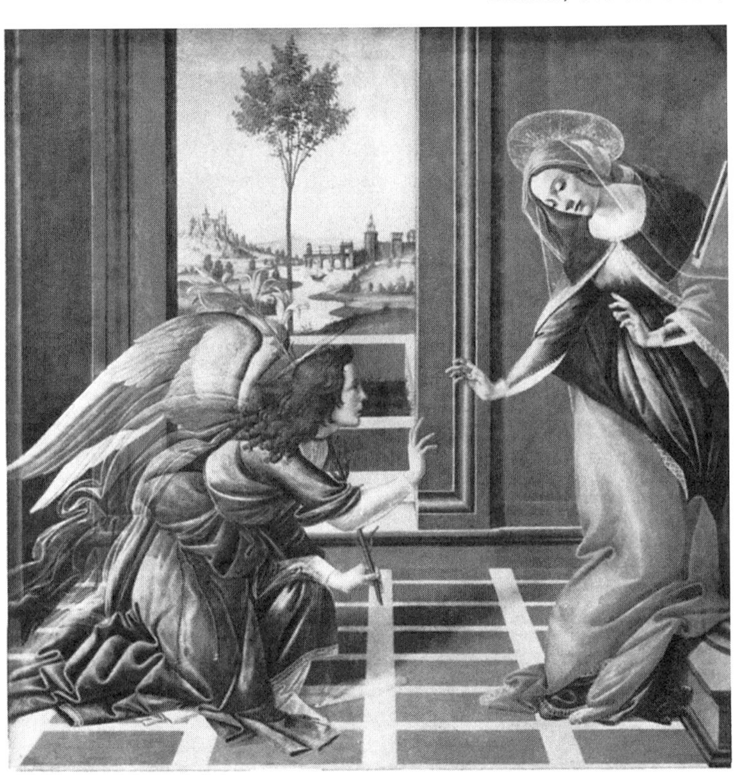

The angel seems "to wish to chase Our Lady from her room . . ." See no. 85.

the painter's work. We shall discuss this diversity later.

71. Why does one see a painting better in a mirror than without it ? *

72. *Judge with a mirror* *How the mirror is the master of painters.* To see whether your painting as a whole corresponds to the thing represented, take a mirror and set it so that it reflects the model, and compare this reflection with your picture, and carefully examine the whole surface to see whether the two images of the object are similar . . . And since the mirror can create the illusion of relief by means of lines and of light and shadow, you, who have among your colors more powerful shadows and lights than those of the mirror, if you know how to combine them as you should, will also be able to make your work seem like the reality seen in a great mirror.

73. *Painting and its elements* Painting consists of two principal parts : the first is form, that is, the line circumscribing the forms of bodies and their details, the second is the color enclosed within these limits.

74. *The principal divisions of painting* Painting is divided into two principal parts : the outline which surrounds the forms and the objects painted — that which one calls drawing — and the second which is called shadow. But this drawing is of such excellence that it not only investigates the works of nature but also innumerable others that are not part of it . . . Hence we conclude that drawing is not only knowledge but a divine power that should be named with veneration, a divine power capable of reproducing all the visible works of the Highest Power.

NEEDS AND PREFERENCES

That which is more important in painting, the shadows or the outlines. In painting the shadow takes much greater knowledge and skill than the outlines, and the proof of this is shown by the fact that the outlines can be traced by means of " veils " or panes of glass * placed between the eye and the object to be copied ; but this method cannot be employed for shadows because of the uncertain nature of their limits, which usually fade out, as we will show in the Book on Shadow and Light. 75. *Shadow versus drawing*

Levels of painting. What is beautiful is not always good. I say this for those painters who love the beauties of colors so much that, most unfortunately, they give them only very weak and almost invisible shadows, not considering their relief ; and this too is the error of fine orators whose words have no substance. * 76. *Shadow versus colors*

Of beauty. The beauty of the face may be equal in several persons, but its form can never be identical ; and there are even as many kinds of beauty as there are persons to whom it belongs. * 77. *Multiplicity of beauty*

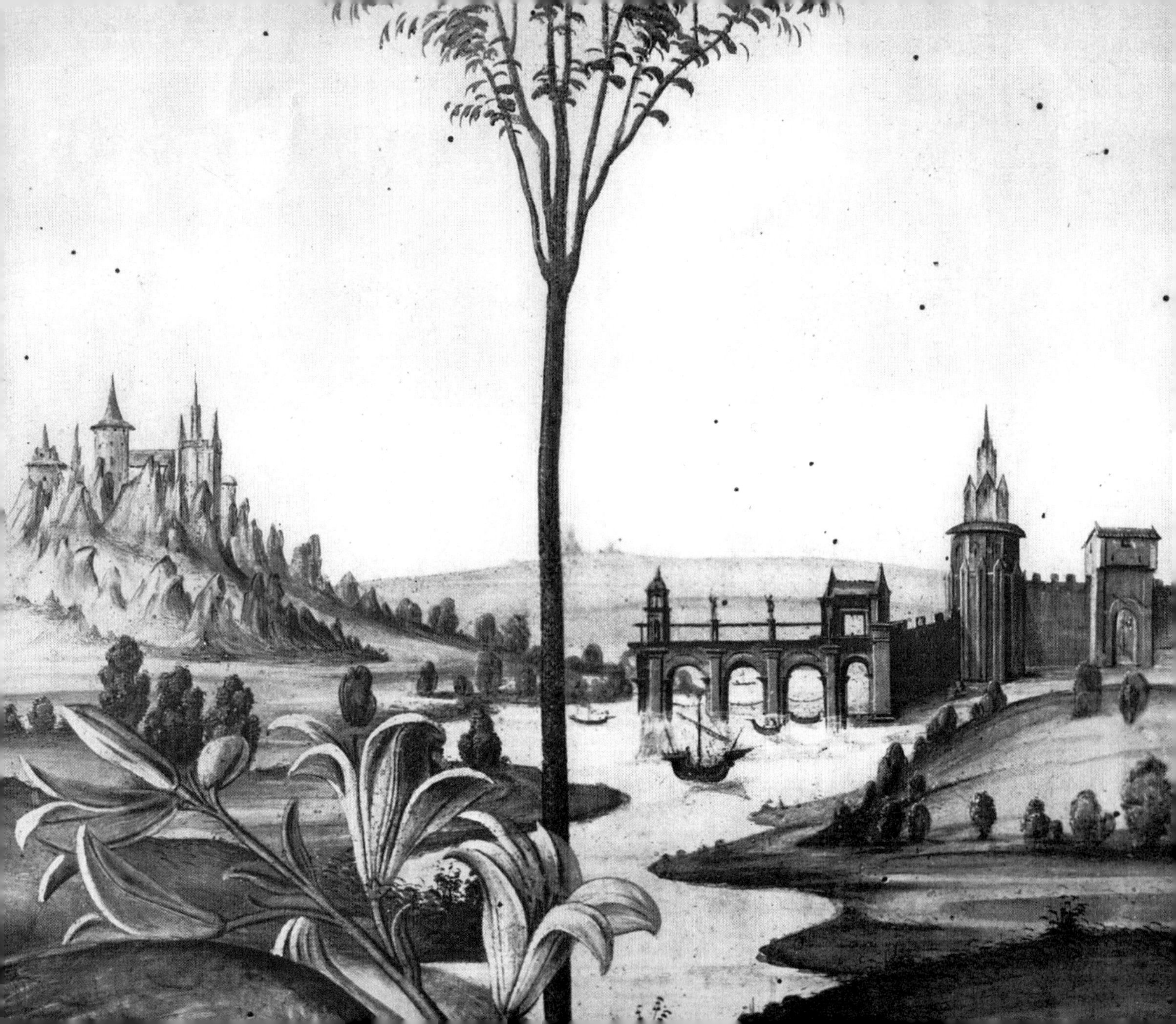

78. *Of not ornamenting figures in narrative paintings.* In narrative compositions do not give too much ornament to your figures and other objects, for it obscures the forms and poses of the figures and hides the structure of the other objects.

79. How narrative pictures should not be crowded and confused by too great a number of persons.

80. *Of judges of different beauties of equal excellence in different bodies.* Although there are different beauties of equal grace in different bodies, different judges of equal intelligence will judge that there are great differences between one and the other which they prefer.

81. *Be natural*

Discourse upon practice. Painter, strive to make works that attract spectators and make them stop in admiration and pleasure, instead of first attracting them and then driving them away, as does the air to someone who at night leaps naked from his bed to see whether the sky is overcast or serene and, driven by the coolness of the weather, quickly returns to the bed from which he came....

Do you not see that, among human beauties, it is the beautiful face that stops passersby and not the rich ornaments? I say this to you who encumber your figures with gold and other rich trimmings. Do you not see that the beauty of youth loses its brilliance through excessive and affected ornament? Have you never seen women in the hills, wrapped in their poor and plain draperies, more beautiful than women who are much adorned? Leave off affected curls and hair styles like those of empty-headed persons who think themselves disgraced because one more lock is on the right than on the left and believe that everyone around them thinks of nothing else and looks at nothing else and censures them. Such people have the mirror and comb for their advisors, and the wind is their mortal enemy, for it disarranges the sleek hair.

◀ Botticelli, *The Annunciation*, Detail, landscape; see no. 88.

Therefore, give your figures hair which an invisible wind causes to play about their youthful faces, and enhance them with various kinds of curls and do not imitate those who plaster it down with glue and give their faces the appearance of glass — another increase in human folly for which there are not enough mariners to bring gum arabic from the East to prevent the wind from disarranging the symmetry of the hairdos; and other means are still being sought out!

82. *Against tours de force*

Of composing narrative paintings. Painter, when you depict a single figure, take care to avoid foreshortening, both in the members and in the whole, for you would have to contend with the ignorance of those not versed in the arts. * But in narrative compositions make all kinds of foreshortenings wherever you wish to, and especially in battles where there are inevitably innumerable bendings and contortions among those taking part in this fight or, rather, in this bestial folly.

83. *Avoid profiles or sharp edges for objects.* Do

not make the contours of your forms of a different color than that of the background itself against which they are set ; that is, do not detach your figure from the background by means of a dark outline.

84. *Of gracefulness* Choose figures that are delicate rather than dry and wooden.

THE OPPOSING FACTIONS OF PAINTERS

85. *Personality in painters* *Statement of precepts for the painter.* I have always noted that, among all the portrait painters, he who gives the best likeness is worse at composing narrative paintings than anyone else, and this occurs because he who does one thing best is certain that nature has disposed him to do that thing rather than some other, and that is why he prefers it ; and this greater love has made him more diligent, and all the love he has brought to bear on one part is lacking in the rest of the painting, for he has made of this one thing his pleasure, abandoning the universal for the particular. Since the whole power of this talent has been limited to a narrow area, it becomes weak when it has to expand ; and this talent is like a concave mirror which, catching the rays of the sun, reflects them, and the wider the dispersion the lower the temperature. And when they are all reflected into a smaller space, then the rays are of immense warmth but act only in a limited area. That is what those painters do who love no other part of painting than the human face, and, what is worse, they do not recognize or appreciate any other aspect of art. Their paintings being without movement because they themselves are lazy and inert, they criticize works that are more animated and free than their own, saying that the figures seem like persons possessed or like masters of a Moorish dance. It is true that one ought to observe decorum and that movements express the emotions of the soul that is their mover. If one wishes to represent a person showing timid reverence, one should not depict him so violent and forward that his movements seem those of one in despair or of one giving a command to . . . * I saw, recently, an Angel of the Annunciation who seemed to wish to chase Our Lady from her room, with such rude movements as one might show to a most vile enemy, and Our Lady looked as though she wanted to throw herself from the window in despair. Be careful not to fall into such errors . . . .

In speaking of painters and their tastes, I say that he who gives his figures too much movement believes that he who gives them the proper amount of movement depicts persons that are asleep ; and he who gives them too little movement believes that those who have given them due movement have made them as if they were possessed. That is why the painter must take into consideration the manners of men who converse either coldly or warmly and, knowing the matter of which they speak, see

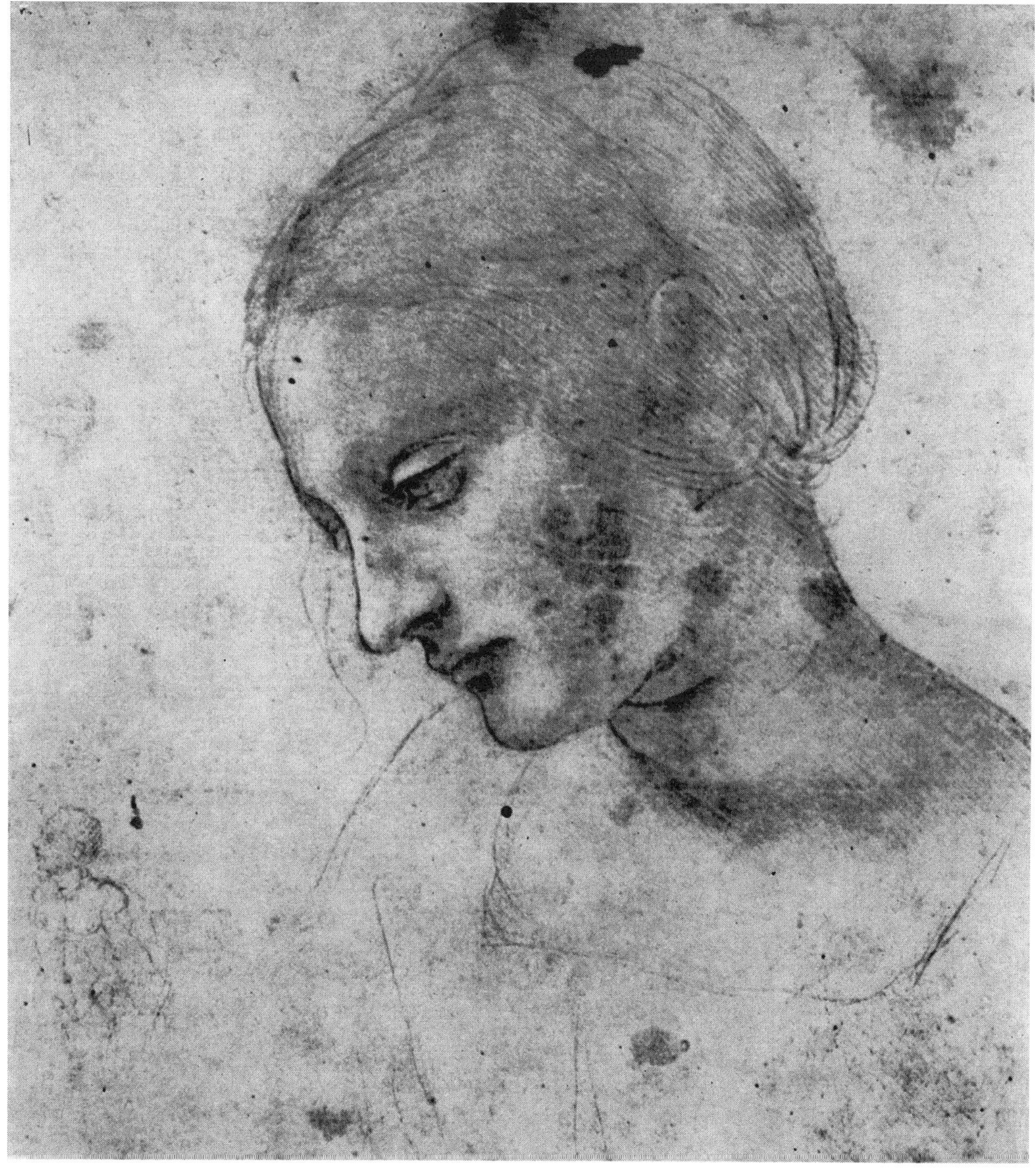

Study for the Head of
The Madonna Litta.

that their movements are appropriate to the subject of their conversation.

86. *Pros and cons of reflections*

Of the reflections of the lighted areas surrounding shadow. The reflections from the lighted parts rebound to the shadows opposite them, and more or less relieve their darkness, depending on their distance and their degree of brightness. This observation has been applied by certain painters, but others ignore it, and each of these two parties laughs at the other.

But if you wish to avoid the reproaches of both the first and the second party, employ each practice where it is necessary, but be sure to make the causes clear; that is, one should see with clarity that which produces the reflections and their colors, and even show why certain things do not have any reflections. If you do this, you will not be entirely condemned nor entirely praised by the different judges; and, except for complete ignorance, those of both parties should approve of you without reservation. *

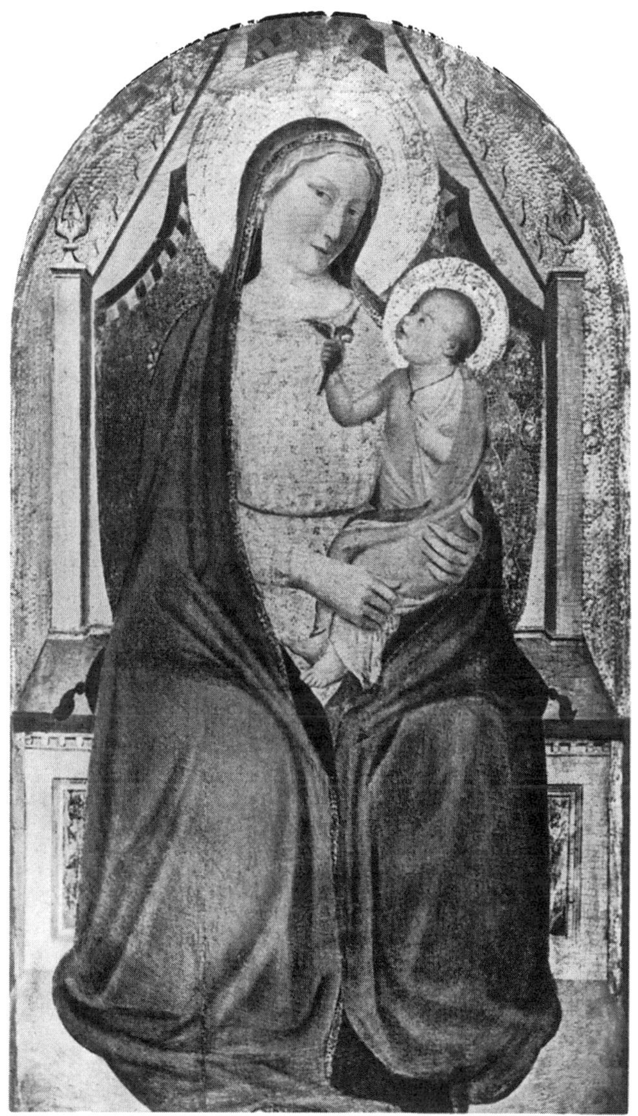

Italian School fourteenth century, *Madonna and Child.* "They give a little child of one year the proportions of a man of thirty." see no. 90.

CRITICISMS OF OTHER PAINTERS

87. *Pollaiuolo and his "anatomies"*

Of painting. It is necessary for the painter, if he is to render accurately the members of the nude in the attitudes and gestures of which they are capable, to know the anatomy of the nerves, bones, muscles, and tendons in order to know for each movement and effort which tendons or muscles occasion them ; and he should make only these stand out more and become larger, and not all at the same time, as do those who, in order to appear to be great draftsmen, make their nudes wooden and without grace, resembling sacks of nuts rather than human forms, or indeed a bundle of radishes rather than muscular nudes.

88. *Botticelli and landscapes*

Precepts for the painter. He who does not love equally all that belongs to painting is not universal. For example, if he does not like landscapes, he will say that it is an easy and simple matter to understand ; thus our Botticelli said that it was a vain study, for by merely throwing a sponge full of various colors at a wall, a stain appeared on the wall in which one could see a fine landscape. It is true that in such a stain one can see different compositions of things * one wishes to look for — human heads, various animals, battles, rocks, seas, clouds, woods, etc. It is like the sound of bells in which you can hear what you like. But while these stains supply you with compositions, they do not teach you to complete any detail.

And the above-mentioned painter produces very poor landscapes.

89. *Architecture in Trecento painting*

Avoid disproportion in the settings. Many painters have this great fault, that they make men's houses and the other elements in the setting in such a way that the gates of the cities do not come up to the knees of their inhabitants, even when they are closer to the spectator than the man who wishes to enter into them. We have seen galleries crowded with men on them, when the columns supporting them fitted into the fist of a man who leaned against them as against a thin reed. Great care should be taken to avoid things of this type.

90. *Against the followers of the Byzantine manner*

Which is the better painting. That painting is most worthy of praise which resembles most closely what it imitates. I say this in opposition to the painters who think they correct the works of nature — for example, those who in representing a child of one year, whose head should be a fifth of its height, make it an eighth ; and though the breadth of the shoulders equals that of the head, they make the head half as wide as the shoulders ; and in this way they give a little child of one year the proportions of a man of thirty. And they have so often made this mistake and seen it made, and this practice has so penetrated and become established in their corrupt judgment, that they have convinced themselves that nature and those who imitate nature err greatly in not doing as they do.

91.

That the art of painting declines from age to age and is lost if painters have no other guide than what was done before them. The painter will produce a work of little value if he takes the works of others as his model, but if he studies and follows the creations of nature he will have good results. We have seen this with the painters who came after the Romans and who continually imitated each other, and art declined steadily from age to age. After them came

Giotto of Florence who, having been born in the solitude of the mountains inhabited only by goats and other beasts, was not satisfied with imitating the works of his master Cimabue; this Giotto, then, having been brought by nature to art, began to draw on the rocks the poses of the goats he was tending, and he began to draw all the other animals that there were in that region, so that after much study he surpassed not only all the masters of his time but also all those of many preceding centuries. After him art again declined, for all imitated work done before their time, and it continued to decline from generation to generation until such a time as Tomaso of Florence, called Masaccio, showed by the perfection of his work that those who followed models other than nature, the teacher of masters, expended their energies in vain.

About our studies of mathematics I wish to say that those who study only the masters and not the works of nature are in art the grandsons and not the sons of nature, mistress of all good masters. O what supreme folly to reproach those who learn only from nature and do not spend their time on masters, the disciples of this nature! *

NEW VALUES: UNIQUENESS AND ORIGINALITY

92. *Of imitable sciences.* The imitable sciences, that is, those in which the disciple becomes the equal of the discoverer and can produce similar works, are useful to the imitator but are not as excellent as those which cannot be left as an inheritance the way other things can.

Among the latter painting takes first place; it cannot be taught to those who are not talented by nature, as is the case with mathematics, where the disciple acquires all that the master presents to him; it cannot be copied as the written word can, where the copy is worth as much as the model; it cannot be cast as sculpture can, where the copy equals the original in value, insofar as the excellence of the work is concerned. It does not produce multitudinous progeny as do printed books. Painting alone remains noble; it alone honors the author; it alone remains precious and unique and never brings forth offspring that equal it, and this uniqueness makes it more excellent than those things which are spread abroad.

Do we not see the greatest kings of the Orient go about veiled and covered, certain that they will diminish their prestige by making their presence generally known and public? Do we not see the painting representing the highest deities always covered with precious cloths? And when they are uncovered, great ecclesiastical feasts with many chants and diverse music are first celebrated. And at the unveiling a great multitude assembles, and people throw themselves upon the ground, and adore it, and pray to the One for whom it was painted in order to regain their lost health or to gain eternal salvation — just as though this Divinity were actually there, alive and present.

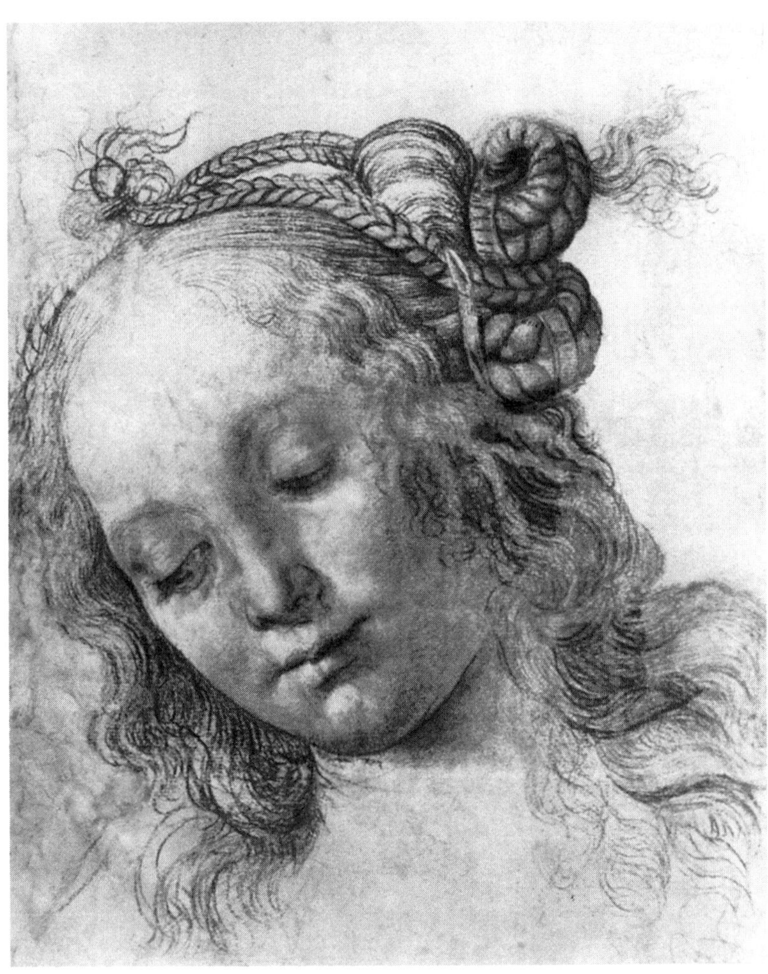

Verrocchio, *Study of a head.* A typical example of the work that influenced Leonardo during his formative years.

This does not happen in the case of any other science or any other human work ; and if you say this is not due to the merit of the painter but is in virtue of the thing represented, you would be answered that in such a case the people would be content to remain in their beds and not go on pilgrimages to places that are difficult and dangerous to reach, as is constantly being done. And as these pilgrimages continue, what is it that causes them without reason ? You must surely admit that it is the image, and that all the writings that wish to portray that Divinity and to paint it actually do not achieve this result.

Francesco di Simone, two pages of studies. A typical example of the work of a mediocre student at the time when Leonardo was an apprentice. ▶

It would therefore seem that the Divinity loves these images and those who love Him and revere Him ; and He prefers to be adored in such images rather than in others representing Him, wherefore He grants grace and gifts of health according to the belief of those who assemble in such a place. *

Of imitating other painters. I say to the painter that no one should ever imitate the manner of another painter, for in respect to art he will be called the grandson and not the son of nature. Given the great wealth of natural objects, nature requires and demands that we have recourse to her rather than to the masters who have learned from her. And I do not say this for those who wish to become rich through art, but to those who wish to acquire fame and honor. 93.

He is a poor pupil who does not surpass his master. 94.

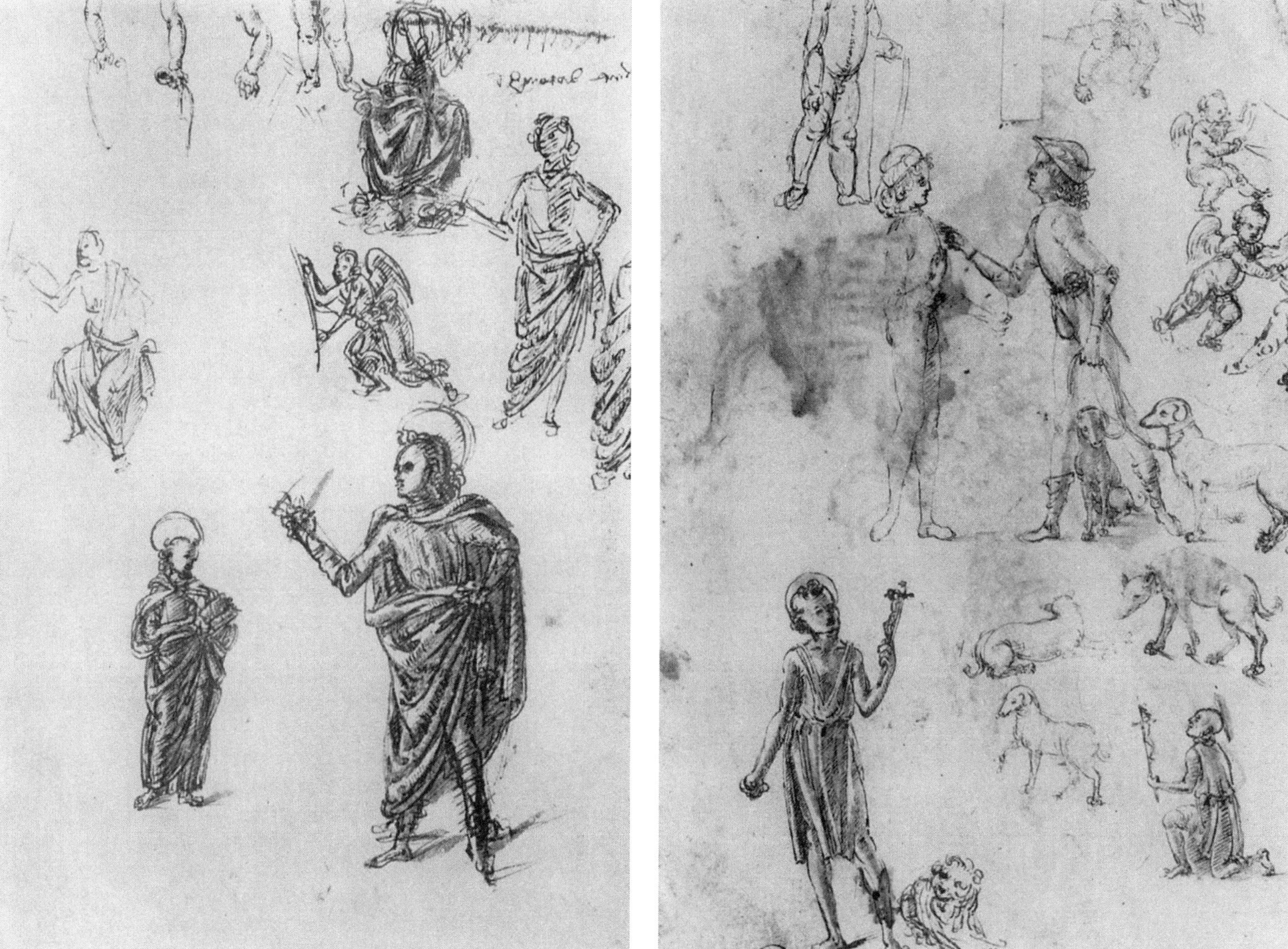

Space and Light

Although the section on space and light is the best known one of the Treatise, it is also the least original. Leonardo here builds on a particularly sound foundation because the Florentine neo-Platonists on the one hand and Alberti and Piero della Francesca on the other had already formulated the basic concepts : the primacy of vision which, when considered with mathematical rigor, is identical with intellectual activity ; and the boundless marvel of light, which is a principal element of both the visible universe and sight, through which the former is observed.

As is his habit, Leonardo approaches these ideas through nature : to understand sight, he studies its organ, the eye ; to understand light, he studies shadows and reflections. He thus substitutes observable phenomena for intellectual symbols. In analyzing these phenomena he discovers contradictions and problems which ultimately take the place of what was initially assumed. As a result he often deals with pictorial considerations by isolating interesting alternatives : linear perspective, instead of being seen as the only solution, becomes merely one method ; the other is spherical or " natural " perspective to which Leonardo constantly returns as his reflections ripen and which he eventually accepts as preferable.

But the problems of space are not exhausted by mathematical perspective. Leonardo isolated and finally evaluated the rules of color gradation, that is, aerial perspective. He came to consider this subject of prime importance and made innumerable observations of trees, clouds, distant views, etc., which paved the way for his com-

prehensive study of landscape. In respect to light, his concern with relief seemed at first to compel him to choose between color and modeling. He avoided the choice but this brought about a more insidious difficulty : the conflict between outline and reflection, a problem that arose at an early stage and was finally resolved by the use of chiaroscuro. As an introduction to the study of color Leonardo had planned a little chapter on the rainbow that would have been a gem ; as has been remarked, Leonardo's interpretations here are closer to Goethe than to Newton.

If linear perspective and its basic rhythms relate to the function of the eye responding to the infinite expansion of luminous space to what relate the shadows and the transparent " veils " of air that trouble space and disperse vision and color throughout the visible universe ? Here the cosmologist's curiosity prolongs the painter's investigations. The blue of the atmosphere, caused by humidity in the air, is a diffused element that blurs outlines and changes colors. It is to be connected with the quiet and unceasing action of water which, as we know, came to play an increasingly important role in Leonardo's speculations. Water, an active and pervasive force, moves objects and corrodes forms : it is the enemy of geometry. It destroys the organization of space and dissolves stable formations : it is the enemy of permanence. It freezes and extinguishes : it is the enemy of heat and fire, the radiant principles of the sun. The battle of the elements and the eruptions of air, water, or earth became a dominant interest during Leonardo's last years. The great themes of floods and natural catastrophes are related to it. The problems of the painter develop with his vision of the world.

THE CONDITIONS OF VISION

95. *The eye*

Here figures, colors, and all aspects of every part of the universe are contracted to a point ; oh how marvelous is this point ! O admirable, oh astounding Necessity, you, who by your law constrain all effects to relate to their causes in the most direct manner possible. These are the miracles . . .

That in so narrow a space *(the image)* may be recreated and reconstructed according to its full extension. Describe in your anatomy what the relations are of the diameters of all the images in the eye and what their distance is from the crystalline lens. *

96. *Light and perception*

Painting. First : The pupil of the eye diminishes in size in proportion as the light reflected in it increases.

Second : The pupil of the eye becomes larger in proportion as the light of day or any other light that reflects in it diminishes.

Third : The eye sees and knows better the objects before it the more the pupil is dilated ; and this can be proven by means of nocturnal animals, such as cats, and birds like the owl, and others, in which the size of the pupil varies greatly, dilating and contracting, etc., according to whether it is dark or light.

Fourth : The eye, placed in an illuminated atmosphere, can distinguish nothing behind, windows of houses *(though their interior is)* lighted. *

Fifth : All colors appear equally dark when in a dark place.

Sixth : But in lighted places all colors show their true nature without alteration.

97. *Dilation of the pupil*

The larger the pupil, the larger will be the things it sees. This will become evident when we look at luminous bodies, especially celestial ones. When an eye emerging from darkness suddenly looks at them, they seem larger and then diminish. And if you look at these bodies through a small hole, they will seem smaller to you, because a smaller part of the pupil is exercising its function. *

98.

Observations on the dilation and contraction of the pupil through the movement of the sun or another source of light. The darker the sky is, the larger the stars will seem, and if you light up the place, the stars will show themselves less, and this phenomenon is due entirely to the pupil which expands and contracts according to the amount of light in the atmosphere between the eye and the luminous body. Experiment by holding a candle above your head while you look at a star ; then gradually lower the candle until it reaches the line going straight from the eye to the star, and you will see the star diminish until finally you will have lost it from sight.

99. *Binocular vision*

Why a painting can never have as much relief as the things themselves. Painters often despair of being able to imitate nature, seeing that their works do not have that relief and realism that have things seen in a mirror, although they say they have colors that are much brighter or darker than the light and shadows of the objects seen in the mirror ; and they blame their ignorance for it and not the true reason, which they do not know : that is, that it is impossible for a painted object to appear to have as much relief as that object seen in a mirror, although both are on a single plane, unless one looks at it with one eye only. The reason is that the

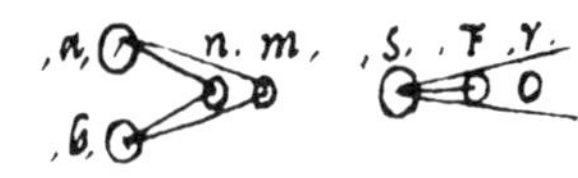

two eyes see two objects that overlap as *a* and *b* see *m* and *n*. Now, *n* cannot entirely hide *m*, because the base of the visual pyramids is large enough to contain the second body behind the first. But, if you close one eye, as in *s*, the body *f* will hide *r* because the pyramid has its origin in a single point and its base in the first body, so that the second, which is of the same size, cannot be seen.

Text and diagrams on the mechanics of vision. Leonardo imagined the lens as a sphere in the center of the eye, an error common to all anatomists of his time, and from it he attempted to reconstruct the supposed double reversal of the image in the eye. ▶

Proof that objects come to the eye. If you look at the sun or another luminous body, and then close your eyes, you will see it again inside the eye for a long time. This is proof that the image entered it. 100. *Intromission of images*

How the images of objects received into the eye intersect within the crystalline humor. An experiment showing that the images or appearances of objects transmitted into the eye cross in the crystalline humor : this is demonstrated by 101. *The eye and the dark room* letting the images of illuminated objects penetrate through a small hole into a very dark room. You will then intercept these images on a sheet of white paper placed near this hole and inside the room and you will see all the aforesaid objects on this sheet of paper in their true forms and colors; but they will be smaller and upside down because of the said crossing. These images, if they emanate from a sunlit place, will actually seem to be painted on the sheet of paper, which should be very thin and seen from the back; and the hole should be made in a very thin sheet of iron....

102. *The reversed image*

All that the eyes see through the little holes *(of the pupils)* is inverted but is known right side up.

103.

That things which are on the right will only seem so to the sense of sight if the images undergo a double inversion. *

104.

Of the ten functions of the eye, all contained in painting. The painter is concerned with all the ten functions of the eye, that is, shadows, light, volume and color, figure and placement, distance and proximity, movement and rest.... *

LIGHT AND SHADOW

105. *An infinity of images*

Any opaque body will fill the surrounding air with an infinite number of images representing it completely everywhere and at each point by virtue of the infinite numbers of pyramids filling this air. Each pyramid, formed by

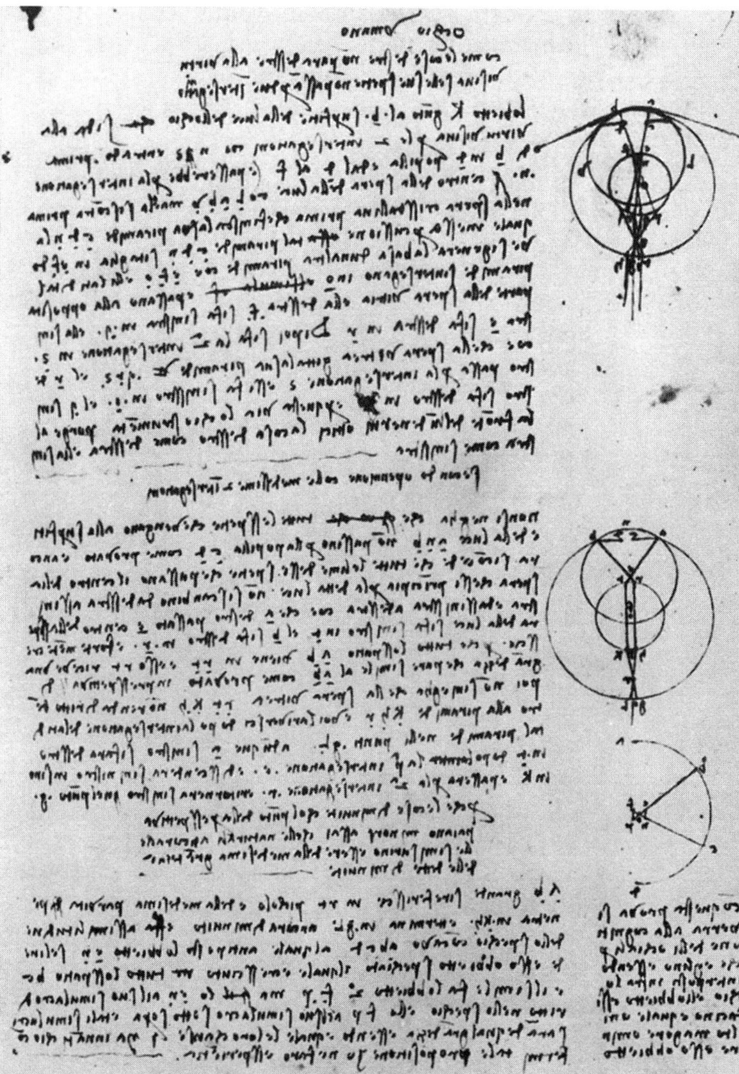

long rays, encloses an infinite number of pyramids, and each one contains all of them in its power, and all each. The points of the pyramids placed at an equal distance from the object will form equal angles, * and the object will seem of the same size to each observer. The body of the air is filled with an infinite number of pyramids, made up of radiating rays which are caused by the surfaces of the opaque bodies found there ; and the farther the pyramids are removed from their origin, the more acute they become. And although their passage is full of crossings and intersections, they nonetheless do not become confused one with the other, but, progressively diverging, spread out throughout all the surrounding air. And they are of equal power, all equal to each, and each equal to all, and by means of them the images of the forms are transmitted, all in all and all in each part, and each pyramid receives in its smallest part the whole form of its cause. *

106. *Introduction* ... Shadow is the absence of light. It seems to me that shadows are indispensable to perspective, for without them it is difficult to grasp the opaque bodies or the volumes or the manner of filling the outlines ; and the outlines themselves would be unclear if the forms are not set against a background of a different color from them. That is why in my first proposition on shadows I state that every opaque body is surrounded and on its surface is clothed with shadows and lights, and this I elucidate in my first book. Moreover, the shadows themselves are of various degrees, because they are caused by the absence of luminous rays of varying intensity, and these I call primary shadows, for they are the first shadows to cover the forms to which they attach themselves, and to these I shall devote the second book. From these primary shadows there issue rays of shadow which are diffused in the air, and of these there are as many different kinds as there are variations of the primary shadows from which they derive. These I shall then call derived shadows, because they originate in other shadows, and this I shall make the subject of the third book. Next, when these derived shadows fall on an obstacle they produce effects as varied as the different types of places they strike, and of this I shall make the fourth book. And since the place where a derived shadow strikes is always surrounded by the striking of luminous rays, which through reflection are always projected toward that which causes the shadow, and as it there meets the primary shadow, with which it mingles, thus slightly altering its nature, on this I shall base my fifth book. Next, I shall make a sixth book which will deal with the numerous varieties of reflected rays, which will modify the primary shadows by as many varieties of colors as there are different points from which these luminous rays issue. Furthermore, the seventh section will deal with the various distances between its point of origin and the point at which the reflected ray strikes, as well as with the variety of the colors of the reflection which it projects onto the opaque body on which it falls. *

Definition of Shadow and Light

107. *What shadow and light are.* Shadow is the absence of light or simply the opposition of opaque bodies that intercept the light rays. Shadow is of the nature of darkness ; light is of the nature of brilliance. One conceals, the other reveals. They are always connected with bodies, and shadow is more powerful than light, for it can prohibit all light and entirely deprive bodies of it, while light can never dispel all shadow from a body, at least from opaque bodies.

108. . . . Shadow may be of infinite obscurity or display an infinite variety of changes toward light.

. . . Shadow is the expression by bodies of their shapes. The shapes of bodies will not show their particulars without shadow.

109. *Of the essence of shadow as such.* Shadow is of the same nature as everything that exists, that is, it is more powerful at its origin and becomes weaker toward its end. I speak of the beginnings of forms and qualities, visible or otherwise, and not of things brought from a small beginning to a great expansion by time as, for example, an oak tree, the beginnings of which are a weak acorn. I shall even add that the oak is most powerful at its origin, near the earth, for there is its greatest thickness. Darkness, then, is the first degree of shadow and light is the last. Therefore, painter, you should make the shadow darkest near its beginning and its end should be converted into light, that is, it should appear without limit.

Light and Luminosity

How one can determine what part of a body should be more or less luminous than the others. 110. *The impact of light*
Let *A* be the light, and a head the body, illuminated by it : that part of the head which receives the rays at an angle closest to the perpendicular * will be the most illuminated, and that part which receives the rays at the most acute angle will be the least illuminated.

This light acts like a blow, for the blow that falls perpendiculary has the greatest strength, and if it falls obliquely, it will be as much less powerful than the former as its angle is greater. For example, if you throw a ball against a wall, the extremities of which are equidistant from you, the impact will fall on the perpendicular, but if you throw the ball from one of its extremities, it will fall obliquely, and the impact will not be effective.

Proof that light from everywhere converges 111.
at a point. Although balls *a b c* are lighted from a single window, you will, nevertheless, find that if you lengthen *(forward)* the *(median)* lines of their shadows, they will intersect at a point at the apex of angle *n.* *

All shaded bodies that are larger than the 112. *Against the light and in the light*
pupil and interposed between the eye and the source of illumination will appear to be dark.

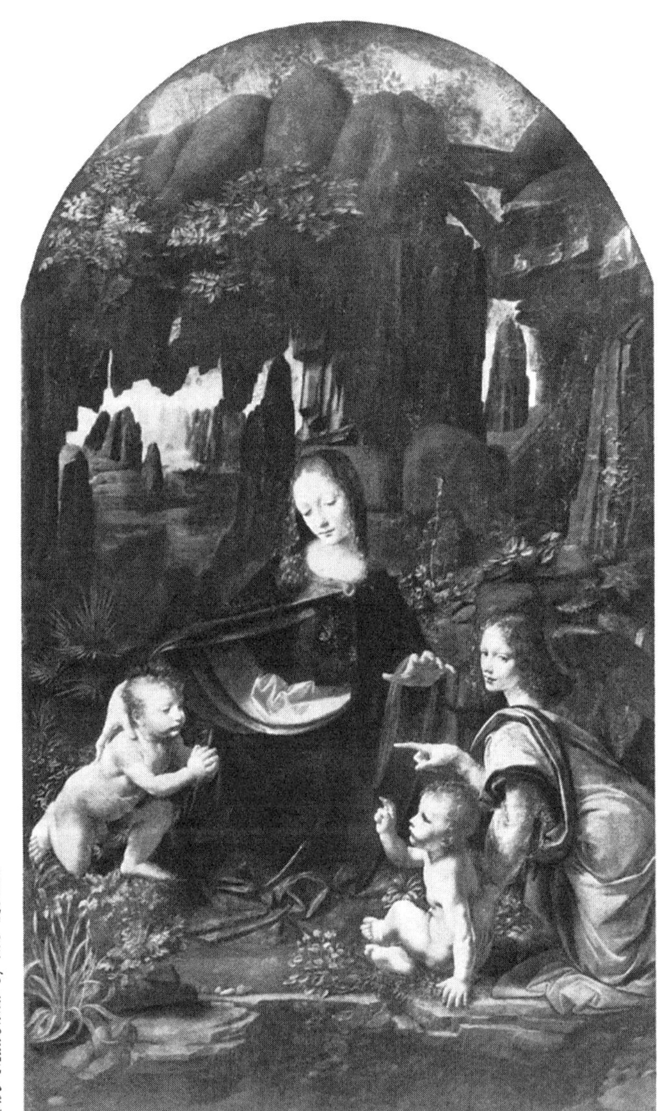

The Madonna of the Rocks.

The eye, when placed between the source of illumination and the bodies illuminated by it, will see these bodies without any shadow.

Directed light gives greater relief to opaque bodies than diffused light, as may be seen by comparing objects in a landscape when one part is lit by the sun and another, hidden by a cloud, merely receives the light diffused through the air. 113. *Lighting and relief*

That shadows should always participate in the color of the body they cover. No object appears to us in its natural whiteness, for the place where it is seen renders it more or less white to the eye, according to whether this place is more or less dark. For example, we learn this from the moon, which by day appears in the sky with little brightness, but at night with such brilliance that it drives away darkness like the sun or like daylight. This comes about for two reasons : the first is the tendency of nature to show colored images as much more clearly as the colors are different ; * and the second, that the pupil is larger at night than during the day, as has been proven . . . 114. *Relativity of luminosity*

Light striking the profile ; see no. 110 ; on the left three small balls illuminated from a single window ; see no. 111. ▶

Study of the length of primary shadows ; see no. 115. ▶

The Geometry of Shadows

The part of an opaque body that is seen in a smaller quantity of light is also less illuminated. The part *m* of the body is illuminated in the 115. *Construction of primary shadows*

[illegible]

[illegible]

[illegible]

[illegible]

[illegible]

[illegible]

[illegible]

[illegible]

[illegible]

[illegible]

first degree, because it faces the whole window *ad* along the line *af* ; *n* is in the second degree, because it faces the light *bd* along the line *be* ; *o* is in the third degree, because it faces the light *cd* along the line *ch* ; *p* is in the next-to-last degree, because it faces *cd* along the line *dv* ; and the part *q* is the last, because it does not face any part of the window.

By as many times as *dc* goes into *ad*, *nrs* is darker than *m* and all the surface without shadow. *

116. *Construction of derived shadows*

The darkest shadow is the simple derived shadow, because it does not face either of the two sources of light, *ab* or *cd*. *

The second, less dark shadow is the derived shadow *efn*, being half as dark, because it faces and is illuminated by a single light, that is, *cd*. And it is of a uniform *natural* quality, because in all its parts it faces a single source of light ; but it varies *according to the condition of position* in the sense that the further it is from the source the less it participates in its brightness.

The third is the middle shadow, but its *natural* depth is not uniform, for it becomes darker in proportion as it is nearer to the simple derived shadow, and, moreover, it alters according to the uniform diminution *according to the position*, that is, the further removed it is from the two sources of light, the darker it becomes. *

The fourth is the shadow *krs*, and its natural depth becomes darker the closer it comes to *ks*, because it then faces the smaller portion of *ab*, but it is illuminated *according to the position* because it comes closer to the light *cd* ; and this shadow always faces both sources at the same time.

The fifth is the least dark of all, because of the two sources it always faces one of its two sources in its entirety and the other in at least a part ; it becomes increasingly lighter as it comes closer to the two sources and also as it approaches the outer side *xt*, for it is then more exposed to the second light *ab*.

Why the shadow, when it is larger than the body throwing it, is not like it. The distortion of a shadow larger than its cause stems from the fact that the luminous source, being smaller than the object, cannot be equidistant from the extremities of the object, * and the shadow of the more distant parts becomes larger than that of the nearer parts . . . . 117.

118. *The construction of reflected shadows and reflections of "rays of shadows"*

That part of the surface of a body on which the images of the bodies facing it falls at the largest angle will take on their color most. * At point *8*, at the bottom, the angle is larger than at *4*, because the base of *8* is *an (on the wall opposite)* and the base of *4* is *en* (in the figure below one should consider only the part *a-n-4-8*). The illuminated part of the wall that is closest to the shadow on it will be the brightest. Just as a thing touched by a greater quantity of luminous rays is brighter, so that touched by a greater quantity of shadow rays will be darker. . . . *

The First Principles

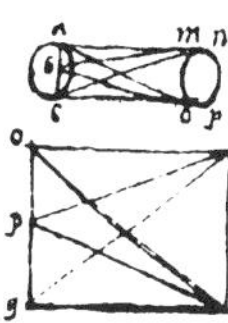

119. *Principles of the science of painting.* The plane surface has its complete image on the plane surface opposite it. . . . *

120. *Of the second principle of painting.* The second principle of painting is the shadow of the body represented by it ; and we shall give the laws of shadow and show how the surfaces are thus given relief. *

Analogy of all Optical Phenomena

121. *Luminous rays and visual images*

Perspective. That images of all things are spread through the air may be shown with the aid of several mirrors placed in a circle: for they will reflect each other for an infinite number of times, and *(the image)* of each, having reached the other, again rebounds to the first, then returns, and does this again for an infinite number of times. If at night you place a light between two flat mirrors a *braccio* (*arm's length*) apart, you will see in each an infinite number of lights, one smaller than another, in succession. And if at night you place a light between the walls of a *(room)*, every part of these walls will be covered by the images of this light, and all that shall be seen by that light will, in turn, see the light, as long as there are no obstacles to interrupt the transmission of the images. All this is even more clear in the transmission of solar rays, which all together and each alone bring the image of their cause to the object. And these examples clearly show that each body separately fills all the air around it with its images and that this air can receive the images of an infinity of these bodies all there at the same time. And each body appears in its entirety in all that air and in all its parts ; all throughout it and in each part ; each throughout it and all in each part.

The air is full of an infinity of straight lines and rays which cut and cross each other without displacing each other, and which reproduce the true form of their cause on whatever they encounter. 122. *Images propagated by rays*

Just as the stone thrown into the water becomes the center of several circles, and as sound is diffused in circles through the air, so all bodies put into the luminous air spread and transmit to the nearby parts an infinity of images and appear in their entirety everywhere and in every part. This may be proven by experience, for if you close a window facing west and make a hole in the shutters . . . * 123. *Images propagated in circles*

There is no difference between the source of light and the eye in regard to the function of perspective. 124.

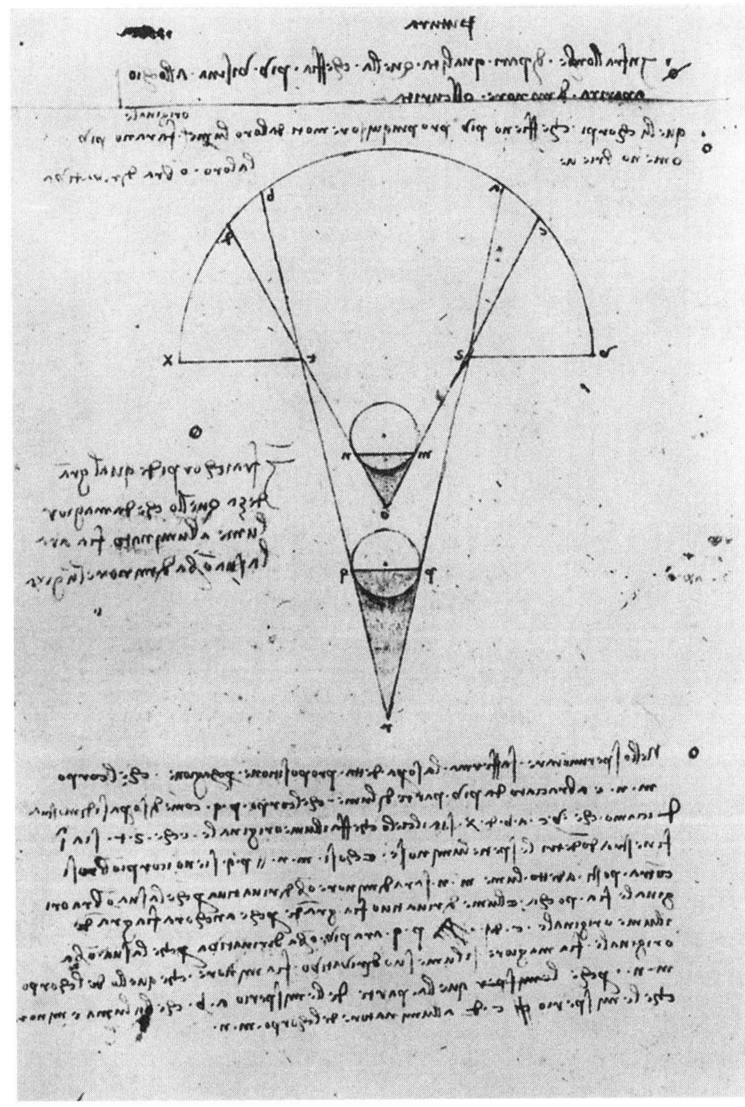

Diagram for the study of the length of shadows; see no. 128.

125. *Visual pyramids and cones of light*

Perspective. If you let rays of light pass through a hole in the form of a star, you will get some beautiful effects of perspective in the spot where the light coming through it will fall. *

126. *Visual pyramids and cones of shadow*

. . . Whatever the inequality of the surface or the projection, the shadow will always coincide in its outlines with the body that causes it, as long as the eye is placed so that it is at the center of the luminous source.

Applications of these Analogies

127. *The projection of a shadow and perspective vision*

If you wish to paint a figure on a slanting or curved wall and want this figure to appear in its true form and detached from the wall, you should do as follows : get a thin sheet of iron and make a small, round hole in its center and bring it close to a light that you will place immediately in front of it. Then put the object or the figure you have chosen close to the wall, so that it touches it, and note its shadow on the wall and draw *(the outline)* where the shadow and light meet ; place whoever wishes to see this figure before the hole where the light had been placed before, and you would never believe that this figure is not actually detached from the wall.

128. *Pyramids of light and visual pyramids*

Isolated bodies in rooms lit by a single window will have derived shadows that are more or less short, depending on whether they are more or less directly opposite the window... The reason why opaque bodies placed more directly facing the center of the window have shorter shadows than those obliquely placed is that they see the window larger and in its true shape, while those placed obliquely see it foreshortened... The one in the center sees the larger arc *ef*, and those at the two sides the smaller, that is, *qr* sees *ab* and *mn* sees *cd*. The body in the center receives a greater quantity of light than those at the sides and is illuminated well beyond its middle line, and that is why the shadow will be shorter; and the relation of *ab* to *ef* is exactly equal to that of *g4* to *ly*. ... *

LINEAR PERSPECTIVE

For Renaissance painters the problem of the third dimension was reduced to the task of reproducing an imaginary cross-section on a single plane by means of the " pyramid " of rays going from the object to the painter's eye. This cross-section can be projected on a flat pane of glass, and that is why a painting is frequently described as a window giving onto the scene depicted.

The various geometric constructions all aim at reproducing this cross-section by starting from the coordinates in the imaginary plane of objects in the space to be represented. Leonardo seems to have been the first to question the possibilities of this procedure. He found that it was limited since certain specific conditions had to be assumed :

1. *that the spectator has only one eye.*
2. *that this eye is immovable.*
3. *that the eye in front of the image has to be in the same place and at the same relative distance (taking the change of scale into account) as the painter was in relation to the subject when he painted it.*

The third point is of primary importance and Leonardo begins his criticism with it. He points out that objects at the edges of the painting do not appear on the projection plane as they do to the eye. If the perspective is to be accurate it would have to intercept them on a spherical surface (see nos. 139, 140). In fact, traditional perspective foreshortens only in depth while actually the breadth should also be diminished. For example, the tiles of a tiled floor should decrease toward the sides as well as toward the back, and the space of a narrow street should diminish in its height as well as in its depth. In short, all straight lines, except those of the horizon and the vertical axis, should appear curved. As Gioseffi has pointed out, we have an image of the world seen in a slightly concave mirror.*

Leonardo called this spherical perspective " natural " and seems to have discovered it. (This type of perspective is found in some of Fouquet's miniatures though it is not applied consistently. See J. White.) He himself states that his new method is not indispensable and not necessarily the only true one, for when we look at the painted surface, it undergoes a spherical distortion similar to that of any object we see :

For instance, when we stand close to Leonardo's Last Supper *and directly in front of the figure of Christ, the ends seem considerably foreshortened in comparison to the center of the fresco. Therefore, although the extremities of the image are unduly large when rendered in traditional " flat " perspective, the eye of the spectator standing in line with the central axis of the painting restores them to their proper proportion. It can easily be proven that these opposing distortions cancel each other out (so that plane perspective is useful) if, and only if, the spectator stands exactly at the apex of the visual pyramid of which the painting is a cross-section. The third condition given above is then fulfilled. At all other times the distortion of flat perspective is added to that of the " natural, " spherical perspective imposed on the painting by the viewer, and interferes with it instead of canceling it out, so that the image seems out of all proportion.*

Leonardo suggests two solutions. One is to reproduce the " natural " perspective faithfully. It is more independent of the eye, it might be said, because the spectator has to adjust to only one distortion, the subjective one, without having to correct the objective one because that is actually drawn on the canvas. The other is to " combine the natural with the accidental perspective, " that is, to make the spectator look at the painting from a predetermined point of view as though he were looking at it through a hole in a wall. In that case the " natural " perspective of perception and the " accidental " (artificial) perspective painted on the wall " combine " by canceling out their respective distortions.

From here it is only a step to the last and most curious of Leonardo's inventions on this subject. He is well aware of the fact that his " combined " method does not have to be limited to the traditional point of view located on the central axis relatively distant from the painting. As long as the spectator remains in one set spot, this spot can be any place, such as at the side and fairly close, as though the picture plane were a cross-section of the pyramid made at an angle to its base. Out of this arise the amusing tricks called anamorphosis or, less accurately, inverted perspective. To follow Leonardo's terminology, these are merely " combined " perspectives, that is, with a fixed point of view. In all honesty it must be added that traditional perspective, which is still taught today, and which was justly criticized by Leonardo, is, because of its third condition, merely one instance of anamorphosis.*

The Codex Urbinas is particularly fragmentary and short on the subject of perspective, perhaps because Leonardo's various statements on the subject are so difficult to reconcile. However, Mss. A (dating ca. 1492) and BN 2038 (which originally was a part of Ms. A) are much richer in this respect. It is noteworthy that a collection of material copied from Leonardo's notebooks that included a remarkable section on perspective was in circulation toward the middle of the sixteenth century. Cellini's comments suggest that it consisted of a presentation of " natural perspective. "

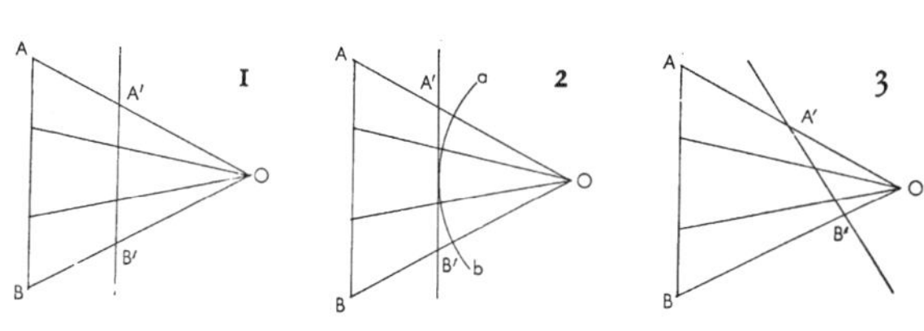

Figure 1. Flat perspective. *The lateral sections of the area AB are seen at a more acute angle and therefore appear smaller than the center one ; however, in the painting A'B' all three sections are of the same size. This error is without consequences as long as the eye is precisely at O, because then the spectator also sees the lateral sections of A'B' at a more acute angle than its center one. (The diagram is based on Gioseffi's theory.)*

Figure 2. Spherical perspective. *The painting A'B' instead of showing the direct projection of AB shows it on the curve ab. The representation thus avoids the distortion of perspective to which the actual painting is subjected. As a result, the spectator can move freely before the image since its " truth " as well as its lighting now moves with him.*

Figure 3. Anamorphosis. *The cross-section A'B' is at an angle to the spectator and if he were to stand directly in front of it the image would appear to be distorted almost beyond recognition. But when the eye is at O the image that appears to the spectator is identical with that of AB as seen from directly opposite.*

Among all the studies of causes and natural agents, light gives those who consider it greatest joy ; among the glories of mathematics it is the certainty of the proofs that most elevates the investigator's mind. Perspective, which shows how linear rays differ according to definite conditions, should therefore be given first place among all the sciences and disciplines of man, for she crowns both mathematics and the natural sciences and is adorned by the flowers of one as well as of the other ; and its theorems, proven in a hundred ways, I can sum up with conclusive brevity, adding proofs taken from mathematics and physics as the subjects require them, at times deducing the effects from the causes, at times the causes from the effects ; and I shall also add to my theories certain ones which, if they are not implicit in their causes, can, nonetheless, be taken from them. If the Lord, light of all things, deigns to enlighten me I may treat of light ; and wherefore I shall divide the present work into three parts. * 129. *The basic science of light*

Of the three kinds of perspective. There are three kinds of perspective : the first deals with the objects as they recede from the eye and is called diminishing perspective ; the second is concerned with the manner in which colors change as they recede from the eye ; the third and last consists in showing how objects ought to be less sharply defined proportionately to their distance. And the names are these : 130.

Linear Perspective
Perspective of Color
Vanishing Perspective

131. *Agreement between the three perspectives*

Painter, do not diminish the colors in perspective more than the forms carrying those colors.

And do not increase the linear perspective more than that of the colors, but diminish the one and the other according to the eighth and seventh rules. *

It is true, however, that in nature the perspective of colors always follows this law, while that of size is arbitrary, for one may find a small hill near to the eye and a huge mountain in the distance ; and the same is true of trees and buildings. *

132. *Definition of linear perspective*

... Perspective is the rational law by which experience shows us that all objects send their images to the eye in a pyramid of lines ; and bodies of equal size will produce pyramids that are more or less acute depending on their respective distances. I call " pyramid of lines " the lines that emanate from the surfaces and outlines of the bodies and, in converging from a distance, arrive at a common point ; one calls a point that which cannot be divided in any way, and that point, situated in the eye, receives in itself the apexes of all the pyramids.

133.

The wall of glass. Perspective is nothing other than seeing a scene behind a flat and very transparent pane of glass on the surface of which one marks all the objects that are on its other side ; these things are connected to the eye by pyramids ; and the pyramids are intercepted by the pane of glass.

134. *How to determine the apex of the pyramid*

Concerning the point in the eye, you may find it more easily comprehensible as follows : if you look into the eyes of anyone, you will see your own image there ; and if you now suppose two lines that emanate from your ears and go to the ears of your image in the eyes of the person facing you, you will clearly recognize that these lines converge in such a manner that they would join in a point very little behind your reflected image . . . .

135.

Why an object close to the eye has indistinct outlines. All objects opposite the eye and too close to it have indistinct and confused outlines. A source of light gives objects that are very close to it large and confused shadows ; the eye does the same thing when it judges exterior things, for in all instances of linear perspective the eye acts in the same way as a source of light does.

The explanation may be found in that vision has a principal axis that is enlarged by distance and that can grasp large objects far away and little objects nearby with precision. But as the eye sends out a multitude of lines around this main central axis that are much less capable of perceiving with exactness the things that it * finds farther from the center of this circle, the object close to the eye does not have *(all its parts)* close enough to the central axis for their outlines to register with clarity ; and these necessarily fall into the area of lines of less power of discernment, which are to vision what pointers are to hunting—able to raise the hare but not to take it ; thus they cannot grasp but are the reason

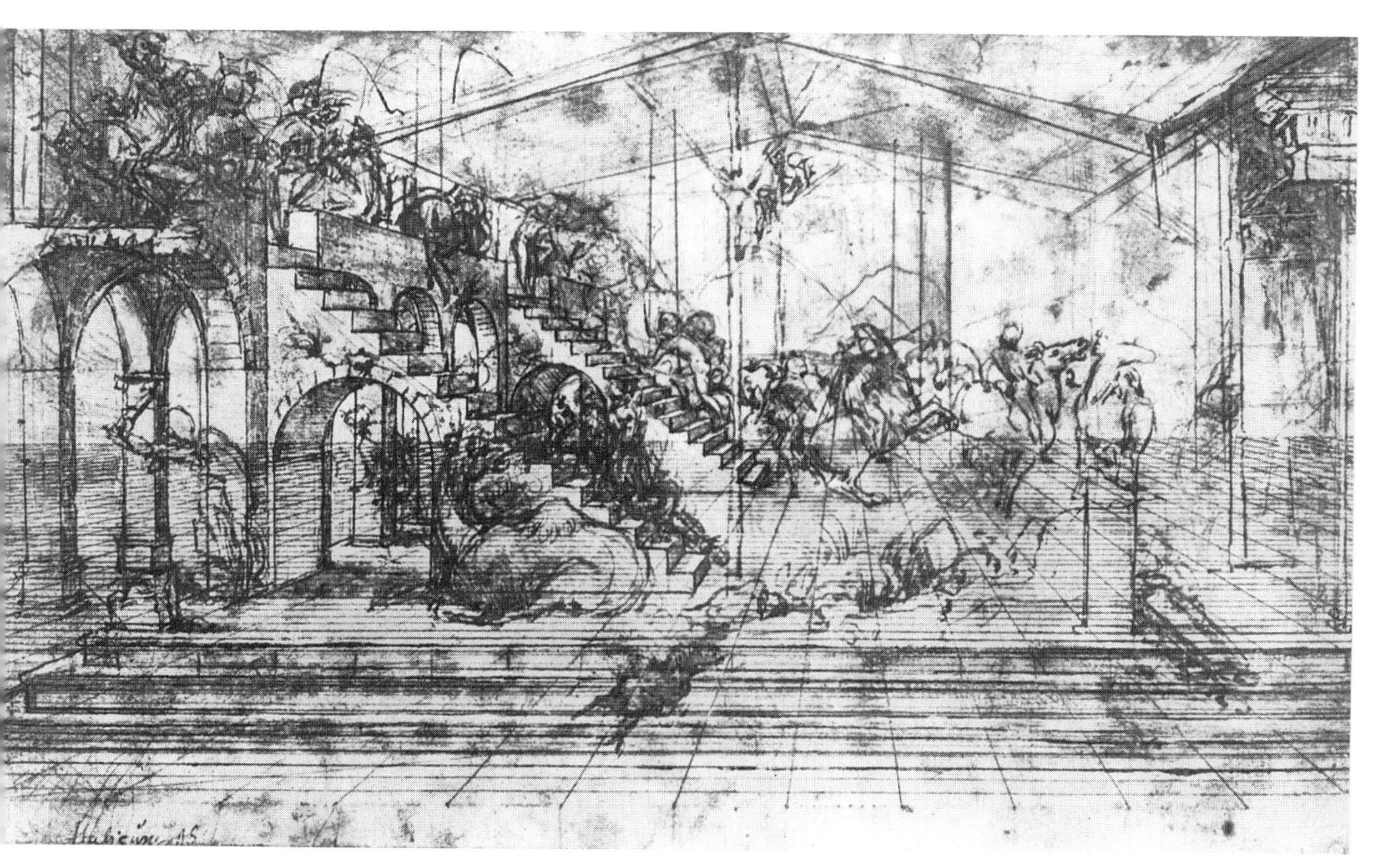

Perspective study for *The Adoration of the Magi.*

why the central axis turns toward the object they have raised. The objects of which the outlines are perceived through these lines, therefore, remain confused. *

136. *What is the true location of the horizon.* Horizons are at varying distances from the eye, for one calls horizon that place where the luminous air is next to the earth. And on a given vertical it appears at as many different places as there are different heights for the point of view. If the eye is placed at the level of the surface of a calm sea, the horizon is at the distance of about a mile, but if one rises and brings the eye to its normal height, the horizon will be seven miles away from him ; and thus to each higher level of elevation corresponds a horizon that is farther away ; and so it happens that those who are on the tops of high mountains, near the sea, see the circle of the horizon very far away, but those who are inland do not have the horizon always at the same distance, for the earth is not everywhere the same height in relation to the center of the earth, and it is therefore not perfectly spherical like the surface of the seas ; and it is this that makes the distance between the eye and the horizon vary . . . .

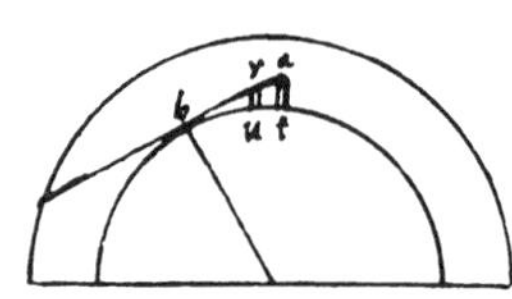

The horizon seems very distant when, from the seacoast of Egypt, one looks up along the Nile toward Ethiopia over the plains of the two sides *(of the river)* : the horizon is blurred or even invisible, because there are three thousand miles of plain which always rise with the level of the river ; * and between the eye and the Ethiopian horizon there is such thickness of air that everything becomes white and the horizon can no longer be distinguished. In painting, horizons of this type have a very beautiful effect. It is true that one should make some mountains at the sides, gradually diminishing the intensity of the colors, as is required by the rule for the diminution of colors at great distances. *

But to prove that the pyramid of perspective includes infinite space let us take *ab* for the spectator who *(with his eye)* measures the segments *dnmop* of an infinite line, intercepting the visual rays on the wall *cd*. * These visual rays pass through the wall *cd* at higher points in proportion as their point of origin is farther away, but they will never reach the height of the eye. And since the wall *cd* is a continuous quantity, it is divisible to infinity and can never be filled with the *(intersections of)* the visual rays to its top, even if the last is of infinite length ; and if the distance *bs* were infinite, one would still achieve only a parallel line. *

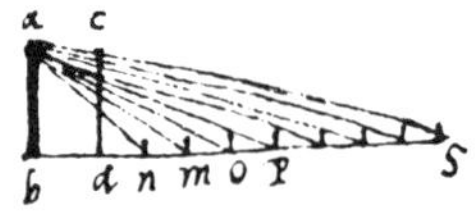

Figures that are little diminished are also close to the eye ; from which it follows that the natural horizon is at the level of the eye of the person represented *(in the foreground)*.

Diminution

137. *Note taken from Euclid*

A small object nearby and a large one far away, when seen between equal angles, will seem to be of the same size. *

Of the diminution of objects according to their distance. If the second object is as far removed from the first as the first from the eye, it will seem half as large, although in fact they are of the same size.

138.

The degrees of diminution. If you place the vertical plane one *braccio (arm's length)* away from your eye, the first object, four *braccia* from your eye, will be diminished to three-fourths of its height on the plane; and if you move it to eight *braccia* from your eye, it will have diminished to seven-eighths; and if it is at sixteen *braccia,* it will have diminished to fifteen-sixteenths of its height; and so on progressively as you double the distance the diminution will double. *

The Systems

139. *Spherical and flat perspective*

Simple perspective. Simple perspective is that which art uses on a surface all the parts of which are at the same distance from the eye. Complex perspective is that which is used upon a surface of which no part is at the same distance from the eye as any other. *

140. *The inconsistency of plane perspective*

Among things of equal size the more remote seem smaller. . . . Let the plane be *de,* above which are represented three equal circles that are placed behind it, that is, circles *a, b,* and *c*; you now see that the eye, *h,* will perceive the images of the distant object on the plane as being larger than those that are nearer. *

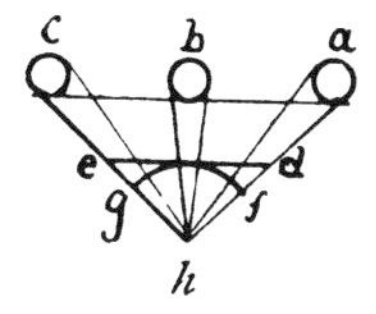

141. *Classification of the perspectives*

The practice of perspective is divided into . . . parts, * of which the first deals with objects seen by the eye at whatever distance they may be; and it shows all these objects diminished as the eye sees them, and the spectator is not obliged to stand in one place rather than another, provided that the wall does not produce a second effect of foreshortening.

But the second practice is a combination of perspectives caused partly by art and partly by nature, and, in a work made according to this rule, there is no part that is not a combination of natural and accidental perspective.

By natural perspective I mean that the wall on which this construction is represented is flat, and even though it may have the sides parallel, two by two, * it is necessary to diminish the sides more than the parts closest to the spectator, and this diminution is natural. And accidental or artificial perspective acts *(as compensation)* in the contrary way, that is, it enlarges bodies that are in themselves of equal size on the wall, and does this in proportion as the natural perspective intervenes * and whether the spectator is nearer to the surface of the wall and whether the place on which one paints is further away from the spectator. . . . *

142. *Against perspective with a fixed point of view*

. . . But this invention * forces the spectator to stand with his eye close to a hole, and then, through this hole, it will seem correct. But since many spectators will come at the same time to see a work made this way, and this perspective works only for one among them, it remains confused for the rest. It is therefore necessary to shun this combined perspective * and keep to the simple, which does not assume walls that are foreshortened but wants them as close as possible to the true form. And of this simple perspective, in which the intersection cuts the pyramids that carry the images to the eye *(everywhere)* at an equal distance from the center of vision, the model for it is furnished by the curve of the eye * where the pyramids are cut at a distance that is *(everywhere)* equal from the center of the eye.

143. *The three kinds of linear perspective*

Of natural perspective combined with accidental perspective . . . . . . Natural perspective is as follows : among things of equal size, the one farthest away seems smallest, and conversely, the one nearest seems largest, and the diminution is in proportion to the distance.

But accidental perspective give the appearance of unequal size to things of the same *(size)* painted at different distances *(on the wall from the eye),* leaving that which is smaller than all the others in the place nearest the eye, and placing the largest at a distance so that is seems smaller than all the others — and all this because of the wall on which the scene is represented,

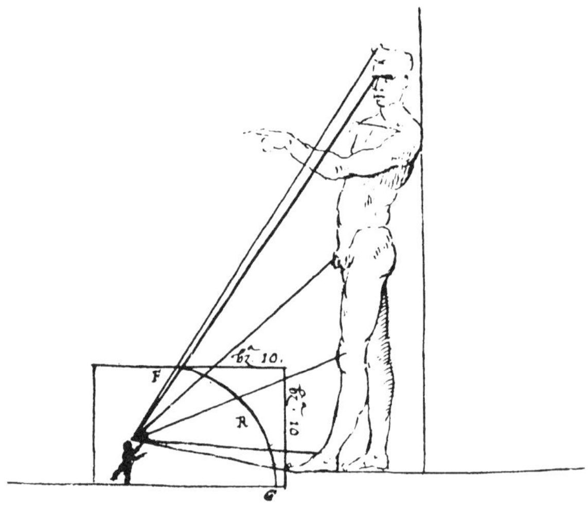

"Accidental" perspective. The figure to be represented on the curved surface FG has to be distorred "monstrously" in order to appear well-proportioned to the tiny spectator on the left.

and all the parts of which, in its length, are at unequal distances from the eye ; this diminution of the wall is natural, but the perspective painted on it is accidental, for it does not agree in any way with the true diminution of the said wall ; * hence, if the eye looking at this representation in perspective moves slightly, all the images will appear monstrous to it, which is not the case with the natural perspective defined

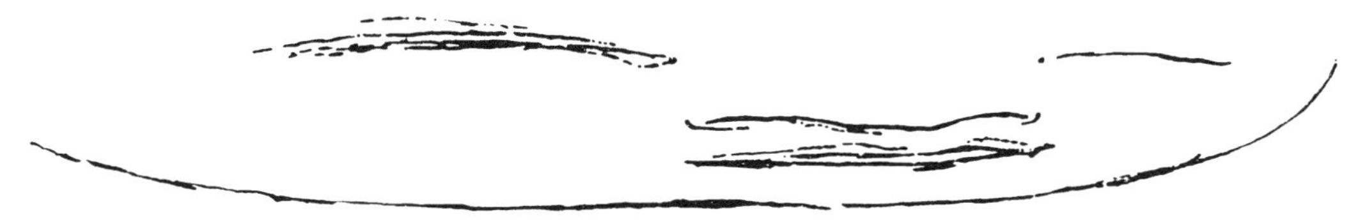

Anamorphosis : head of a child.

above, etc. Therefore, we say that the quadrilateral *abcd* drawn below* is *(according to plane*

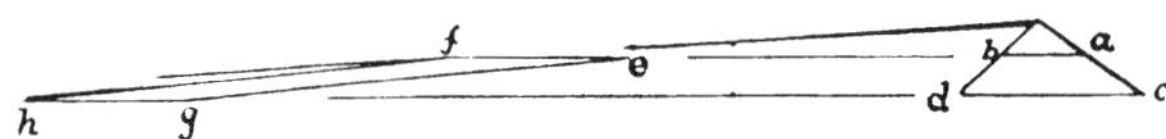

perspective) a foreshortened square seen by a spectator placed opposite the center of its base.

144. *Anamorphosis*

... The eye, *m*, that sees the intervals, *ovx*, barely perceives the differences between them (*although* vx *is larger than* ov) and this is so because it is close to them *(so that as a result the apparent diminution of* vx *is more accentuated than that of* ov). If the same intervals are indicated on the wall *no*, the interval *ov* will be

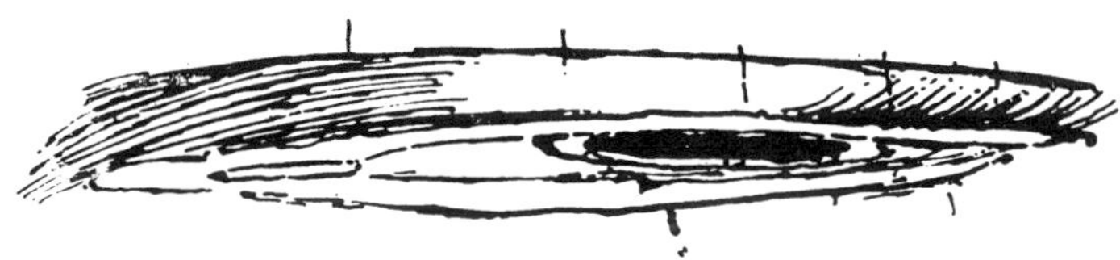

Anamorphosis : the eye.

But accidental perspective combined with the natural * may be seen in the so-called *el main* * quadrilateral, that is, *efgh*, which should be similar to *abcd* for the eye that remained in its original position between *c* and *d*, and the effect will be good, for, because of its natural perspective, the wall will conceal the error of this monstrosity.

seen as *or*, and in the same way *vx* will become *rq*. And if you paint this on a wall before which you can move freely, it will appear disproportionate to you because of the great difference between *or* and *rq*. This occurs because the eye is so close to the wall *(no)* that the latter seems foreshortened. And if you wish to paint this nonetheless, your perspective will have to be viewed through a single hole placed at *m* .... The wall *op*, because it is everywhere at an equal distance from the eye, will both show the objects correctly and in a way that they may be seen in all directions. *

AERIAL PERSPECTIVE

Light and Forms

145. *The diminishing visibility of objects* In a figure placed at a great distance, the smallest details will be the first to become invisible, and the larger divisions will be preserved longest though their contours will become indistinct; they become oval or spherical forms without precise limits.

146. *The law of diminishing visibility* Any material object has, in relation to sight, three properties : volume, outline, and color. With distance, the image of volume disappears more slowly than the color or the outline; secondly, the color remains visible for a longer time than the outline. But this rule is not applicable to luminous bodies . . .

147. *Aerial perspective of luminous bodies* *Of light.* A luminous body will appear to be smaller when veiled by dense atmosphere, as may be seen by the moon or the sun covered by mists. . . .

148. *An illusion of aerial perspective* Finding myself on a branch of the sea that was equally far from a beach and from a cliff, the beach seemed much farther away to me than the cliff. *

Proof that luminous bodies seem larger from a distance than they actually are. If you place two lighted candles at a distance of half a *braccio* (arm's length) from each other and then go two hundred *braccia* away from them, you will see that because of their enlargement the two lights will form a single luminous body and will seem to be a single light, one *braccio* large. . . 149.

A shaded body will appear smaller when it is surrounded by a more luminous background; and a luminous body will appear larger when its background is darker. This is shown by the *(apparent)* size of buildings at night when there are flashes of lightning behind them, for during the lightning one has the sudden impression that the building is diminished in size. And this is the reason buildings appear larger in a fog, or at night when the air is pure and illumined. 150. *The body and its background : contrast in light*

Perspective. No visible object can be clearly perceived by the human eye except through contrast with the background against which the outlines are drawn and delineated; and no object will have the lines of its contours detached from the background. * And, although the moon is very far away from the body of the sun, when there is an eclipse it finds itself between our eyes and the sun, and will appear to human eyes to be united with and attached to the sun. 151. *Contrast flattens*

Color Vision

Of aerial perspective. There is another pers- 152. *The blue of distant views* pective which I would call aerial because the differences in the color of the air can show us the respective distances of several buildings, the bases of which are cut off by a single line, as when one sees them above a wall. Let us assume that above this wall they all appear to be of the same size and that you wish to show that some are at a greater distance than others and are in a comparatively thicker atmosphere. You know that in such an atmosphere the objects the farthest away that one can make out, as for example mountains, seem blue, almost the color of air when sun is in the east, because of the great mass between these mountains and your eye. Therefore, you will give the nearest building above the wall its true color, and the one that is farther away you will make less clear and bluer. And the one you want to show still farther away, paint much bluer ; and the one that should be five times as far away, make it five times bluer. And by this rule concerning buildings above a line, which seem to be of the same size, it will be clearly understood which of them are more distant and therefore *(in reality)* larger than the others.

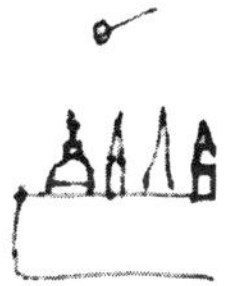

153. *At what distance from the eye the colors of objects are lost.* The distance at which the colors of objects are lost varies according to the time of day and the thinness or density of the air through which the images of the colors of the said objects pass to the eye. And for the present we shall not give any other rules.

Of the color of the atmosphere. I say that the blue which we see in the atmosphere is not its true color but is caused by hot moisture that has evaporated into very tiny and invisible particles and which are struck by the rays of the sun, becoming luminous against the black of the immense darkness of the region of fire that envelops them on the outside. * This may be seen, as I myself saw, by anyone who climbs the Monboso * at the ridge of the Alps that separates France from Italy. At its base, this mountain gives birth to the four rivers that water all of Europe and flow in different directions, and no other mountain around it has such height. It rises to so great a height that it almost passes above all clouds and *(hence)* snow seldom falls there, but only hail in the summer when the clouds rise to their greatest altitude ; and this hail is so well preserved there that, were it not for the infrequency of the clouds rising so high and its hailing — it does not happen twice in one generation — there would be an enormous accumulation of ice carried there and piled up by the hail, and this I found very large in the middle of July. And I found the air above me dark and the sun that illuminated the mountain, far more bright than in the lower plains, for there was less thickness of air between the summit of this mountain and the sun. 154.

As a further example of *(my theory of)* the color of the air, we may take the smoke produced by old, dry wood. As it comes out of the chimney, it seems very blue when it is between the eye and a background ; but as it rises higher

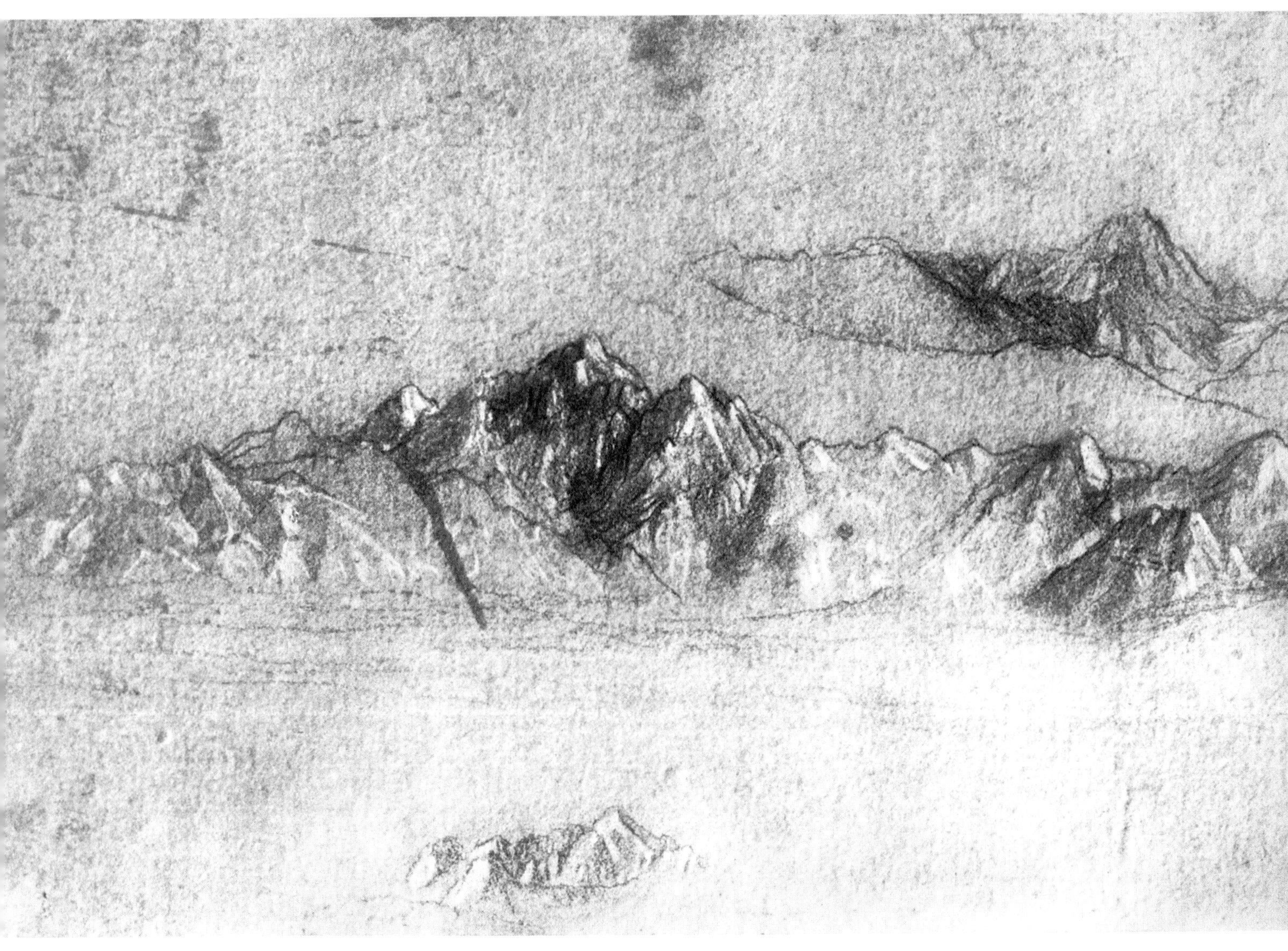

Chain of the Alps.

and comes between the eye and the luminous atmosphere, it immediately takes on the color of ashes ; and this occurs because it no longer has darkness behind it but in its place the luminous air. If the smoke is from fresh, green wood, however, it will not take on a blue color because it is not transparent but full of excess moisture ; hence it will have the effect of a dense cloud, which retains light and well-defined shadows, as if it were a solid body. The air does the same thing when excess moisture, dispersed by the heat, makes it dark, and gives it a dark blue color. And this is enough to explain the color of the air.

One might, however, add that if the air had transparent blue for its natural color, it would follow that where there was a greater quantity of atmosphere between the eye and the region of fire, the blue would be darker, as may be seen in blue grass or in sapphires, which appear darker in proportion as they are thicker. But the effect of the air under these conditions is the exact opposite . . .

We may also see, in the dark shadows of mountains far from the eye, that the air between that shadow and the eye will appear to be of a very strong blue, while the parts of the mountain that are illuminated alter their true colors very much less.

But whoever wishes to have definite proof, should paint a board with several colors, among them a very fine black ; and over this he should put a very thin and transparent layer of white lead. He will then see that the lustre of this white lead will not have as beautiful a blue appearance over any other color as over the black ; but it must be very thin and finely ground.

155. *Lighting and color*

Of flesh tones and shapes seen from a distance. . . . And remember that shadows are never so deep that their darkness obscures all traces of the color of the place they cover, except when the place where they are is already in darkness. * And do not make *(sharply cut)* profiles, do not isolate individual hairs, do not make white high lights except on white objects, and let these high lights display the full beauty of the color they touch.

156. *Blue shadows*

Of painting. Since white is not a color, but has the power to receive every color, all its shadows appear blue when seen out-of-doors. And this is explained in our fourth proposition which says : the surface of every opaque body partakes of the color of the object it sees. Take a white surface deprived of the light of the sun by the interposition of some other object between it and the sun ; it must be concluded that the white facing the sun and the air *(at the same time)* will partake of the colors of the sun and the air, but that the part not facing the sun stays in the shadow and partakes *(only)* of the color of the air. And if the white did not face the green of the fields stretching to the horizon, nor the whiteness of this horizon, undoubtedly it would have the simple color of the air.

157. *Colored lighting*

Of light on opaque bodies . . . If you take a white ribbon and put it in a dark place and illuminate it, through three holes, by the sun, by fire, and by the light of day, this ribbon will be of three colors.

158. *Of the nature and of the crossing of the rays that transmit the visual images of objects. . . .* The rectilinear rays which carry the forms and colors of things through the air from where they emanate do not color the air and do not taint each other through contact where they intersect, but color only the place where they destroy themselves, * for that place sees the source of the rays and is seen by it, and no other object near by that place of origin can see the place where the intercepted ray destroys inself, and leaves the prey it has carried.

And this is proven by the fourth proposition on the colors of bodies, which says that the surfaces of all opaque bodies partake of the color of that which they see. As a result of this, in fact, the place which, through the rays carrying the image, sees the source of that image and is seen by it, is tinted by the color of that source. *

159. *Color and apparent size*

Of ordinary perspective. An object of uniform color and breadth, seen against a multicolored background, appears to be of varying size.

And if an object of uniform size and varying colors is seen on a monochrome background, it will appear to be of varying size. . . .

Reflection

160. *Reflections in water*

Perspective. The shadow or the image of a thing reflected in moving water, that is on little waves, will always be greater than the object on the outside causing it.

Of the difference between splendor and luster ; and that luster is not numbered among the colors but is a sen*(sation ?)* of white. * It arises on the surface of humid bodies. Splendor is of the color of the body that originates it, such as gold or silver, or the like. 161. *Splendor, luster, and color*

Of painting. The high light, that is the luster of a thing, will not be situated in the center of the illuminated part, but will follow the movements of the eye perceiving it. 162. *Luster*

Of where there can be no luminous reflection. . . . There can be no luminous reflection on the parts of the objects that are turned toward bodies in shadow, such as shadowed scenes, fields with grass of varying height, woods, whether green or bare, where, although a part of each branch illuminated by daylight takes on the quality of that light, there are, nevertheless, so many shadows belonging to each branch or cast by one branch on another, that the total result is so much darkness that the light no longer counts ; that is why bodies like these cannot throw any reflection on the bodies that are near them. 163.

Of light and shade. Each part of the surface enclosing a body takes on to a greater or lesser extent the colors of the things facing it. 164. *Colored reflections*

Example : If you place a spherical body in the midst of several objects, that is, if there is sunlight on one side, and on the other a wall that is green or of some other color, illuminated by the sun, and that the ground on which it rests is red, and the two lateral sides dark : you will then see the natural color of that body partake of the colors it sees. The strongest *(reflection)* will come from the luminous source ; the second from the illuminated wall ; the third from the shadow. Finally there remains a part that retains the *(original)* color of the surface.

165. *Optics as a general theory of reflections*

Of shadows which are not consistent with the illuminated parts. . . . The color of illuminated faces having opposite them black surfaces, will be combined with black shadows ; and the same is true for yellow, green, blue, or any other color placed before the face. This happens because all bodies send their images through all the surrounding air, as is proven in perspective and as is shown by the observations concerning the sun, for all objects that see it, receive its light and reflect it on other objects, just as the moon and other stars reflect toward us the light they receive from the sun. And darkness acts in the same manner, for it clothes in its obscurity everything that is hidden therein. *

166. *Qualitative laws*

Of reflections. The surfaces of bodies assume more readily the reflections of objects when the images reach them at more nearly equal angles. *

Of the colors of reflected images that objects send to surfaces of bodies facing them, the angles of reflection being equal, the most powerful will be the one of which the rays of reflection are the shortest.

Of the colors of reflections with equal angles that are at the same distance from the surfaces of bodies opposite, the most powerful will be the brightest.

The object that sends the most intense reflection of its color to the bodies opposite is that which is surrounded only by colors that are similar to its own.

Of luster. Luster takes on much more of the color of the light that is reflected on the body than of the color of the body itself ; and this occurs on dense surfaces. 167. *Quantitative laws*

In several kinds of opaque bodies the luster is entirely in the color of the body that is illuminated, as is the case with polished gold and silver and other metals and similar bodies. . . .

The luster produced inside the depth of dense and transparent bodies has the most beautiful color, as may be seen in balas rubies, *(stained)* glass, and similar materials. This is so because the natural color of the transparent body is interposed between the luster and the eye.

The light reflected by dense and lustrous bodies is more beautiful than the natural color of the bodies, as is seen in the folds of garments adorned with gold threads or in other similar objects when a surface is reflected in another that is in front of it, and the other in it, and so on to infinity. . . .

Color

Of the colors that result from the mixing of other colors, which are called secondary colors. 168. *How to make a systematic table of colors*

There are six simple colors of which the first is white, although some philosophers do not include either white or black among their number because one is the origin of all color and the other its absence. But as the painter cannot do without them, we shall classify them among the number of colors and say that in this order of simple colors white is the first, yellow the second, green the third, blue the fourth, red the fifth, and black the sixth.

We shall put white for the light without which no color can be seen, yellow for the earth, green for the water, and blue for the air, and red for the fire, * and the black for the darkness that is above the element of fire, * for there, there is no matter or density that the rays of the sun can penetrate and hence illuminate.

If you wish to represent the diversity of all the composite colors with ease, take pieces of colored glass and through them look at all the countryside that is behind them. You will thus see that all the colors of the things behind these pieces of glass are combined with the color of the glass, and you will note which colors are strenghtened and which are weakened by such a mixture.

For example, if the piece of glass is yellow in color, I say that the image of the objects seen through this piece of glass may be impaired or improved ; when seen through a piece of glass of this color, deterioration will occur in the case of blue, black, and white before all others ; and improvement in the case of yellow and green. And thus you will review the mixtures of colors, and you will make new discoveries of mixtures and compositions, and you will then proceed to do the same thing with two pieces of glass of different colors *(super)*imposed one over the other before the eye ; and thus you may continue at will. *

169. *Harmony of colors*

Of colors. Colors that go together harmoniously are green with red or purple * or violet, and yellow with blue.

170. *Lighting favorable to each color*

In which way a given color will look most beautiful in painting. It is necessary to observe in which way a color looks beautiful in nature : when it receives reflections, or when it is illuminated, or when it is in a medium shadow, or when it is in darkness, or when it is transparent.

It depends on what the color under consideration is, for different colors will show their greatest beauty in different ways ; thus, we see that black is most beautiful in the shadows, white in the light, blue, green, and brown in the medium shadows, yellow and red in the light, gold in reflected light, and lake blue in medium shadows. *

171. *Transparency*

How to make the colors in your paintings bright and beautiful. For the colors which you wish to give the greatest beauty, first make a preparation of a very pure white ; and I say this for the colors that are transparent, since for those that are not transparent, the white preparation is of no use. This may be seen, for example, in the pieces of colored glass which, when placed between the eye and the luminous

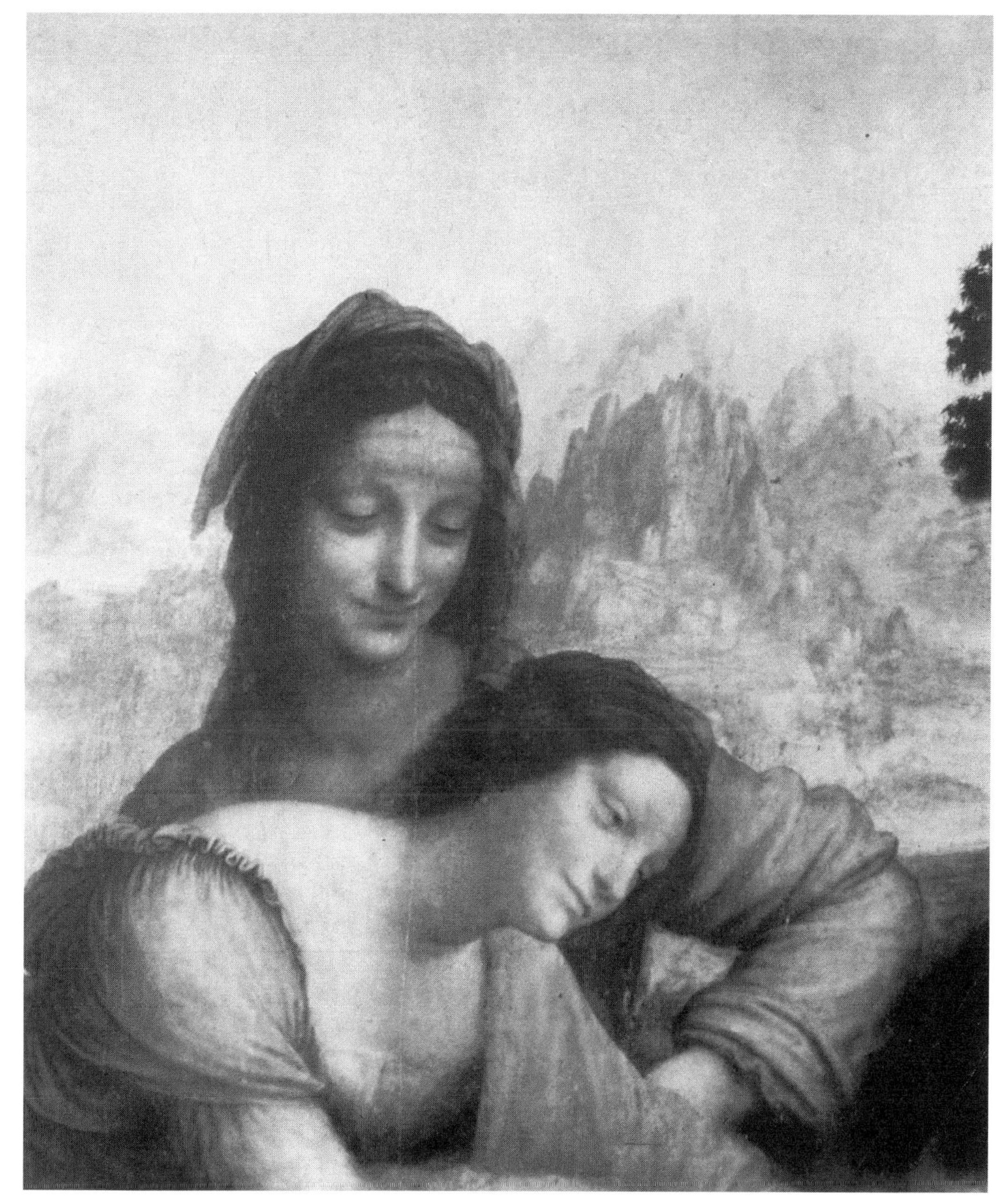

The Virgin and Child with St. Anne. Detail.

air, are of a great beauty ; something that is not so when they have dark air or other black things behind them.

172. *Shades and values* *Whether different colors can take on the same amount of darkness from the same shadow.* It is possible for all kinds of colors to be transformed by a given shadow into the color of that shadow.

This is proven by the darkness of a cloudy night in which one cannot distinguish any form or color of an object ; and since darkness is nothing but the absence of light, direct or reflected, through which one can distinguish all the shapes and colors of bodies, it follows that when the light, its cause, is suppressed entirely, the effect or perception of the colors and shapes of bodies also ceases.

LANDSCAPE AND PAINTING OUT-OF-DOORS

173. *In what way one should paint a landscape.* One should represent landscapes in such a manner that the trees are half illuminated and half in shadow ; but it is better to paint them when the sun is hidden by clouds, for then the trees are touched by the diffuse light of day and the diffuse darkness of the earth. And their parts are darker the closer they are to the ground or to the middle of the tree.

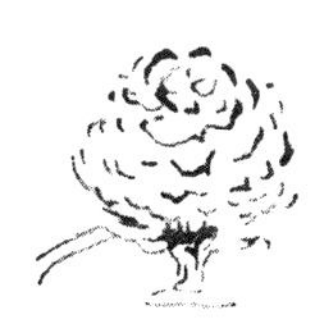

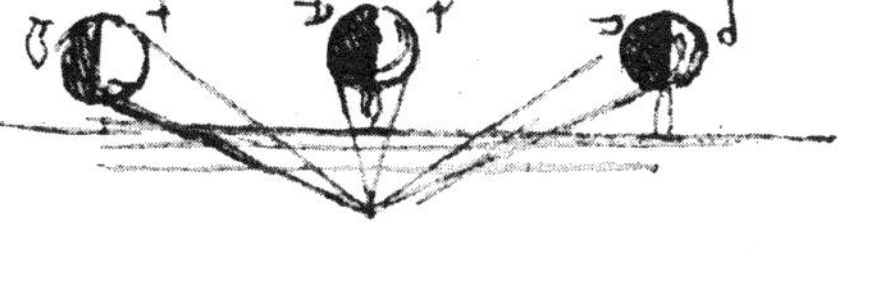

For the spectator facing the three illuminated "trees", the one in the center will have the greatest relief.

174. *How to paint distant views.* It is easy to see that one part of the atmosphere, the one close to the plain, is denser than the other ; and the higher it rises the lighter and more transparent it becomes. The bases of high and large objects, far away from you, will not be seen much for they are seen at the end of a line that passes through the densest and thickest atmosphere. But the summits of these heights are seen at the end of a line which, although it originates at your eye, in a dense atmosphere, nevertheless, when it arrives at the summit of the object looked at, culminates in an atmosphere that is much finer than at the base ; hence, as that line extends farther away from you, it passes through air that becomes progressively finer. Therefore, painter, when you paint mountains, be careful to make the bases from hill to hill in lighter tones than the summits, and the farther away they are the more the color of the bases will be light, and the higher the mountains rise the more they will show their true form and color.

175. *Of the color of mountains.* Among mountains far from the eye, the one that is darkest by nature will be of the most beautiful blue ; and the darkest will be the one that is highest and most wooded, for since these woods are situated

very high, * they will show the lower part of their trees; and the lower parts are dark because they do not see the sky. Moreover, the wild plants of the woods are in themselves darker than cultivated ones; oaks, beeches, firs, cypresses, and pines are much darker than olive trees and all kinds of fruit trees....

176. *Landscapes at nightfall* When the sun is setting, the mist that falls makes the air thick, and the objects not touched by the sun remain obscure and indistinct, and those illuminated by the sun turn reddish or yellowish, according to the color of the sun at the horizon; and also the houses illuminated by the sun stand out very clearly, and especially the buildings and houses of cities and villages, because their shadows are dark; in their conspicuousness they seem to stand out against an indistinct and uncertain background, for all things, unless they are touched by the sun, seem to be of the same color. *

177. *Trees* When it happens that a cloud casts a shadow on some part of a hill, these trees will change *(color)* less than those in the plains; for trees on heights have thicker branches because they grow less each year than those down below; and since these branches are naturally dark and more infiltrated with shadows, the darkness of the clouds hardly makes them any darker. But the bare spaces between the trees, not being covered by shadows, change very much in tone, especially if they are not green, as for instance, cultivated land, the ravaged mountains, the barren parts, and the rocks. Trees set against the skyline all appear of the same color, unless they are very close together and have thick foliage, such as the pine, and others. If you look at the trees on the side on which the sun illuminates them, you will see that they are almost uniformly light, and the shadows within them will be hidden by the illuminated leaves that are between your eye and these shadows....

The smoke of the cities. Smoke is seen better 178.
and more distinctly in the east than in the west when the sun is in the east; and the reason for this is twofold: the first is that the rays of the sun shine through the particles of this smoke and render them visible; the second is that the roofs of the houses are in shadow when seen toward the east at this hour, because the sun cannot illuminate their slopes. And the same thing happens with dust. Both the one and the other become more luminous as they become denser, and their greatest density is toward the center.

The variations in the color of trees. The colors 179.
of the leaves of trees are varied by four factors, that is: shadow, light, reflection, and transparency.

Of the visibility of these variations. At a great distance the gradations of the leaves of the trees become a mixture in which the shade that occupies the most surface will predominate.

Of opaque leaves placed before transparent 180.

ones. When there are leaves between the light and the eye, those nearest to the eye will be the darkest and those farthest away will be the lightest, unless they are set against the sky . . .

181. *Trees seen from below*

Do not forget, painter, when you make a tree nearby that your eye is a little lower than the tree so that you will see the leaves from the right side and from the reverse, and the parts that are on the right side will be bluer as their foreshortening is greater, and the same leaf will sometimes show part of the right side and part of the reverse, and that is why you should paint it in two colors.

182. *Trees in the wind*

The part of the tree farthest away from the force that strikes * it is the one that feels the impact most strongly ; that is why nature has taken care to give it greatest thickness there where the risk of its breaking is greatest, particularly with trees that grow to great heights such as pines, and others.

183. *Study of mists*

What things are visible at a great distance. A dark object appears lighter the farther away it is from the eye ; and it follows, conversely, that the dark object will seem darker the closer it is to the eye. Therefore, the lower part of anything placed in thick air will seem farther away at its foot than at its upper part, and for that reason the base of a nearby mountain will seem farther away than its summit, which is actually more distant.

184. *An optical illusion caused by mists*

The upper parts of buildings seen in mist . . . . A tower with parallel sides, seen in mist from a distance, seems narrower toward the base. The reason for this is the preceding proposition, which says that the mist is whiter and denser in proportion as it is closer to the ground ; and

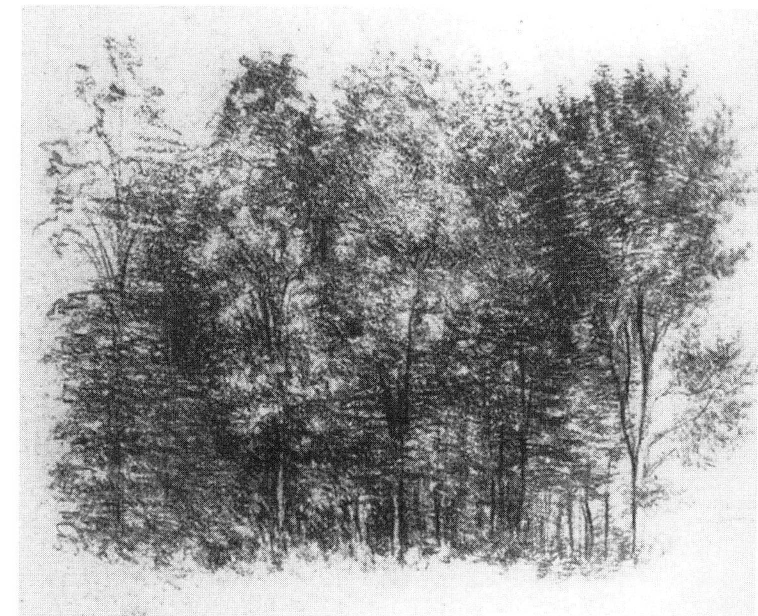

Study for trees.

the second proposition of this book, which states that a dark object seems proportionally smaller as its background is more intensely white. Therefore, as the mist is whiter toward the base than toward the top, the dark tower necessarily appears narrower toward the base than toward the top.

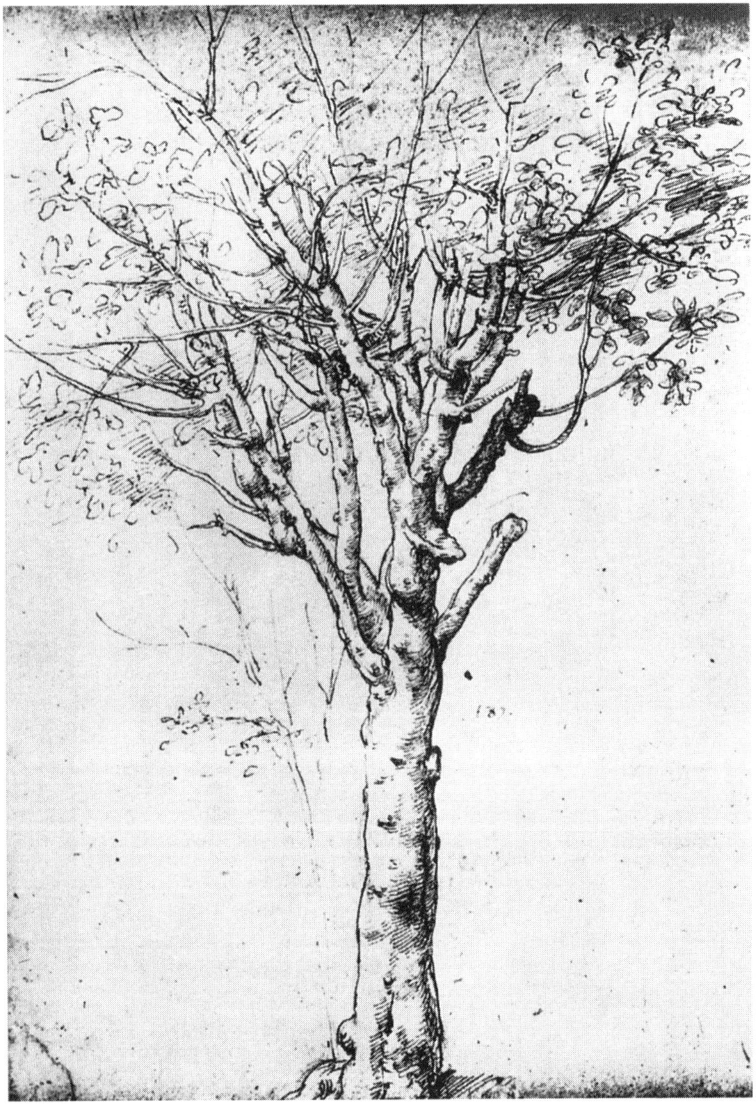

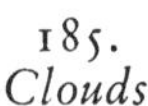

185. Clouds

Of clouds, smoke, and dust, and of flames from ovens or burning kilns. The roundness of clouds is evident only on the side that is seen by the sun, and the others, being in shadow, are invisible. If the sun is in the east and the cloud in the west, then the contours of the roundnesses of the clouds appear dark to the eye situated between them and the sun ; and the interior incircled by these contours appears light . . . .

Clouds, like trees, display no roundness in the parts that are in shadow. *

186. *Landscapes at dawn*

In the morning the mist is thicker above than below because the sun raises it ; that is why the tops of large buildings, although not farther away from you than their bases, are invisible. For the same reason the sky seems darker toward the zenith than toward the horizon, and its color is not blue but is tinged by the smoke and dust . . . .

The buildings to the west show their illuminated parts, those reached by the sun, and the rest is hidden by the mist. When the sun rises and drives away the mist, the hills on the side from which it is being dissipated are illuminated and become blue and smoke in the direction of the departing mist, and the buildings show both the sides that are illuminated and those that are in shadow at the same time, while they show only their illuminated side where the mist is thinner, and nothing at all where it is denser. And this is true when the departing mist moves horizontally, and in that case it is not clearly distinguished from the blue of the sky, but below the horizon it is like dust rising. As the air is

Study of a tree. Leonardo's drawing was gone over by Cesare da Sesto.

thicker, the buildings in the cities, and the trees of the fields appear thinner for only the largest and thickest are visible . . . .

187. *Of meadows. . . .* When the sun is in the east, the color of the meadows and the small plants is a very brilliant green because they are transparent to the sun, which is not the case with the meadows at sunset ; and those to the south and to the north are of a moderately brilliant green.

188. *Vegetation in the mountains*

Painting ; to represent the characteristics and parts of mountainous landscapes. Grass and plants will become paler as the soil that nourishes them becomes poorer and has less humidity ; and the land is poorer and drier on the rocks composing the mountains. And the trees will be smaller and frailer the nearer they are to the summits of the mountains, and the land will be poorer the closer it is to the mountain peaks, and the rich soil will be more abundant the closer it is to the concavities of the valleys.

Therefore, painter, you will show the peaks of the mountains and the rocks that constitute them in large part not covered by soil ; and the grass that grows there is small and sparse, and for the most part pale and dry for lack of moisture ; and one should be able to see the poor and sandy soil showing between pale grass and small plants that are stunted and aged without having reached full size, with short thick branches with few leaves, the roots, arid and blighted, in large part exposed, interwoven with the cracks and broken places of the decomposed rocks, growing among trunks mutilated by men and wind. And in several places one should see rocks protruding from the slopes of the high mountains, covered by thin and pale grit, but in other places showing their true color, laid bare by the impact of lightning from the heavens, whose descent is often stopped by these rocks, and not without their suffering from it.

And the farther one descends toward the base of the mountains, the more vigorous the vegetation will be, and the thicker the branches, and leaves and their green will be of as many different shades as there are kinds of plants in these forests ; and the trees will vary in structure and in thickness of the branches and leaves, and in shape and in height ; certain kinds will be narrow, such as the cypress, and in the same way others will be thick and broad, such as the oak and the chestnut, and others ; some will have very small leaves, others slender ones like the juniper and the plane tree, and the like ; some groups of trees of the same age are separated from each other by variable spaces, others close together without being separated by fields or other open spaces.

Of the birth of branches on trees. The beginning of the ramifications of new branches upon the principal branches is the same as the beginning of leaves of the same year upon the shoots. And these leaves have four rules of disposition from the bottom to the top : the first and most general is that each leaf corresponds to the sixth one below it ; the second is that once in three times each group of two leaves corresponds to the one below it ; the third is that the third leaf corresponds each time to the third leaf 189.

189. Distribution of leaves

below it ; the fourth is that for pines, which distribute them in layers.

190. *A botanical analysis for painters*

Of the leaves of the walnut tree. The leaves of the walnut tree are distributed over the whole outgrowth of that year and are the farther away from each other and greater in number, as the branch from which the outgrowth springs is younger . . . . The fruits grow at the end of these shoots ; and the largest shoots grow on the lower side of the branches from which they spring. This occurs because the weight of the sap of the tree is more apt to descend than to rise and that is why the shoots that start above them and rise to the sky are small and weak. And when the branches look toward the sky, from the beginning the leaves have their tips uniformly distributed ; * and if the shoot is horizontal, the leaves remain flat, and this comes about because all the leaves turn their reverse side toward the ground.

191. *Trees :* High, short, thin, thick — that is, concerning the leaves — dark, light, reddish, with branches that rise, are horizontal, * or descend, with white trunks, letting the air show through or not, close together or spread out.

APPENDIX : THE RAINBOW

192. *Colored light and colored material*

Treat of the rainbow in the last book on painting, but first write the book on colors produced by the mixture of other colors, in order to be able to show the genesis of the colors of the rainbow by means of these colors of the painter. *

193. *The rainbow is not an objective phenomenon*

Whether the colors of the rainbow stem from the sun. The colors of the rainbow are not the product of the sun because they are produced in many ways without the sun, as occurs when you bring close to the eye a glass of water in which there are tiny bubbles that one usually finds in glasses made of impure material ; although the sun may not be visible, these bubbles will produce all the colors of the rainbow on one of their sides. . . .

194. *The rainbow is not a subjective phenomenon : experiment with the prism*

That the eye plays no part in the creation of the colors of the rainbow. In the experiment described above it would seem that the eye took part in the creation of the colors of the rainbow, because the bubbles in the glass do not alone display these colors without the eye that looks at them. But if you place this glass full of water on the window sill so that the rays of the sun strike it from the outside, you will then see the above-mentioned colors producing themselves in the image made by the rays of the sun that have traversed the glass and terminated on the ground below the window in a dark place ; and, as the eye does not enter into this process, * we can say with certainty that it plays no part in the creation of these colors.

195. *An optic phenomenon related to the conditions of observation*

. . . The rainbow is neither in the rain nor in the eye that perceives it, but is originated by the rain, the sun, and the eye. The rainbow in the heavens is always seen by an eye that is between the rain and the body of the sun ; thus, when the sun is in the east and the rain in the

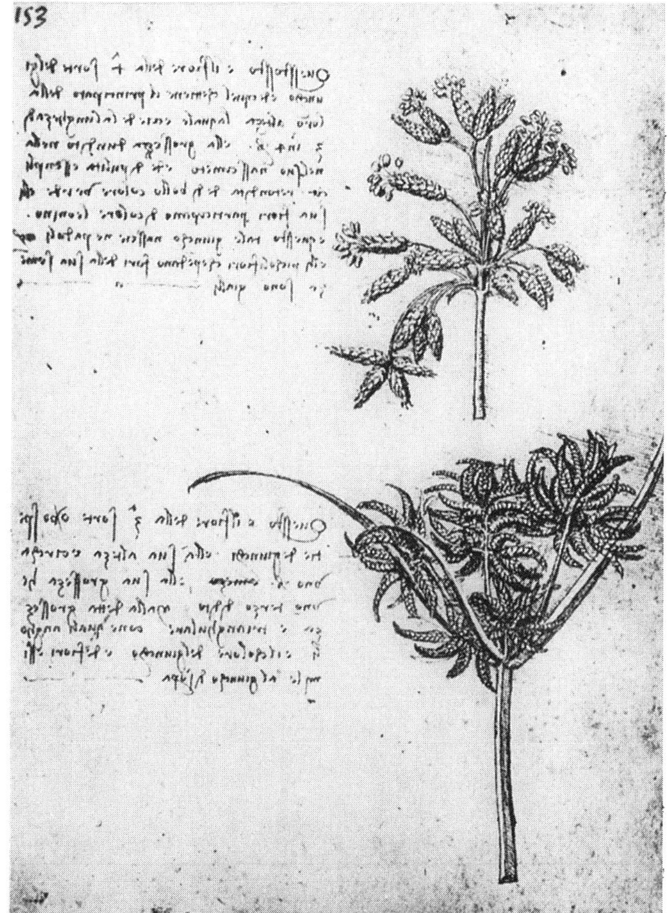

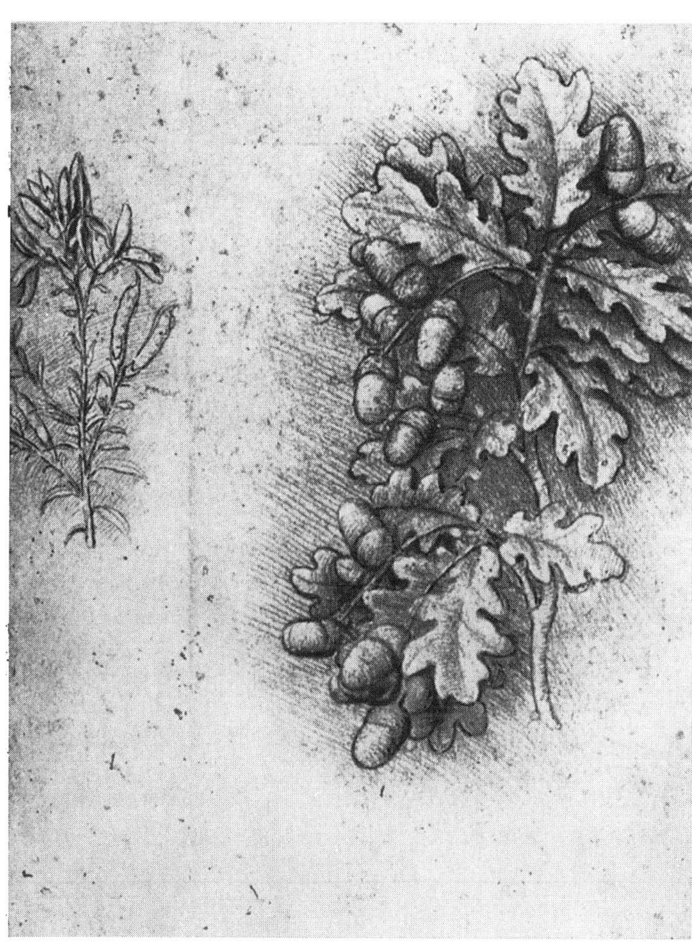

Studies of plants.

west, the rainbow appears in the rain to the west.

196. *The conditions of the phenomena*

Why dense air becomes red near the horizon. . . . and that redness, as well as the other colors (of the rainbow), is more intense when the rain is made up of larger drops, and the smaller the drops are, the paler the colors will be, and if rain is in the form of a mist, the rainbow will become white and completely devoid of color. But the eye must be between the mist and the sun.

197. *Iridescence*

Of the colors found in the feathers of certain birds. There are many birds in different parts of the world whose feathers exhibit the most beautiful colors when they make various movements, as happens among us with the feathers of peacocks and those on the necks of ducks or pigeons.

The same occurs on the surface of ancient glass found buried and on the roots of radishes when they have been at the bottom of a well or other stagnant water for a long time, for each of these roots is enclosed by bands of colors similar to those of the rainbow in the sky.

This may also be seen on oil spread out over water or again, in the solar rays reflected from the surface of a diamond or beryl ; through the facets of a beryl * every dark object seen against the sky or other light background appears surrounded by this sequence of colors where the dark object touches the air. And I am omitting many other such color sequences for the ones given will be enough for this subject.

Man and the Emotions

Leonardo alternated studies of subjects like anatomy and physiology with investigations of the forces of nature. He was well aware that the human body is the ultimate subject of painting and he realized that the painter could go further than he had in exploiting the " magic of expression. " The human form can act directly on the sensibilities and, when properly used, can open to art a whole new range of stupendous effects. The painter should be the master of the emotions he arouses at will — but at what price?

*Because Leonardo substituted knowledge acquired from direct observation for book learning, he studied anatomy by means of dissecting cadavers. He let no prejudice stop him, not even the very natural repugnance at handling corpses. He was sensible to the sublime paradox that the living organism is comprehensible only through the examination of the dead. * In opposition to the "verbal" sciences of the Universities, where nomenclature of the organs was taught from the texts of Galen and others, Leonardo developed a descriptive method based on the practices of the Florentine workshops. This is what he called turning to experience — forbidden "to scholars who impede anatomy and to its abbreviators" * — which consisted of precise exploration and graphic representation, so that it is not unlike the* anatomical topographies *generally used by artists. For Leonardo this "topography" was only the beginning and he went beyond it by studying the functions of the various parts. He observed how each muscle, each organ works, how it moves, wears out, and dies. * Finally this "functional anatomy" served as basis for further*

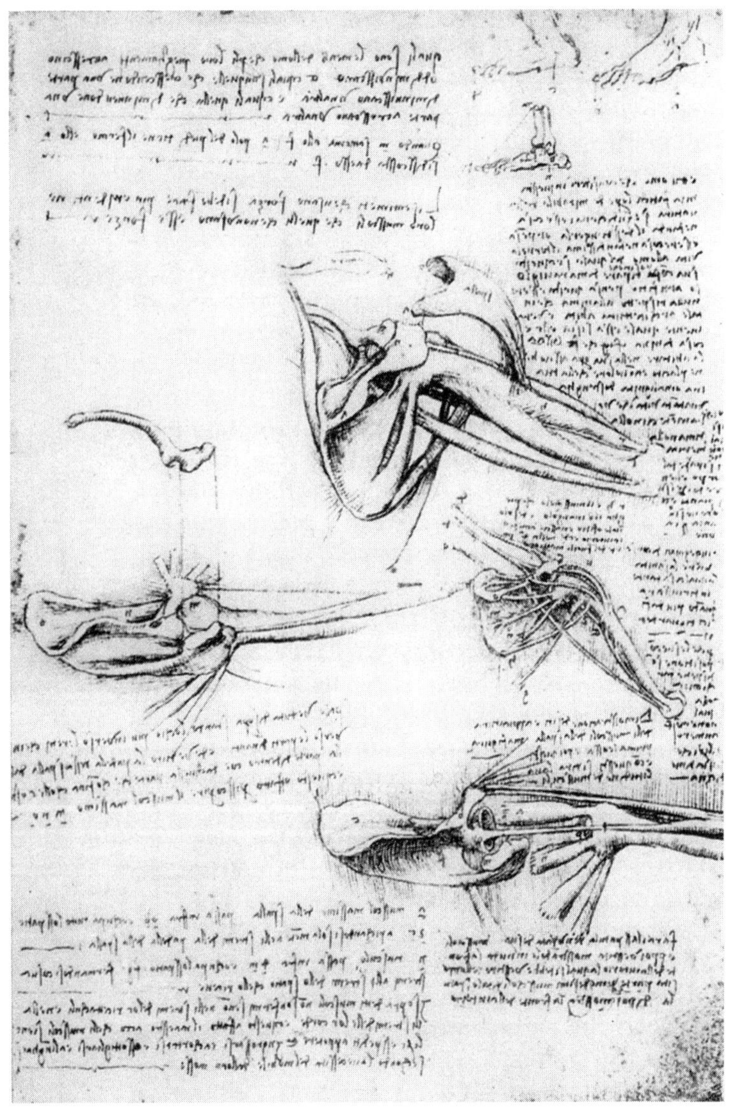

studies in which he considered the place of each organ within the whole and out of this developed the reconstructions he presented in masterly drawings and in which he substituted, by analogy, similar animal organs when human ones were not available to him : the famous fetus in utero shows * the unborn child in the uterus of a cow, as is indicated by the placenta ; the larynx inside the human throat is that of a dog and the thyroid gland is that of a pig.* Moreover, as part of his project he had planned a general anatomical study with sections entitled : Man, The Lion, The Horse, The Bull.

Finally, Leonardo, aware that "All parts of any animal exist in relationship to the whole," * reconstructed this totality and studied the functions of each member. He then turned to the significant positions the body takes in the process of movement. In sum, he had acquired the information necessary to introducing innumerable variables into his figures. For instance, he could show the effects of age or temperament. The painter, who now knew how to depict all kinds of movements, at last had a full repertory at his command and was no longer limited to using a single, monotonous type of figure in a favorite position. The imperceptible movement of the organs and the play of emotions is extended by the visible movements of the passions and all activities expressed through gestures. Hence the injunction : "The most important things that can be found in the analysis of painting are the movements appropriate to the states of mind of each living creature, such as desire, contempt, anger, pity, and the like." * Here too

Anatomical study. In order to make the mechanics of movement clearer, Leonardo made the muscles look like ropes.

there are a wealth of parallels between man and animals. The many drawings of facial types — now often referred to as caricatures — are sketches turned into useful exercises.

The wealth and variety of expressions are the rewards of a long investigation that began with the study of anatomy. It is, therefore, understandable that Leonardo craved the greatest possible variety of types, and had recourse to contrasts and the multiplication of nuances. From 1480-81 on, when he worked on the Adoration of the Magi *(which remained unfinished), he showed the fascination that lay in bringing together many faces of different ages, character, and kinds of expression. Here he had to obey the laws of composition : this demands a harmonious grouping and meaningful interrelation of the forms, and especially of all the suggestive forces that are appropriate to the laws of decorum.* The theorist here multiplied the material of which the painter can display the value. Nor did he forget the importance of clothing. Drapery was one of the traditional elements best known to the language of painting, and Leonardo wrote a lively little history of his time's fashions.*

MEASUREMENTS

198. *The drawing as the digest of logical observation*

The Anatomist at Work

The things of the mind that have not passed through the senses are vain and give rise only to invisible truths ; such discourses spring from poor intellects and their authors are poor ; if they are born rich, they will die poor in their old age. For nature seeks to punish those who wish to work miracles ; they have less than calmer men. Those who wish to become rich in one day will have a long life of poverty, as happens, and to all eternity will happen, to alchemists, the would-be creators of gold and silver, and to engineers who wish to have dead water animate itself into perpetual motion, and to the supreme fools, the necromancer and the enchanter.

You who believe that it is better to watch an anatomical demonstration than to look at these drawings, you would be right if one could see all the details shown in my drawing in a single figure in which, with all your talents, you will not see or get to know more than a few veins. To obtain an exact and complete knowledge, I have dissected more than ten bodies, destroying all the other parts and removing everything to the least little particle of flesh surrounding these veins, without any bleeding other than that, almost imperceptible, of the capillary veins. A single body did not suffice for so long a time ; it was necessary to proceed by stages with several bodies to achieve complete knowledge. And this I did twice, in order to verify the differences.

Despite all your love of these investigations, you may be deterred by repugnance ; and if that does not deter you, then by the fear of having to spend the night hours in company of corpses that have been cut up and flayed and become horrible. And if this does not deter you, then perhaps you do not have the skill in drawing necessary for such representations ; and if you know how to draw, perhaps you do not have any knowledge of perspective ; and if you have it, you may not be versed in mathematical exposition or in the methods of calculating the forces and energy of the muscles ; or perhaps it is patience that you lack so that you will not be diligent.

199. O investigator of this machine of our body, let it not distress you that your discoveries come through another's death ; rejoice, rather, that the Creator, in His intelligence, has provided an instrument of such excellence. *

200. O man, thou who through my endeavor examines the admirable works of nature, if you consider it atrocious to destroy these, * reflect that it is altogether atrocious to take the life of a man ; if the organization *(of his body)* appears to you like a marvelous creation of art, remember that it is nothing compared to the soul that inhabits this structure and that whatever it is, it is a thing truly divine. Therefore, let it dwell within this work at its pleasure and let not thy rage or malice destroy such a life (truly, he who does not value it, does not deserve it) for it leaves the body with extreme reluctance, and I believe that its lamentations and sorrow are not without justification. *

201. *Program for observation*

O painter of anatomy, beware lest excessive knowledge of bones, tendons, and muscles turn you into a wooden painter when you wish your nudes to be too revealing ; hence, to remedy this, note how the muscles of old or thin people cover and hide the bones and, moreover, according to what rules these muscles fill out the spaces that separate them and what muscles remain visible even in the most obese persons and what muscles disappear under the least layer of fat ; and often several muscles come together to form a single one when anyone becomes fatter, and often as one ages or becomes thinner a single muscle will become several . . .

And, furthermore, you should not fail to observe the variations of the forms of the muscles around the joints of the limbs of each animal caused by the diversity of the movements of each limb . . . .

And you should do the same for the child from its birth until the time of its decrepitude, through all the stages of its life from the lowest, beginning with infancy, then childhood, adolescence, youth, and so forth.

The Canon

202. *Canon of beauty and average stature*

If a man of two *braccia* is small, one of four is too large and it is the mean that is best. Now the mean between two and four is three ; therefore take a man of three *braccia* and measure him according to the rule that I will give you. And if you say that I could make a mistake and consider a man well proportioned who is not, I say you should see many men of three *braccia* and choose among their number several who have similar limbs ; and take the measurements

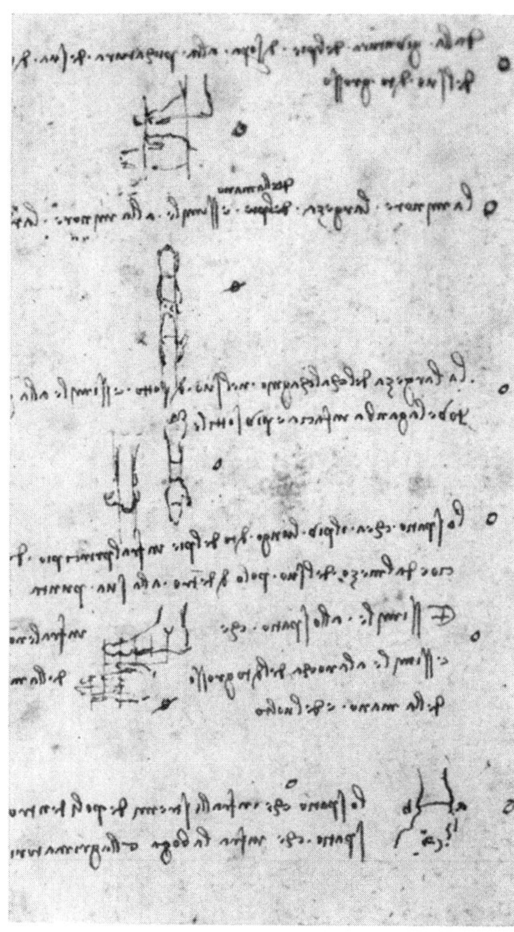

Comparisons of lengths of different members.

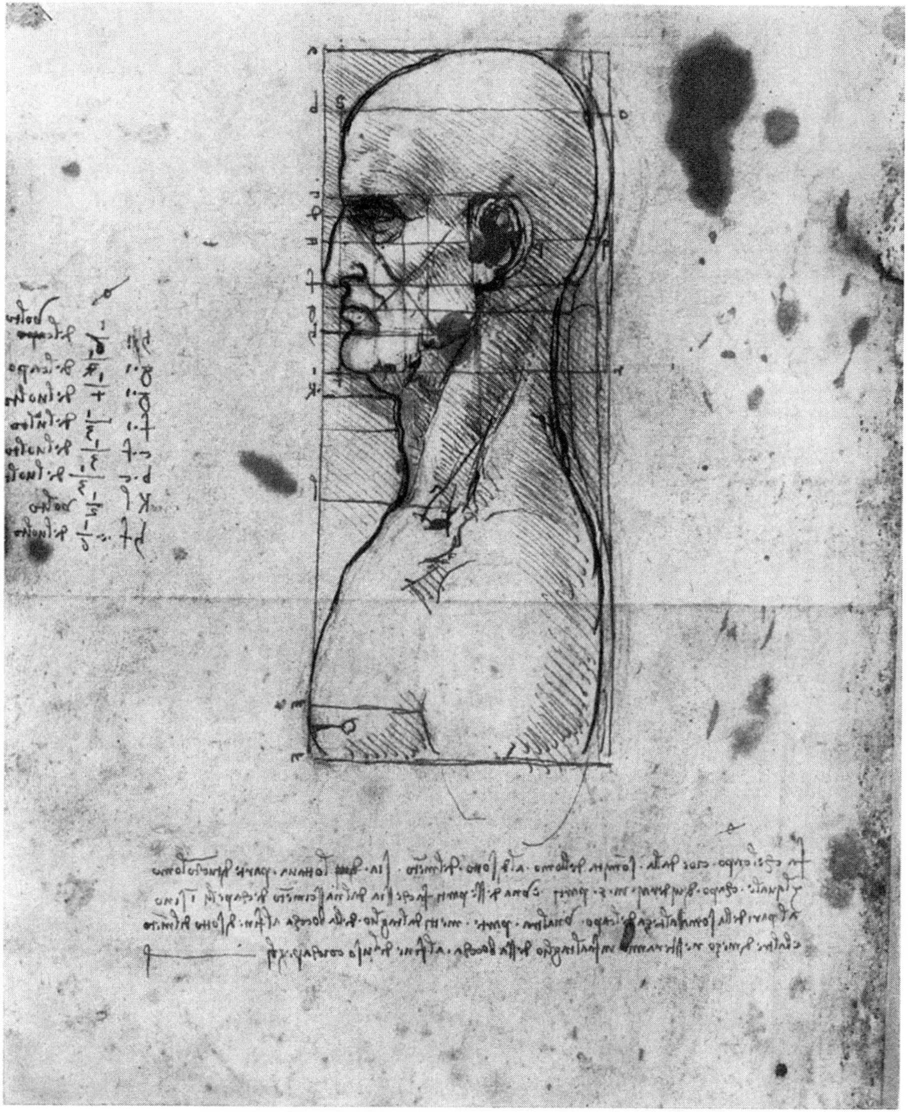

Geometric scheme of the proportions of the head.

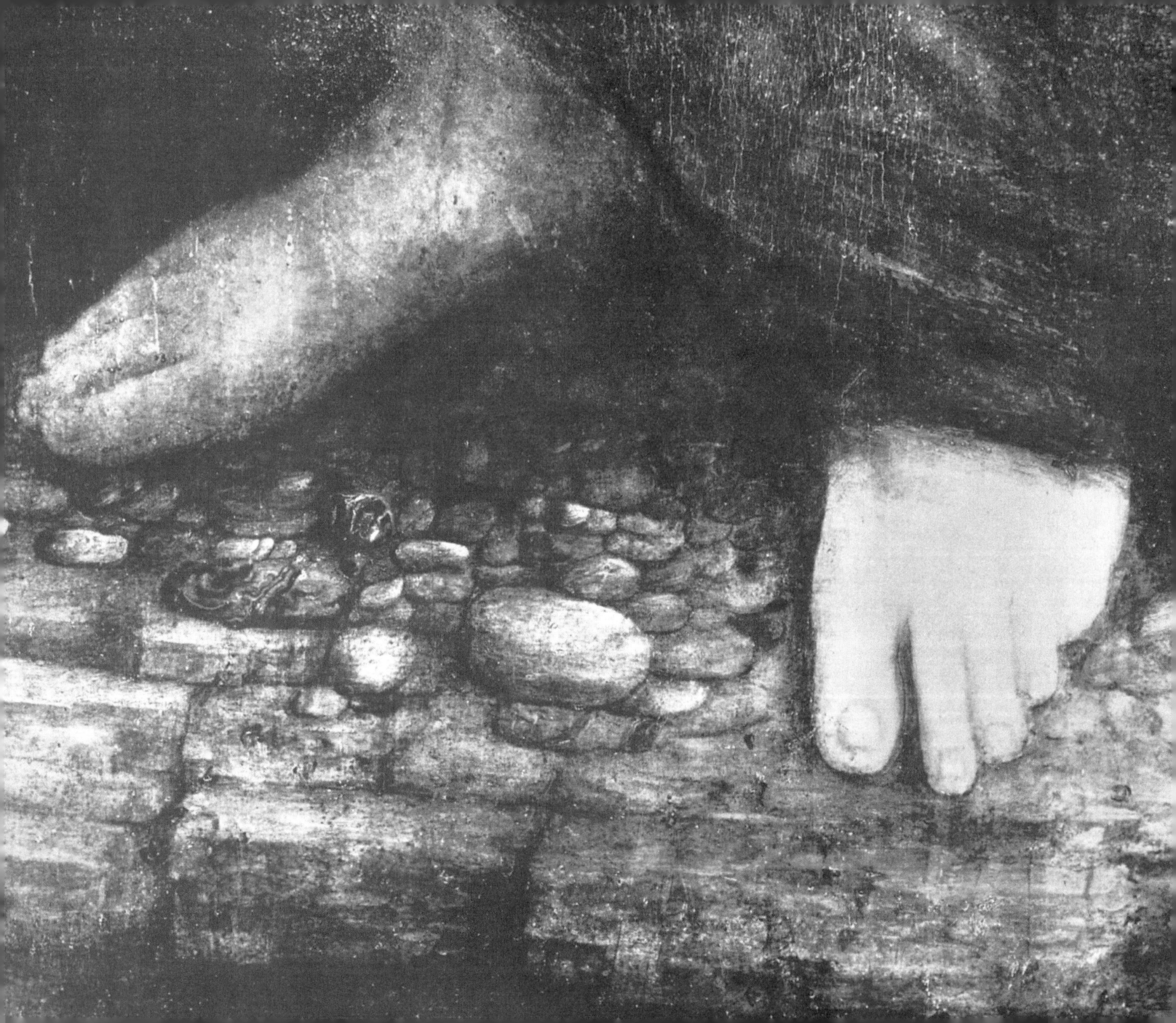

of one of them, who is comparatively agreeable to look at.

The length of the hand is a third of the arm, and it goes into the height of the man nine times ; the same is true of the length of the face and of the distance from the hollow of the throat to the shoulder, and from the shoulder to the nipples and from one nipple to the other and from each nipple to the hollow of the throat.

203. *Proportions of the face*

The distance from the eyebrow to where the lip joins the chin, and from there to the *(posterior)* angle of the jaw, and from there to the upper limit of the ear, near the temple, will form a perfect square the sides of which measure half the head.

And the hollow below the cheekbone is halfway between the tip of the nose and the rear of the jaw, that is, the angle just below the ear in the drawing opposite. *

From the edge of the eye socket to the ear, the distance is the same as the length of the ear, that is to say, a third of the head.

204. *Proportions of the foot*

The big toe is a sixth part of the foot, measured in profile, on the inside of the foot, from where the toe springs at the extremity of the ball of the foot to its tip, *ab ;* and it equals the distance from the mouth to the bottom of the chin. If you show the outside profile of the foot, make the little toe begin three quarters up the length of the foot, and that way you will find the distance from the beginning of the little toe to the extreme tip of the big toe.

The Virgin and Child with St. Anne. Detail, St. Anne's feet.

205. *Corresponding measurements in the human body*

There will be room for the whole foot between the elbow and the wrist or between the elbow and the armpit when the arm is bent. The foot is as long as the whole head of the man from the bottom of the chin to the very top of the skull, as is shown in the illustration.

206. *Body measurements when kneeling or sitting*

A man who kneels will lessen his height by a fourth.

A kneeling man who holds his hands on his chest will have his navel and his elbows at the halfway point of his height.

The halfway point of a man who is sitting — measuring from the seat to the top of the skull — will be at *(the level of)* the arms below the breast and the shoulder blade, and the seated portion (that is, from the seat to the top of the skull) will be more than half the *(full length)* of the man by a length equal to that of the testicles.

207. *The central axis of man when standing*

(Profile view), the opening of the ear, the joint of the shoulder, that of the hip, and the foot fall on the same vertical . . .

208. *Vitruvian man*

The architect Vitruvius states in his book on architecture * that the measurements of the human body are arranged by nature as follows : four fingers make one palm, four palms make one foot, six palms one cubit *(elbow)*, and four cubits the height of a man. And four cubits make a pace, and twenty-four palms the height of a man ; and these measurements he used in his buildings. *

If you spread your legs far enough apart to diminish your height by one-fourteenth, and if you open out and raise your arms so that your middle finger is on a level with the top of your skull, know that your navel will be the center of the circle formed by the spread of the limbs, and that the space formed between the legs will be an equilateral triangle.

The span of a man's outstretched arms is equal to his height.

From the beginning of the hair to the bottom of the chin is one-tenth of a man's height ; from the bottom of the chin to the top of skull is one-eighth of a man's height ; from the top of the chest to the crown of the head is one-sixth of the man ; from the top of the chest to the beginning of the hair, a seventh of the total height ; from the nipples to the top of the skull is a fourth of the man.

The maximum width of the shoulders measures a fourth part of the man ; from the elbow to the end of the hand is a fifth part of the man ; and from this elbow to the angle of the shoulder is the eighth part of the man ; the hand stretched out is a tenth part ; the penis begins at the center of the man ; the foot is a seventh part of the man ; from the sole of the foot to the lower edge of the knee is a fourth part of the man ; from the lower edge of the knee to the beginning of the penis is the fourth part of the man.

The distances from the chin to the nose and from where the hair begins to the eyebrows are each equal to the ear : a third of the face.

The Types

209. *The law of consistency of type*

Painting. Each part of a whole should be in proportion to this whole. Thus, when a man is short and thick, he should be the same in each of his limbs, that is, with short, thick arms, large, heavy hands, fingers short, with joints of the same character, and so with the rest. And I would have the same understood for all animals and plants that are variable in size while maintaining the proportionality of the dimensions.

210. *The muscular type*

That muscular men are short and thick.* Muscular men have thick bones and are short and thick in stature, and lack fat, since the muscles, because of their size, are drawn one against the other and leave no room for the fat that would otherwise lie between them. And in the case of men who are thin the muscles, being in close contact with one another and not having space in which to extend, grow in thickness, and particularly in the part farthest away from the ends, that is, toward the middle of their length and breadth.

211. *Age*

Of the harmony of limbs. And I remind you to take great care when you give the figures limbs that they will not only appear suitable to the size of the body but also to its age, that is, not too muscular and without veins for young men, with the surfaces well rounded and smooth and agreeable in color ; mature men should be sinewy and full of muscles ; old men have

Study of proportions ; see no. 206.

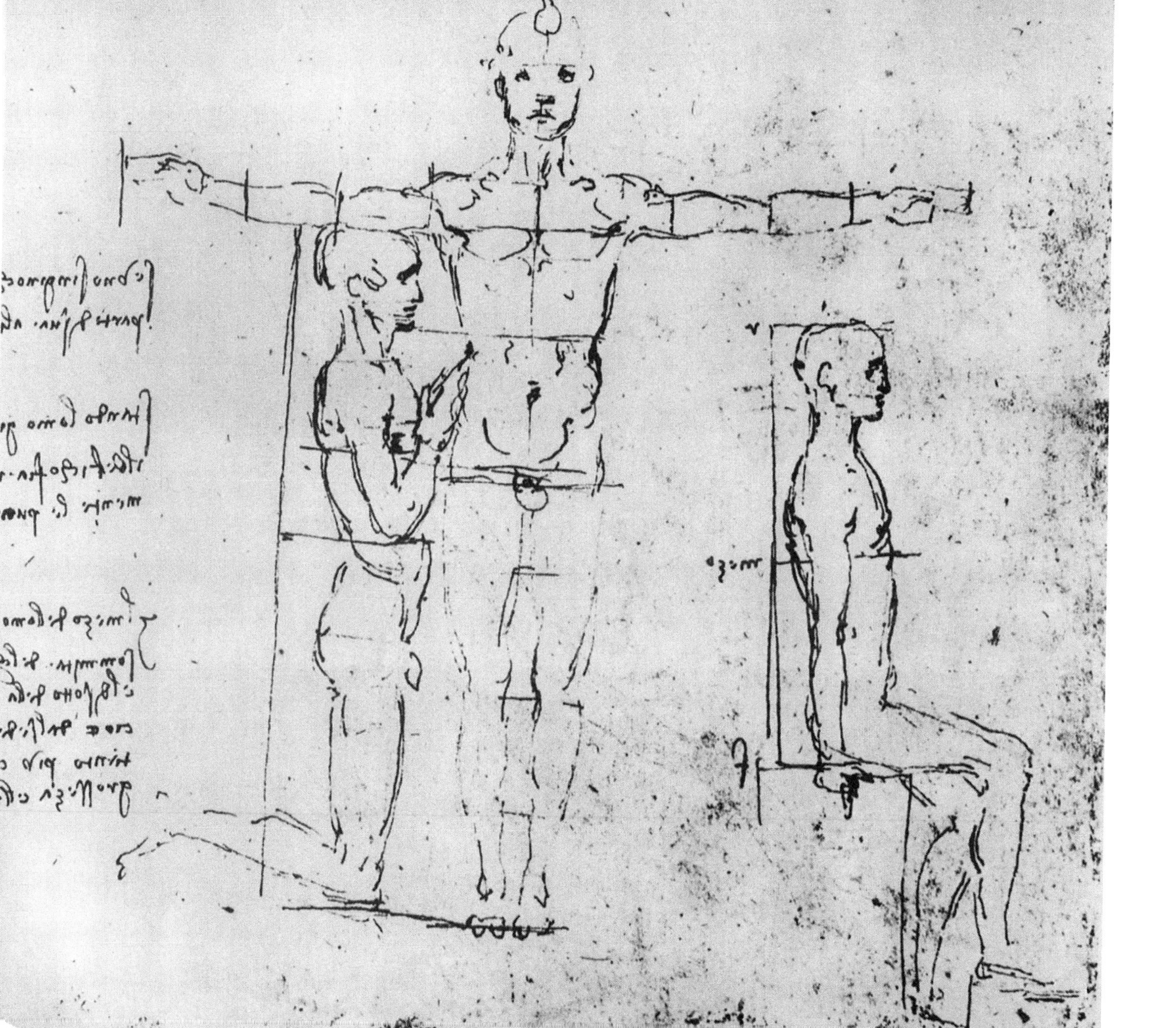

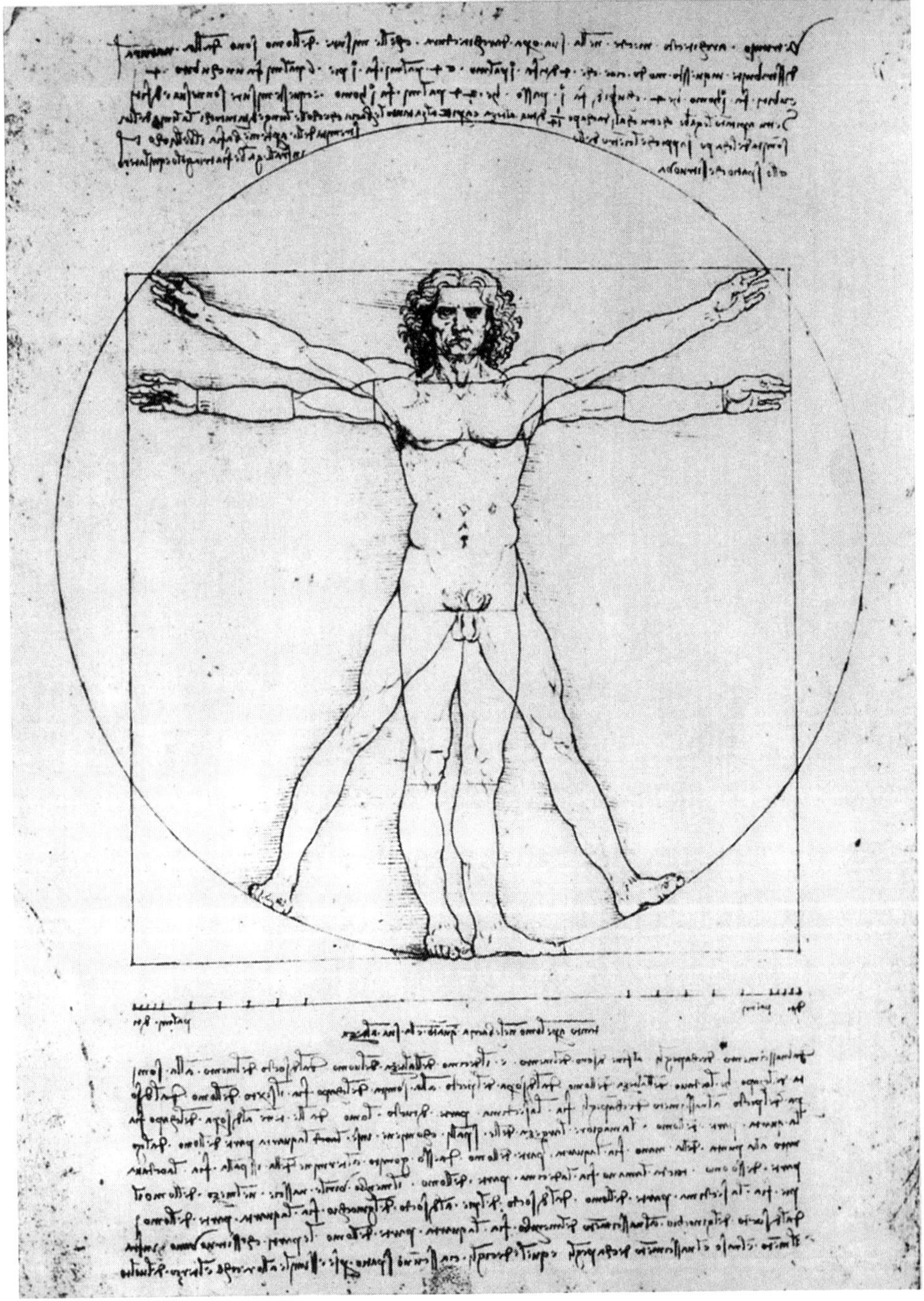

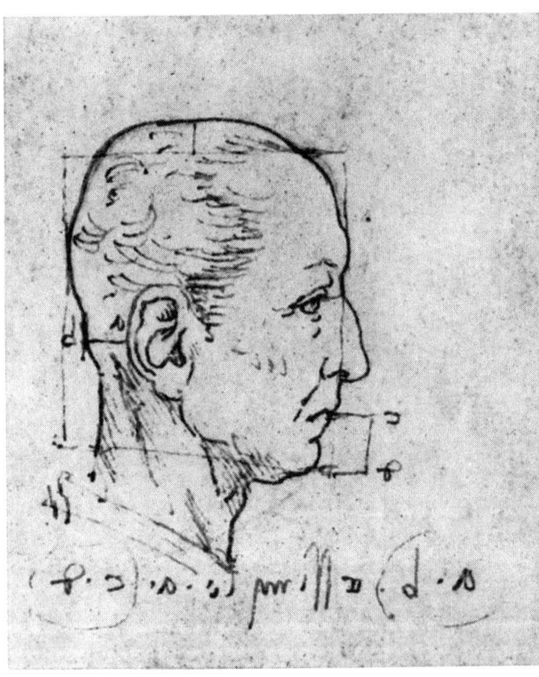

Proportions of the face.

Proportions of the human figure after Vitruvius; see no. 208

wrinkles on the surface, with folds and veins and prominent sinews . . . .

212. *To make a portrait of a man in profile after having seen him only once.* It is necessary, in this case, to pay attention to the varieties of the four separate parts of the profile, that is, the nose, the mouth, the chin, and the forehead.

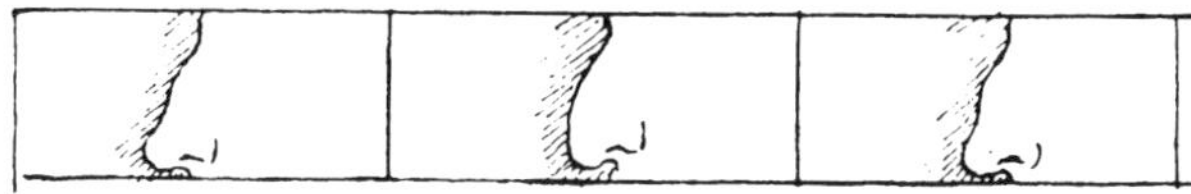

First we will speak of the nose, of which there are three kinds, to wit : straight, concave, and convex. Of the straight there are only four kinds, that is, long, short, with the tip raised or lower. Concave noses are of three kinds, of which some have the concavity on the upper part, others in the center, and still others on the lower part. In the same way convex noses are of three kinds, that is, some have the hump on the upper part, others in the middle, and still others on the lower part. The sections that surround the hump are of three kinds, that is, they are straight, concave or yet convex.

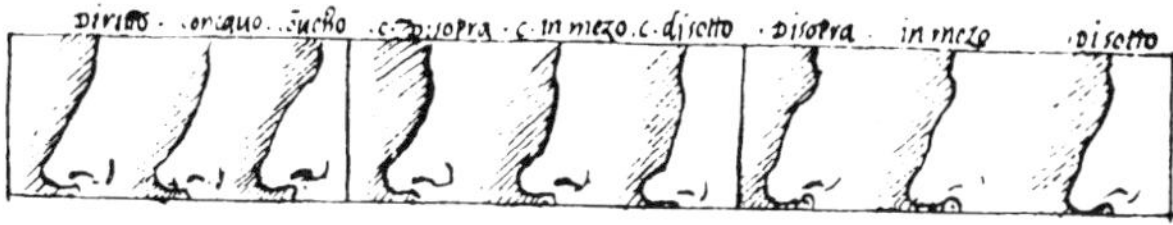

213. *Plan for a general anatomy*

Man. A description which will also include similar species : baboons, apes, and others like them, which are numerous.

Second book. The lion and those which go with him, like panthers, cheetahs, tigers, leopards, wolves, Spanish cats, civet cats, ordinary cats, and the like.

Third book. The horse and those which go with him, like mules, asses, and others that have teeth above and below.

Fourth book. The bull and those that go with him, which have horns and are without upper teeth like buffalos, stags, bucks, chamois, sheep, goats.

THE MOVEMENTS

Of the parts of the body. Each part of the body exercises that function for which it was destined. In the dead or the sleeping no part seems alive or awake. The foot that receives the weight of the man should lie flat, without play of the toes, except when the weight is on the heel. 214. *The principle of function*

When a limb is bent everything that was prominent in the joint becomes a hollow ; and in the same way all the hollows around the joints become protuberances when the limb is completely straightened. And in this respect, those who do not know this science and rely only on themselves and do not have recourse to the imitation of nature make serious mistakes. These variations are more noticeable in the center of the sides than in front, and behind more than at the sides. 215. *Alterations in the limbs through movement*

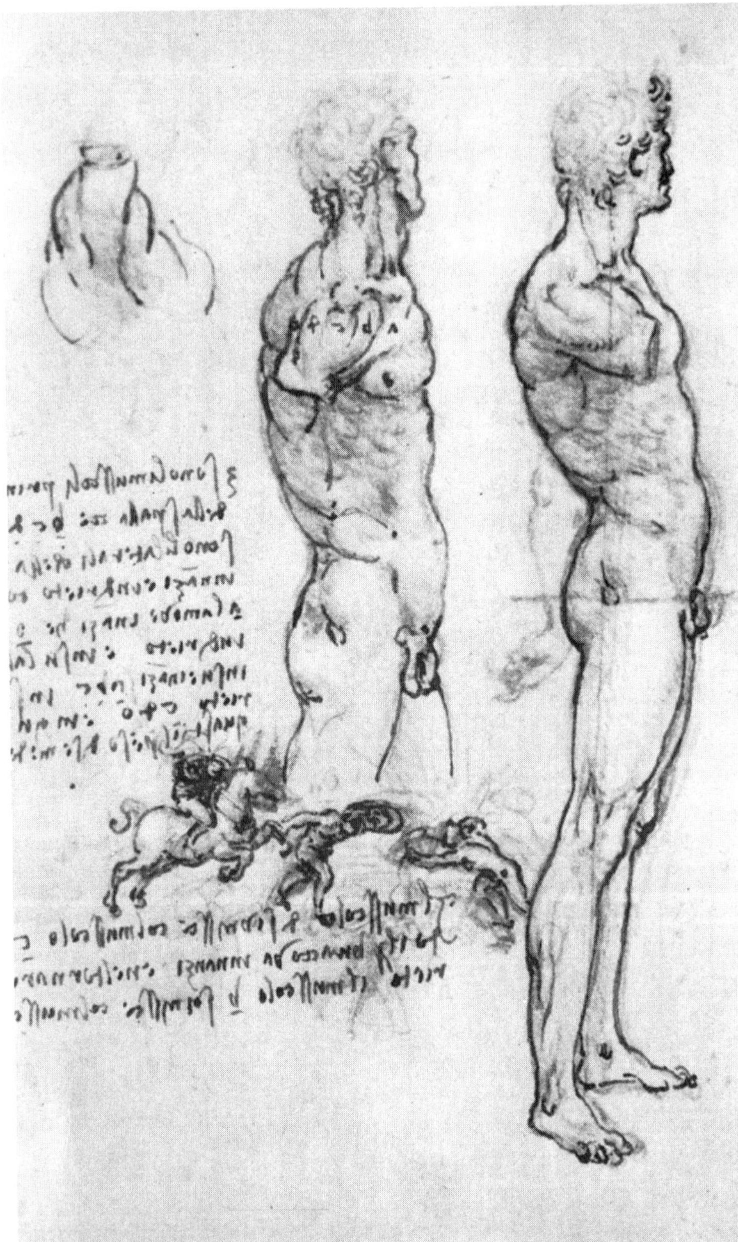

Studies of shoulder movement; see no. 216.

Observe how the shoulder changes with all the movements of the arm, up, down, inward, outward, backward, forward, and also in circular motions and so forth. 216.

And do the same for the neck, the hands, and the feet, and the chest above the hips.

Of the lengthening and shortening of the muscles. The muscles at the back of the thigh vary more in their extension and contraction than any other of man's muscles ; second are those of the buttocks ; third, those of the back ; fourth, those of the neck ; fifth, those of the shoulders ; sixth, those of the abdomen, which begin below the chest and end at the pubis ; in this way all others will be determined. 217.

Represent the cause of a catarrh, of tears, of sneezing, of yawning, of trembling, of epilepsy, of madness, of sleep, of hunger, of sensuality, of anger, how it works on the body, fear, likewise fever, disease, where poisons act. Why thunder kills a man without injuring him, and if a man blew his nose he would not die, because it affects the lungs. Write what the soul is. Of nature : that it of necessity produces the instruments of life and action in their suitable and necessary shapes and positions. 218.

How necessity is characteristic of nature.

Represent from where the semen comes, from where the urine, from where the milk. How nourishment is distributed through the veins. From where intoxication comes, from where vomiting, from where stones, from where pains in the side, from where dreams, from where delirium during sickness, why man falls asleep because of a contraction of the arteries, why a man drops dead from a prick in the nape of the neck, from where come tears, from where the movement of the eyes, that of one eye drawing the other after it. Of sobbing.

219. Of the muscles that raise the shoulders
and raise the head
and lower it
and make it turn
and bend it diagonally.

To lower the back, to bend it, to turn it, to raise it.

You will write of physiognomy.

I find that the veins have no other function than to heat, for example, the muscles or the organs that produce sensations. *

220. *Classification*

The way to represent the eighteen actions of man. Rest, movement, running, standing upright, leaning, sitting, bending, kneeling, lying down, hanging. Carrying, being carried, pushing, pulling, striking, being struck, pressing down, raised up.

221. *The movements of the hand*

The principal movements of the hand are ten, that is : inward, outward, to the right and to the left, in a circle, up and down, closing and opening, spreading the fingers and bringing them together.

222. *Elastic alterations of the torso*

Of loins when bent. If the loins or the back are bent, the nipples are always lower than the shoulder blades of the back.

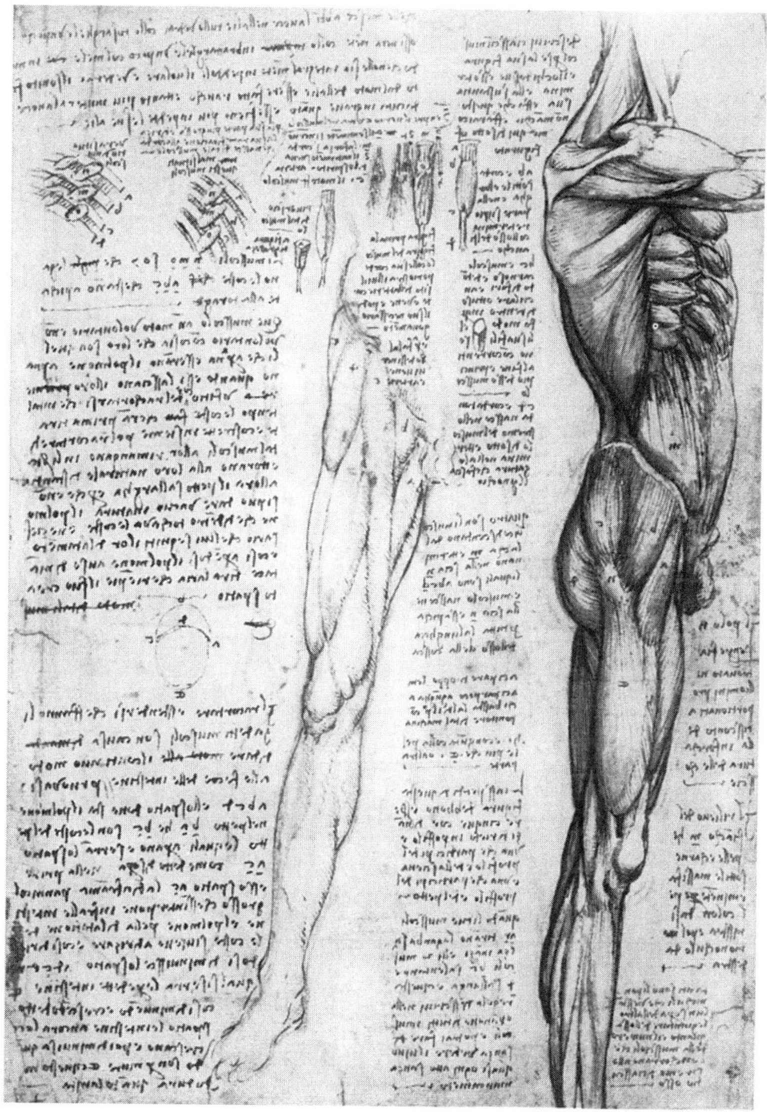

Studies of the muscles.

Studies of movements. ▶ If the chest is arched, the nipples are higher than the shoulder blades of the back.

If the back is straight, the nipples are always on the same level as the shoulder blades.

223. *An observation on the knee* *Of the limbs that diminish when they are bent and increase when they are extended.* Among the articulations of the flexible members only those of the knee diminish in size when they are bent and increase when they are extended.

224. *Balance in movement* A man who is seated cannot get up without the aid of his arms, if the part in front of the vertical axis * does not weigh more than the part behind.

A man going up an incline must put more weight on the foot in front than on the one behind, that is, more weight in front of the vertical axis than behind it ; and a man always moves a larger part of his weight in the direction in which he is moving than in the other.

The faster someone is running the more he leans toward the place to which he is running and puts more weight on that which is in front of the vertical axis than on that which is behind it. Someone running down hill has the center of gravity fall on his heels, and someone running up hill places it above the tips of the feet ; someone running on flat ground first puts it on his heels and then on the tips of his feet.

The man opposite* cannot carry his weight unless he throws his body

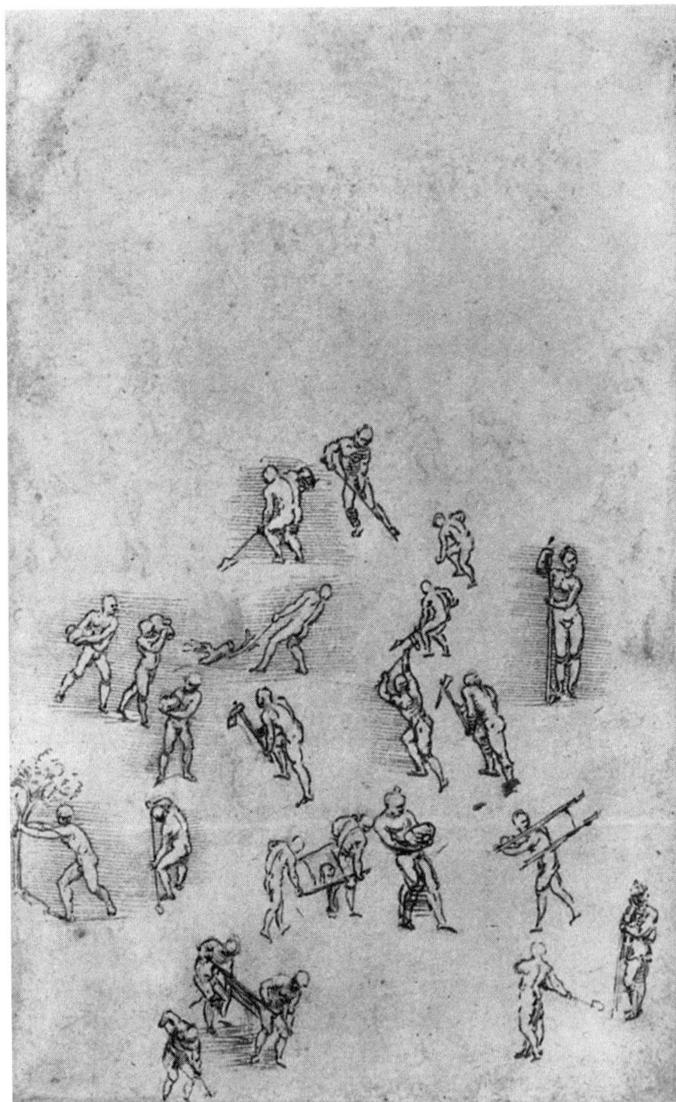

back, in order to balance the weight in front ; then the foot on which he is standing will support the center of gravity.

225. A man who is running puts less weight on his legs than a man standing still ; similarly, a horse feels the weight of his rider less when he is running. From this stems the fact that many look on with surprise, that a horse can keep on its course on one foot. Therefore, it may be concluded that a weight moving in the horizontal weighs less toward its center in proportion as it moves faster.

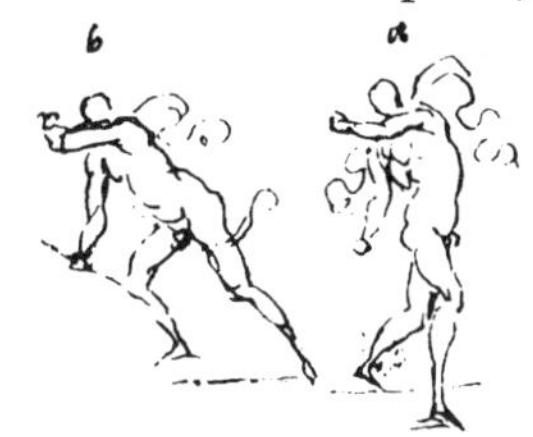

226. *An observation on balance*

How the extension of an arm that was bent modifies the whole distribution of a man's weight. The extension of an arm that has been bent changes all the weight of a man to the leg which supports the whole, as is apparent in a man who, with arms spread out, walks a tightrope without any pole.

227. *How to carry a weight*

Painting. If you have to represent a man who is moving, or lifting, or carrying, or raising a weight equal to his own, how would you place the legs under his body ?

228. *How to draw a bow*

Whoever wishes to send an arrow a great distance should have all his weight on one foot and raise the other foot to the height that precisely balances the body which is behind the *(supporting)* foot ; he should not extend his arm completely, and in order the better to sustain the effort, he should hold a piece of wood that goes, as it does in the crossbow, from the hand to his chest ; and when he wishes to discharge the arrow, he should quickly and at the same time jump forward and extend the arm that holds the bow and release the string ; and if he does all this at the same time with dexterity, the arrow will go very far.

EXPRESSION

Dispute between the poet and the painter ; and of the difference between poetry and painting . . . And if the poet says that he can inflame men with love, which is a principal thing among all animated beings, the painter has the power to do the same, and more so, since he places the image of the beloved before the lover ; and often the lover kisses this image and speaks to it, which he would not do were the same beauties represented by the writer ; still better, the painter so affects the minds of men that they fall in love and come to love a painting that does not represent any living woman. And it happened to me that I made a picture with a religious subject that was bought by a lover who wished to have the divine attributes removed so that he could kiss it without scruples ; but at last conscience overcame sighs and desire, and he had to remove the image from his house. * 229. *The power of painting the passions*

. . . The painter will move to laughter but not to tears, for tears are a stronger emotion than laughter.

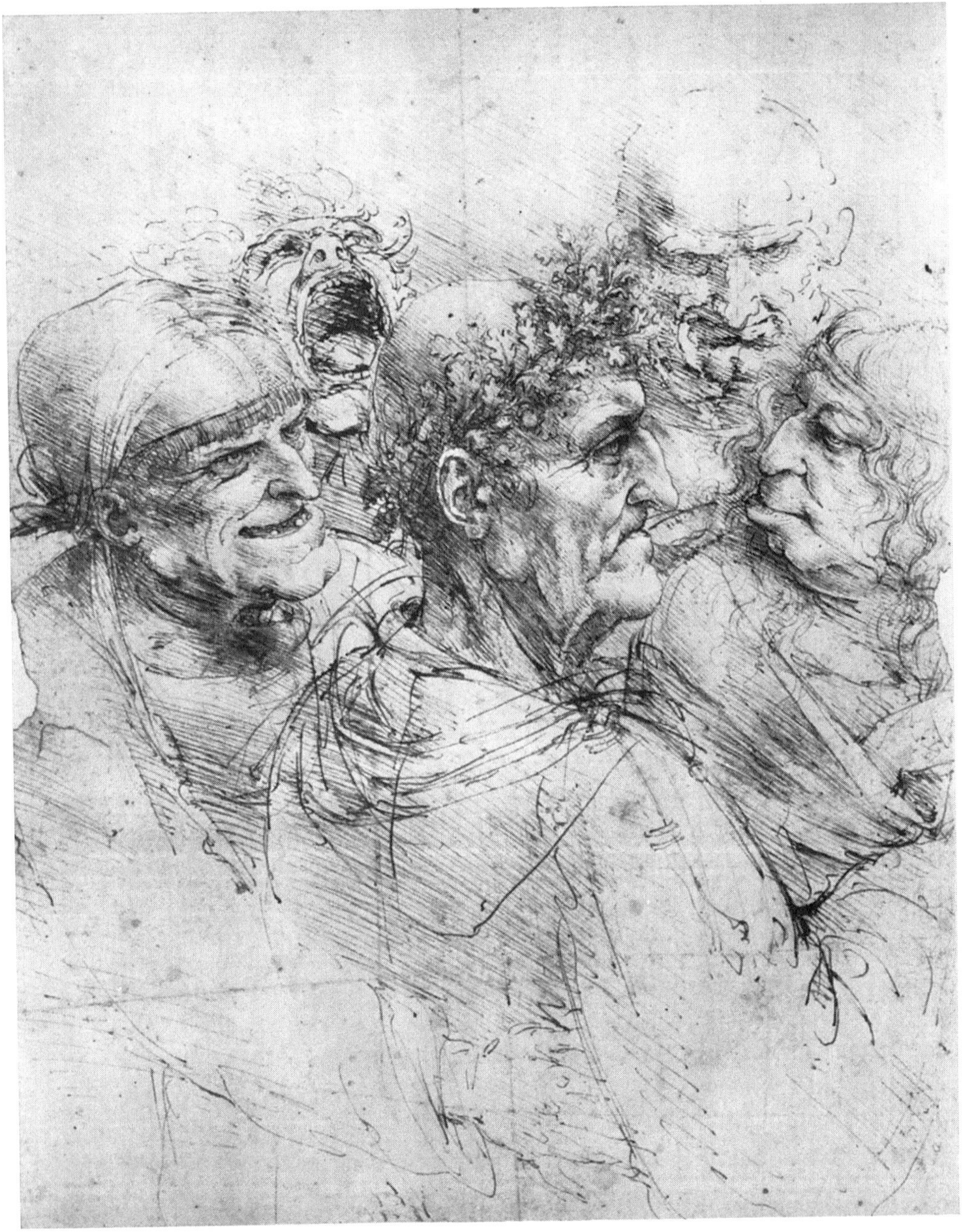

Study of a mimic, after Leonardo.

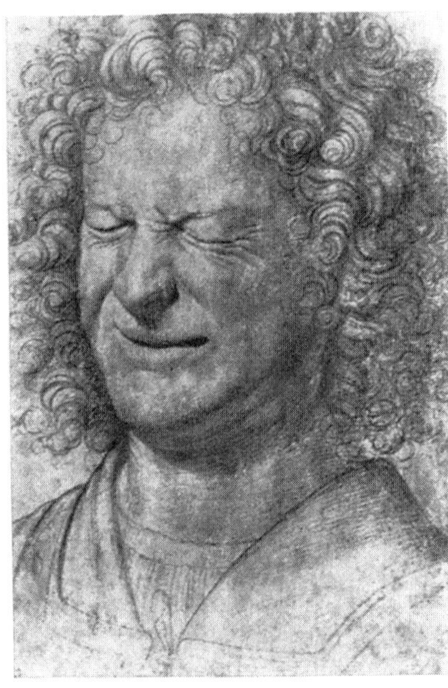

Study of facial expressions.

A painter once made an image that made the spectator yawn immediately and not stop yawning as long as he looked at it, and it represented a person yawning. Others have represented erotic scenes so voluptuous that they incited the spectator to the same joys, which poetry cannot accomplish . . .

230. *How to study expressions*

Of study and its order. I say that one should first learn about the limbs and how they work, and when one knows this one should study their actions in the situations in which man finds himself and, thirdly, one should compose narrative scenes, for which one should study the natural movements that men make according to the situations in which they find themselves. And notice these in the streets, and squares, and fields and record them by rapid indications of outlines, that is, for a head make an O, for an arm a straight or broken line, and the same for the legs and chest ; then, having returned home, give these aids to memory a complete form . . .

231. *How to recognize a good painting and through what qualities.* The first thing to consider, if you wish to recognize a good painting, is that the movement should be appropriate to the state of mind of the person moving ; second, that the greater or lesser relief of the objects in shadow should be adjusted to the distances ; third, that the proportions of the parts *(of the body)* should correspond to those of the whole ; fourth, that the choice of poses should be appropriate to the decorum of the actions ;

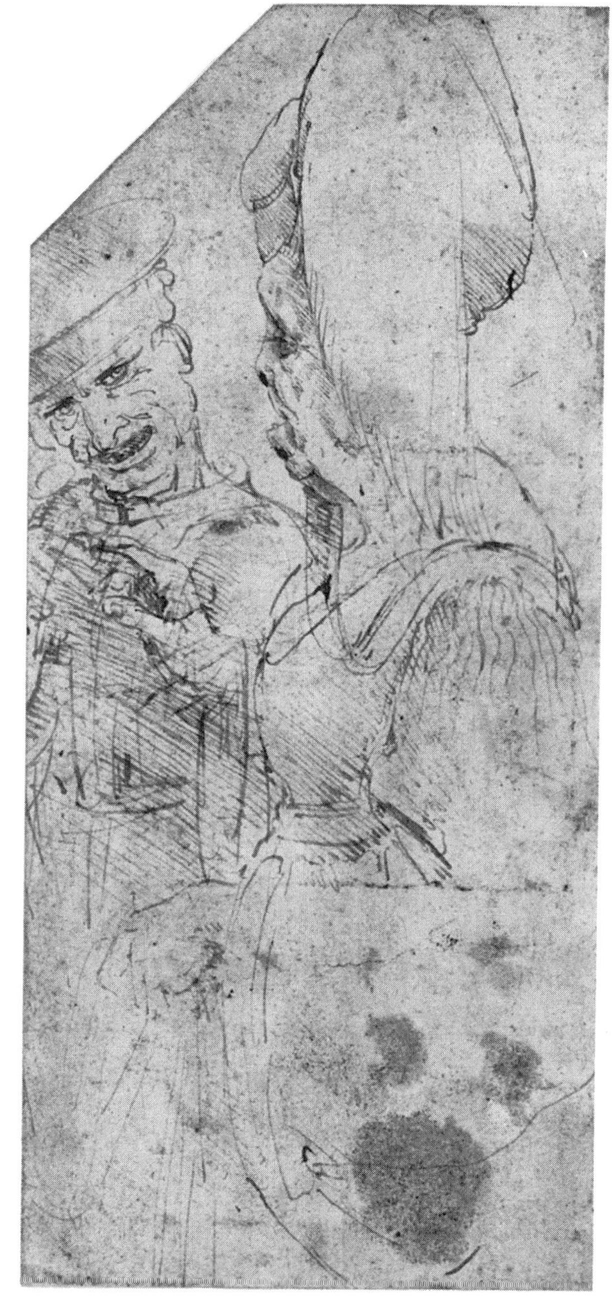

Grotesque heads.

fifth, that the details of the structure of the figures should correspond to their type, that is, delicate limbs for the delicate, thick limbs for the thickset, heavy limbs for the fat, and so forth.

232. *How to study the movements of man.* The movements of man are acquired from a knowledge of the parts of the body and of the combination of all the positions of the limbs and joints ; finally in quick sketches catch the actions of people with their characteristics without their being aware that you are observing them ; for if they realize this, that will interest them, and the act that formerly occupied all their mind will lose energy ; as for example, when two angry men argue and each thinks he is right, they move their eyebrows, and their arms, and their other limbs with much violence, making gestures that are appropriate to their intentions and their words. You could not get the same result if you asked them to pretend anger or some other passion, such as laughter, tears, sorrow, amazement, fear, and the like. Therefore, take care always to have a small notebook with you, with pages prepared with gelatin, and with a silver point briefly note the movements, and also note the poses of the participants and their grouping ; and this will teach you to make compositions. And when your notebook is full, put it aside and save it for your later projects ; take another and continue. And this will be useful to the art of composing, about which I shall write a separate book which will follow the study of figures and the separate parts and their different articulations.

That the good painter has to represent two things : the person and his mind. Fundamentally, the good painter has two things to depict : the man and his state of mind. The first is easy, the second difficult, because it has to be done through the gestures and the movements of the parts of the body ; and this can be learned from the mute who do this better than any other kind of man. * 233. *Expressive painting*

Of spontaneous movements that reveal the passions of him who moves. The movements and attitudes of a figure should display the state of mind of him who makes them, and in such a way that they cannot mean anything else. 234. *The principle of pantomime*

. . . In the same way a deaf-mute who sees two people talking, being deprived of hearing, understands the subject of their discussion from their gestures and poses. Once I saw a man in Florence who had become deaf, who could not understand if you spoke loudly to him, but if you spoke softly without giving it much voice, he understood from nothing other than the movement of the lips. Now, you will say to me, 'Does not a man who speaks loudly move his lips like a man who speaks softly ? And since they move the lips in the same way, will one not be understood like the other ?' To this I will let experience give you the answer : have 235. *Clarity in gestures* someone speak softly and then loudly * and observe the lips.

236. *How to represent an angry man.* You will show an angry man holding another by the hair, pulling the head down, pressing his knees into the other's ribs, raising the right hand in a fist. His hair should stand on end, his eyebrows should be lowered and drawn together, his teeth clenched, and the corners of his mouth pulled down in a curve ; and as he is bending over his enemy, his neck should be swollen and full of wrinkles.

237. *How to represent a desperate man.* Give the desperate man a knife and have him tear his clothes with his hands, and let one hand be shown tearing open his wound. He should be standing, the legs slightly bent, and also his whole body bent toward the ground, and his hair in disorder and straggling. *

238. *The observance of decorum.* Observe decorum, that is, appropriateness in the gestures, the clothing, and the place ; and observe the degree of rank in the things you depict, that is, the king should be bearded, and serious of expression and attire, and depicted in an ornate setting, and the participants should be standing with respect and attention, dressed with dignity as is suitable to a royal court.

And common people should be poorly attired, in disarray and abject, and the bystanders should be similar, with low and vulgar gestures, and all the parts should correspond to the character of the whole ; and the movements of an old man should not be the same as those of a youth, nor the attitudes taken by a woman those of a man, or those of a man like a child's.

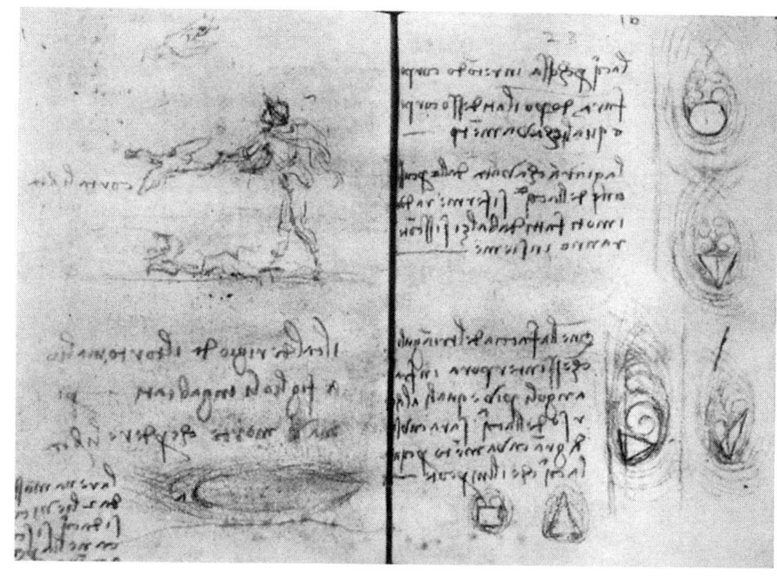

Movements, currents, and eddies.

Of the attention of bystanders at an unusual event. The bystanders at any kind of an unusual event will, while watching it, react with various gestures of surprise, as when justice punishes malefactors ; and if the event has a religious character, such as at the elevation of the host and the like, all the bystanders will watch with diverse gestures of devotion ; and if the occurrence in funny or lamentable, it is not necessary 239.

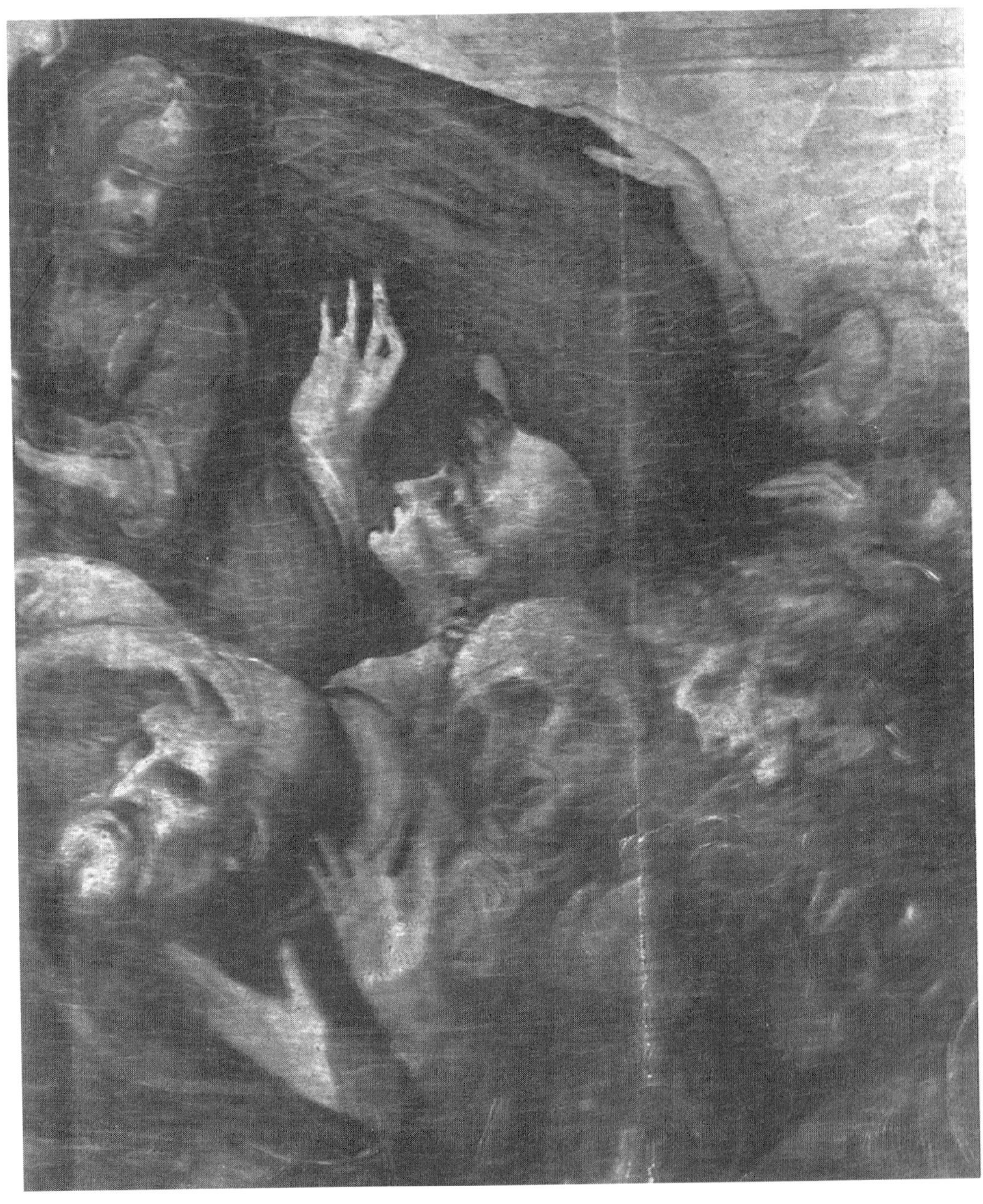

The Adoration of the Magi. Detail.

Chained beggar. Costume study. ▶

that all bystanders turn their eyes to it; they should have different movements, but a large part of them should rejoice or lament together; and if the event is frightening, the terrified faces of those fleeing should clearly express fear and flight with various gestures, as we will show in the fourth book on movement.

240. *How to represent someone who is speaking among several people.* If you wish to show someone speaking to several persons, you should consider the subject of his speech, and make the gestures appropriate to that subject. That is, if it is a matter of persuading, the gestures should be such as are required for this; and if it is a matter of explaining something with numerous reasons, he who is speaking should hold a finger of his left hand with the fingers of his right, while the fourth and fifth fingers remain bent; and he should turn toward the people, the face animated, the mouth half-opened, so that he seems to be speaking; if he is sitting, he should seem to rise a little with the head forward; if he is standing, he should bend his chest and head slightly toward the people. These latter should be represented silent and attentive, all looking the speaker in the eye, with gestures showing that they are impressed; and have the mouth of some old man reveal his astonishment by having it tightly closed with the corners pulled down so it produces folds in the cheeks; and the eyebrows should be raised and pulled up, so that there are many wrinkles in the forehead. Some seated figures

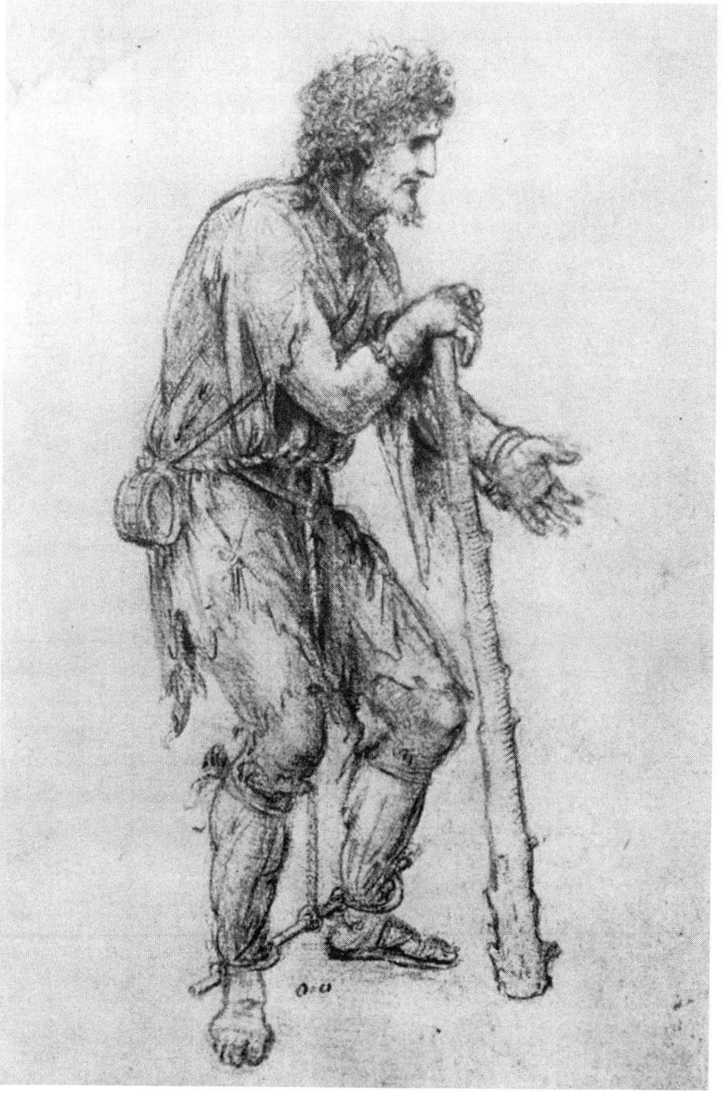

hold up their tired knees with interlaced fingers ; another bent old man, having crossed his legs, has placed a hand on the upper knee which holds the elbow of the other arm, the one supporting his bearded chin.

241. *Of laughter and weeping and the difference between them.* You will not give the face of one who weeps the same expression as one who laughs although *(in reality)* they often resemble one another ; for it is best to differentiate them, just as the emotion of laughing is different from the emotion of weeping.

In those who weep the eyebrows and mouth vary according to the different causes of the tears ; for one weeps for anger, another for fear, some for tenderness and joy, others for anxiety, others for pain and misery, and others for pity or in mourning for having lost a relative or friend ; and among this weeping, some seem desperate, others moderate ; some only shed tears, others cry out, and some raise the face to heaven and lower the hands with the fingers interlaced ; others are fearful, with the shoulders raised to their ears ; and so on according to the causes mentioned.

He who sheds tears raises the eyebrows from the inside and draws them together and brings on wrinkles between and above them ; the corners of the mouth will be lowered, but he who laughs raises them, and his eyebrows will be open and apart.

242. *Characteristics of age*

How old men should be represented with slow and sluggish movements, the knees bent when they are standing, the feet apart and parallel, the posture bent, the head bowed and forward, the arms not too far extended.

How women should have modest poses, the legs close together, the arms folded, the head inclined and held sideways.

How old women should be depicted decisive and without restraints, with angry movements like the infernal furies ; and the movements of their arms should seem more lively than those of their legs.

How small children should have quick movements and complex twistings when they are sitting and timid and frightened ones when they are standing.

Of physiognomy and chiromancy. I do not concern myself with false physiognomy and chiromancy because there is no truth in them, and this can be proven because these chimeras have no scientific foundations. 243.

It is true that the features of the face display a part of men's nature, their vices and complexions. If the lines in the face that mark the separation of the cheeks from the lips, of the nostrils from the nose, of the eyes from the sockets are accentuated, the man is gay and laughs much ; and those in whom they are not much accentuated engage much in thought ; and those in whom parts of the face are very prominent or very deep set are bestial and choleric, and without reason ; and those who have deep and noticeable lines between the eyebrows are irascible, and those in whom the horizontal lines on the forehead are deeply marked suffer torments, concealed or evident ; and it is possible to interpret many other parts of the face in this manner.

But as for *(the lines of)* the hands, you will find whole armies that have fallen by the iron at the same hour and not one man has a line in the hand that is identical to that in any other ; and the same is true in shipwrecks.

244. *Of the ways of dressing figures, and of diverse garments.* The figure's clothing should be appropriate to its age and to decorum : old men should wear long robes, youths be adorned in garments that do not hide the neck above the shoulders unless they are in holy orders, and if the persons have not taken holy orders avoid contemporary clothing as much as possible, keep these for portraits similar to those of the dead entombed in the churches, so that our descendants can laugh at the mad inventions of man, or else be inspired by them to admiration for their beauty and nobility.

I can today remember having seen in my childhood men, both small and great, with all the edges of their garments scalloped all around, from the head to the toes and on the sides. And at the time, the invention seemed so beautiful to them that they even scalloped the scallops ; they wore hoods of the same kind, and shoes, and they scalloped the cockscombs that came out of the seams of their motley garments. I saw shoes, headdresses, purses, weapons, the

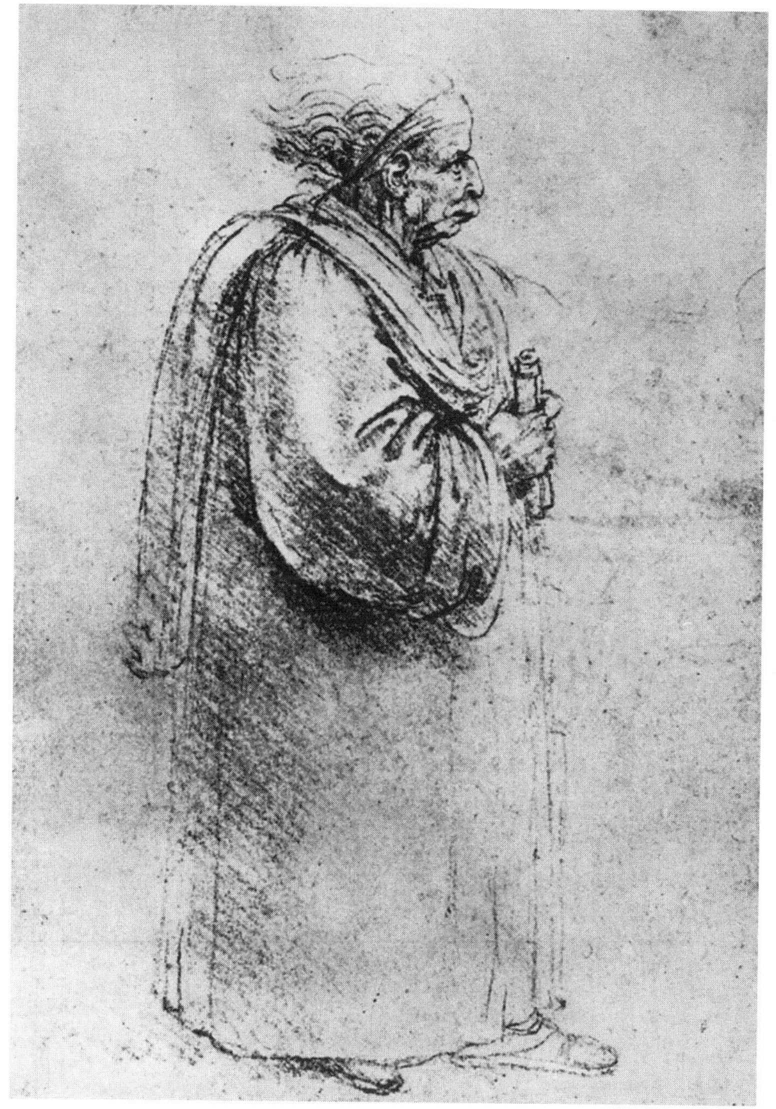

Study of a man of importance.

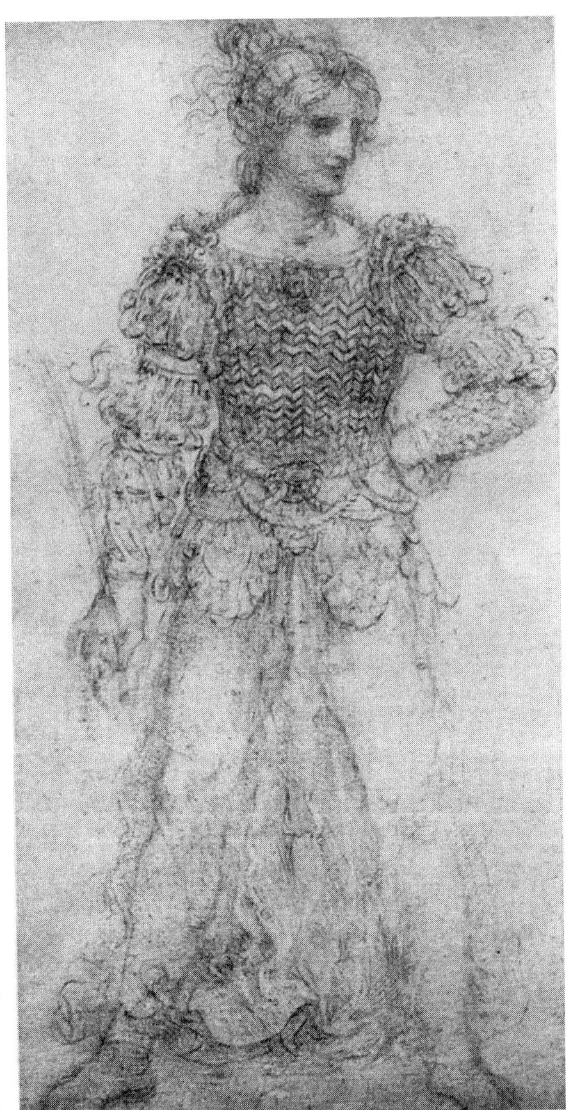

Costume study.

collars of the garments, the edges of robes reaching to the ground, the trains of gowns, all in this manner, and whoever wanted to appear beautiful was covered up to the mouth with long, pointed scallops.

In the next period the sleeves began to grow, and they became so enormous that each by itself was larger than the garment ; then the garments began to rise above the neck and ended by covering the whole head ; then *(the neck)* was left completely free so that the material could not be held up by the shoulders because it did not cover them ; then the garments began to become longer so that people constantly had their arms full of clothing, so that it would not drag underfoot. Finally it went so far that men were clothed only around the hips * and necks, and the garments were so tight that they suffered great torments, and several burst inside ; and the shoes became so tight that the toes pushed against each other and became covered with corns.

Of the way of dressing the figures. Observe 245.
decorum by clothing your figures according to their rank and age ; and above all, see that the materials do not hide the movements, that is, the limbs, and that these limbs are not crossed by folds or the shadows of folds, and imitate as much as you can the Greeks and the Latins in the manner in which they showed the limbs when the wind presses the draperies against them. And make few folds, except for the old men who wear long robes and are in authority.

The Approach to Beauty

Leonardo approaches beauty through the painter's technical skill in producing effects, and for the most part these exploit the possibilities of space. Thus he points out that by combining a given position with the play of light, the illusion of relief is intensified and enhanced. At the same time he studies the subtle interrelation of movement and underlying intention, for only when the action corresponds to a well-defined inner emotional state can the artist win ascendancy over the spectator and create the true magic of painting. Furthermore, this illusion and this magic must be the vehicle for an intimate revelation carried by the painter's conviction. The development of Leonardo's argument, as always based on antitheses, permits one to predict that in his eyes this revelation could only be a complex and subtle instance — a secret and essential moment of Being : this is what he calls beauty. Beauty cannot be approached directly, and it would be difficult to isolate a definition from the innumerable passages in which the word appears. According to Leonardo, beauty is precisely that superiority archieved by nonconceptual thought — which is that of painting, and which nonetheless includes all the properties of mental (or scientific) discussion.

The analyses that preceded it can do no more than prepare the mind by displaying all its characteristics. The only two manifestations that are rich enough to hold the painter's attention and to justify the effort of painting are analogy *and* ambiguity. *No text states unequivocally that they are the keys to beauty, but Leonardo's finest pages, which he devoted to their praise, have the ring of true conviction.*

*He has insistently stated the analogy between the microcosm and the macrocosm. At times it has been seen as an imaginative and provisional foundation, a survival of medieval doctrines that gratified his taste for the marvelous and lent itself to fantastic guesses. However, it is permissible to see this key analogy as the principal component of knowledge concerned with the manifestations of the visible; it is the effective tie between science and art. This analogy, in fact, is only a consequence of the continuity of things; having defined a sort of " physiognomy " of nature in the landscape, Leonardo is only too willing to see human life connected with animal life through the passions and with telluric life through the humors and the bodily structure in which the elements recur. Indeed, as is indicated above, he once again puts forward certain correspondences, that of water and blood, for example. * But that is only after having fully exploited an analogy which has, above all, the effect of giving forms a noteworthy consistency. He is equally interested in the curve of a spiral or interlace in a drawing as in the rhythmic arrangement of leaves on a stem; he can identify this arrangement with that of tributaries flowing into a river; he sees a resemblance in the movement of the surface of water and the waves of hair. This kind of universal identification unites motifs which, thus, take on a striking symbolic value. It enhances them infinitely; it lends them a mysterious dignity by referring them back to primal forms.*

The correspondence between the microcosm and the macrocosm is only one part (one that is eventually abandoned) of a more general " law " demanding a profound concentration in its analysis: each form is in some way the instrument of an active force, or the conclusion — in a sense, the scar — of its operation. Here water or fire are unmoving pivots for imagination, while in the Madonna with St. Anne, *for example, there is a spontaneous search for the correspondence between cosmic continuity and the ages of man. Leonardo's brief suggestions tempt one to figure the odds on an analogical science, a concept he had certainly thought of but which he rarely discusses outright in his works, though he hints at it occasionally. For example, he does not hesitate to speculate about an arrangement of space analogous to that of music (see below, no. 269). In this context his taste for the fantastic, his remarks on making imaginary monsters believable, his interest in whatever seems impossible open up surprising vistas about which he leaves us free to speculate.*

In the long run, however, these ideas are less interesting than his investigations of ambiguity and his concern with vagueness in appearance. His famous evocation of an artist at the entrance of a cave, at the same time experiencing fear and desire, fortunately gives the passage the full scope the theme deserves. It connects Leonardo's intellectual libido *with the incisive probings of his sensibilities (which Freud did not interpret so inaccurately). Above all, it marks the point at which the uneasiness of knowledge, or rather the confusion of thought, coincides with the triumph of chiaroscuro. Hence its increasingly insistent application — from the* Madonna of the Rocks *(1482) to the* Bacchus-St. John *(after 1506) — becomes more intelligible; and the short notes jotted down at random, such as (no. 294) "Observe the softness and grace in the faces of men and women in the streets as night falls when the weather is bad" and others given later take on their full value. The transition from the supple form to the twisted one — which Leonardo practiced as well as preached — is like a supplementary contribution of the play of analogies to the charms of ambiguity. The intentional blurring of color and outline are the price that has to be paid for this enigmatic beauty which is the exact opposite of splendiferous display. The ideal of painting "in relief," of smooth and glossy forms is also sacrificed to the delights of the indistinct. But here, in near disaster, he retains the reward of a subtle and durable discovery, stated at the end of the Treatise: the* non-finito, *the unfinished.*

ANALOGY

246. *The geography of the body*

I shall reveal to you in fifteen figures the cosmography of the microcosm in the same order that Ptolemy used before me in his Cosmography; * and I will divide the members as he divided the provinces and then I shall describe the functions of each part in all its aspects, placing before your eyes the description of the figure and the capacities of man in respect to the local movements stemming from these members.

247. *The macrocosm*

Nothing grows where there is no sentient, vegetal, or rational life; feathers grow upon birds and change every year; hair grows upon

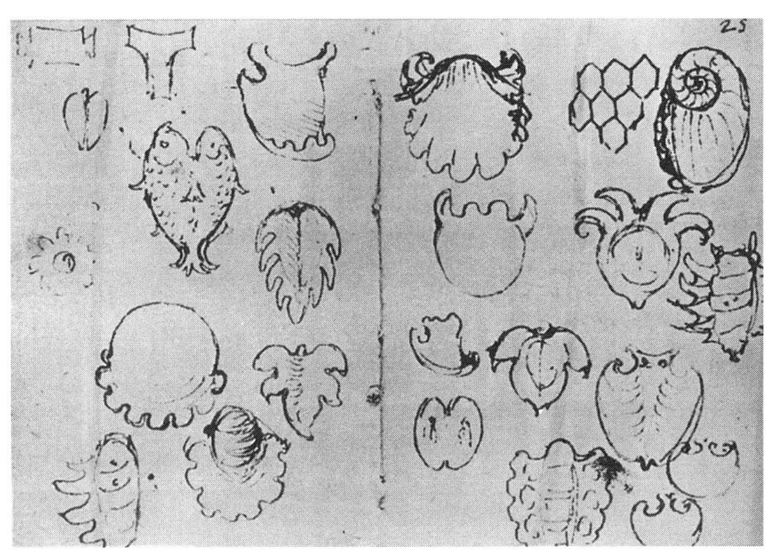

Comparative study of leaves, shells, and similar forms.

animals and changes every year, except some parts, such as the hair of the whiskers of lions and cats and others; grass grows in the fields and leaves on the trees and in large part are renewed each year; therefore, we may say that the earth has a germinating soul, and that its flesh is the soil; its bones are the successive strata of rocks of which the mountains are made up, its cartilage is the tufa stone, and its blood

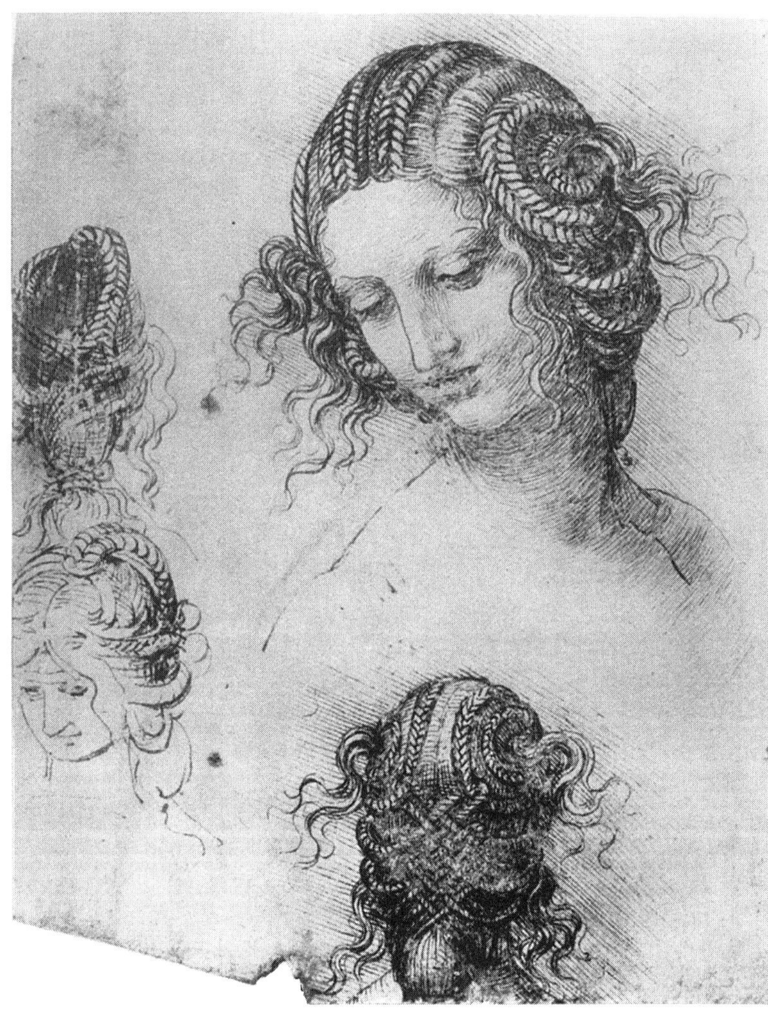

Studies for *Leda*; see illustration p. 158.

the running water; the lake of blood that surrounds the heart is the ocean, and its breathing and the rise and fall of the blood in the pulses, and similarly, in the earth, is the ebb and flow of the sea; and the vital heat of the world is the fire diffused throughout the earth, and the seat of the germinating soul is the fires which breathe in diverse places, in the baths and sulphur mines, and in the volcanoes and in Mount Etna in Sicily, and in many other places.

The body of the earth is of the nature of fish, sea monsters, or whales, for it breathes water instead of air. 248.

Man was called the *microcosmos* by the ancients, and surely the term was well chosen; for just as man is composed of earth, water, air, and fire, so is the body of the earth. As man has bones as support and framework for the flesh, so the earth has rocks as support for the soil; as man carries a lake of blood in which the lungs inflate and deflate in respiration, so the body of the earth has the ocean which waxes and wanes every six hours in a cosmic respiration; as the veins emanate from the lake of blood and are ramified throughout the human body, in the same way, the ocean fills the body of the earth with an infinity of veins of water. The body of the earth lacks muscles, because they are made for movement, but the earth, endowed with perpetual stability, is without movement, and, being without movement, has no need of muscles. But in all else they resemble each other very much. 249. *The microcosm*

Currents and eddies in water. ▶

▶ Currents and eddies in the blood stream.

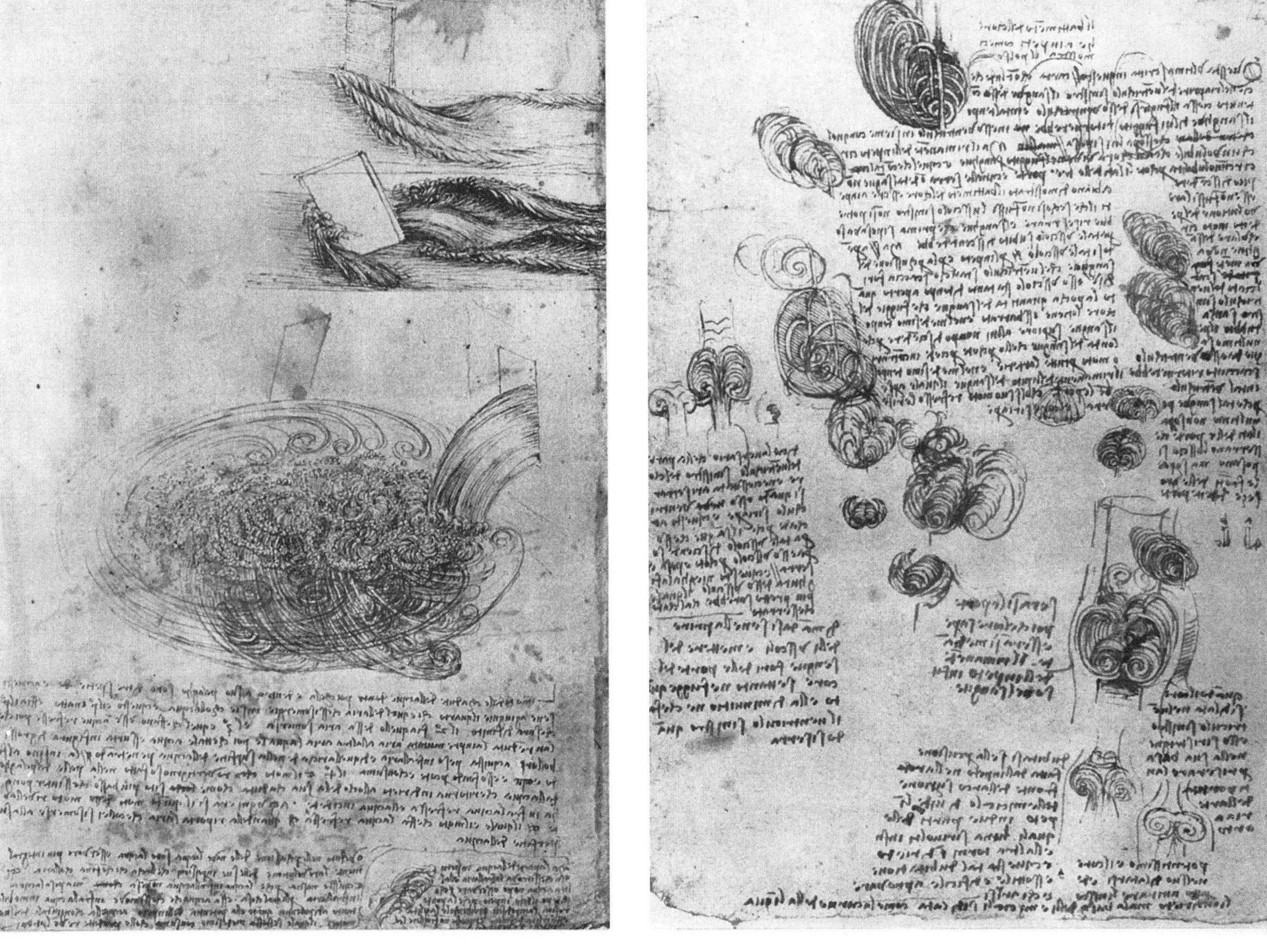

250. The origins of the sea are the opposite of those of blood; for the sea receives within itself all the rivers, which are caused by the vapors of water that have ascended into the air; but the sea of blood is the source of all the veins.

251. *Of the soul.* In the movement of earth against earth pressing down upon itself, the parts struck are moved very little.

Water struck by water creates circles around the point of impact; the voice in the air goes farther; still farther in fire; the spirit still farther into the universe, but being finite, it does not reach infinity. *

252. *Water and hair*

Observe how the movement of the surface of the water resembles that of hair, which has two movements, one of which stems from the weight of the hair and the other from the waves and curls. In the same way the water has its turbulent curls, a part of which follows the force of the main current, and another obeys the movement of incidence and reflection.

253. *The "hydraulics" of the growth of plants*

All the branches of a tree, at any stage of their height, if brought together and united, equal the thickness of the trunk.

All the ramifications of the waters at any stage in their course are, if the current is of the same speed, equal in size to the body of the main stream. *

254. *What to do to make an imaginary animal appear natural.* You know that there is no animal that does not have members that are individually similar to members in some other animal. Hence, if you wish an animal imagined by you to appear natural — let us say it is a dragon — take the head of a mastiff or a pointer, the eyes of a cat, and the ears of a porcupine, and the nose of a greyhound, the eyebrows of a lion, the temples of an old cock, and the neck of a water tortoise.

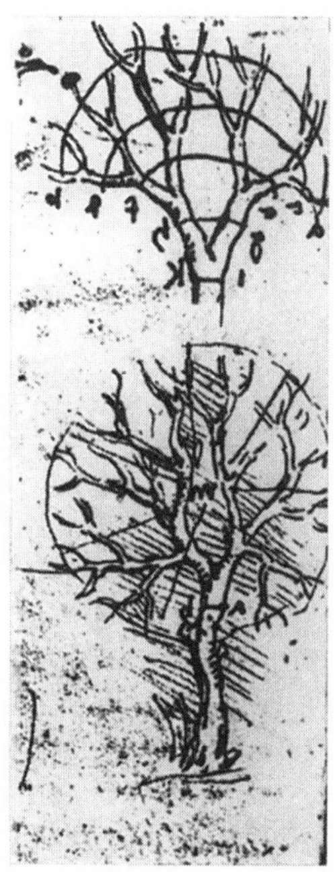

AMBIGUITY

255. *The cave*

The sea does not roar so loudly during a tempest when the north wind strikes between Charybdis and Scylla with foaming waves, nor Stromboli or Mount Etna when the pent-up, sulphurous flames break out and rend the mountain asunder and hurl into the air stones and rocks in belching fire, nor when the inflamed caverns of Mount Etna let escape the elements they can no longer contain, throwing them out and sending them back into their own

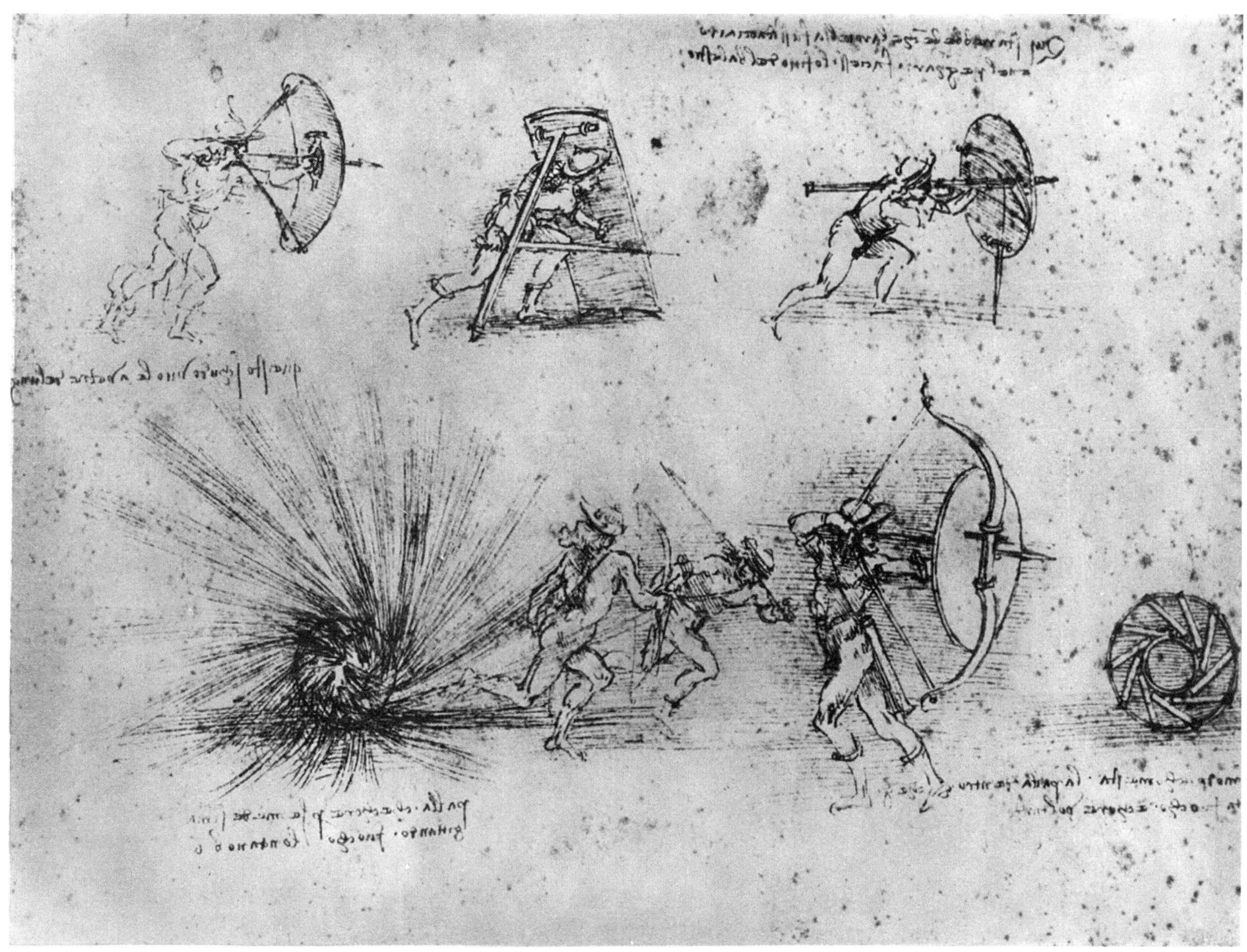

War machines and shields.

sphere * with fury, impetuously pushing away all obstacles in their way . . .

And abetted by my ardent desire, impatient to see the great abundance of strange forms created by that artificer, Nature, I wandered for some time among the dark rocks ; I came to the mouth of a huge cave before which I stopped for a moment, stupefied by such an unknown thing ; I bent my back into an arch, rested my left hand on my knee and with the right screened my lowered and contracted eyebrows ; several times I leaned to one side and to the other in order to see whether I could distinguish anything ; but the great darkness that reigned there rendered this impossible. At the end of some time, I was overcome by two emotions : fear and desire — fear of the dark and menacing cave, desire to see whether it did not contain some extraordinary marvel.

256. *Under what conditions a face is to be represented to give it grace through shadow and light.* Shadow and light give a high degree of grace to the faces of those sitting in the doorways of dark buildings in such a way that the eye of the spectator sees the shadowed parts of the face obscured by the shadows of this building and the illuminated parts animated by the light of the air. Through the greater contrasts of shadow and light, the face is given a more pronounced relief, with almost invisible shadows in the illuminated part, and with almost invisible high lights in the dark part. Through the increase of shadow and light, such a representation gives the face great beauty.

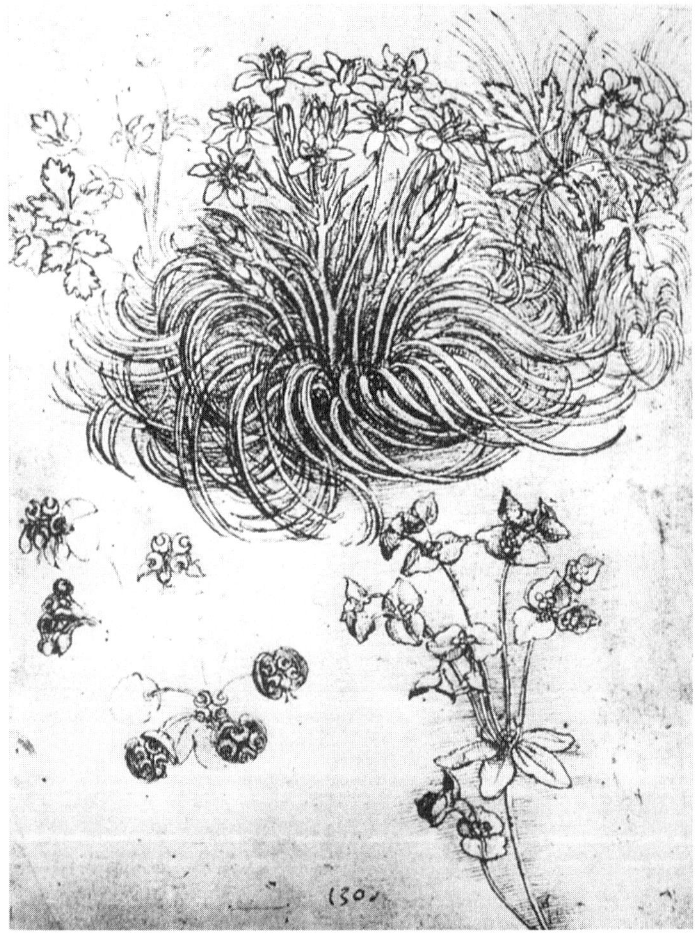

Studies of plants. Leonardo finds swirls and lunules everywhere.

The Madonna of the Rocks. Detail, the Madonna's head. ▶

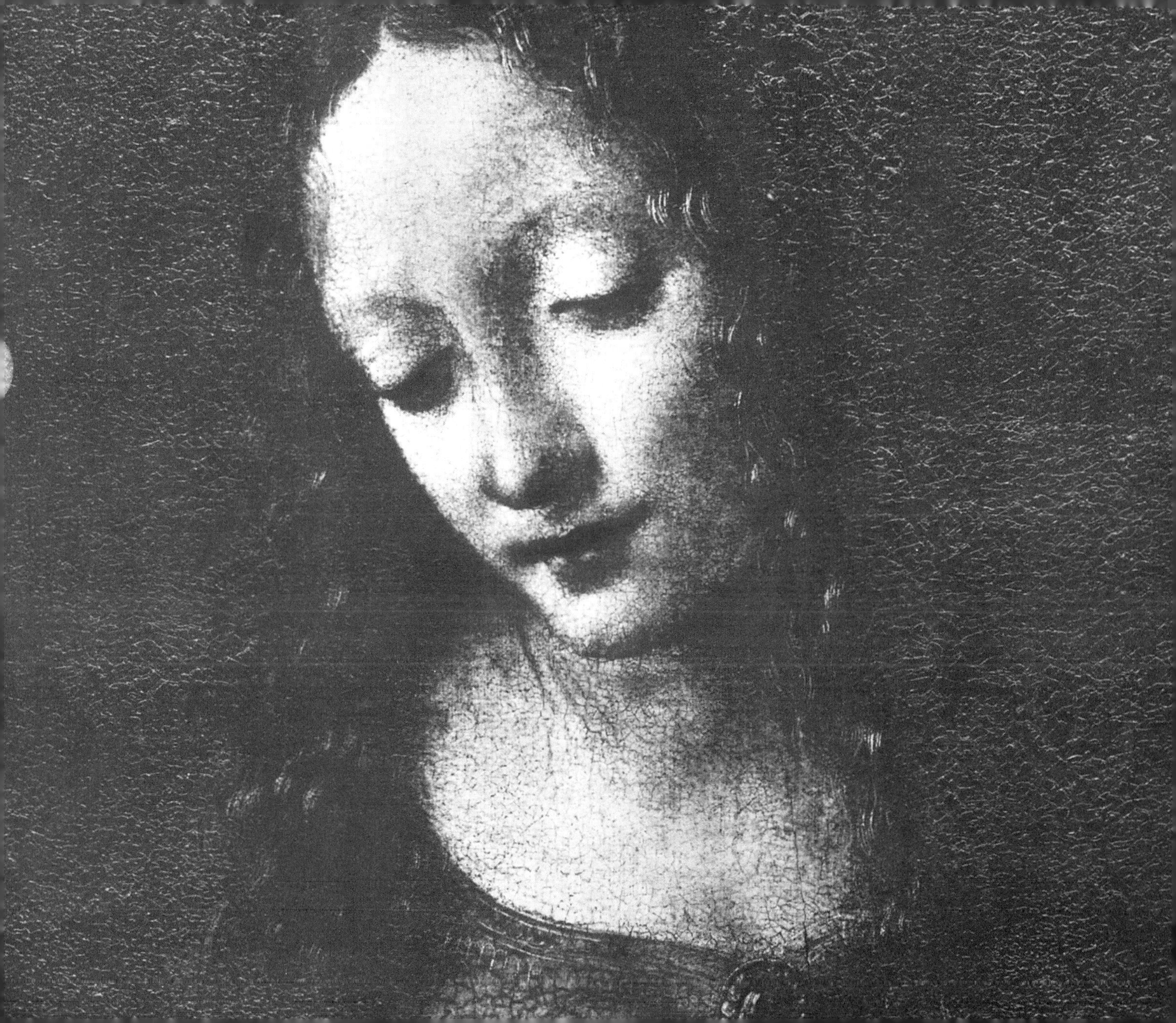

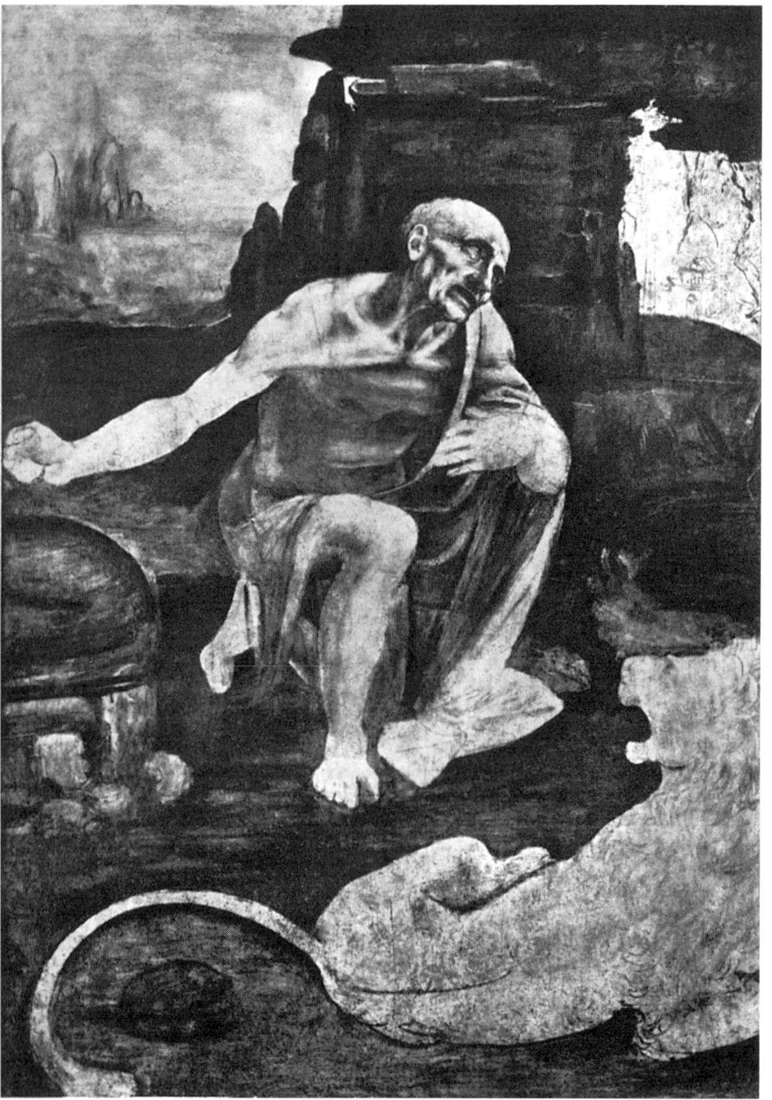

St. Jerome ; see no. 256.

What lights should be chosen to render the shapes of bodies. The forms of any body whatever oblige you to choose the light in which you will represent these figures ; that is, if you paint them out-of-doors, they will be surrounded by a great quantity of light, the sun being obscured ; * but if it reaches them, the shadows will be very black as compared to the illuminated parts, and the outlines of both the simple and the derived shadows will be very sharp. These shadows will be in little accord with the light, for on one side the light comes from the blue of the air, which tinges everything it touches with its own color (and this may be seen very clearly on white objects), but on the other side the light will come from the sun and partake of its color . . . and whoever sees these bodies will think they are of two colors ; and when you show the causes of the shadows and lights, you cannot help but also modify the shadows and lights through these causes ; if not, your work is vain and false. 257. *Against painting people in direct light*

But if your figure is inside a dark house and you see it from outside, it will have shadows that are black and more veiled, when you stand in line with the light. And a figure painted in this way will have grace and do honor to its author, because it will have much relief and its shadows will be soft and veiled. . . . *

Of the grace of the limbs. The limbs and the body should be in harmony with the action you wish to have your figure perform ; and if you wish him to have charm give him elegant and 258.

Botticelli, *The Entombment.* Detail. Three arms and a leg are in a single vertical line; see no. 259. ▶

attenuated limbs without too many muscles ; and the few that you let him display, according to his position, you will indicate gently, that is, not very prominently and without shadows that are too dark ; and the limbs, especially the arms, should be free, that is, that none should continue in a straight line with the adjoining part.

And if because of his position, the two hips, which are the poles of the body, are placed so that the right is higher than the left, you should make the shoulder so that it is exactly above the highest part of the hip, and so that it is lower than the left shoulder, and that the hollow of the throat be exactly over the middle of the joint of the foot supporting the weight ; and that the knee of the free leg be lower than the other leg and near it.

The positions of the head and arms are infinite, and I shall not undertake to give a rule for them, except that they should be easy and pleasing, with various turnings and angles, with the articulations free so that the limbs do not appear like pieces of wood.

259. . . . Never make the head of a figure turn to the same side as the chest, and the arm should not be parallel to the leg, and if the head is turned to the right shoulder, the parts on the left will be lower than the right ; and if you make the chest turn outward and the head turn to the left side, then the parts on the right side will be higher than those on the left.

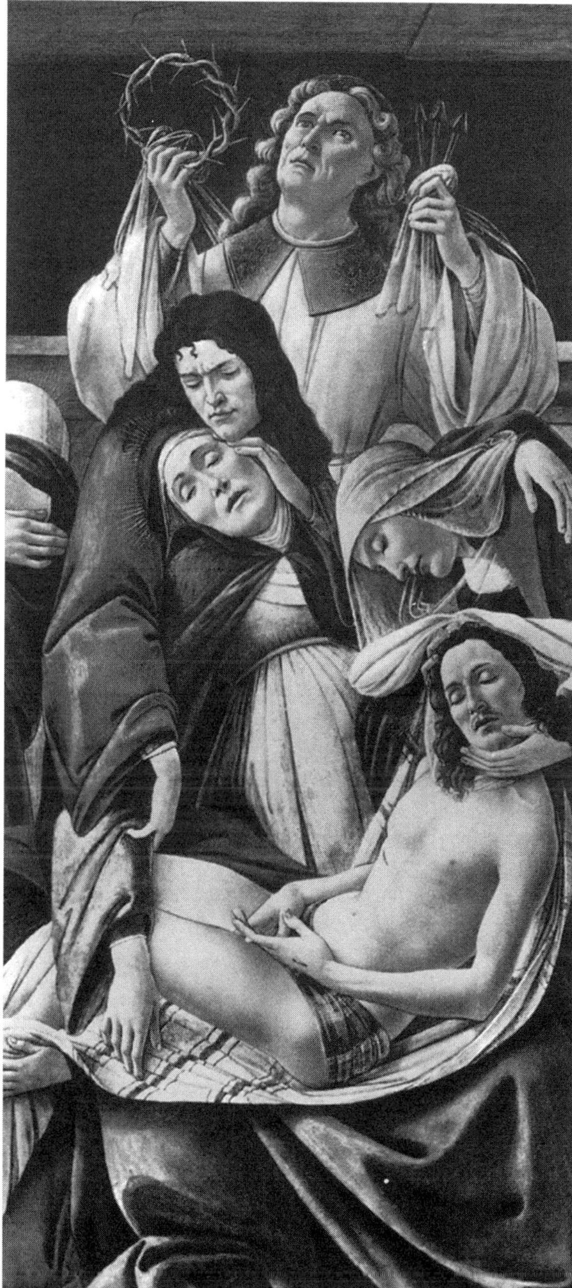

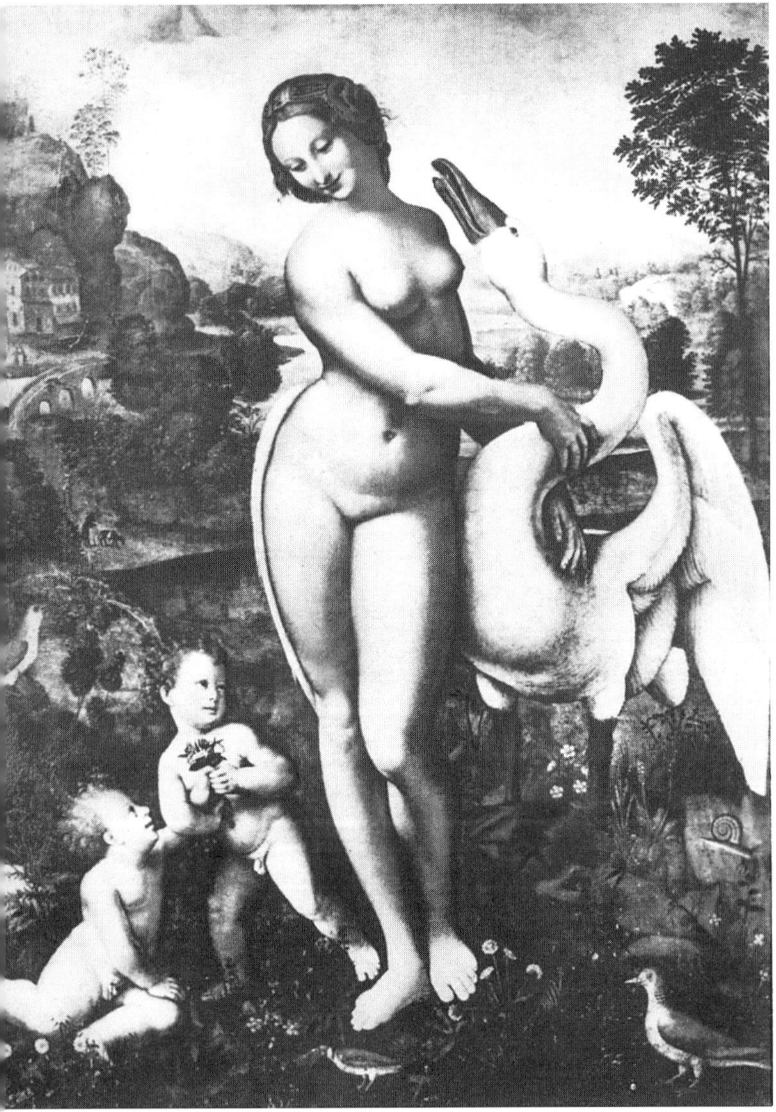

260. *Contrapposto*

Of the arrangement of the limbs. Concerning the arrangement of the limbs, remember that if you wish to represent someone who for one reason or another turns backward or sideward, you should not have him move his feet and all his limbs in the direction in which he is turning his head, but you should show the action proceeding in stages through the different joints . . .

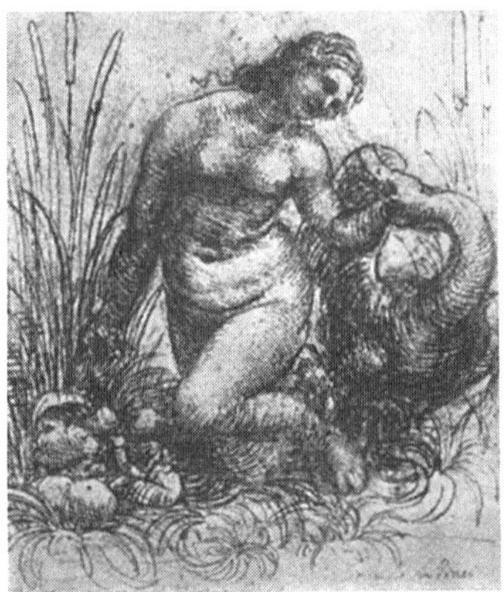

And always make your figures so that the head is not turning in the same direction as the chest, since, for our convenience, nature has invented the neck which turns in various directions with ease when the eye wants to observe different places ; and the movements of the other joints are in part ruled by the same aim. And if you paint a figure that is seated, whose arms may have something to do at his side, depict him so that the chest turns upon the hips. *

◀ *Leda.* Copy of a lost work by Leonardo. The figure follows the rules set down in no. 258.

Study for *Leda.* Here the movements are exaggerated.

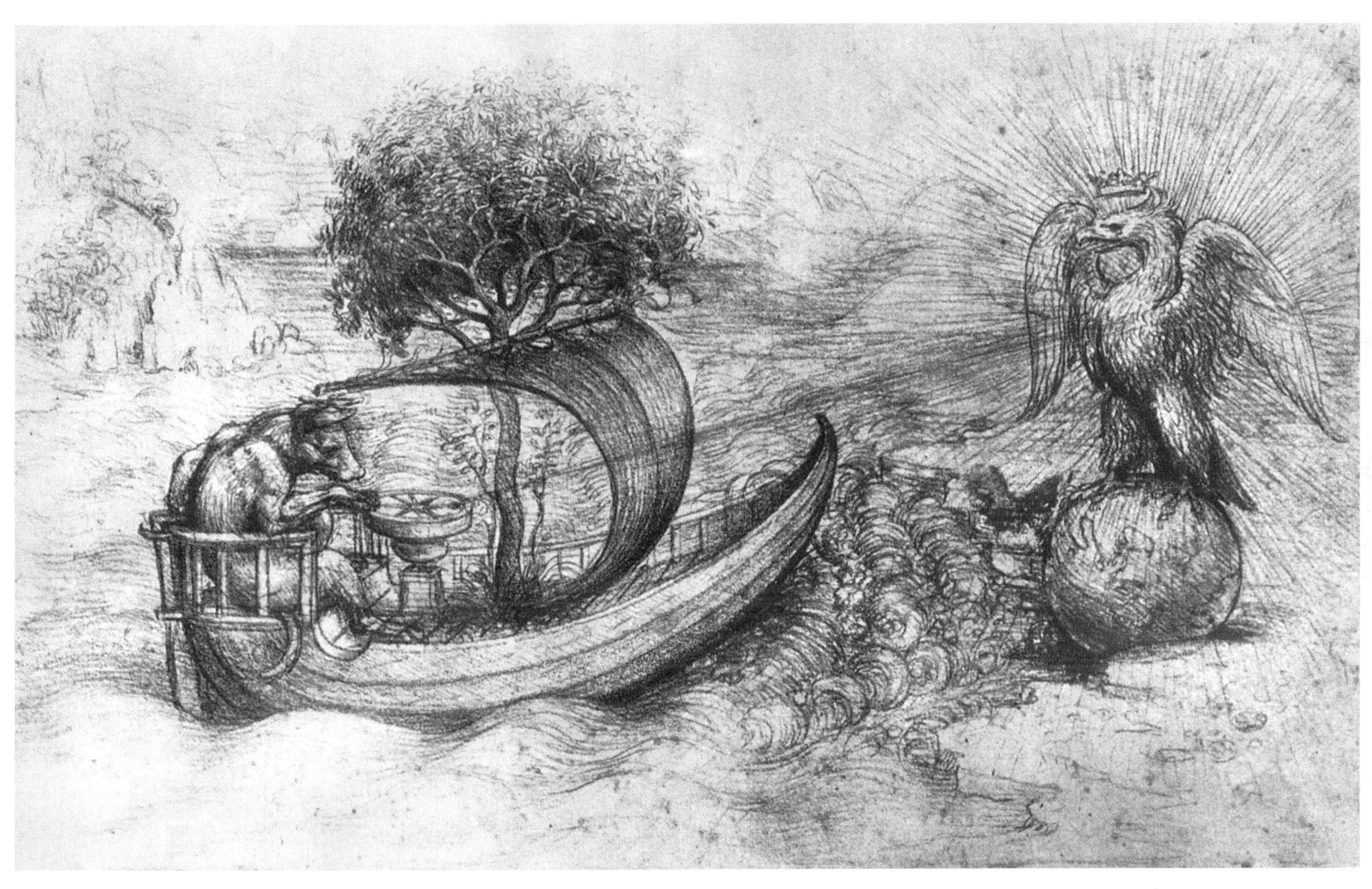

Allegory. The meaning probably is that the king of France, the eagle, is the guiding star for the ship of Cesare Borgia, the wolf.

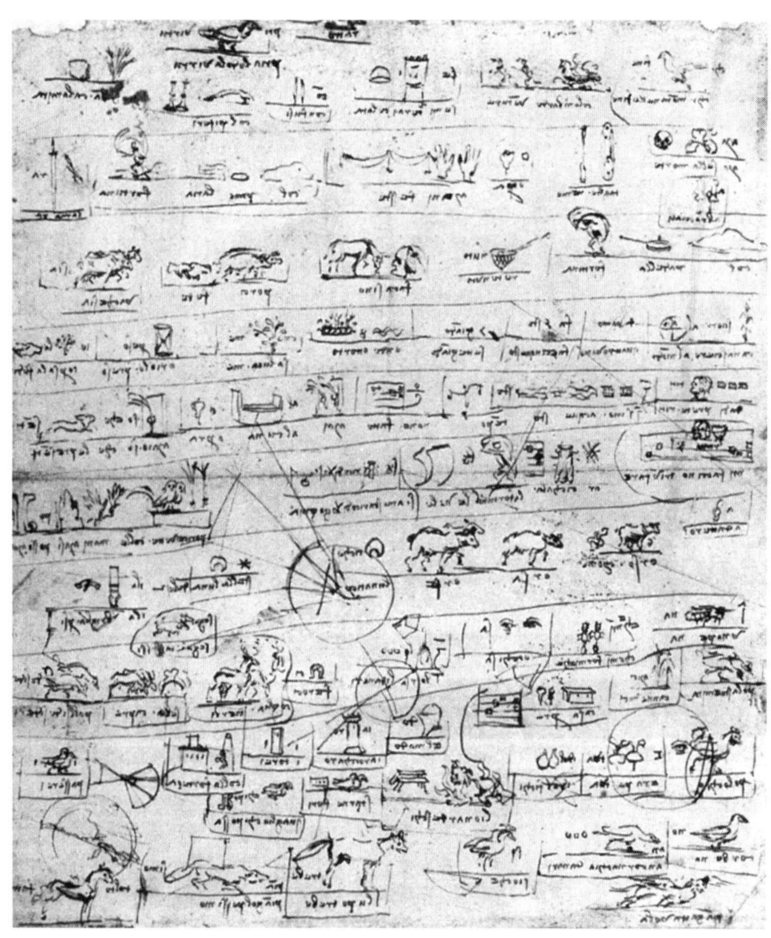

Rebus.

Of the shadow that moves with a man. There shall be seen shapes and figures of men and animals that will pursue these men and animals wherever they flee ; and the movements of the one shall be like those of the other, but the changes in their size shall be wondrous. 261.

And many creatures of the earth and of the sea will rise up among the stars. That is, the planets. 262. *The constellations*

The bones of the dead, by their rapid movements, will decide the fortunes of those who move them. The dice. 263.

The dead being buried. O human folly ! O living madness ! Simple people shall carry many lights to illuminate the route of those who have lost their sight. 264.

One may cross the division between two hemispheres at any point. All men will suddenly be transferred from one hemisphere to the opposite. 265.

The ditch. (To say as in a delirium, frenzy, or mental aberration.) Many will toil to remove from a thing which is enlarged in proportion as one takes away from it. 266.

What is the thing that cannot be given, and if it were, it would not be ? It is infinity . . . 267.

The Painter's Studio

The flow of Leonardo's thought turns from the conditions of painting itself to investigate nature in all its aspects, only to return to it with new authority. However, one cannot help being struck by the gap between the mass of preliminary knowledge thus brought together for the Treatise and the little put into practice in executed works. The conflict that this gap suggests is not of an intellectual nature in the sense that his scientific interest gradually took Leonardo away from painting, as has been believed since the sixteenth century and frequently reiterated, but of a practical kind. Each painting, and even each incident in it, brings into play the generalized reflections of both the philosopher and the practicing artist. The cause of Leonardo's slowness in working is the interruption of methodical revery and uncommon deduction. It is a matter of making two equally attractive and demanding orders of reality coincide : nature and its mirror. It would have been more than surprising had Leonardo not felt and stated the clash between the two, a clash that is the true cause of the painter's torment.

In following his purely analytical and scientific tendency, Leonardo is led to emphasize that any perceptible quality exists in relation to another : there is no light without shadow, and size varies not only in relation to distance but also in relation to lighting and color. The result is a general relativity in all effects of interest to their painter. But when he begins to work, the artist must arrest this movement of the phenomena. To do so, Leonardo establishes ideal conditions which do not belong to scientific

Interlaces. Detail of the ceiling of the Sala delle Asse. ▶

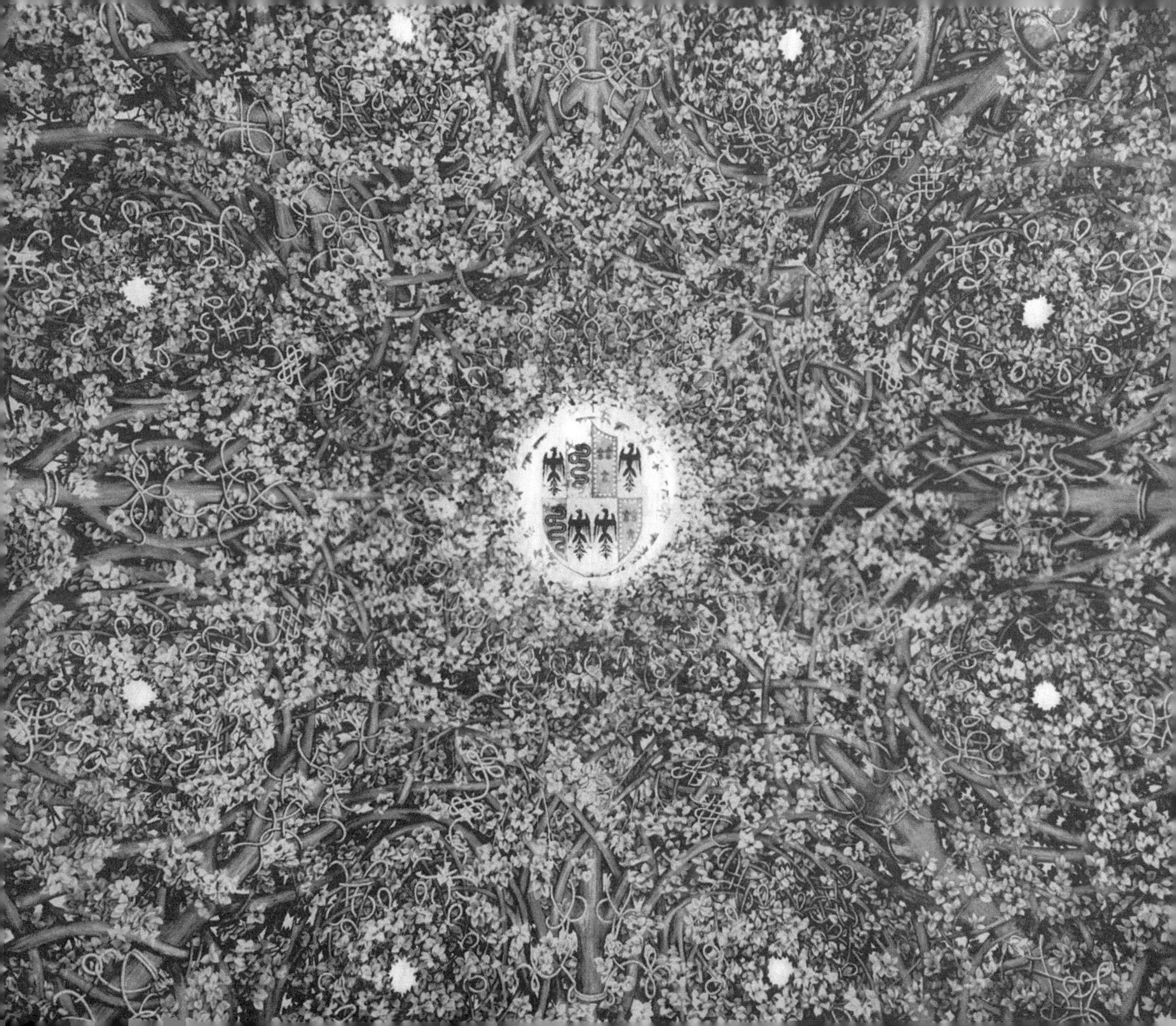

truth but to representation. This is the meaning of the passages on the true colors, true shadows, and true proportions of things. These qualities are essential to the existence of the painting and prepare the way for the reflections on methods of selection, of bringing together, and of co-ordinating that are necessary from the point of view of the artist at work. As soon as knowledge, which is properly a part of painting, is realized, it becomes evident that art must be considered and accepted as the receptacle of a fascinating and necessary illusion. This might be called the workshop point of view. As a result of this attitude, no care in preparation is too great. With minute care, Leonardo gives details of installations in order to further and facilitate the artist's work. Even from the very fragmentary extant notes concerning brushes, palettes, and the mixing of colors, one can discern Leonardo's interest in all practical operations. He is not interested in the instruments then in use, such as the quadrilles for perspective, but employs them for his own purposes.

Out of all this emerges the image of a workshop that is extremely well ordered and no doubt as busy as it is silent. Vasari's description of Lorenzo di Credi's studio may help to visualize that of Leonardo since both of them were apprentices in Verrocchio's workshop at the same time. Nor should one forget that Leonardo vaunted elegance and cleanliness as the privilege of the painter (see (no. 30).

It is surprising that there are so few notes on oils and varnishes. Most likely they were in notebooks that the compiler of the Codex Urbinas neglected and that are now lost. Verrocchio's workshop was one of the first to adopt the Flemish technique of oil painting, and Leonardo's experiments with transparent shadows, thin glazes, and particularly his invention of chiaroscuro would have been impossible without as ductile a medium as oil because it permits building up successive layers of paint. The importance of his studies in this area are attested by many early witnesses, such as Leo X, as well as by a study of his works. In fact, the spirit of experiment and the instinct for research into subtle effects led to results that hardly ever give up the secrets of their processes to x-rays.* It must be remembered that Leonardo also became famous through the spectacular failures caused by his disdain of accepted techniques and his need to alter them at all cost, as in the case of the* Battle of Anghiari *where the underlayer on the wall decomposed in 1506 and brutally interrupted work.*

The Conflict of Science and Art

Of painting. Of the darkness of shadows, or rather, of the brightness of lights. Experienced painters distinguish four values for each color in everything represented — trees, fields, hair, beards, furs. First, a dark foundation, second, a *(lighter)* stain that follows the shape of the part, third, a lighter and more sharply defined part, and fourth, the high lights that catch the eye more than does the rest of the object. But it seems to me that the variety *(of shades)* on a continuous surface is infinite and divisible to infinity . . . 268. *Continuity in transitions*

The painter establishes the degree for the objects of sight as the musician does for sounds, the objects of hearing. Although the things submitted to sight form a continuous series, I will, nonetheless, make my rule * of twenty *braccia* intervals as the musician does for sounds that are united and joined together but have, nevertheless, been given small intervals from sound to sound called first, second, third, fourth, and fifth and thus from degree to degree with the names of all the variations of the voice upward and downward. 269.

Precept for imitating the color of leaves. Those who do not wish to rely wholly on their own judgment in imitating the true color of leaves, should take a leaf from the tree they wish to represent and mix their colors on it, and when 270. *Of the "true" color of things* the color they have mixed can no longer be distinguished from the leaf you can be certain that it exactly represents that leaf, and you can proceed in like manner with other *(matters)* to be painted. *

271. *That the most beautiful shades of a color should be saved for the parts that are highlighted.* Since the quality of color obviously becomes known to us through light, we can conclude that there, where there is most light, one can best see the true quality of the color so illuminated ; and there where it is darkest, the color takes on the tones of the shadow. Therefore, painter, be careful to show the true quality of the colors in the parts that are illuminated.

272. *Of true color.* The true color of any body whatever is revealed in those parts that are not covered by any shadow, nor, if the body is polished, by any reflection.

273. *That no body shows its true color except when it is illuminated by a similar color.* No object will ever show its own color if the light that illuminates it is not of exactly the same color.

This is confirmed in the colors of draperies where the illuminated folds, if they reflect the light and project it onto the folds opposite, make these show their true color. The same thing is true for laurel leaves, * which illuminate one another.

The opposite occurs when the lighting is of another color. *

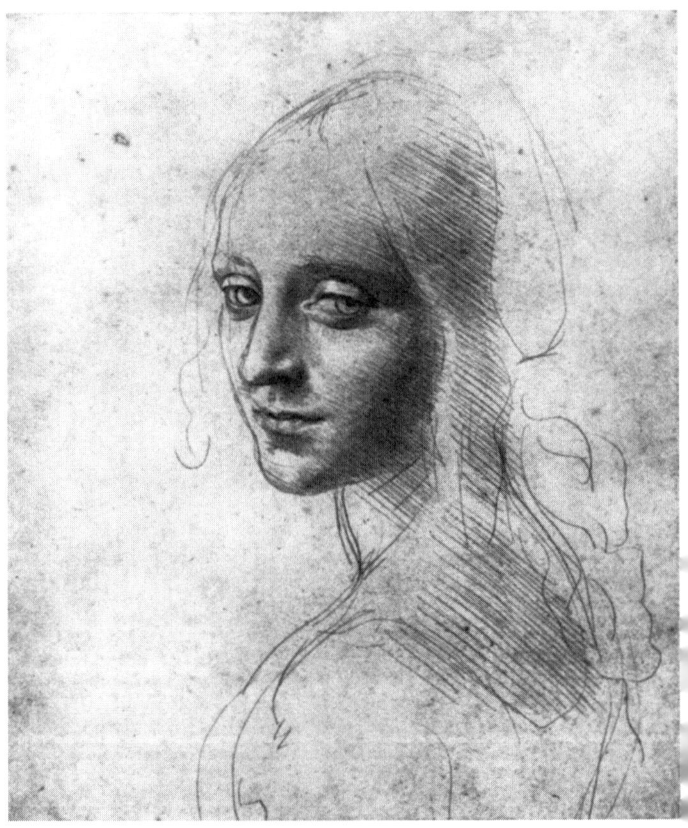

Study for the Angel in *The Madonna of the Rocks.*

274. *Of lights and shadows and their color.* No body ever shows itself entirely in its natural color . . . .

The true color may appear on that part of the body which is illuminated by a colorless source of light, if, with that illumination, it does not have anything else before it but that source of light. These conditions are never fulfilled except in the case of a sky-blue *(material)* spread out flat on the top of a high mountain so that it cannot be exposed to any other object ; or when the setting sun is covered with clouds and the cloth is of the color of the air.

But I have to retract because a pink cloth, too, increases in beauty when it is illuminated by the red sun in the west, with clouds lying in between.

However, if the pink cloth seems more beautiful when illuminated by a reddish light than under any other condition, that is an indication that the beauty it loses under an illumination of another color was its own by nature. *

275. *True shadow*

What is, in fact, the true shadow of the colors of bodies. The shadow of a body should not take on any other color than that of the object it touches ; therefore, it is black, which does not count among the colors, that gives the shadows to all the colors, more or less dark, according to what the spot requires ; but the *(actual)* color of the said body is never completely lost, except in the parts contained below the surface of an opaque body.

Therefore, painter, if you wish to work after nature, slightly tinge the walls of your workshop with white mixed with black, because white and black are not colors.

Precept of painting. Perspective is the bridle and rudder of painting. 276. *True size*

It should be possible to tell the distance from which a painted figure is seen from its size.

If you see a *(painted)* figure that is life-size, you know that it is conceived as being near the eye. *

SELECTION, COORDINATION, AND CONTRAST

Perspective of colors. In the foreground, one should place the simple colors and the degree of their diminution should be in accordance with their distance, that is, the dimensions of the objects will become more and more like a point in proportion as they approach it, * and the colors will become more and more like the horizon in proportion as they approach it. * 277. *Showing distance*

Of the consistency between shadows and the lights that accompany them. Here you must pay careful attention to the objects surrounding the one you wish to represent, for the first proposition of the fourth book says that the surfaces of all opaque bodies take on the color of whatever is in front of them. But you should intentionally arrange to have the reflections * of green things fall on green bodies, for example, 278. *Avoid ambiguity* fields, and obtain other such agreements ; this should be so that the reflection that takes on the color of its object should not degenerate and not appear to be the reflection of a body that is not green ; for if you have a bright red take on a green reflection, this reflection would become reddish so that its color would be very ugly and very different from the reflection of a green.

And what I have said concerning this color is also appropriate for all the others.

279. *Against confused representation of foliage*

Never paint transparent leaves in the sun because they are always indistinct ; this occurs because the shadow of one leaf will be imprinted upon the transparence of another, below it ; and this shadow will have precise outlines and a definite shade, and at times it may cover a half or a third of the leaf ; and such foliage will be indistinct and should not be painted.

280. *Show the causes of phenomena*

Of shadows on bodies. If you represent shadows on opaque bodies, always show their cause ; and you should do the same for reflections, for dark shadows stem from opaque bodies and reflections from objects of not too great luminosity, that is from diminished lights. And there is the same relation between the part of the body illuminated *(directly)* and that illuminated by reflections as between the cause of the direct light on the object and the cause of the said reflection.

281. *A useful compromise in perspective*

An object represented in *(flat)* perspective * should be looked at from the same distance, height, and direction as the position of your eye *(when you drew it)* ; otherwise your knowledge will not bear fruit. And if you will not or are not able to apply this principle — because the wall you are painting must be seen by several people *(at the same time)*, which would require several points of view, and make the work disproportionate and false — remove yourself to a distance of at least ten times the size of the object *(painted)*.

In that case you will commit the least error, that of giving all the objects in the foreground their true form ; * and wherever you stand, the things you see represented will of themselves take on the proper diminution of perspective ; * but the spaces between the things will be distorted. For, if you stand before the center of a row of columns, you will see that after a few interstices the columns will begin to seem to touch each other, then to cover each other, so that the last will be barely visible behind the one before the last ; thus the spaces between the columns finally disappear altogether. And if your projection of perspective is good, it will reproduce the effect that occurs when someone stands close to a row of columns. But this method will

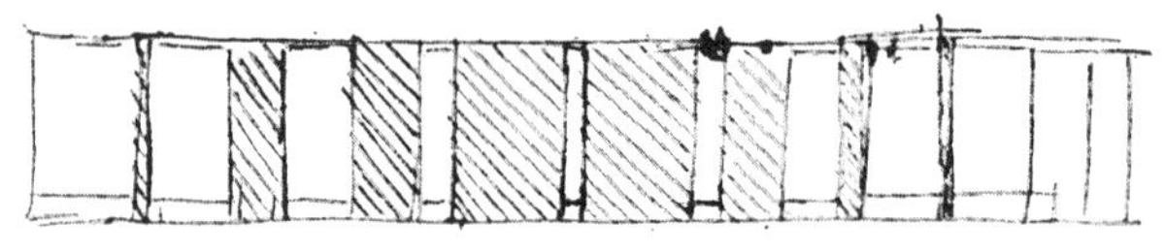

Colonnade drawn in anamorphos[is] with a fixe[d] central poi[nt] of view v[ery] close up.

not work if the painting is not seen through a small hole at the center of which you have located your point of view ; and if you do this, your work will be perfect and convince the spectators who will see the columns represented as described above.

Here the eye is in the center, opposite point *a* and close to the columns. *

282. *Contrast with the background* *Backgrounds.* Of backgrounds for figures ; a light figure against dark and a dark one against a light background.

White against black or black against white reinforce each other. Opposites always appear more powerful one because of the other.

283. *The background and relief* The background on which a thing is painted is of great importance in painting. Against the background, the outlines of things that have some roundness are revealed, as well as their forms ; and this happens even if their color is the same as that of the background. The cause of this is that a given light does not illuminate the convex surfaces of objects in the same way that it illuminates the background, the surfaces being several times lighter or darker than it. But if you give the surface the same shade as the background, then undoubtedly this part of the painting does not permit the figures thus surrounded to be visible. And by his judgment a good painter should avoid such parts in his art, for the aim of painting is to make the figures appear detached from their background, while in the instant mentioned the contrary occurs, not only in the painting but also in reality.

284. *Indicate depth* *How to heighten the appearance of relief in a painting by the clever distribution of light and shadow.* To increase the relief in a picture, you should place between the figure represented and the object shown that receives its shadow a line of bright light that separates the figure from the one it puts in shadow.... And the same for limbs that are to be somewhat separate from their body, particularly arms crossing the chest, show how between the impact of the shadow of the arm on the chest, and the part of the arm itself that is in shadow, there is a little light that seems to pass through the space between the chest and the arm ; and the more distant you want the arm to appear, the more you will extend that light....

An object depicted in white and black will always appear in greater relief than any other. And for this reason I advise you, O painter, to clothe your figures in lighter colors. For if you make them in dark colors, they will have little relief and, from a distance, will not stand out much ; this is because the shadows of all things are dark : and if you make the clothing dark, there will be little contrast between the light and the shadow ; and on light clothing the contrast will be pronounced. 285. *Choose colors that heighten relief*

OPTICAL AND MENTAL ILLUSIONS

How shadows deceive the judgment which evaluates their degree of darkness. Among 286.

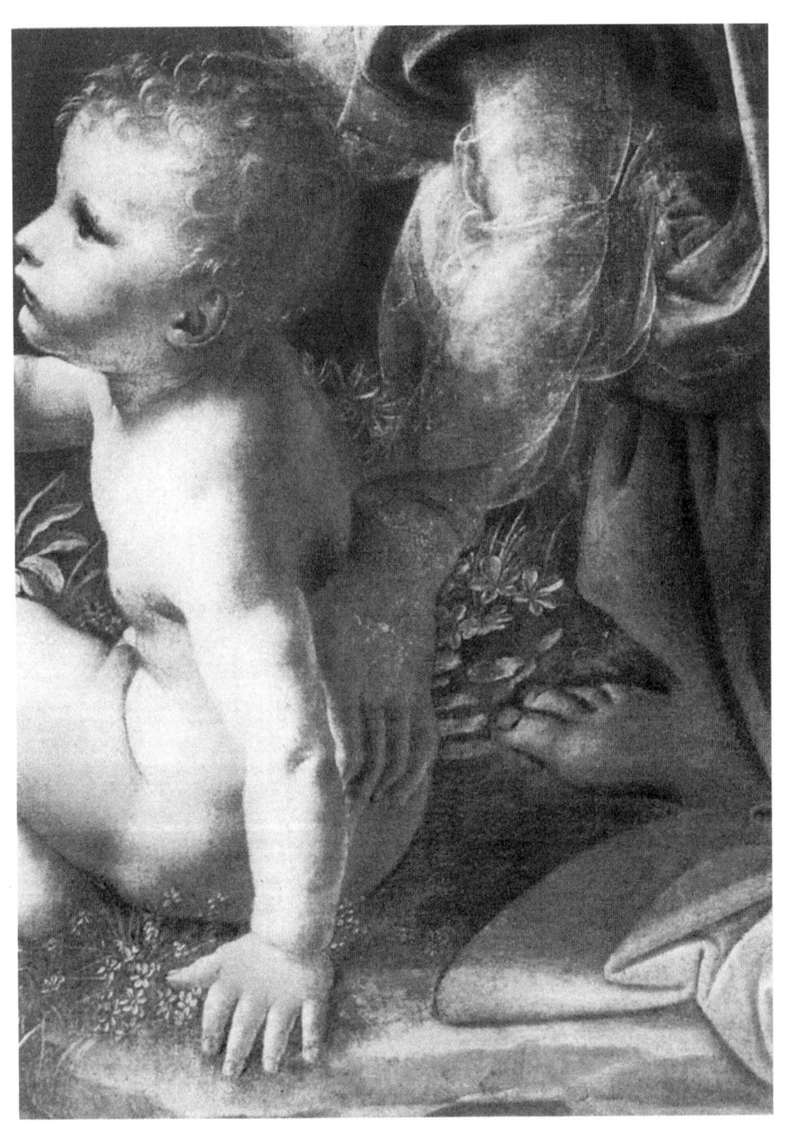

equally dark shadows the one surrounded by weaker light — as for example the gleam of luminous reflections — appears less dark. Therefore, painter, be careful not to deceive yourself by changing this shadow. *

Of lights among shadows. If you draw an object, remember that the eye is often deceived when comparing the intensities of the brightness of illuminated portions, and takes for lighter that which is less so; and this comes from comparing them to adjacent parts . . . 287.

Perspective. It is asked of you, painter, why figures that for reasons of perspective you have painted small, do not appear, despite the indications of distance, as large as real persons of the height of those you depicted on the wall *(when placed at the same distance as these).* 288. *Illusion in linear perspective*

And why the objects in the foreground appear larger *(on the canvas)* than in reality when seen at the same distance. *

Of bodies seen in a mist. Things seen in a mist appear much larger than in reality, and this comes about because the perspective of the middle lying between the eye and the object does not give the color appropriate to its size. Because mist is similar to the indistinct air lying between the eye and the horizon in clear weather, a body close to our eye seen through the near mist seems to be at the distance of the horizon — where a high tower would seem smaller than this man near us. * 289. *An illusion in aerial perspective*

◄ *The Madonna of the Rocks.* Detail, the Christ Child; see precept no. 284.

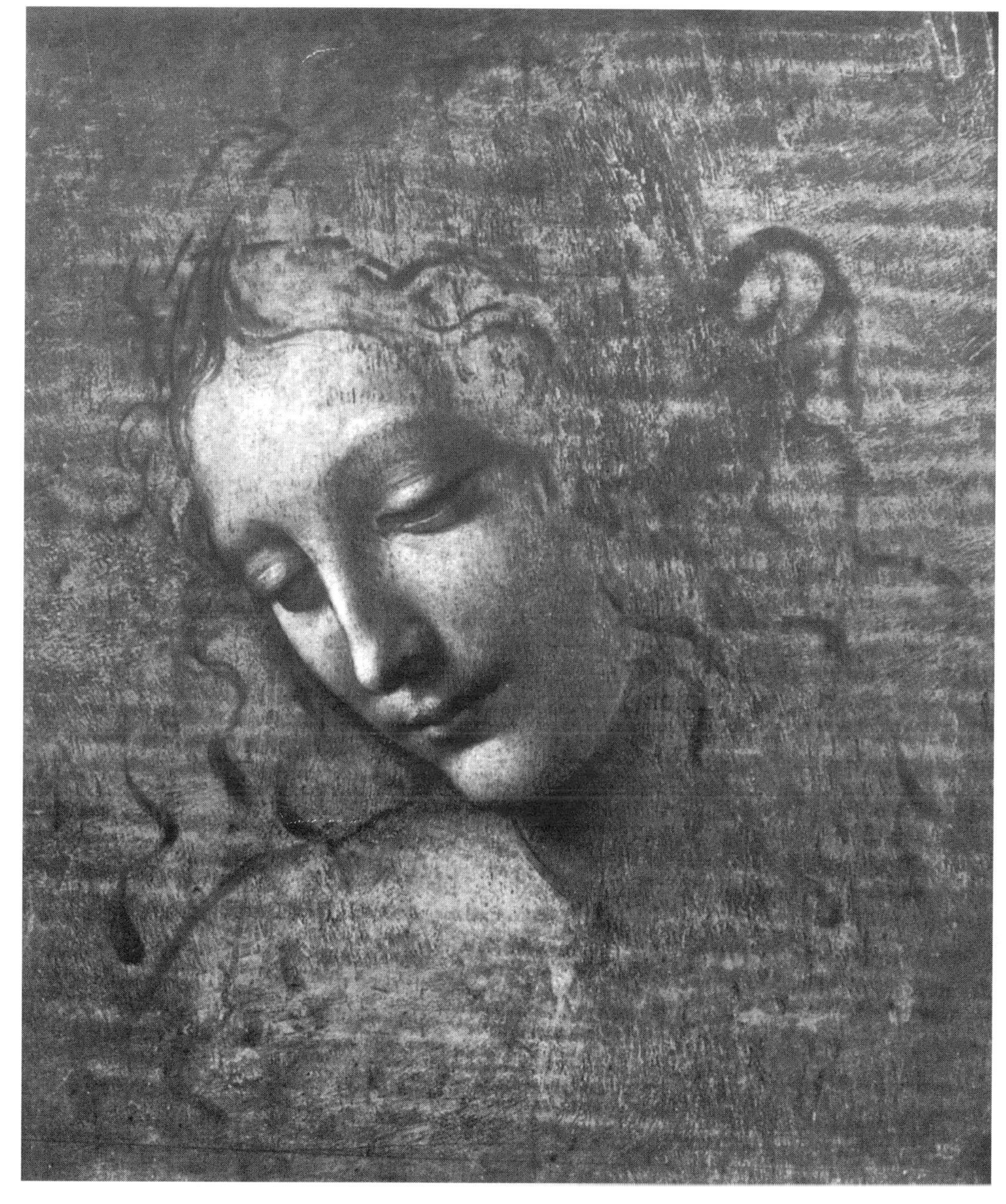

Head of a Girl.

The Studio

Small rooms or domiciles awaken the spirit, 290.
large ones distract it.

The quality of light. The plane *ab* is as much 291.

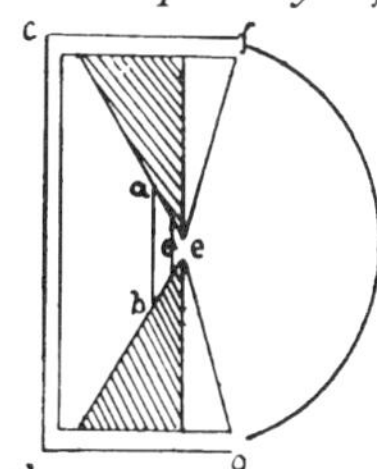

lighter than *cd* as it is smaller; and in the same way the opening *e* is as many times lighter than *cd* as it is smaller. This sort of light is useful for those who have precise work to do. *

Of small sources of light. . . . Light cast from 292.
small windows causes strong contrasts of light *Lighting*
and shadow, especially if the room thus illuminated is large; and this is not good for work. *

The painter's window and its use. The 293.
painter who works from nature needs a window he can raise or lower, because at times he may wish to finish his painting near the window.

Let *abcd* * be the frame in which he can lower or raise his work so that it is the work and not the master that is moved up or down. And every evening you can lower the work to the bottom and lock it in, as in a chest which, when closed, also serves as a bench. *

How to choose the light that gives most grace 294.
to faces. If you have a courtyard and you can cover it with a linen awning, the light will be excellent. Or else, when you wish to portray

someone, do so in bad weather or toward evening and place the model with his back against one of the walls of the courtyard. Observe the softness and grace in the faces of men and women in the streets as night falls when the weather is bad. Therefore, painter, you should have a courtyard provided with walls tinted black and with a roof that projects beyond this wall ; and this courtyard should be ten *braccia* wide and twenty long, and ten high, and when the sun shines you should cover it

Text and illustration of no. 293.

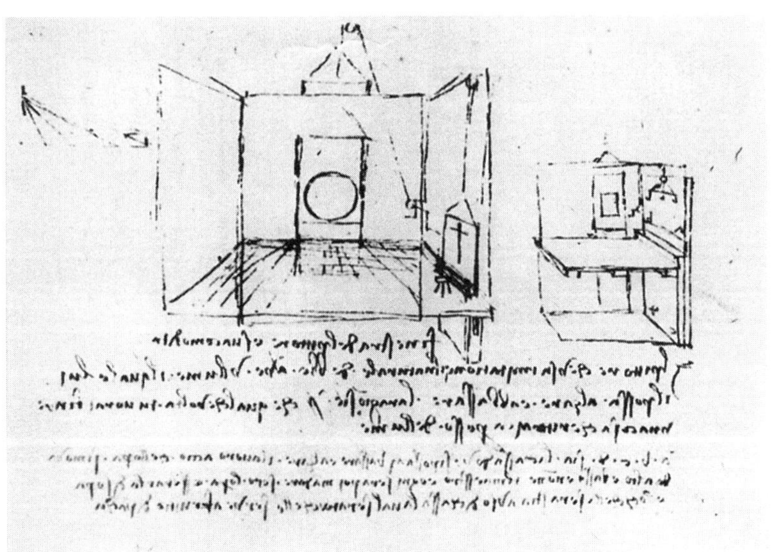

with an awning. Or else paint your pictures toward evening when there are clouds or a mist, and this atmosphere is perfect.

Materials

295. *Colored crayons*

To make points (of crayons) *for coloring dry.* Bind *(the powdered color)* with a little wax so that it will not crumble. This wax should be dissolved in water so that when you have mixed the lead white with it, the distilled water will disappear in vapor, and the wax will remain, and this makes good crayons, but you must know that you have to grind the colors with a hot stone. *

296. *Paper for herb books*

This paper should be colored with candle soot attached with thin glue ; then coat the leaf with a fine layer of lead white in oil, as is done with the letters in printing, then print it on the paper in the usual way. Thus, the leaf appears dark in the parts that are hollowed out and light in the parts in relief, but like a negative. *

297. *Colors*

To make a beautiful green take the *(powdered)* green and mix it with bitumen, and you will thus make the shadows deeper. Then, for the lighter greens, mix green and ochre, and for still lighter greens, green and yellow ; and for the highlights use pure yellow. Then mix green and saffron from India and put a glaze of it over the whole.

To make a beautiful red, take cinnabar or red chalk or burnt ochre for the deep shadows, and for the lighter shadows, red chalk and vermilion, and for the lights, pure vermilion, and glaze the whole with a fine lake.

To make oil that is good for painting : one part oil, one part turpentine once distilled, and another of turpentine distilled two times.

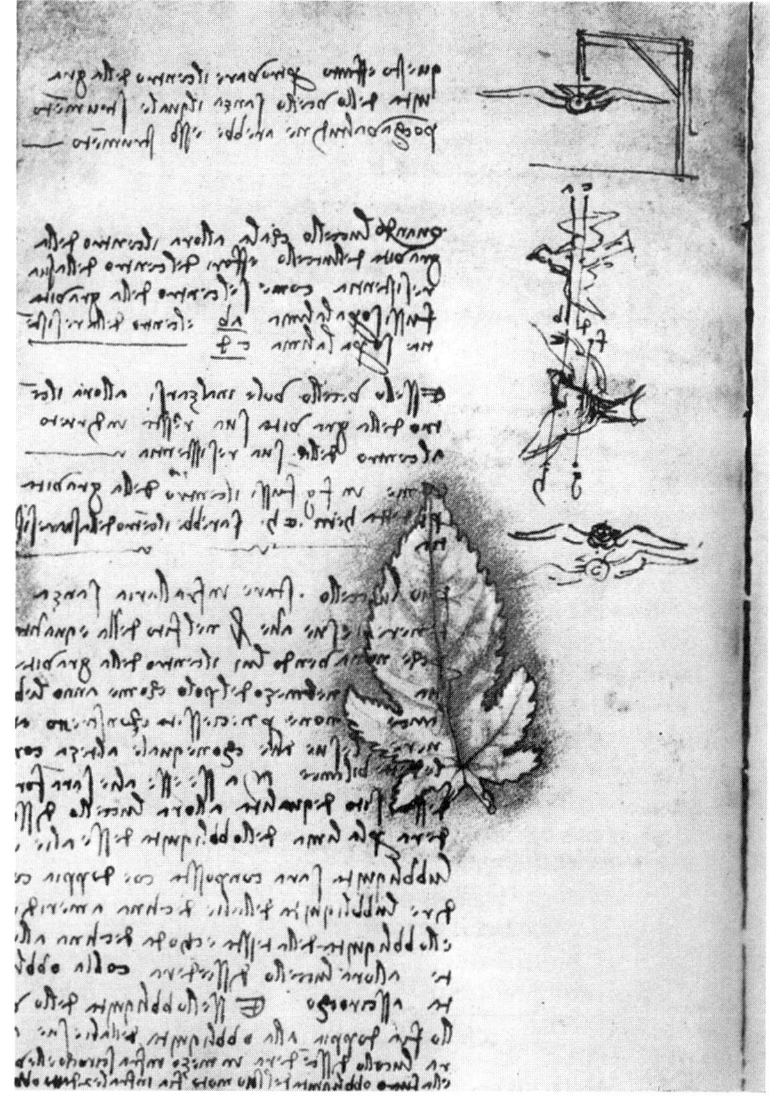

Page with the imprint of a leaf ; see no. 296. ▶

298. *To increase the beauty of gray-green.* Gray-green will gain much in beauty if you mix it with cavalline aloe, and would gain even more with saffron if it did not evaporate. This cavalline aloe is known to be good when dissolved in warm alcohol, which is a better solvent than when cold.

And if you have finished your work with this simple green, and then have covered it with a thin layer of aloe dissolved in water, it will have a very beautiful color. But this aloe can also be used in oil, ground alone or with gray-green, or with any other color you choose. *

299. *Proportions of colors.* If one ounce of black mixed with one ounce of lead white makes a shadow of the first degree, a shadow of how many degrees will two ounces of black to one of white make ?

300. *To prepare a wooden panel for painting on it.* The wood should be cypress, or pear, or service tree, or walnut that you harden with mastic and turpentine that has been distilled twice and with white, or rather lime ; and put it in a frame so that it can expand or shrink according to the degree of humidity. Then cover it with a layer of a double or triple solution of arsenic or of corrosive sublimate in alcohol ; next cover it with boiled linseed oil so that it will penetrate throughout and before it cools off again rub the panel well with a cloth to dry it ; after this apply liquid varnish and lead white and then, when it is dry, wash it with urine. Finally, pounce it and lightly draw your design and cover it with a coat of thirty parts gray-green to one of a mixture of one part gray-green and two yellow. *

Of the panels that keep straight best. Panels made from the part of the tree turned toward the north bend less and best keep their natural flat form. 301.

And the reason for this is that the sun hardly ever reaches that side or moves the sap of the tree, while the southern side is exposed to the sun all day long which, on this side, results in the movement of the sap from east to west, following the course of the sun.

Of trees and panels which of themselves never bend. If you want a cut panel to keep straight, saw it in the center along its length, and turn the two halves in opposite directions, laying them one against the other ; that is, place the head *(of the one against)* the foot *(of the other),* and the foot *(against)* the head and then reunite them this way, and such a construction will never bend. * 302.

How to use color on canvas. Put the canvas on the stretcher, give it a thin coat of glue, let it dry, and draw on it ; paint the flesh tones with brushes of silk, and on the fresh color make the shadows as you wish. The flesh tones will be made of white lead, lake, and earth of Cologne ; the shadow will be black and red with a little lake, or, if you wish, hard red chalk. 303.

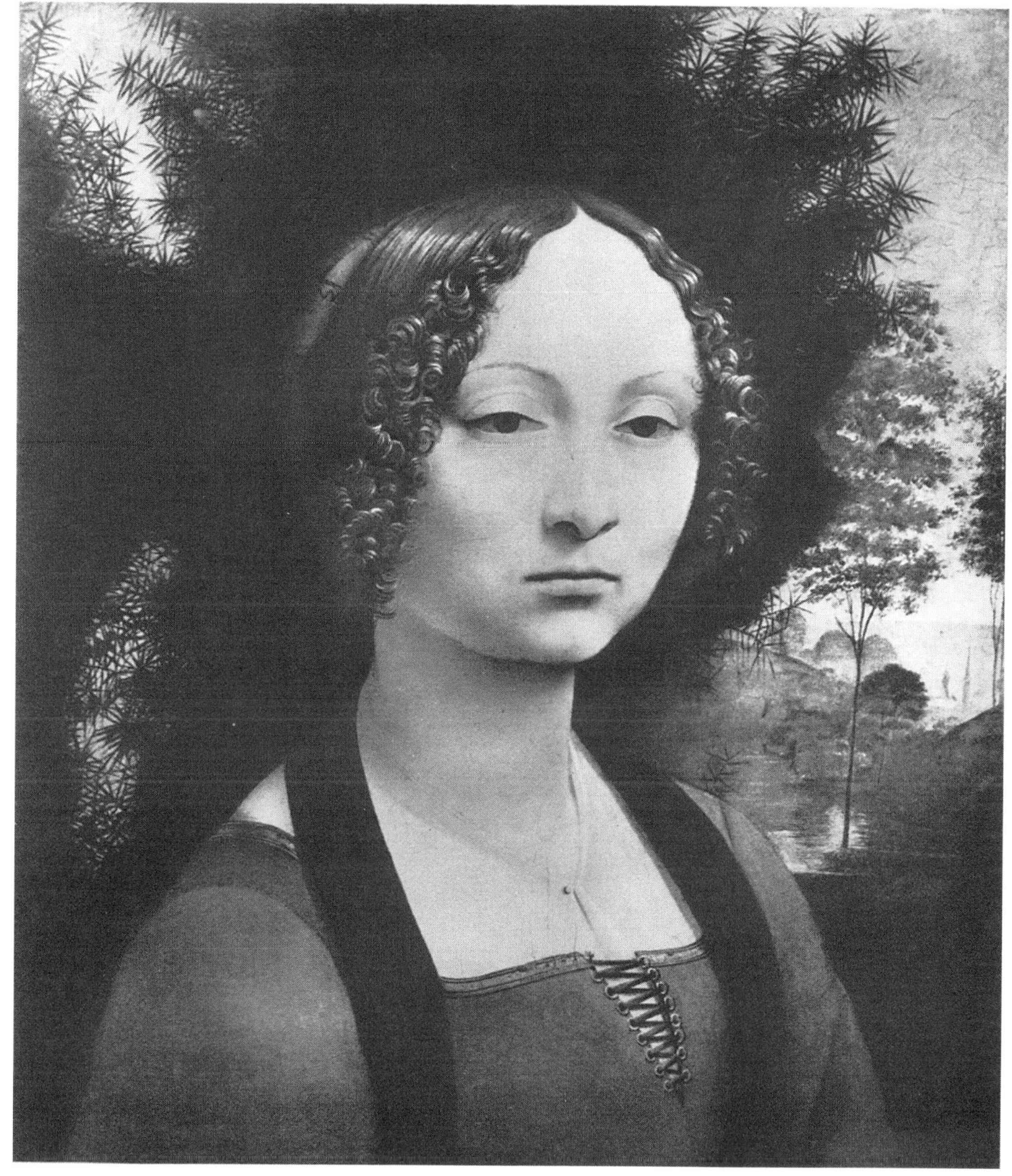

Portrait of Ginevra de' Benci.

When you have put in the shadows, let it dry, then retouch *a secco* with lake and gum that has been kept in its own liquid a long time, which is better because it fulfills its function without shining. Or else, for the darkest shadows take the lake gum mentioned above and ink, and with that you can shadow many colors because in this way the layer is transparent; you can shadow blue and lake on the dark side *(of objects)*; I say dark side, because on the light side, above the lake color, you will shadow with pure lake gum without binder, for one paints without a binder over vermilion with a binder that has dried.

304. *Oil.* Make oil from seed of mustard; and if you wish to make it more easily, mix the ground seed with linseed oil and put them under the press together.

305. *How to obtain clear oil*

Walnuts are covered with a certain thin skin which is of the nature of the shell; if you do not remove it when you make the oil, this skin will color the oil, and when you use it in your work, it will become separated from the oil and come to the surface of your painting and change it.

306. *Varnish.* Tap a juniper and water its roots, and mix the liquid it exudes with the oil of walnuts and you will have a perfect varnish, like the varnish of amber; and do the same with the cypress and you will have a varnish of excellent quality. And do this in May or April.

Tricks, Techniques, and Processes

307. *The use of transparent panes*

How the painter should practice the perspective of colors. If you wish to be able to apply this perspective to the variations or changes or diminutions of the natural colors, you should observe objects in the landscape that are a hundred *braccia* apart, for example, trees, buildings, persons, and places. Then, for the first tree, you will take a pane of glass set in one place, and also keep your eye in one position, and you will draw this first tree on the glass by tracing its outline; then move the glass sideways until the outlines of the real tree and the drawn tree touch; then color your drawing in such a way that in color as in form it is so similar, and that, when you close one eye, both appear to be painted on the glass at the same distance. And apply the same process to the second and the third tree, each a hundred *braccia* farther away; and from then on let these trees act as guides and models that you use in your own works wherever they are applicable; and they will give your works great depth.

But I have found it is a rule that the second tree, at twenty *braccia* from the first, is four-fifths the size of the first.

308. *Drawing with a weighted thread*

To draw a nude or other object from nature, hold a line with a lead weight in your hand to see the position of things in relation to this line.

309. *Squaring*

How to learn to place a figure well. If you wish to learn correct and good positions for your figures, make a frame that is divided into squares by threads and put it between your eye and the nude you are drawing, and you will trace the same squares lightly onto your paper on which you intend to draw your nude. Then place a small wax pellet on some spot on the net to serve as marker which each time you look at the nude, you will place over the hollow of the throat (or, if he is seen from the back, over one of the vertebrae of the neck); and these threads will tell you for each position of the body, which parts of the body are *(precisely)* below the hollow of the throat, below the angles of the shoulders, the breasts, or the hips, or other parts of the body. And the transverse lines of the network will show you how much higher the figure is on the side of the supporting leg than on the other side; and the same for the hips, the knees, and the feet . . .

Later, when you paint it, remember the rule of correspondence between the limbs as you learned it from the network. And the frame should be three and one half *braccia* away from you and one from the nude.

310. *Foreshortening on a curved surface*

How to make a figure on a wall of twelve braccia appear to be twenty-four braccia high. If you wish to represent a figure or another thing so that it appears to be twenty-four *braccia* high do as follows: First execute the *(lower)* half of the man you wish to represent on the wall *mr*, then paint the other half of the figure on the vault *mn*. *(To do so)*, first sketch *(a vertical plan)* of the wall and ceiling on which you wish to paint your figure on the floor of the room; then, behind this outline of the wall, draw the figure in profile, in the size you desire; and unite with lines its *(characteristic)* points with point *f*. And according to where they cut the outline *mn*, you will have the heights and projections of the figure on the *(real)* wall similar to the outline *mn*.

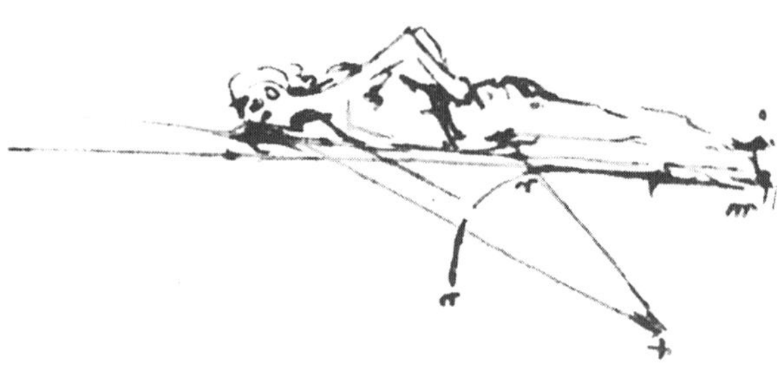

311. *Of drawing the shadow of bodies by the light of a candle or oil lamp.* Place in front of this nocturnal light a frame with paper, either made transparent * or not, but use only one whole sheet of chancellery size; and you will see the shadows as smoky, that is, without outline. If you remove this frame, the light will produce reflections on the paper on which you are drawing.

312. *Rule for giving the right degree of illumination to the sides of a many-sided body.* * Take a color similar to that of the bodies you wish to paint and take the color of the principal light that illuminates these bodies.

Then, if you find that the angle of incidence is larger and is double the smaller, * take one part of the natural color of the body you are to paint and add two parts *(of the color)* of the light needed to illuminate it, and you will thus have a light that is double the lesser *(light)*; and if you wish to have half the illumination, take only one part of the color of the above-mentioned body, and add to it only one part of the said light; in this way you will have two lights for the same color, one of which is double the other . . .

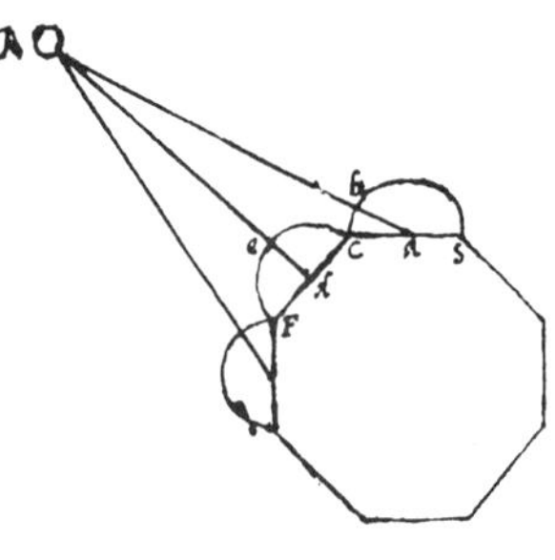

And if you wish to measure these quantities of colors precisely, use a small spoon with which you can take equal portions, as is shown in the drawing here; and after having heaped it with your color, * level it with a small straightedge, as is done with the measures in selling grain. *

313. *A drawing technique*

To give relief to the objects he draws, the painter should stain the surface of the paper in a medium shade and then make the shadows darker, and finally make the strongest highlights with little strokes that will be the first to be lost to the eye with distance.

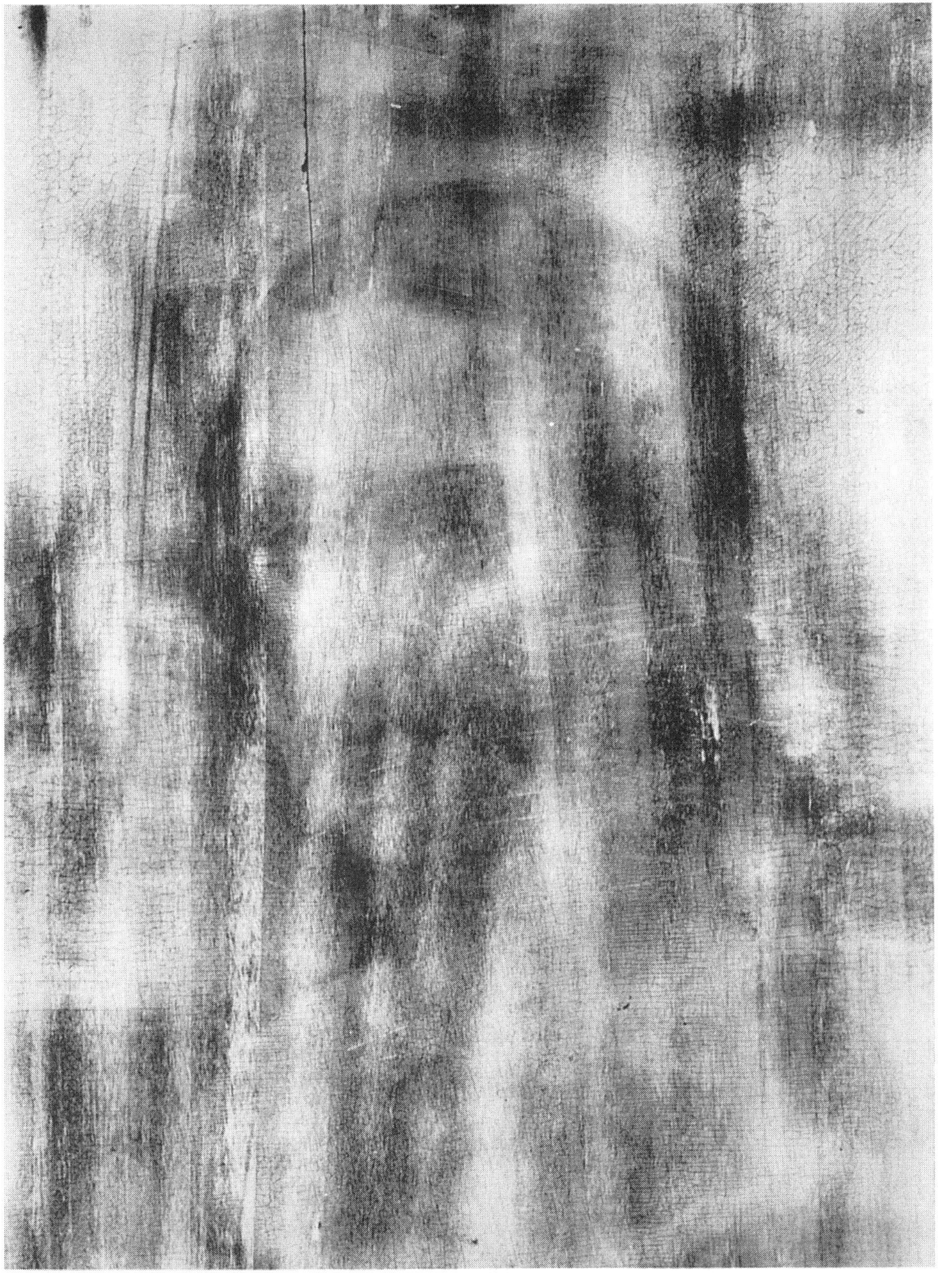

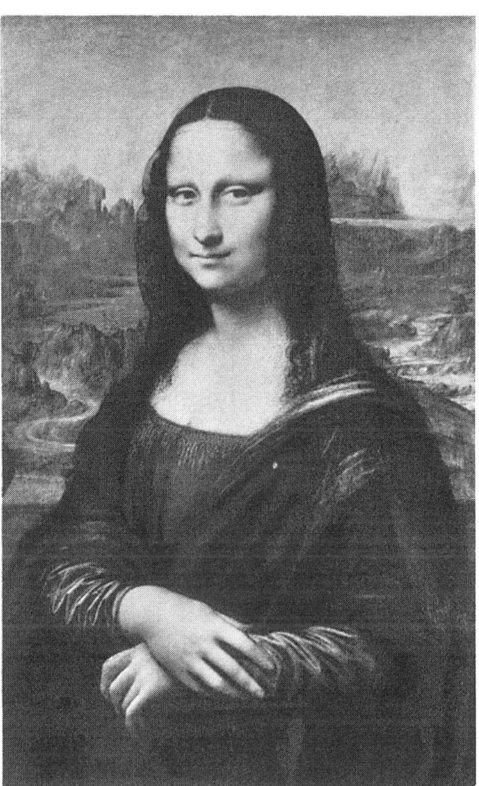

Mona Lisa. On the left an x-ray of the head showing the panel it is painted on; see nos. 300-302.

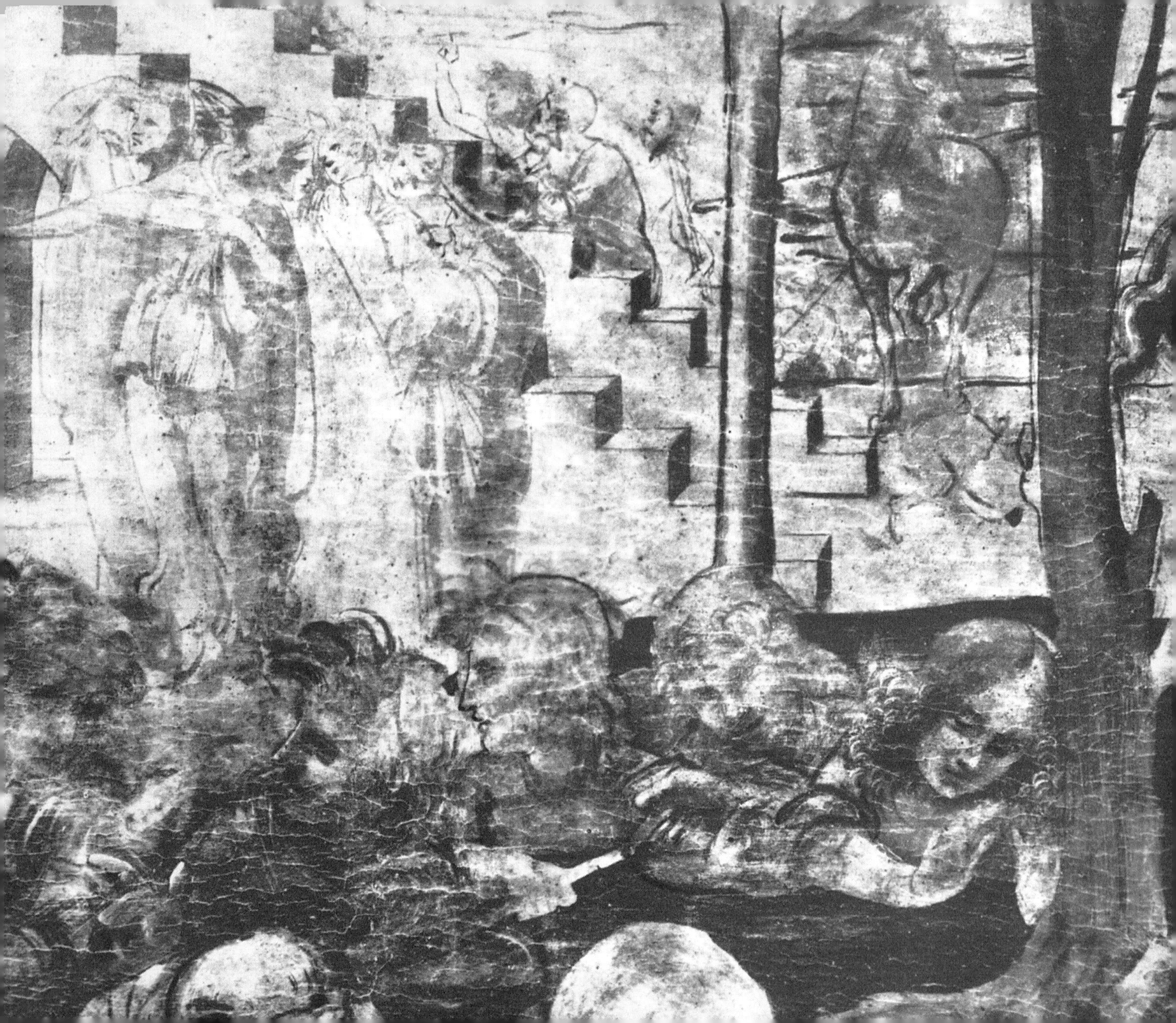

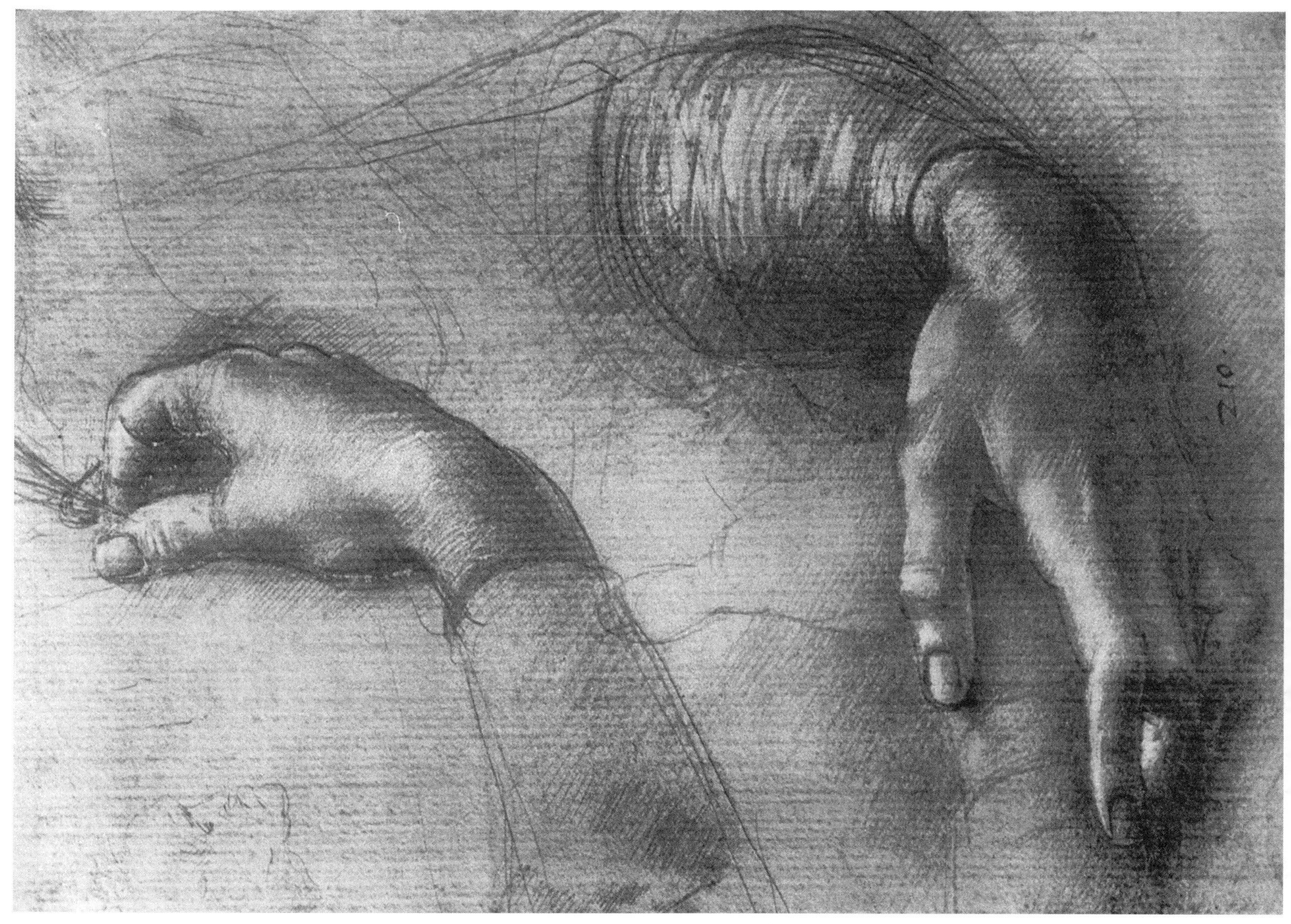

◀ *The Adoration of the Magi.* Detail of a roughly sketched-out part.

Study of hands.

Advice on Working Methods

Precepts of painting. Sketch the narrative subject rapidly ; do not go too far in the execution of the limbs but be satisfied to indicate their position ; you can finish them later at your leisure if you wish. 314. *Sketching*

When you draw nudes, always sketch the whole and then finish the part which seems best to you ; and this you will use later in your work with the other limbs. Otherwise you will get into the habit of putting the limbs together badly. . . . * 315. *Preparatory studies*

Of illumination. First paint a general ground of shadow for all the parts that are not directly illuminated ; then add the medium and darkest shadows, contrasting one against the other. In the same manner, paint the general diffused light and the weak direct light, then add the medium and principal lights, always contrasting them. 316. *Order of painting light*

How to paint colors at different distances. When you reproduce a color, remember that if you are in a shadowed place, you should not attempt to paint an illuminated place, for in doing so you will deceive yourself. In such a case, if you wish to work with certainty, as is appropriate to mathematical demonstrations, * you should compare the imitation and the model in the same light for each color, making your color approach the color perceived on the natural object. 317. *Avoid errors caused by lighting*

Let us say that you wish to represent the side

Ceiling of the Sala delle Asse. Detail showing that the shape of the vault was utilized for the trompe-l'oeil effect. ▶

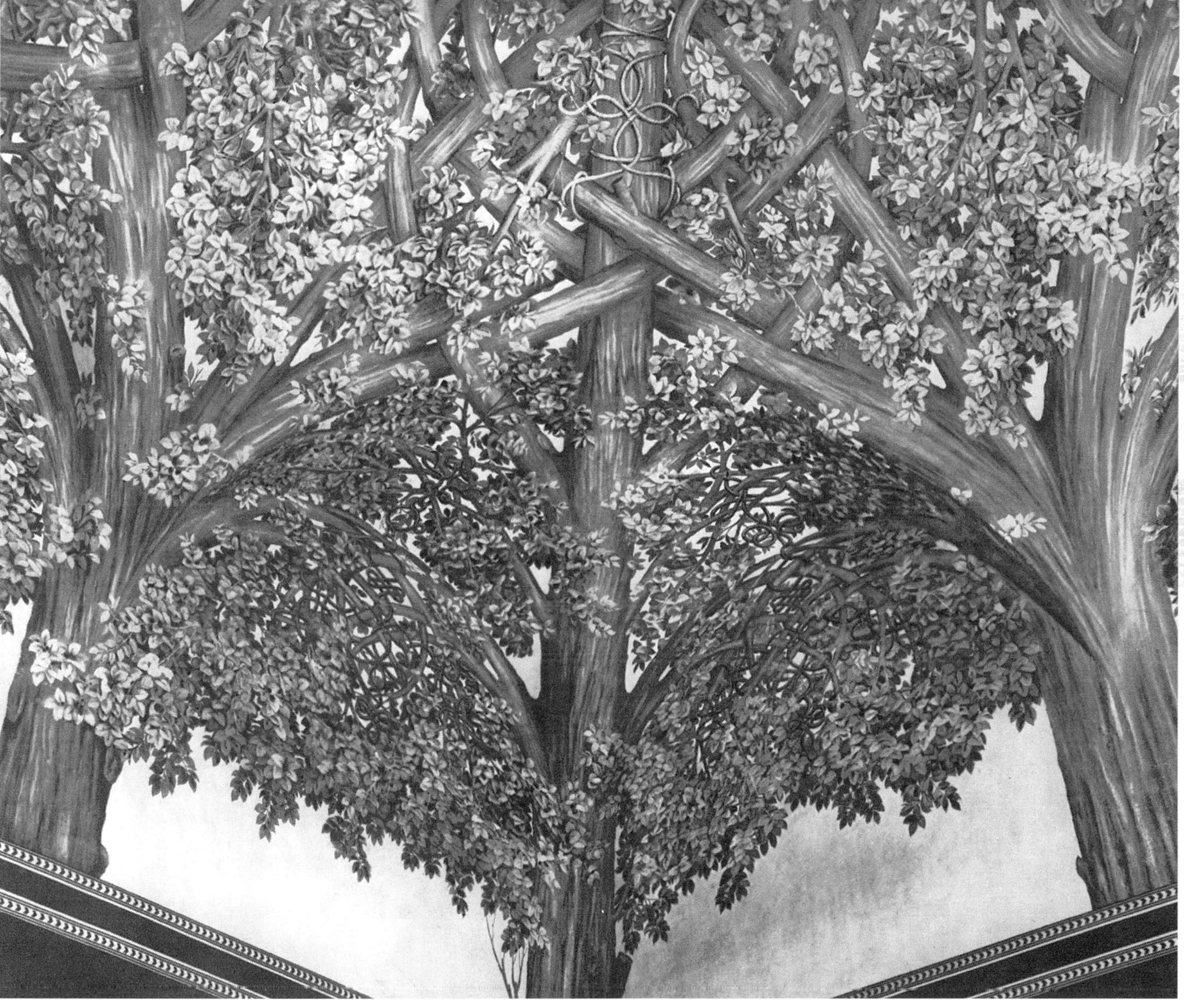

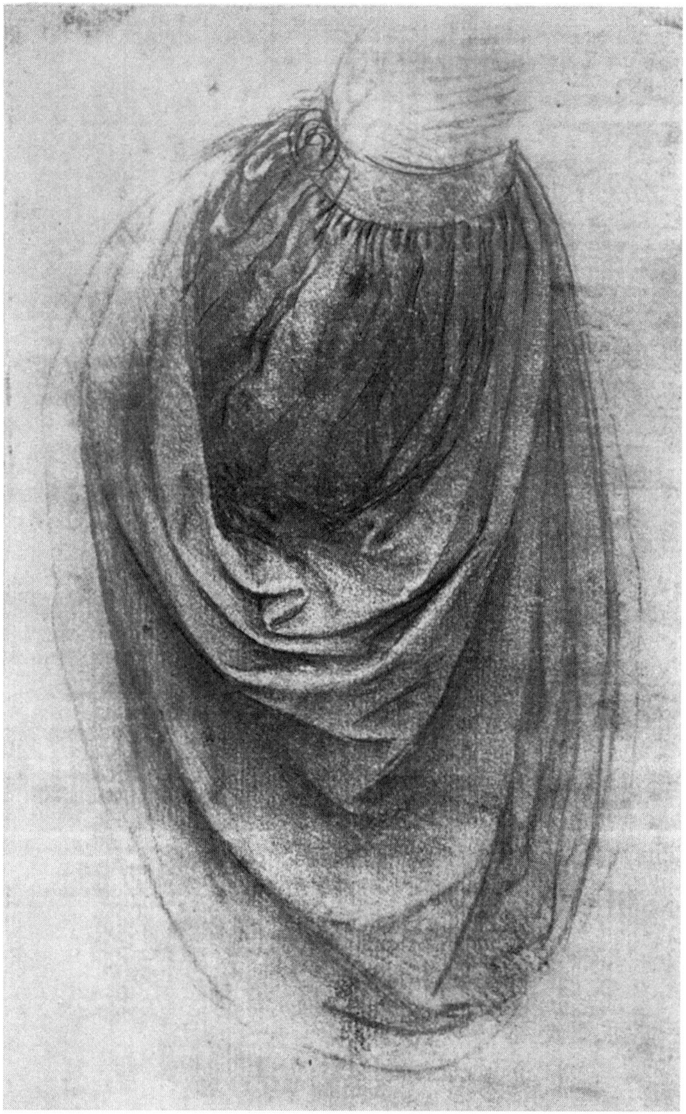

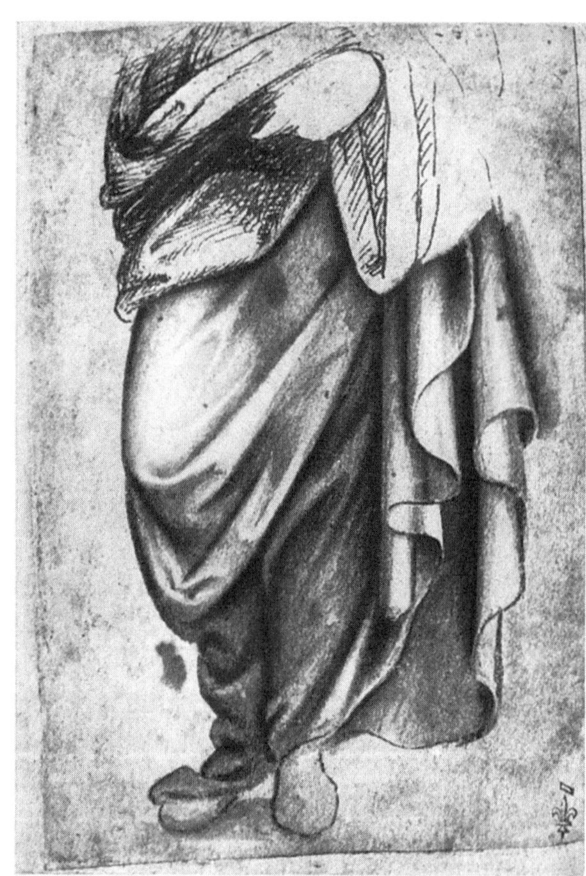

Drapery studies; see nos. 322-325.

of the mountain that is illuminated by the sun : expose your colors to the sun and make the mixtures in the sunlight, and compare them in the same light, holding your color close to the one you are reproducing . . . .

318. *Selecting a point of view : position of the horizon*

At what height to place the (vanishing) *point.* The *(vanishing)* point should be at the level of the eye of a man of medium height, and the end of the plain, where it touches the sky, should be at this level . . . except for the mountains, which are changeable. *

319. *The position to take in making frescoes high up*

How to represent figures in narrative paintings. On the wall he is to decorate, the painter should always take into consideration the height of the place at which he intends to place his figures and everything he has to paint from nature, according to his purpose. And he has to place himself as much lower in relation to his model, as the object he is to represent will be higher in relation to the spectator. Otherwise the work will incur criticism. *

320. *Distance*

Of drawing. If you wish to draw from nature, you should be three times as far from the object you are drawing as it is high.

321. *Distance and plane perspective*

If you cannot arrange it so that whoever looks at your work has a set point of view, * be at least twenty times the maximum height or width away from the model when you are composing your work, and in that case, the spectator's changes of position will make so little difference that they will hardly be noticeable, and your work will be very praiseworthy. . . . *

Of the nature of drapery folds. The part of the fold that is farthest from its cause will turn most toward its original form. 322.

By nature, everything desires to remain in its own state. Drapery, having the same density and the same thickness on the right side and on the reverse, desires to remain flat ; hence, whenever any fold or pleat forces it to modify this state, the nature of the *(disturbing)* force will be expressed where the constraint is strongest ; and you will see that the parts farthest away from this disturbance tend to return most to the original state of the drapery, which is free and full . . . .

. . . Draperies should be painted from nature : 323. *How to paint cloth*
If you wish to represent woolen cloth, paint the draperies according to their nature, and if it is to be of silk, or a thin material, or a coarse one, or linen, or crepe, vary the folds accordingly ; and do not make costumes as some do, who cover the model with paper or thin leather, for you will deceive yourself greatly.

Of the infrequency of folds in draperies. That 324.
a figure dressed in a cloak should not reveal its shape in such a way that the cloak seems to be next to the skin (unless you wish to create this effect) ; but you should remember that there is other clothing between the cloak and the flesh, which keeps the forms of the limbs from appear-

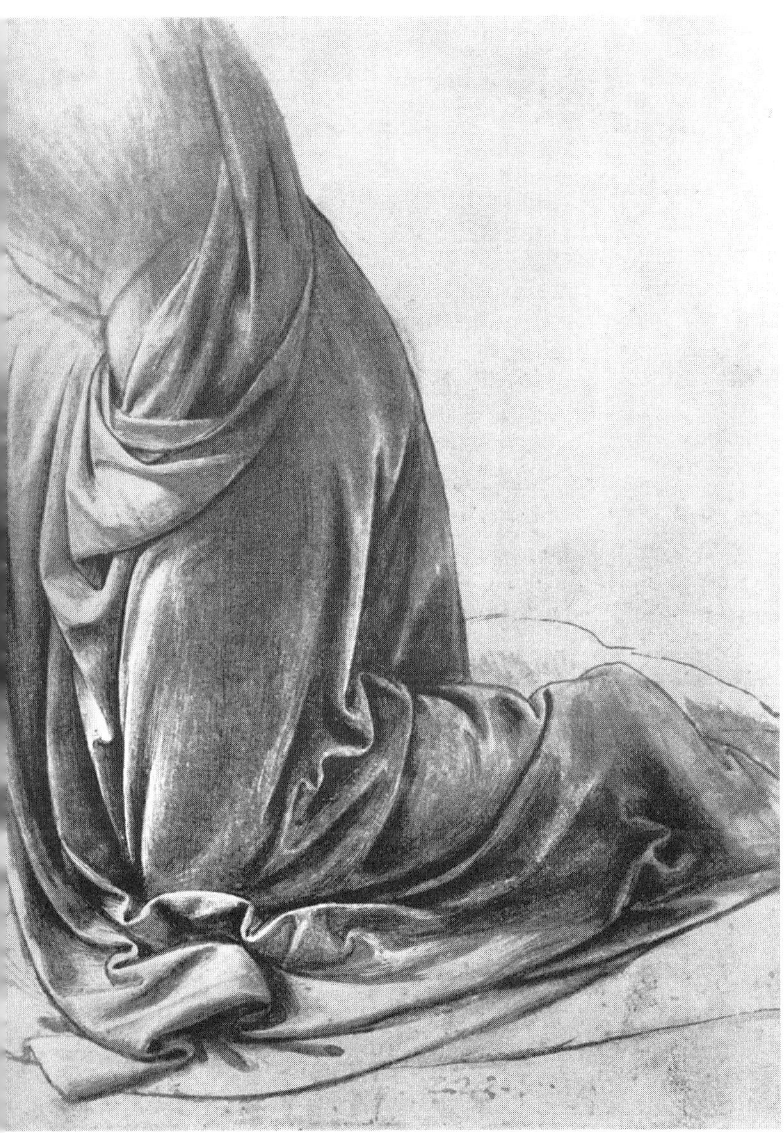

ing as in a nude or from showing through the cloak. And the limbs you permit to be distinguished, depict them thickly so as to suggest the other garments under the cloak, and you will reveal nearly exact dimensions only in the limbs of nymphs or angels who are represented clothed in fine materials, pressed against the limbs of the figure by the blowing breeze.

Of the draperies clothing figures, and their folds. The draperies clothing figures should have folds suitable to the limbs they cover so that in the illuminated parts there will not be folds with shadows that are too dark and in the shadowed parts folds with too much light ; and so that the outlines of the folds should somewhat follow the limbs they cover, without lines that cut the limbs and without shadows that sink below the surface of the body so clothed. In short, the drapery should be arranged in such a manner that it does not seem to be a collection of drapery left behind by the wearer as may be seen in the works of several painters who are so much enamored of diverse groupings of various kinds of folds that they cover the whole figure, forgetting the purpose for which draperies exist and that they are meant to clothe and surround gracefully the limbs supporting them,* instead of completely covering the illuminated projections of the limbs by puffed-up forms or blown-up bladders. I do not deny that some beautiful folds should be made, but they should be made around the figure, where the limbs assemble and pull together the drapery between themselves and the trunk . . . . 325.

Drapery studies.

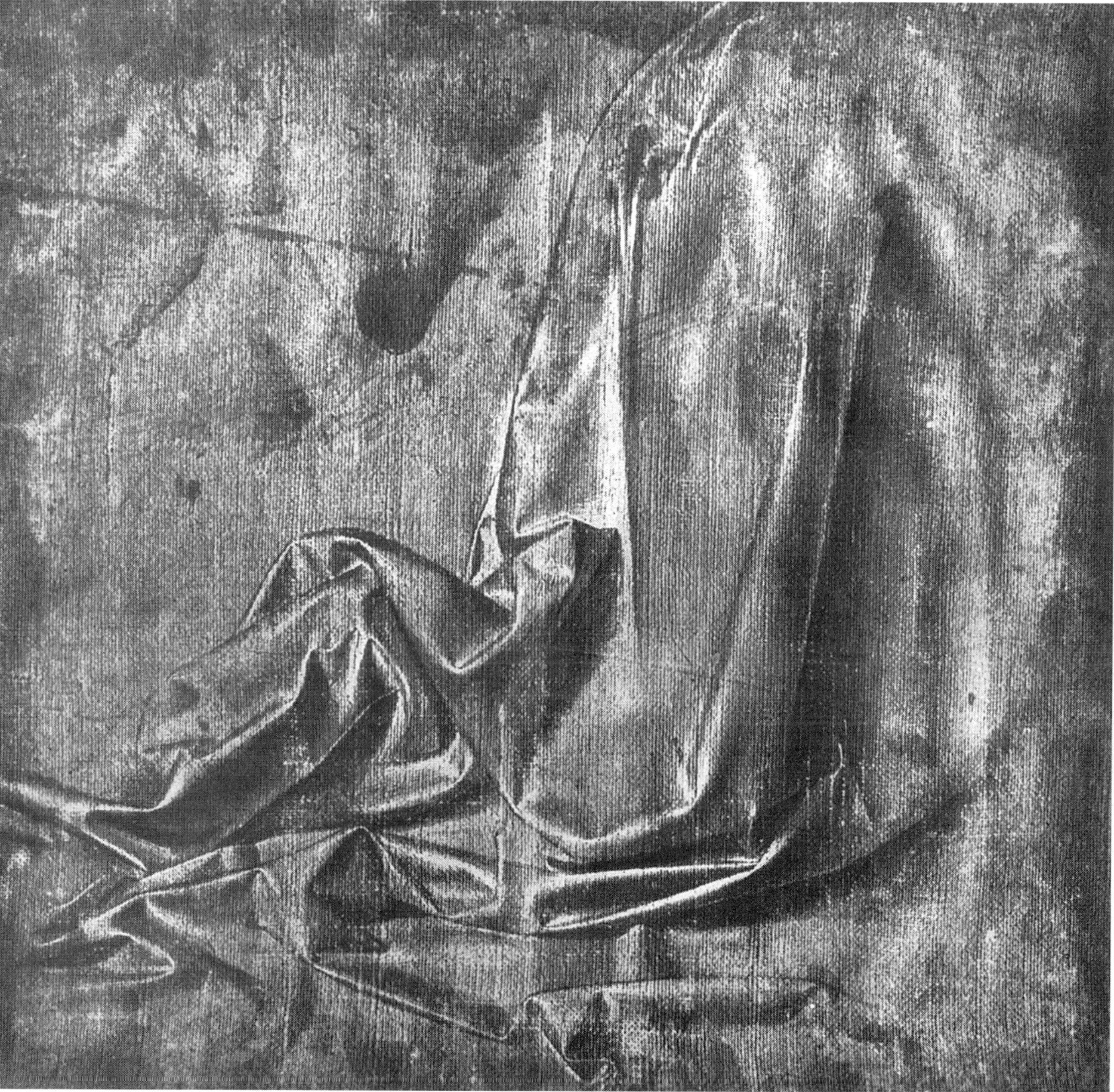

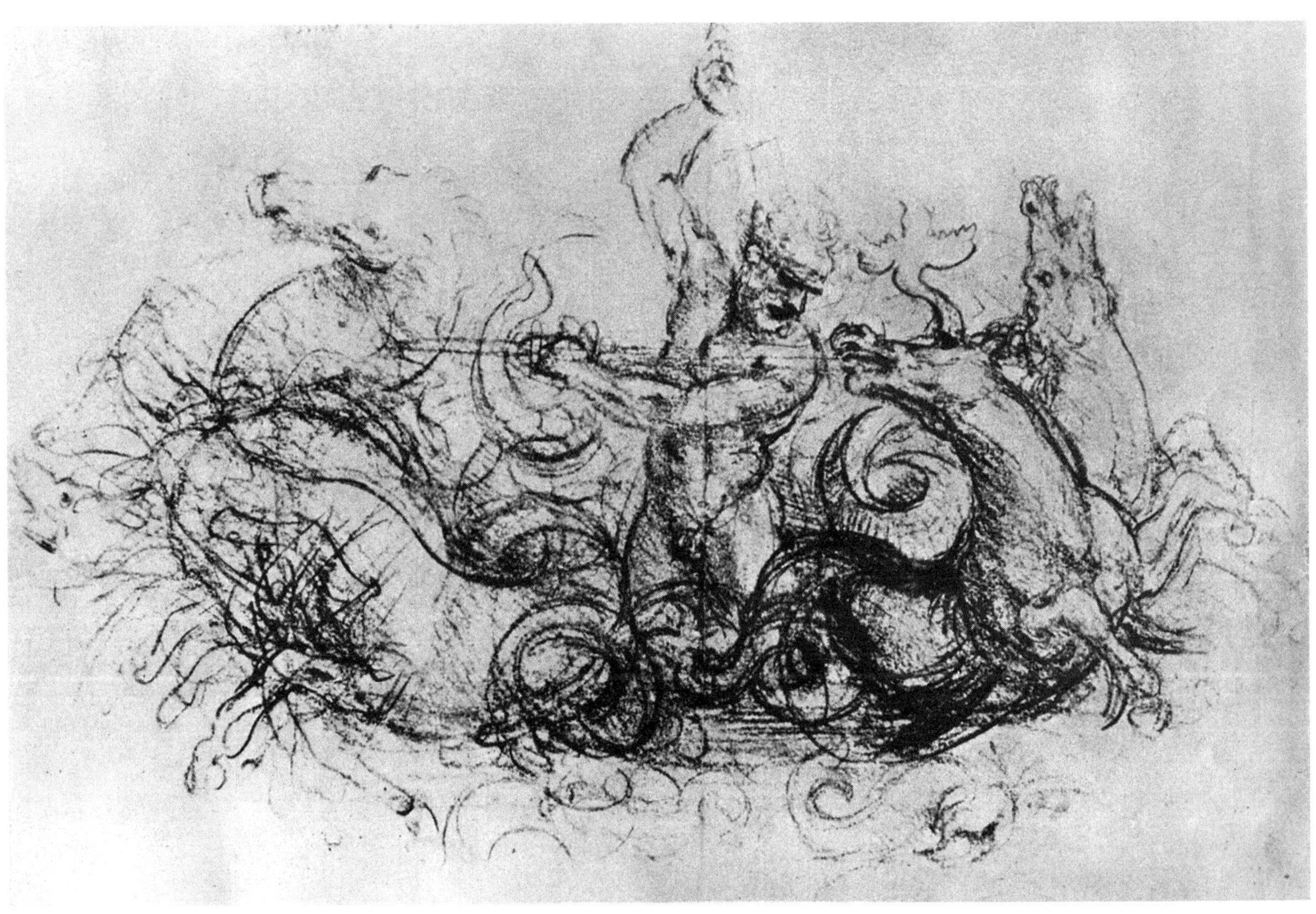

Neptune with his Horses; see no. 350.

The Painter's Activity

More than once the investigations of the ends and means of painting have revealed a shaky foundation. The more Leonardo attempts to rationalize the process of painting the more he realizes that in the final analysis painting depends on a number of attitudes and abilities. It must then be asked how these grow naturally and how they can be acquired. It is remarkable that the majority of these reflections were already written down in a manuscript (BN 2038, Institut de France) dating about 1490.

With his usual insight, Leonardo discovered that the activity of the painter cannot be wholly separated from a fascination with the self. The artist is in search of himself and finds his own image in the multiplicity of forms. Hence, the education of the painter must begin, as far as is possible, with a concealed attempt at "depersonalizing" the initial situation. The order of study must not only be conceived as a series of exercises geared to technical accomplishment but also as an ascetic discipline to free the soul from the pitfalls of subjectivity. Only after the painter has become detached and flexible can — and indeed should — he identify with the manifestations of universal life : The painter's ideal is a gradual union with the highest forms of existence — a final penetration into the most mysterious principles of Being.

There is a distinct ethic for the painter, and one can well imagine that nothing could have suited Leonardo better. This ethic is based on a generosity and openness that is both indulgent and demanding and that assumes love and disinterestedness. Perhaps Leonardo's alterna-

tions, the pendular rhythm reaches its apex : the love of mankind and respect for its state, based on a keen awareness of its precarious condition, has as a counterpoint a horror of bestiality and animality that conscience can neither redeem nor control. Leonardo has written some striking pages on these two subjects. The area between solitude and love is covered by the ironic eye of the observer. Leonardo has an impressive reservoir of sarcasm that finds a healthy outlet in the jests and jokes which, like most Tuscans, he enjoyed thoroughly. But in him this behavior goes beyond the usual, for Leonardo senses that the world of games belongs to the world of art. The former required a detachment and effort that suited him. How far did he go in generalizing the idea? To what extent does an intellectual orientation toward the unusual and difficult heighten a "higher playfulness"? One need do no more than mention that the questions arise. Leonardo's activity at court as master of ceremonies, his pleasure in amusing tricks and puzzles are well known, and he treated games as an art form worthy of full development.

Leonardo is adamant about the dignity of the painter. His position as an "intellectual" artist, and his campaign for painting as a mental activity forced him to condemn the artisan-painter, the mere craftsman who more or less conscientiously employs fashionable or traditional formulas and uses the advantages this method has for him to justify his actions. Leonardo derogates this lazy attitude with a severity applicable to all hack work in all periods. Instead, the

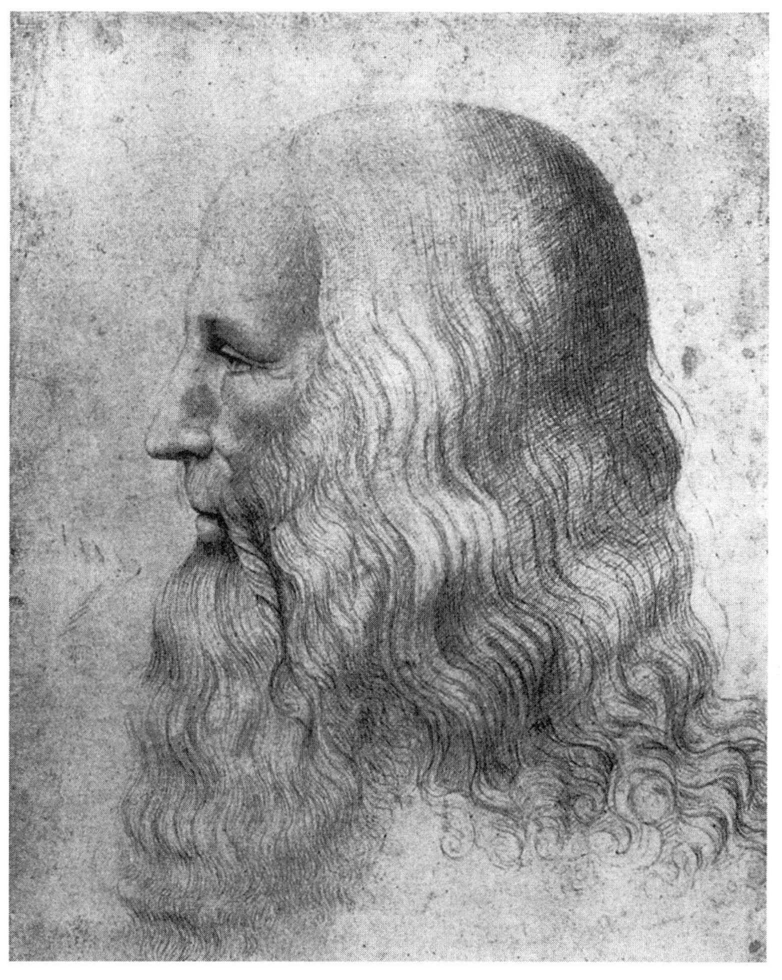

Anonymous, *Portrait of Leonardo* (?).

*artist should seek out useful criticism and never give in to self-complacency. He must be a master or nothing and does not have the right to renounce perfection (the road to which is outlined in the Treatise); obviously, such a standard brooks no limitations. One or two rather sharp passages against "hypocrites" * show that Leonardo reacted violently against the revival of pietistic art and traditional forms that swept Florence at the end of the fifteenth century and brought on a dangerous conflict between art and religion.*

It is when he gives personal advice that Leonardo is most appealing. For the first time in the history of art, a painter analyzes, criticizes, and defines his basic course. Leonardo saw clearly that the intellectual mastery of nature is useless without observation and memory. These make the formal truth of things emerge and put the artist at the hub of the relations between the mind and the universe. This, however, is not Leonardo's ultimate legacy. In conclusion I have assembled some extraordinary and well-known texts in which Leonardo gives the painter his own secret — what Leonardo calls the componimento inculto, *the informed sketch. Contrary to all tradition, this consists of putting down on paper the mass of forms dictated by the unconscious without first working out the details. It is objectified when the painter daydreams before confused stains and splashes on old walls, and it is intended to make the observation more pliable and to give practice to the rapid interpretation of the inexhaustible depths of things. * Thus the painter may correct and change his work the way the writer does (indeed, Leonardo points out that the painter then works like the poet); but most important, this "secret" permits him to freeze the instant at which the mind feels actively connected with the totality of things, for this "chaos" that the artist projects and explores on paper is like an outcry from nature itself.*

This discovery throws some light on the fate that led Leonardo to leave several important works unfinished. The importance of these statements is confirmed by Leonardo's decision, about 1501 or 1502, to introduce non-completeness (non finito) *into painting in order to enhance its fullness. * Finally, it should not be overlooked that the master who sets such store by the possibilities of the informed sketch, takes pleasure in the drawings of his last years in swirling and roiling visions of catastrophes and cosmic disasters that turn even chaos and the blind forces of the universe into the final aims of his art. The confusion of elements in nature, the turbulent stains in the visual, and the incomplete in art confirm and complement one another. The conclusion of the unprecedented effort to be objective — to embrace the structure of things, the organization of forms, and the perfection of relief — is the final triumph of the subjective. **

All Painters Paint Themselves

Of errors in judging the limbs of the body. The painter who has misshapen hands will give similar ones to his figures, and he will do the same for all the other members unless long study has prevented it. Take note of the ugly parts of your body and concentrate your studies on correcting them. For, if you are brutish, your figures will be the same and without grace ; and in the same manner, everything that you, painter, have within you, whether it leans more toward good or toward evil, will be revealed in your figures in some way. 326.

How to select beautiful faces. It seems to me that it is no small quality in a painter to be able to give his figures a pleasant appearance ; and whoever does not possess this grace by nature can acquire it artificially by study, as follows: Look at the good parts of a great number of beautiful faces, whose beauty is confirmed by public opinion rather than by your own judgment, for you might make the mistake of selecting faces similar to your own. In fact, it does happen that we love that which resembles us ; if you are ugly, you might choose faces without beauty and you will make them ugly as do many painters whose figures resemble the author. Therefore choose beautiful faces according to the standard I have told you and commit them to memory. 327.

Of the greatest defect in painters. It is the greatest defect in painters to repeat the same movements and the same faces and draperies in a composition and to make most of the faces resemble their author. This has often surprised me, for there are some who have made self- 328.

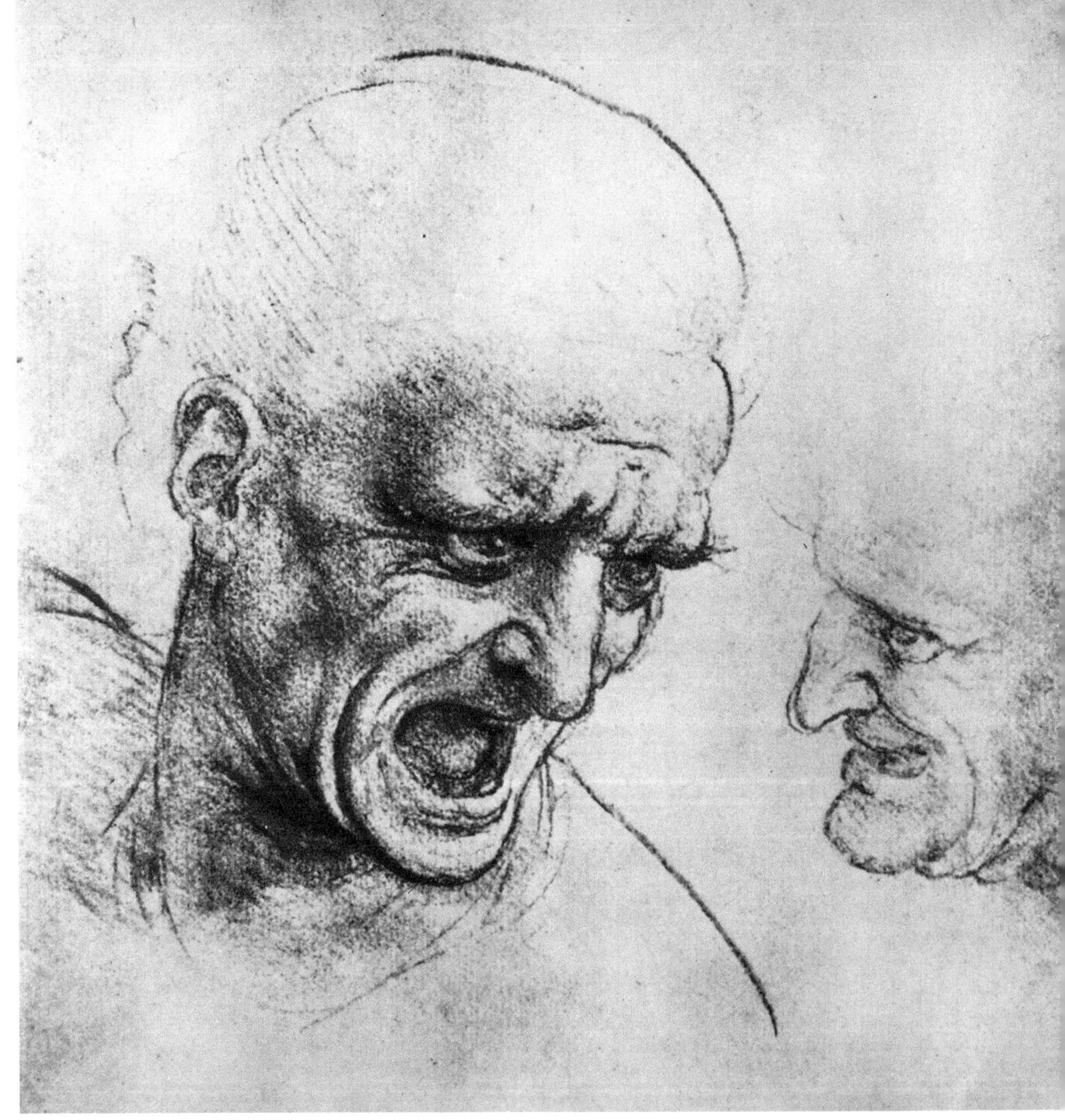

Heads of warriors.

portraits of all their figures, all with the manners and movements of him who painted them. And if he is lively in his speech and his gestures, his figures are equally lively ; and if the master is devout, the figures appear to be the same, with their necks bent ; and if the master does little, his figures seem to be portraits of laziness personified ; and if the master is poorly proportioned, the figures are of the same kind, and if he is mad, this is amply revealed in his pictures, which are deprived of all logic, the figures not attending to what they are doing, but looking here to the right, there to the left, as if they were dreaming. And thus, every characteristic of the painting corresponds to a characteristic of the painter himself.

Having repeatedly thought about the cause of this defect, it seems to me one must believe that the soul, which rules and governs the body, also forms our judgment, even before we have formed it ourselves ; * thus it is the soul that has shaped the whole figure of the man as it judges best, with the nose long, or short, or flat, and in the same way determined the height and general appearance ; and this judgment is so powerful it moves the arm of the painter and makes him copy himself, because it seems to the soul that this is the true way to paint a man, and that whoever does not do as it does, is mistaken. * And when it finds someone who resembles the body it has composed, it likes him and often falls in love with him ; and that is why many men fall in love with and marry women who resemble them and often the children born to them resemble their parents.

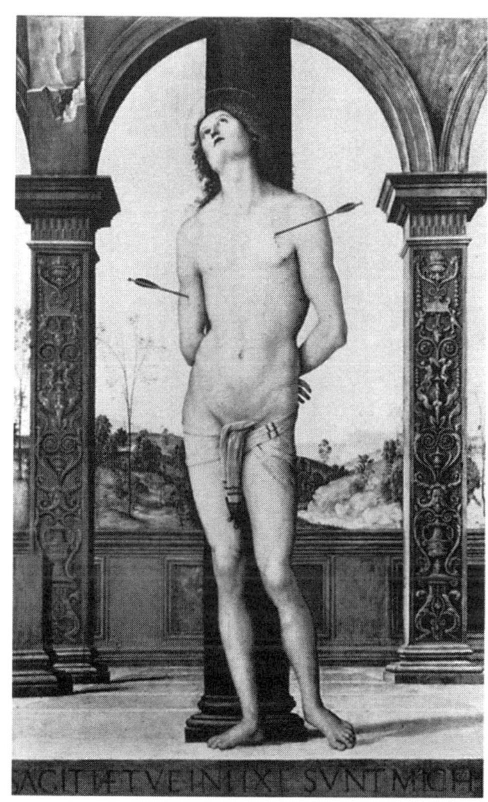

Perugino, *St. Sebastian* ; see no. 328.

Learning and Practice

The young man should first learn perspective, 329. *Training o the painte*
then the proportions of all things, next, he should work after a good master so that he becomes accustomed to beautiful forms ; next, after nature, to confirm the principles he has learned ; he should then study the works of various masters for some time ; and finally he should learn to apply and put into practice his art. *

Of drawing. Which is better, drawing from 330. *Appren-ticeship*
nature or from the antique ? And which is more difficult, outlines or light and shadow ? *

How to study. The painter should study me- 331. *Atten-tiveness to detail*
thodically and commit the least little thing to memory ; and he should note the differences between the members of the *(different)* animals and between *(their)* articulations.

How a young man should proceed in his stud- 332.
ies. The mind of the painter should concern itself continually with as many arguments as there are forms of notable objects that he sees ; and he should dwell on them, and remember them, and deduce rules from them, taking into consideration the place and the setting and the lights and shadows.

Of the sculptor and the painter . . . . Thus, 333. *Of acquirec knowledg*
many painters return to nature because they are not schooled enough in the theories of light and shadow and of perspective, and that is why they copy nature, for only in that way can they

apply *(these sciences)* without knowing and without reasoning in this regard about nature.

And among these painters there are some who look at the works of nature through panes of glass or other sheets or transparent nets, and they trace them on these transparent surfaces and then trace the outlines, enlarging them according to the rules of proportions, * and then fill the outlines with lights and shadows by noting the position and extent of the forms of the shadows and the lights. But this should not be praised except in those who know how to reproduce natural effects from imagination, and only employ these means in order to lighten their work-load a little and in order not to deviate in anything from the precise imitation of a thing that should be made with exact similitude. But that invention should be condemned when those who use it cannot do without it or think on their own, for through this laziness they destroy their mind and they do not know how to do anything well without this aid ; and they are always poor and mean in invention and in narrative compositions, although this is the final aim of this discipline, as I will show in another place . . . .

334. *Of studies and their order.* * . . . My opponent says that to acquire practice and make many works, * it is better that the first period of study be devoted to copying compositions in drawing or fresco by the different masters, for in that way one acquires rapidity in execution and good habits. The reply to this is that this practice would be good if founded upon excellent works by diligent masters. But as such masters are so rare that one hardly finds any, it is much safer to go to the works of nature rather than to those that have been imitated from nature with serious deviations ; for one thus acquires bad habits, and whoever can go to the fountain should not go to the water jar.

335. *Against routine work*

That in a work of importance a man should not trust to memory so entirely as to neglect to work after nature. Any master who wants it believed that he can recall all the forms and phenomena of nature * would seem to me to be endowed with great ignorance, for these phenomena are infinite, and our memory does not have a capacity sufficient for everything . . . . Therefore, painter, through the drawing you will first try to give to the invention or project that you had previously conceived in imagination, a form visible to the eye ; then add or remove whatever is necessary to satisfy you ; then pose the draped men or the nudes according to the arrangement of your work, and be careful that in regard to dimensions and relations of sizes according to perspective, there is nothing in your work that is not approved by reason or conforms to nature ; and this way you will be celebrated for your art.

336. *Paintings at every price*

Of the sad excuse given by those who call themselves painters without being worthy of it. There is a certain class of painters whose limited knowledge forces them to maintain themselves on the strength of the beauty of their gold and blue, * and who stupidly aver that they cannot give good work for poor payment, and that they would do as well as any other if they were well paid. Now, see how foolish these people are! Can they not make some works of worth, saying: these are masterpieces, and these are of

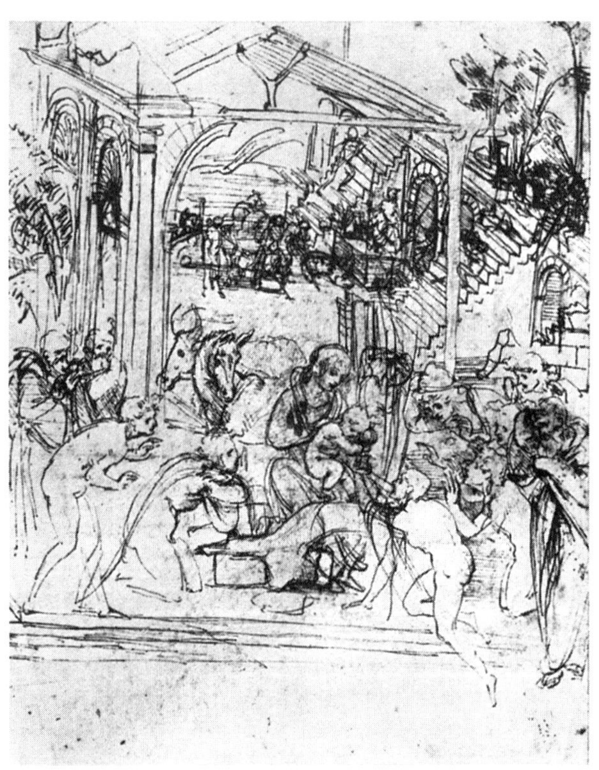

Study for *The Adoration of the Magi.*

moderate cost, and these are produced in large quantities? In this way they could have works at all prices.

337. *Stepping back from the work*

How to judge your own work .... I say that in painting you should have a flat mirror and often look at your work in it, which, when seen in reverse, will seem like the work of another to you and you will the better be able to judge its faults. It is also good to stop at times and engage in some recreation, for, when you return to your work, you will be able to judge it better while you make a serious mistake in staying at your work too long. It is also useful to go some distance from your work because it then appears smaller and it is easier to take it in at one glance and see the lack of harmony and proportions of the parts and colors of things. *

338. *That the painter should always wish to hear everyone's opinions of his work*

That the painter should always wish to hear everyone's opinions of his work. While one is painting, one should never refuse to hear the general opinion, for we know that a man, even if he is not a painter, knows the form of another man and can tell whether he is humpbacked, or has one shoulder higher than the other, or has too large a mouth or nose, or has other defects. And if we know that men can judge correctly the works of nature, we shall have to admit that they can judge our errors even better; for you know how much one errs in one's own work, and if you have not noticed this yourself, you can recognize it in others, and you will profit from the errors of others. Therefore, listen to others, always wish to hear everyone's opinions of his work, consider if the criticism is right or not and if so, make corrections, but if not, act as if you had not heard him or, if he is a man whom you esteem, show him the reasons why he is wrong.

Of the Painter's Ethics

The painter at work — rules for him. I remind you, painter, that if you discover some error in your work, either through your own judgment or through the advice of another, you should correct it so that when you show this work publicly, you will not show your shameful weakness * at the same time. And do not find excuses to make to yourself by persuading yourself that you will make up for your mistake in your next work, for the painting does not die at its birth, as music does, but bears witness to your ignorance for a long time ; and if you say to yourself that in making corrections you lose time which, if you would spend it on a new work, would bring you much profit, you should understand that the money you make beyond your daily needs is worth little, and if you want it in abundance, you will not be able to spend it, and it will not be yours . . .

339. *Against cupidity*

But if you will study and go over your works well, according to the two perspectives, the works you will leave will bring you more honor than the money *(you would make),* which is esteemed only for itself without regard to who owns it. The owner always arouses envy and is a target for thieves, and the fame of the rich man ends with his life, and only the fame of the treasure remains, but not of the treasurer. The glory of the excellence of mortals is much greater than that of their riches. How many emperors and princes have passed away without being remembered, although they sought out estates and riches in order to leave a great name behind ? And how many are there who lived in poverty, as to money, to become rich in excellence ? And this desire has been more successful for the worthy man than for the rich in proportion as his excellence surpassed riches . . . .

And if you excuse yourself by saying that you have children to feed, *(I say that)* they need very little ; and rather see to it that they are nourished on excellence, for this is a faithful wealth that does not abandon us except at death ; and if you say that first you wish to acquire a capital of money and an endowment for your old age, remember that the studies you have made will never fail you and do not let you grow old . . .

340. *Of the draperies that clothe figures and of their folds* . . . . And I do not say this for the masters, but for those who do not wish to teach and are certainly not masters, for whoever does not teach is afraid that he will be deprived of gain and whoever esteems gain abandons the study of what is taught by the works of nature, the teacher of painters. And these forget what they have learned, and what they have not learned they will not ever learn.

341. *Love and knowledge*

Of persons who blame him who works on feast days and investigates the works of God. Among the number of fools, there is a certain sect called hypocrites, who are constantly occupied with fooling themselves and others, but others more than themselves, though in fact they fool themselves more than others. These people blame painters who, on feast days, study the things belonging to the true knowledge of all the aspects of nature's works and who diligently contrive to acquire this knowledge as far as it is possible.

But let such critics be silent ; for through these means one learns to know Him who made so many marvelous things and in this way one comes to love the Inventor of all these things for, in truth, great love is born of a profound knowledge of the thing loved, and if you do not know it, you can only love it a little or not at all ; and if you love it because of the good you expect from it, and not because of its excellence, you are like the dog who wags his tail, stands on his hind legs, and fawns on him who may give him a bone, but if he knew the goodness of this man, and knew that it was directed toward him, he would love him all the more. *

342. *Contemplate in solitude*

Of the life of the painter in his studio. So that the health of the body should do no harm to that of the mind, the painter or draftsman should remain solitary, particularly when he is occupied with considerations and problems that, being constantly before him, furnish ample food for his memory. Alone you belong entirely to yourself ; with a companion, you belong only half to yourself, and all the less as his intercourse is less restrained ; with several companions these inconveniences will be multiplied.

"But," you say, "I behave as I see fit ; I will keep myself apart the better to study the forms of nature." I say that you will succeed poorly, for you cannot help frequently lending an ear to the chatter of your companions. And as one cannot serve two masters, you will not succeed in being a good companion, and even less in

Study for *The Madonna with the Cat.*

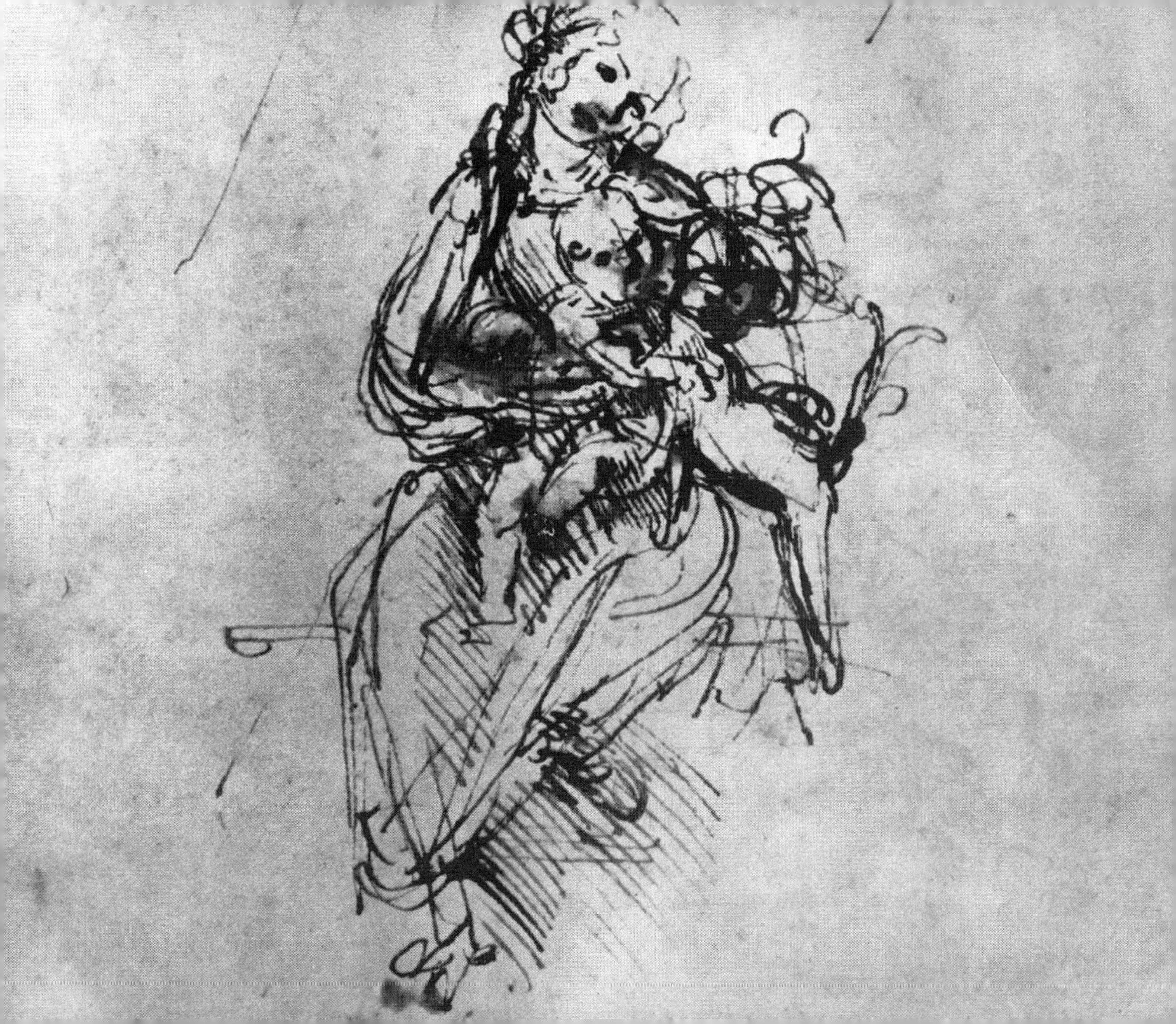

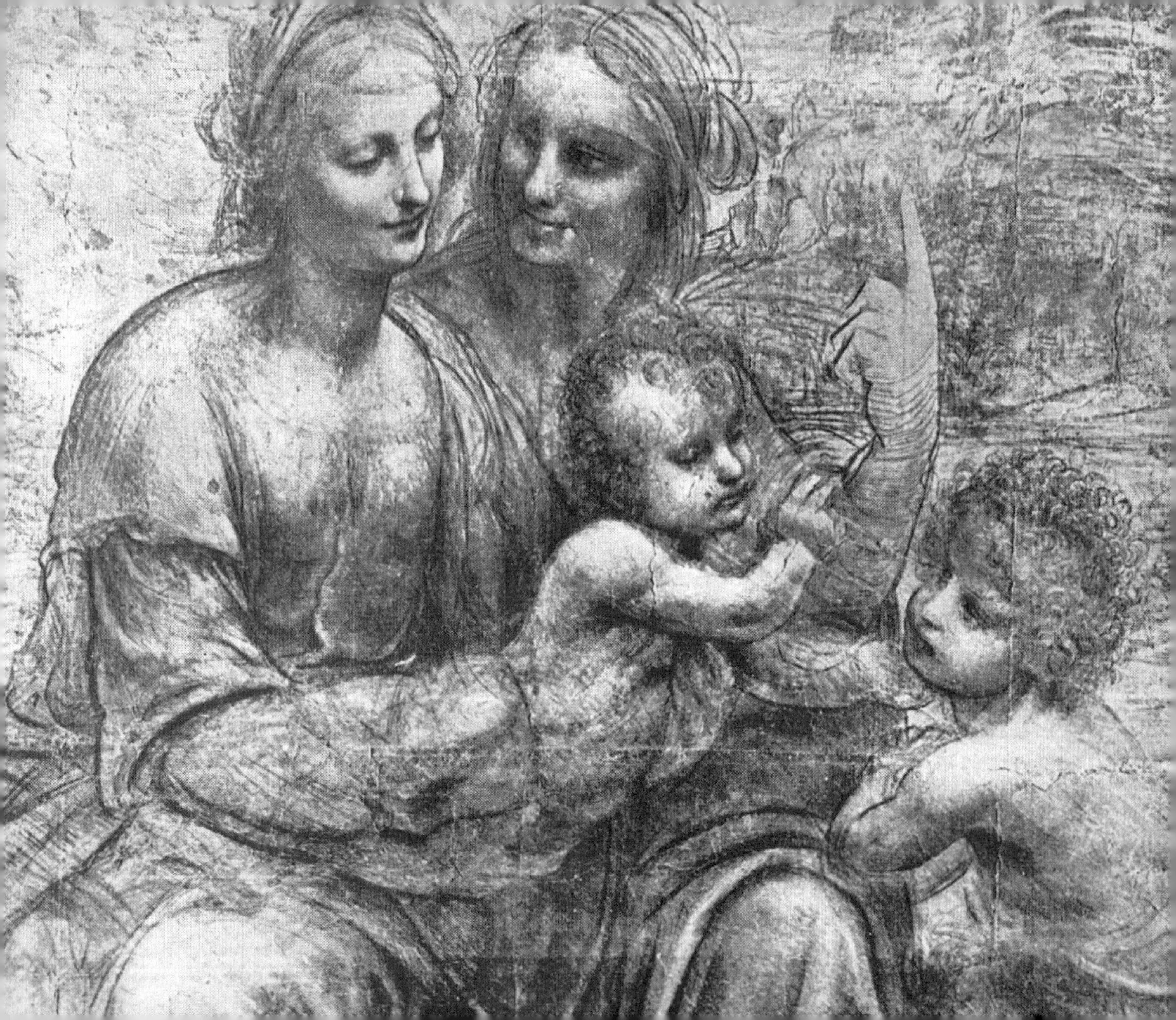

conducting your investigations concerning art. If you say, "I will go so far away from them that their words will not reach me to disturb me," I reply to this that you will be considered a madman. And remember that in so doing you will be alone in any case. If you, however, insist on having a companion, choose him with your studies in mind; this may be useful to you in those discussions to which one may be led by one's investigations. All other companionship would be very dangerous to you.

343. *Draw in company*

Whether it is better to draw in company or alone. I say and insist that it is better to draw in the company of others than alone, for several reasons: the first is that you will be ashamed to show yourself inferior to the other draftsmen, and this shame will lead you to study well; in the second place, rivalry will make you attempt to equal those who are more highly esteemed than you, and the praise given others will be a spur to you. Another reason is that you can learn the methods of those who do better than you, and if you do better than the others, you will profit by their mistakes, and the praise others will accord you will increase your strength. *

344.

Of the games in which draftsmen should exercise themselves. Draftsmen, if you wish to find profitable recreation in games, choose them so that they will be of use to you in your profession, that is, useful in forming the judgment of the eye in evaluating lengths and widths of objects. And to accustom the mind to such things, let one of you draw a straight line anywhere on a wall and let each one of you take a little twig or a straw in his hand and, at a distance of ten *braccia*, cut it to the length that the first line appears to him; then each should go close to the model and compare it to his guess; and he whose judgment is closest to the length of the model should be considered best and the winner and receive from all the others a prize agreed on in advance.

◄ Cartoon for *The Virgin and Child with St. Anne.*

Furthermore, you should judge distances in depth, that is, take a dart or stick, and then choose a point in front of you at a certain distance; and let each one say how many times he thinks the measure goes into the distance. Or again, *(see)* who can best draw a line of one *braccio*, which can be tested with a string. And games of this kind help the eye to acquire good judgment, which is the first thing for painting.

345. *The enclosure of mirrors*

Mirrors. If you take eight flat mirrors, each two *braccia* high and three *braccia* wide, and put them in a circle, they will constitute an eight-sided figure with a perimeter of sixteen *braccia* and a diameter of five. Whoever is inside can see himself in each direction an infinite number of times. Four mirrors placed in a square will do the same. *

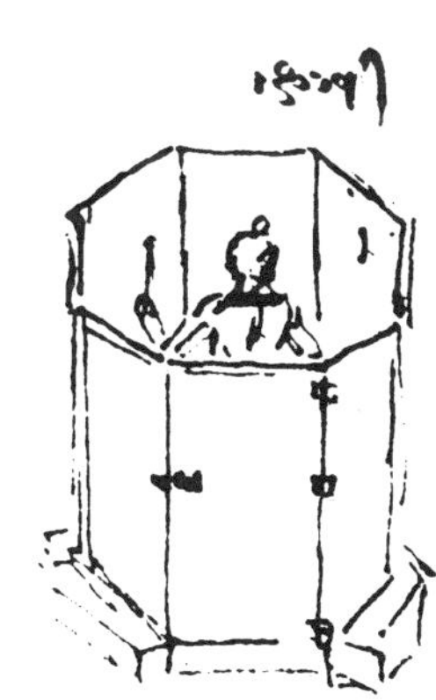

A figure enclosed in a structure of mirrors.

Memory and Attention

What rules to give to apprentices. We know well that sight is one of the quickest actions there is ; in an instant it receives an infinity of forms and yet it grasps only one thing at a time. Let us take that you, reader, look at this written page with one glance ; you will immediately judge that it is covered with various letters, but you would not know what letters they are or what their meaning is unless you consider them word for word and line for line in order to acquaint yourself with the text. In the same way, if you wish to climb to the top of a building, you have to go up step by step, otherwise it will be impossible to reach the top. And again, I say to you who are by nature inclined to this art, if you wish to have a true knowledge of the forms of things, begin by learning their details and do not go on to the second until you have committed the first to memory and have practiced it. If you do otherwise, you will waste time and very much prolong your studies. And remember to acquire care rather than facility. * 346. *Of diligence and metho[d] in studyin[g]*

I have experience of the advantage, when you are in bed in the darkness, in going over in the imagination the outlines of forms already studied or other noteworthy objects conceived by ingenious thought ; this is a recommendable practice and useful in fixing things in the memory. * 347. *Sharpenin[g] the memo[ry] at night*

348. *Training the memory*

If you want to be able to remember a face with ease, first learn by heart many heads, eyes, noses, mouths, chins, and throats, necks, and shoulders . . . .

You will find the same variety in the other parts ; you should draw them after nature and so fix them in your mind. Or, when you have to commit a work to memory, carry a notebook in which similar traits are recorded ; and, from the first sight of the face you wish to draw, note for yourself the nose or mouth nearest to it, making a small mark next to it so you can recognize it again at home.

Of horrible faces I do not speak : one remembers them without difficulty. *

349. *Stains on old walls*

I should not forget to mention among these precepts a new device for study which may seem trivial and almost ridiculous, but is, nevertheless, of some use in exciting the mind to diverse inventions. This is it : if you look at walls covered with many stains or made of stones of different colors, with the idea of imagining some scene, you will see in it a similarity to landscapes adorned with mountains, rivers, rocks, trees, plains, broad valleys, and hills of all kinds. You may also see in it battles and figures with lively gestures and strange faces and costumes and an infinity of things which you can reduce to separate and complete forms. And with these walls and colors it is as with the sound of bells ; in their ringing you can find all the sounds and words that you wish to imagine. *

350.

Painter of narrative compositions, do not paint the elements of your painting with sharp outlines, for the same will happen to you as to many painters of all kinds who want the least little stroke of charcoal to be definite ; and these may very well acquire riches but not fame for their art, since the creature represented often does not have movements appropriate to the intention, but when the artist has finished a beautiful and agreeable arrangement of elements, it seems damaging to him to move them either higher or lower, or more to the back or to the front. These masters do not deserve any praise for their art.

Have you never seen poets compose their verses ? They do not become tired of writing beautiful letters and do not object to crossing out certain verses in order to write them again better. Therefore, painter, compose the limbs of your figures in general terms, and first see to it that the movements are appropriate to the state of mind of the beings who occupy your composition, and only then think of the beauty and the quality of the details.

For you must understand that if this unfinished sketch does happen to agree with your idea, it will be all the better when it is enhanced by the perfection of all its parts. I have seen clouds and stains on walls which have stimulated me to make beautiful inventions on different subjects ; and these stains, although in themselves devoid of any perfection in any part, did not lack perfection in the movements and other effects. *

Notes

Page XXI

Windsor Castle : C. Pedretti, *Leonardo da Vinci : Fragments at Windsor Castle from the Codex Atlanticus,* London, 1957.

Page XXII

care : A. C. Pierantoni, *Studi sul libro della pittura di Leonardo da Vinci,* Rome, 1921 ; L. H. Heydenreich, Introduction to P. McMahon, *Treatise on Painting by Leonardo da Vinci,* Princeton, 1956.

system : In fact, the references in the notebooks on classification are inconsistent and the same proposition, such as the one on the basic principle of the theory of reflections, may be given different numbers.

lost : Most recently, C. Pedretti, " La cronologia del trattato della pittura. " *L'Arte,* 1959, 1960.

Page XXIV

misunderstandings : See the concordance in McMahon, pp. 399-424.

Pensées : P. Valéry, *Divers essais sur Léonard de Vinci,* Paris, 1931, p. 58.

followed it : For example, in a passage on landscapes, McMahon, no. 968, " This is proven by the figure in the margin. "

Page XXV

yet : L. H. Heydenreich, in *Kunstchronik,* IV, 1951, pp. 255 ff.; A. Marinoni, "I manoscritti di Leonardo da Vinci et le loro edizioni," *Leonardo, saggi e ricerche,* Rome, 1954.

rendered : B. Migliorini, "Panorama dell'italiano quattrocentesco," *Rassegna della letteratura italiana,* 1955, no. 2; on Leonardo's style see I. del Lungo, "Leonardo scrittore," *Leonardo da Vinci. Conferenze fiorentine,* Milan, 1910; G. Fumagalli, "Leonardo e Poliziano," *Leonardo, ieri e oggi,* Pisa, 1959.

Page 2

Paolo Giovio : For the original Latin text of the *Vita Leonardo Vincii,* see G. Tiraboschi, *Storia della letteratura italiana,* vol. XIII, Milan, 1824, p. 2494-2495, or J. P. Richter, *The Literary Works of Leonardo da Vinci,* vol. I, 1939, p. 2.

Page 4

King Louis : Louis XII of France.

Pisans : Actually the Milanese.

Gaddiano : Codex Magliabecchiano, Florence, Biblioteca Nazionale, cl. XVII, 17. Ed. C. Frey, Berlin, 1892.

Page 5

Valentino : Cesare Borgia.

Martelli : The author confuses Leonardo's stay in Milan (1482-1499), during the reign of Lodovico Il Moro and his return to Florence (1500-1506), interrupted by a short period in the service of Cesare Borgia, with his second stay in Milan (1506-1513) in the service of France.

Page 6

Vasari : *Le vite de' più eccellenti architetti, pittori, e scultori italiani,* ed. G. Milanesi, Florence, 1897, vol. IV.

Page 9

Academia : The print actually has *Leonardi.*

Page 10

Christian : In the 1550 edition, but deleted in the 1568 edition.

Page 13

them : Pinxit Virgilius Neptunum, pinxit Homerus;
Dum maris undisoni per vada flectit equos.
Mente quidem vates illum conspexit uterque,
Vincius est oculis; jureque vincit eos.

The play on words between Leonardo da Vinci's name and *vincius* and *vincit* is lost in translation.

Page 14

Milan : Error, 1482.

Page 15

France : Louis XII.

Page 16

Duke : His father, Francesco Sforza.

desire : Tal che l'opera fosse ritardata dal desio.

Page 17

Florence : April, 1500.

Page 23

repented : Second edition, 1568.

Page 25

sixty-five : He was actually sixty-seven.

legion : Vince costui pur solo
Tutti altri; e vince Fidia e vince Apelle
E tutto il lor vittorioso stuolo.

Page 26

Painting : Qu. An. II, 6r.

delivered : It is difficult to say which treatises have been lost since Leonardo gives no precise information on what he actually wrote. There are two particularly interesting witnesses : Luca Pacioli and Benvenuto Cellini. In a dedication of his *De Divina Proportione* (Venice, 1509), dated February 9, 1498, Pacioli wrote that Leonardo " had already finished with all diligence the worthy books on painting and human movement. " This first Treatise, whose existence cannot be denied, may possibly be identified with Ms. BN 2038 (Paris, Institut de France) according to a very plausible theory suggested by L. H. Heydenreich. This first version of the Treatise, compiled between 1490 and 1495, already contained the most penetrating passages of the *Paragone,* the remarks on the order of study, the management of a workshop, and even on the problems of the human figure and of shadow and light ; however, it is still sketchy on landscape.

Benvenuto Cellini relates in his *Trattati dell' orificeria e della scultura* (ca. 1550 ; ed. Florence, 1857) that in 1542 in France he acquired a manuscript that contained " among other admirable things, the most beautiful discourse on perspective ever composed by any man . . . " This was not an original manuscript by Leonardo himself but a compilation, made from the notebooks in Melzi's possession, which has not come down to us.

Page 30

my own : The only merits of the Patricians are those derived from their ancestors. See Plutarch.

state it : These paragraphs do not represent a continuous argument but are a collection of disparate ideas and pronouncements provisionally brought together, most probably with the intention of eventually making a selection and arranging them. G. Fumagalli has suggested that the passage on the poor peddler, with its irony and false modesty, refers to a collection of jests and light works.

Page 35

certain : At an unknown date a reader who respected theological doctrine crossed out this passage in the Codex Urbinas.

operations : The expression *vere e note* brings to mind elementary mathematics, but Leonardo has turned to the semi-mechanical or applied sciences, such as optics, the theory of mirror images, the arts of military and civil engineering, etc. It is into this catagory that he intends to put art.

repose : The sentence is evidently inaccurate. " Volume, the placing of figures, " etc., are not part of " lighting " but are among the " first principles of painting. " This slip is significant, however, of the side taken by Leonardo and of the predominant role he gives to chiaroscuro (similar lists of the fundamental elements of the visible are traditionally part of treatises on the theory of optics).

Page 36

distance : Here Leonardo reasserts that painting is a purely theoretical or intellectual science, a stand he had opposed in the previous fragment (no. 14), where he found greater nobility in the manual operation. Furthermore, it is surprising that he should class music with the sciences of continuous quantitites. He was not thinking of the audible intervals but of the length of the vibrating strings.

demonstration : To interpret this passage as an apologia for mathematical physics would be an anachronism. Geometry, by its reduction to first principles and by its use of reasoning from then on, is meant only to serve as an example of the method. Experience enters into this reduction and, finally, into the confrontation of reality and the results obtained. The title indicates that the passage is incomplete, and it may be completed as follows : Painting is a deductive science because, like geometry, it begins with basic principles — physics, optics, and mathematics — and, on the basis of these, goes on to explain and demonstrate all aspects of the visible ; but it is also an experimental science because it results in a work which, by its fidelity and clarity, permits verification of the process.

optics : The text has *prospettivi* which is to be understood in its widest sense.

cube : Here he is referring to squaring and cubing as a result of mensuration but in the rest of the sentence he seems to be thinking of the geometric process of extracting roots.

Page 37

levels : According to Aristotle's physics each element has a natural place at a level of the universe corresponding to its specific weight.

places : This eulogy of sight is one of Leonardo's most brilliant and impassioned pieces. It should be noted that in considering sight as coextensive with thinking to the extent that it is concerned with the perception and organization of nature, he amplifies a theme already developed by Alberti. He does not distinguish between sensory perception and mental activity, and this permits him to establish a hierarchy of disciplines in terms of their sensory principles. Leonardo's originality does not lie in this, however, but in his further development of the argument. He attributes to sight all the higher aptitudes by conferring a universality on it that is like the *a priori* intuition fundamental to his philosophy.

words : That is, poetry, grammar, and rhetoric, all the disciplines connected with the trivium of traditional teaching.

Page 38

things : This remark is directed against descriptive poetry. The fragment is a part of a long passage that also includes entries nos. 17, 21 and 43.

Calumny : Plutarch quotes Simonides as saying that " painting is mute poetry, and poetry, speaking painting. " Leonardo changes " speaking " into " blind. " *The Calumny* by Apelles had already been cited by Alberti, who followed Lucian, as the prototype of paintings depicting psychological states. It had been recreated by Botticelli and Mantegna. Moreover, an allusion to it is essential to a confrontation of the two arts before establishing that the "mute poetry" of the picture is by nature more effective than the " blind painting " of words.

judged : Following traditional theories of psychology, Leonardo here assumes that the original sensation passes from the sensory organ to the community of senses or interior sense, which " judges " and compares it in order to recognize the object it stems from. It is also in this community of senses that imaginary images are formed ; they are then transmitted to the memory which retains the most successful ones for some time. In a later stage the content of memory becomes generalized, thus resulting in a universal concept.

darkness : Leonardo calles this interior vision *l'occhio tenebroso.*

to him : Leonardo's discussion vacillates between two points : 1. Vision, and therefore painting, is more immediate than speech, which includes poetry ; and 2. vision is more adept at imaginative creation. Out of this emerges the vital idea of a nonverbal, nonconceptual language.

Page 39

nature : Leonardo's slow and detailed analysis of the resources of each art avowedly intends to establish that neither poetry nor music can compete with painting. By emphasizing that poetry is a verbal unfolding, he underlines the fundamental concept of harmony or *proporzionalità*, which is part of the classical definition of beauty as an entity superior to its components. The very apt reference to the simultaneous chords of music is here interjected in passing, but the actual evalution of music and painting follows later.

painter : The allusion is to the well-known verse in Horace's *Ars poetica : pictoribus atque poetis / quidlibet audendi semper fuit aequa potestas* (Painters and poets have always had the same license to dare all). Having decided to maintain that poetry has no subject of its own, Leonardo forces the conclusion at the cost of a paradox : in the end he attempts to base the superiority of painting on its ability to absorb all the other disciplines and on its imaginative powers, but here he uses these two qualitites as reasons for the weakness of poetry.

Page 41

more : This little incident illustrates Leonardo's liking for moralizing fables. It is about Matthias Corvinus, king of Hungary, who was an important patron of the Florentine workshops and friend of the humanists. The anecdote may have been based on the misadventure of Angelo Poliziano, the friend and court poet of Lorenzo de' Medici. Poliziano had sent the king a poem praising his own art together with a letter in which he offered his services as historiographer and apologist. The letter, copies of which were circulated among the Italian humanists, alluding to the king's generosity toward painters and sculptors, set forth poetry's superiority over architecture in rather haughty terms. The king never replied. His royal position, moreover, enhances the speech given him by Leonardo expressing the principal motif of harmony or *proporzionalità creata in istanti*.

Page 42

noises : The rest of this text discusses technical aspects that are better expressed in our next entry. The contrast between the gentleman-painter and the laborer-sculptor are, no doubt, superficial, but Leonardo handles deftly and brilliantly a theme that was to become one of the platitudes of the Renaissance. Although it would be tempting to see an attack on Michelangelo in this passage there is no evidence for such an interpretation. However, it is likely that Michelangelo, who must have known Leonardo's words either directly or indirectly, had him in mind in a letter stating that he who has written that painting is more noble than sculpture, knows no more than "my nurse" does.

perfect : This personal information adds considerably to the interest of the passage although the compiler's confusion distracts from it somewhat (an omission makes the fifth paragraph almost unintelligible). Nonetheless, the combination of technical observations and specious arguments, which are more fully developed in the next entry, lend the whole passage interest.

Page 43

furnishes it : Volume (the third dimension) is inherent to the medium in sculpture and therefore considered as something supplied by nature. Once the sculptor has made the shape, the shadows that convey the impression of relief are automatically formed.

in any way : Despite Donatello's work, Leonardo considers illusionistic effects in relief weak.

nature : Leonardo's interest in the techniques of glazed terracottas should not be exaggerated. He had ample opportunity to observe their success in Tuscany and here uses them to support an artificial thesis although mosaics, "true painting for all eternity," also then being revived in Florence, would have made a better example.

back : As the two views are complementary, the sculptor does no more with one figure than the painter with two. Leonardo counters the arguments presented by those partial to sculpture who insist that the sculptor creates a multiplicity of contours while the painter produces only one. This argument is actually based on the four main views of a piece of sculpture (front, back, and two sides). Toward the middle of the sixteenth century these arguments were assembled and expanded with tedious care, but

Leonardo already calls attention to them around 1500. About the same time, in a painting that is now lost, Giorgione depicted by means of mirrors and highly reflective surfaces, a single figure from the four principal sides sculptors claimed as uniquely theirs.

Page 44

planes : Distantie interposte infra le prime parte dei corpi et le seconde. Literally, the texts asked for a visible, progressive flattening of the relief of each figure, but it is unlikely that this is what Leonardo wanted.

eye : The naturalistic reliefs of the Renaissance do, in fact, employ two kinds of perspective. One is linear perspective, which is identical to the "flat" perspective of painters, the other consists of a progressive flattening of the relief, which is at first pronounced but becomes less marked as the objects recede into the distance. As a rule the use of both these systems together results in a practically insoluble conflict.

Page 46

painting : This passage is the conclusion of the one cited above that begins by describing the vast difference between the appearance of the sculptor's and the painter's workshop (no. 30).

nature : For Leonardo the concepts "substance" and "nature" of things have been discredited by the way they have been used in scholastic dialectics.

knowledge : This fragment is an introduction to a collection of anatomical drawings with commentaries. Another passage from it is given below (no. 198).

Page 49

divine : The sum of the cosmic images, transmitted to the pupil of the eye through space, constitutes a limited experience, in which the spirit passes from scientific wonder to religious ecstasy. *Emisfero* (hemisphere), or the globe of the eye, suggests an implicit analogy between the cosmos and the eye. The different ways the theme is taken up at different times in the texts corresponds to successive revisions of the concept.

God : The title and opening sentence are quoted from *The Lives of the Sophists* by Philostratus. Beginning with Alberti, the sentence came into general use in apologies of art. The second part paraphrases a passage from Dante (Inferno, Canto XI, verses 100-105 : *Si che vostr'arte a Dio quasi è nipote ;* so that your art is, as it were, the grandchild of the Deity). Dante meant art in its widest, medieval interpretation, which included all the crafts and all the disciplines by which man after having questioned nature, brought its works to their culmination. According to Leonardo, painting closely resembles the medieval arts.

Page 50

perfection : This passage is more than a *pro domo* plea for the artist who is slow and unable to finish a work. The artist must also be superior to what he produces because art is the product of intelligence and because intelligence being universal by nature, the work of art is unique. The quality of the work derives from the mind that conceived it ; and artistic achievement resulting from chance is a contradiction in itself.

mathematician : Intended as a companion piece to the inscription forbidding those who do not know geometry access to Plato's Academy.

sight : This famous exclamation belongs to the debate between the poet and the painter partially cited above (nos. 22, 26, 28). It ends in a hymn to painting which, through design, has become the universal principle of the mind (no. 17).

air : The absent-minded artist, absorbed in his own reveries, was already a well-known figure at that time. For Leonardo, however, attentive observation is essential to art.

of it : The insistence on a conscientious effort and a critical faculty balances the preceding advice and completes the symbolism of the mirror.

Page 51

imaginary : Per esentia, presentia o imaginazione, that is, necessity, either accidental or fictive, is an original variation of the scholastic distinction between the degrees of being.

Page 53

wind : This long, lyric description brings out the cosmic themes (the battle of the elements) that so often occupied Leonardo. As such it expounds an idea for which the solemn formulation of the first sentence has prepared the way. The impassioned though somewhat confused flow of this diffuse reverie attests to its spontaneity as well as to the authenticity of Leonardo's tendency to balance the pleasant with the horrible.

laws : This short fragment is taken from a passage in which Leonardo praises the diversity of visual phenomena that are the subject of painting in order to lessen the prestige of sculpture. Painting is not passively subjected to reality but becomes consciousness. Thus a third faculty is added to universal observation and imaginative creation : the ability to put oneself in the place of nature through reasoning.

Page 54

distance : At different distances different kinds of trees might accidentally take on the same color since aerial perspective will act differently on each, but this cannot occur when all the trees are at the same distance from the eye.

Page 55

defect : Leonardo takes up the reasons for this tendency toward monotony in types of figures when he discusses the psychology of the painter (see no. 328).

insects : In Leonardo's day it was usual in the universities to teach human anatomy by means of the bodies of dead animals. From this naïve expedient Leonardo developped the idea of a comparative anatomy. The theme will be discussed in greater detail later on, but the passage is given here as a reminder that the law of analogy is an indispensable counterpart of the concern with the infinite varieties of forms.

Page 57

writing : Were it necessary to justify the inclusion of such visions in this collection, it should be pointed out that on 79r of the Codex Atlanticus describing a cataclysm similar to *the Flood* (W 12665r ; no. 64), Leonardo abruptly ends with the statement that the rest of the matter will be discussed in the *Book on Painting* (e 'l resto di tal discorso si tratterà nel libro de pittura distintamente): The title on the reverse of the sheet with no. 64, *The Flood and its representation in painting* (W 12665v ; no. 65) is no less significant in this respect.

Tales : The sketches for the stories about the horrible giant and about the catastrophe of Mount Taurus are scattered throughout the Codex Atlanticus, and it is impossible to establish a definite sequence. Plans for the whole work appear amid narrative fragments, descriptions, and essays already given final form. At times Leonardo juxtaposes. The intention of the first passage is literary, for it parodies romances in the same way as Luigi Pulci's *Il Morgante Maggiore* and other comic-heroic poems (a verse of one that Leonardo had copied out in Ms. I, 139r, Institut de France, may have served as model). Benedetto Dei, to whom this tale is addressed, was a traveler and journalist as well as a friend of Leonardo's. His voyages in Asia Minor may have inspired the second fantastic tale in which precise details, worked out with daring and verve, enliven information that is in part taken from Ptolemy's *Geography* (Ulm, 1482).

Page 62

make : By this injunction Leonardo

suggests to the painter within the framework of a picture a point of view that has something of the scope of the film and is beyond the resources of painting. The subject, long familiar to Italian poetry, was again taken up by Poliziano in his *Stanze* : a paradise of edifices and gardens is created but the northern side, with its shipwrecks, counterbalances it with the strange and catastrophic.

Page 63

appearance : In these two fragments the skeleton of a fossilized sea monster, such as a whale, is the starting point for a tribute to the might of an animal that is now embedded in the earth in a spot once ruled by the sea. The biological and geological aspects are united in the theme of universal evolution much as they are in the passage from Ovid *(Metamorphoses*, XV), which served Leonardo as model. The fragment on the cave (no. 255) also seems to date from this period (1480-1483) during which Leonardo was influenced by Ovid whom he had translated and whose ideas on nature and universal life he developed.

battle : This long description with its precise wealth of detail, belongs to the first draft of the Treatise, written about 1490. Thus it antedates the unfinished *Battle of Anghiari*, begun in 1503, by almost fifteen years.

color : The translation rectifies what seems to have been an inadvertent switch of the words *fumo* and *polvere* in the original manuscript.

Page 64

reddish : There is an omission at this point that makes it difficult to reconstitute the original text.

Page 65

flood : This new description was meant to be added to the Treatise and may be dated about 1515.

Page 67

shade : That is, the lower part according to a note in Ar. 127v.

center : This sentence suggests that in the previous one Leonardo had a whirlpool in mind though he may have used as his model water washing up on a beach. Indeed, from here on the apocalyptic fantasy gradually seems to turn into a series of observations on stormy weather on a beach. Moreover, this is borne out by the notes in the margin of the page, which include the name of the coastal village of Piombino among other related notations.

Page 68

speaker : These notes are in a volume from the Foster Collection in the Victoria and Albert Museum, London, which goes back to 1495.

Page 70

Albizzi : Despite the title, leaders of the Florentine (correctly restituted by Fumagalli), this list includes the leaders of both sides. The battle, fought on June 29, 1440, saw the victory of the Florentine forces under Lodovico, Patriarch of Aquilea, over the Milanese, under the *condottiere* Niccolò Piccinino ; they were aided by exiled Florentines who were the enemies of the Medici.

wyvern : The Milanese standard.

troops : In this passage he twice wrote "the enemy" instead of "our troops," a significant slip of the pen as he had just left the services of Milan.

trophy : This note is not in Leonardo's own hand but in that of the friend or secretary who, in 1482, had copied out Leonardo's offer of services to Lodovico Il Moro. It is not known where Leonardo got the information he uses here. Machiavelli is usually suggested but the description in his *Historie Fiorentine* (Vol. V, ch. 33) is quite different. Probably the signoria supplied him with an impersonal outline only.

Page 74

science : CU, 32r ; McMahon, no. 67.

"naturally" and "according to the position" are always given this definition when underlined in the text.

object : Of course, this would not be true of a circular object and when the source is on the perpendicular.

most : See the diagram below :

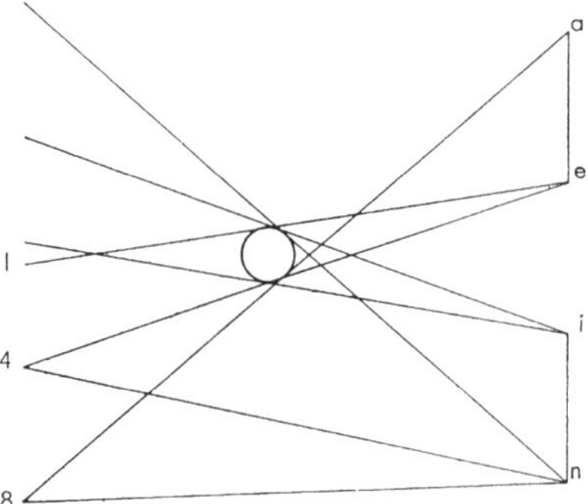

darker : The wall *an* is pierced at *ei.* The problem is to determine the intensity of the shadows on the surface *1-8* and no difficulties arise in the construction of the shadows on *1-4.* As for the others, in the remainder of the note, here omitted, Leonardo explains that point *8* "sees" the whole of wall *an,* hence two parts shadow to one part light result, and that point *4* is lighter because it "sees" only *en,* hence as much light as shadow. However, the reasoning is obviously wrong since he forgets that *4,* instead of "seeing" *ae,* "sees" the dark side of the opaque body in the center. Nonetheless, the text is interesting because of the symmetry he postulates between rays of light and rays of shadow and because of the transition he thus forms to the theory of reflections.

Page 97

it : The note is accompanied by a sketch showing that all the points on a given surface send their images to each point on a parallel surface facing it.

relief : These two statements contain the essence of the theoretical problems of "painting as a mirror" : Perspective — both linear and aerial — and the theory of luminosity and reflection proceed from the sending out of rays and images. Shadow is the "negative" continuation of the "pyramids" and gives rise to the volumes that it causes and that are revealed by it in this empty and vibrant space of rays.

shutters : Despite the opening comparisons, this passage does not introduce a wave theory of light. The unfinished sentence most probably introduces a description of an experiment in a dark room.

Page 98

fall : These effects are probably obtained by varying the distance or angle of the surface on which the image is to fall. This would bring about striking false "diminutions" in perspective and false foreshortenings.

Page 99

to ly : What is particularly interesting in this and the preceding passage is that Leonardo quite naturally combines the idea of the "visual pyramid" of perspective and that of the "pyramid" of directed light or the cone of shadow. When a source of light replaces the eye the shadow of the object lighted "draws" the outline in the foreshortening as it would be seen.

with it : D. Gioseffi, *Perspectiva artificialis ; per la storia della prospettiva,* Trieste, 1957 ; J. White, *The Birth and Rebirth of Pictorial Space,* London, 1957 ; and especially, E. Panofsky, "Die Perspektive als symbolische Form," *Vorträge der Bibliothek Warburg,* 1924-25.

Page 100

perspective : J. Baltrusaitis, *Perspectives curieuses,* Paris, 1955. G. P. Lomazzo, *Trattato della pittura,* Milan, 1584, following Melzi, notes that Leonardo painted a dragon fighting a lion which was an astounding thing to see and also horses meant for François de Valois, King of France, according to the principles of anamorphosis. G. Pedretti, *Studi Vinciani,* Geneva, 1957 pp. 68 ff., has brought together the principle passages on this subject :

Ms. A, 42v, 97v; Ar., 62r; and special uses of the system Ms. A, 38v, this last is also in CU, 139v (McMahon, no. 497).

Page 101

parts : In these lines Leonardo gives an almost word for word translation of the preface to the *Perspectiva Communis* — that is, optics — by John Peckham (died 1292). No text could be more appropriate to Leonardo's *Treatise on Painting.*

Page 102

rules : It is not known to what work these numbers refer.

buildings : It is impossible to check whether linear perspective has been used correctly in a landscape in which the same kind of objects located in different positions may also vary in size.

it : Quando has been amended to read *quanto.*

Page 104

confused : Despite the impression Leonardo's choice of words here gives, he does not believe that the visual rays emanate from the eye (see no. 105). The similarity between the eye and the source of light is here intentionally limited to what relates to all instances of linear perspective, that is, where the geometrical construction does not have to take the propagation of rays into consideration. Furthermore, this fragment gives a good description of the yellow spot of the retina.

river : On a calm sea the horizon is determined by the tangent going from the eye to the curved surface of the water; on the other hand, on a plane tangential to the surface of the earth, that begins where the spectator is located — a condition that would be fulfilled by a gently rising plane — the glance would in theory move on without ever being arrested. According to Leonardo, the Nile Valley approximately fulfills this condition.

distances : Without the mountains to indicate scale, the spectator would be unaware of the great distance and the effect would merely be one of mists.

wall cd : Parte has been amended to read *parete,* which is all the more justifiable since this fragment is taken from the Codex Urbinas, a sixteenth century copy not written by Leonardo himself.

line : It is possible that an error has crept into the text in the process of copying. The idea of infinity and of parallel lines that meet there may not have been clear to Leonardo, but it is not clear how he distinguished between the line parallel to *bs* and the line which goes from the eye to *s* when *s* is at infinity.

Page 105

size : In effect, this proposition completely condemns "flat" perspective on the ground that it gives the same size to juxtaposed objects seen at different angles.

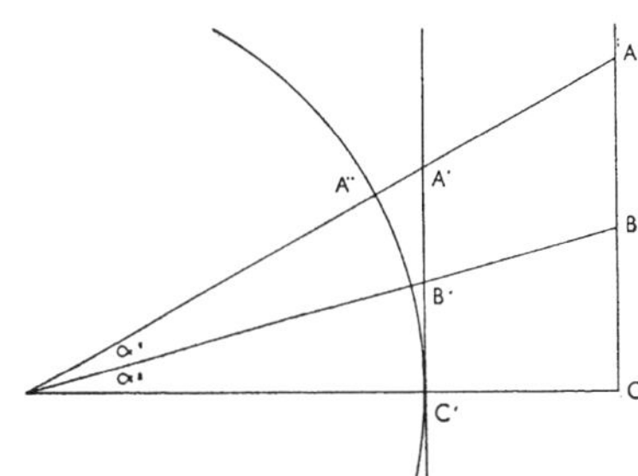

$\overline{AB} = \overline{BC}$; the angle α_1, which "sees" $\overline{AB}$ is smaller than α_2, which "sees" $\overline{BC}$. Therefore, in perspective rendering $\overline{AB}$ should appear smaller than $\overline{BC}$; flat perspective, however, would show $\overline{AB}$ and $\overline{BC}$ as equal. Spherical perspective corrects this by replacing $\overline{AC}$ by the projection $\overline{A''C'}$ on $\overline{A'C'}$.

double : Euclid already noted that the size of an object (y) and its distance form the eye (x) are inversely proportional. But in another place (CU, 146r-147v; McMahon, no. 491), Leonardo claims to have discovered the formula through observation.

other : A comparison with other passages, such as nos. 140 and 142, shows that this simple perspective is the same as the one called "natural" perspective elsewhere. The "surface all the parts of which are at the same distance from the eye" can only be a dome and Leonardo here has just such a surface in mind for the painting.

nearer : The semi-circular cross section made by the wall *gf* results in the correct appearance so that the more distant objects look smaller. Plane perspective, on the other hand, contradicts this rule.

parts : Left blank in the manuscript, see the note *spectator* below.

two : That it should be rectangular.

Page 106

intervenes : The text has *quanto l'ochio è più naturale.*

spectator : Leonardo seems to have changed his mind or his terminology while rewriting this passage. Hence the space left blank for a number of subdivisions. The "first part" is spherical perspective projected on a flat surface; this he also calls "natural" although he uses this term elsewhere for perspective of perception that is not constructed. The "second practice" is perspective with a fixed point of view, that is, both the traditional system and anamorphosis. At times he calls this "accidental or artificial" because it is valid only for a predetermined point of view and at times "combined" because it combines with the "natural" perspective of perception, which rectifies the distortions.

invention : Anamorphosis — but the statement is just as applicable to plane perspective.

perspective : I have already emphasized that in its own way plane perspective is also "combined." The preceding passage indicates that Leonardo was aware of this fact.

eye : That is, presumably, the surface of the eyeball, particularly the part covering the pupil. On the way it cuts the "visual pyramids" see no. 101 and the accompanying drawing (p. 91).

wall : Instead the wall tends to compensate by having the opposite effect.

Page 107

below : The text actually has above but in our edition the drawing appears below.

natural : Anamorphosis.

el main : Term of unknown origin.

Page 108

directions : *ox* exemplifies plane perspective, *op* natural perspective, and *on* anamorphosis.

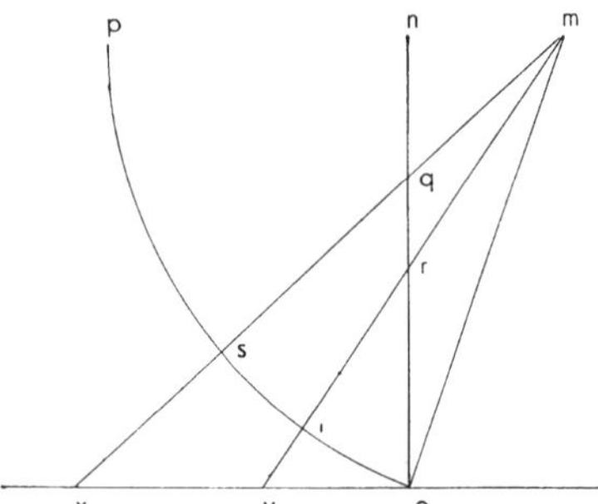

cliff : The explanation, which Leonardo does not give here but which is easily deduced from his principles, is that the air, saturated with humidity, veils the flat beach so that it seems farther away, but that the cliff, whose upper part rises into more transparent air, is seen at its true distance. See, for example, no. 183.

background : Not the outlines but the modeling create the relief.

Page 109

outside : The "region of fire" as an exterior covering of the universe is an Aristotelian concept that Leonardo employs as a mere form of speech since he describes it as "darkness."

Monboso : Possibly the Monte Rosa. The mythical element that creeps into the passage farther along is significant ; thus, in the next sentence the four rivers are reminiscent of the four rivers of Paradise. Leonardo's visionary tendencies are always prone to expression in relation to geographical or geological descriptions.

Page 111

darkness : There can be no doubt as to the reconstruction of the text necessitated by an inkspot on the page.

Page 112

themselves : Where they are intercepted.

source : From its context, it becomes clear that this passage is meant to explain how the visual images cross in the pupil without becoming confused or superimposed. Clearly, however, the solution is connected with the general theory of reflection and the lighting of colors (see no. 165).

white : Leonardo here wavers between the two definitions, white as a color and white as light.

Page 113

therein : Colored reflections emanate from solid bodies in the same way as do visual images ; indeed, they are the same thing, each being a particular aspect of the transmission of light and luster. And, Leonardo adds, the same is true of shadows, for darkness is also an active force and the "shadow rays" also throw their reflections on objects (see no. 118). A non-mathematical law, the unity of type, was to Leonardo's mind proof of the basic unity of such phenomena as colored shadows, the visual image and its "perspective," the radiance of the sun, the reflection of its light, and the obscurity of darkness. It is significant that he uses the same example, only slightly altered, to illustrate the effects of colored light (no. 157) and the presence of colored reflections (no. 164). There are innumerable applications of the fundamental principle that all surfaces take on the colors of the objects facing them, and this even includes the formation of the image on the retina (no. 101). In all probability this synthesis was suggested by the mirror, the body most endowed with the ability to reflect and the "ideal eye."

angles : That is, in the language of the time, the perpendicular. The sentence does not imply an equality in the angles of incidence and of reflection.

Page 114

the fire : The symbolic relation between the four elements and the four "elementary" colors is a traditional one and is in no way meant as a precept to the painter.

of fire : see the note to *outside*, p. 218.

will : The invention of a simple mechanism that can deduce and present all the gradations of possible combinations of colors and which presents a possibility for a strict classification of the components of each shade is characteristic of Leonardo. However, the confusion between colored light and coloring matter makes it useless for the painter.

purple : The precise meaning of the Italian word, *biffa*, is uncertain.

shadows : The criteria for the "beauty" of a color are its brilliance and its depth.

Page 116

high : *Forti* in the manuscript is probably an error made by the copyist and should read *posti*.

color : By playing on the metaphor of illumination for knowledge, the text, which cannot be translated in all its implications, intentionally stresses the contrast between the background that is in darkness and the buildings detached from it. Although the equating of light and knowledge is profoundly rooted in earlier traditions, Leonardo gives it a depth that is uniquely his own.

Page 117

strikes : The force referred to is the wind and the part farthest from it is the base of the trunk.

Page 118

shadow : A similar observation appeared in the Treatise on Painting (now lost) which the doctor and physicist Giovanni Fontana wrote about 1430-1450 and dedicated to the Venetian painter Jacopo Bellini. We hear of it in a chance reference in a book on all natural things, published in 1544 under the name of Pompilius Azalus, though it is actually by Giovanni Fontana himself. The significance of this detail becomes apparent when one considers that Florentine painters and thinkers showed little interest in such observations at a time when Venetian painters were not only well aware of them but also applied them to their work. What one might call the Venetian side of Leonardo should be taken into account.

Page 120

distributed : They form equal angles.

horizontal : The text has : "directed toward the eye."

painter : His constant desire for unity among optical phenomena keeps Leonardo from seeing the distinction between colored matter and colored light familiar today.

process : Leonardo is here probably referring to the fact that, contrary to the experiment described in the preceding entry, the rainbow is formed on the floor and its position does not change when the spectator moves.

Page 122

beryl : That is, a magnifying glass ; beryls were used for this purpose.

Page 123

dead : A. Chastel, "Le Baroque et la mort," *Actes du Congrès d'Études humanistes*, Venice, 1954.

abbreviators : Qu. An. I, 4v.

dies : E. Belt, *Leonardo the Anatomist*, Lawrence, Kan., 1955 ; C. D. O'Malley and J. B. de C. M. Saunders, *Leonardo da Vinci on the Human Body*, New York, 1952.

Page 124

shows : Qu. An. III, 8r.

pig : An. A, 3r.

whole : See CU, 105r, McMahon, no. 286.

like : See CU, 48r, McMahon, no. 111.

Page 125

decorum : The book on the Art of Composition mentioned by Leonardo (CU, 60v, McMahon, no. 249) either has been lost or was never written.

Page 126

excellence : According to a statement he made in 1517 to De Beatis, secretary of the Cardinal of Aragon, Leonardo had dissected thirty bodies in the course of his studies.

these : That is, by dissecting them.

justification : This statement on the relation between the soul and the body is aimed at those who opposed the direct study of the body through anatomy.

Page 129

opposite : See illustration, p. 127.

architecture : The *De Architectura*, by Marcus Vitruvius Pollio (first century B. C.) was known during the Middle Ages and widely read during the Renaissance. In this passage Leonardo bases himself on the antique text and adds many details. The drawing is Leonardo's own invention although it follows tradition in inscribing the figure in a square and a circle. The attempt to establish a simple relation between the limbs, and the idea that the perfectly formed human body is the "model" for architecture are also traditional themes. In this context it is significant that the body is the source for medieval and Renaissance units of measurement and Leonardo plays on these double meanings. The only one that could not be rendered in English was the cubit (called elbow) which is usually the distance from the elbow to the tip of the middle finger.

buildings : He is referring to the fact that four, six, and twenty-four are common ratios in antique buildings and that the module is taken from man, i. e. the palm, cubit foot, pace, etc.

Page 130

muscular : Muscoli in the manuscript has been amended to read *muscolosi.*

Page 135

sensations : These two fragments of quick but precise lists established about 1489-1490 the investigations that were to lead to the anatomy which, in turn, was the foundation necessary to the physiology, the analysis of movements, and the revised physiognomy.

Page 136

axis : Here as in the following passage this inaccurate formulation refers to the plane perpendicular to the ground that cuts through the foot carrying the man's weight.

opposite : A partially erased sketch shows a man standing with one leg stretched forward.

Page 137

house : The anecdote is an adaptation of the one told by Pliny about the passion inspired by the Cnidian Venus *(Historia Naturalis,* XXXVI, 4, 9).

Page 140

man : There is nothing ridiculous or obsolete in conceiving of painting in terms of pantomime. One need only think of the silent movies.

Page 141

loudly : The text as cited in Richter reads *e poi fare* but should probably be amended to read *e poi forte.*

straggling : Despite his concern with careful observation of detail and his faith in empiricism, Leonardo is able to think of the expressive figure in terms of its conveying ideas, that is as hieroglyphs of the emotions. The wealth of plastic and dramatic gestures is more important than the causal truth subordinated here to what the philosophers call the " realism of universals. "

Page 146

hips : Leonardo here seems to allude to the fashion of wearing close-fitting tights that were often flesh colored.

Page 148

example : An. A, 4r (W 19003) : (the origins of the sea are the opposite of the origins of the blood).

Page 149

Cosmography : Ptolemy's *Geographia* was published in Ulm in 1482 and in Rome in 1490.

Page 152

infinity : To this scale of the four elements, in the order of their increasing subtlety, is joined, through a daring extrapolation, a fifth : the spirit. Impacts and impetuses move faster and farther as the medium is lighter, and thought is no more than a wave produced in the mind by a sensation. The extreme naturalism of this passage takes a stand oposed to Platonic doctrine and goes so far as to look for a confirmation in the resistance that the concept of infinity finds in our thoughts. Leonardo had formulated the analogy of the transmission of energy through circular diffusion elsewhere (no. 123), which makes it possible to complete an enigmatic sentence here : The impact of fire on fire, carrying farther than sound, is light.

stream : Unhesitatingly Leonardo

presents as observation something that is clearly a mental image. At the same time it is a fine example of Leonardo's method, a method in which formal analogies play the same part as the abstract formulas to which phenomena were reduced did in the physics of the next age.

Page 154

sphere : That is, above the air.

Page 156

obscured : The " veiled " light illuminates better because it does not throw shadows.

veiled : Until the time of the Impressionists, painters continued to be confronted with the dilemma Leonardo presents here when they painted figures in direct sunlight. Either the painter had to falsify or he had to paint harsh shadows and confused reflections that gave the figures a shockingly motley appearance. Leonardo himself found means of giving his figures indoor lighting : *The Mona Lisa* is placed inside a loggia, *The Virgin of the Rocks* inside a grotto, *Ginevra Benci* is sheltered by juniper trees. In the *Madonna and Child with St. Anne* he chose to falsify.

Page 158

hips : Leonardo carefully follows these precepts in *The Mona Lisa.* She turns toward and imaginary visitor — actually the spectator — who is supposed to have entered the open loggia in which she is sitting. A 90° turn is broken down into successive stages : hips, shoulders, neck, eyes.

Page 160

Riddles : Most of the riddles are stated in the future tense and in their style imitate prophecies and, moreover, in Leonardo's manuscripts they are entitled prophecies. He thus plays with the idea of how terrifying or mysterious things may sound when given an arbitary meaning dependent on one of their formal aspects.

Page 164

Leo X : The anecdote is related by Vasari, see p. 23 and A. Piloty, *La Découverte de Jean Van Eyck et l'évolution du procédé de la peinture à l'huile,* Paris, 1941.

x-rays : M. Hours, " La Peinture de Léonard vue au laboratoire, " *L'Amour de l'art,* XXXI, 1953, nos. 67-69.

Page 165

rule : The rule of aerial perspective.

Page 166

painted : After all Leonardo's observations on the effects of air, distance, and light, such a precept is most surprising. It seems to hark back to Cennini's advice to place a stone on a table in order to paint a mountain " from life. " Leonardo was probably intrigued by the ingenious device of using the leaf whose color was to be imitated as the palette, and allowed it as an aid for painters who were unsure of their own judgment ; nonetheless, he here ignores the relativity in which he has expressed such a firm belief.

leaves : The manuscript is not clear and in place of *laurel leaves* it is possible to read *gold leaf,* an interpretation preferred by McMahon.

color : In choosing an example of the reflection of one body on another of the same material, Leonardo overlooks the fact that this definition of true color depends on a vicious circle.

Page 167

nature : This fragment shows the extent to which Leonardo struggled with the question of true color and how far he involved himself in contradictions. At the beginning he postulates a light without color and the absence of all disturbing reflections. But then, remembering that there is no light without any color since daylight reflects the sky, he changes his mind. In the experiment with the cloth on the mountain top he implicitly admits by his choice of the color blue that the " true " or " natural " color of an object does not exist unless it is " revealed " by colored light. Leonardo expresses the inevitable objection in the form of an example : How can one say that the red light of the sunset that tinges all things with a strange color reveals the " true " color of the pink cloth ? He replies that by definition a color is " true " when it is most beautiful, that is, most saturated ; and that is an admission of a deadlock.

eye : It is doubtful that Leonardo knew how to determine the supposed distance by means of a drawing in perspective. Even if he did, the last sentence is still inaccurate in the strictest sense since he does not take the scale of the painting into consideration. The possiblity arises that this fragment should be understood as a theoretical requirement always to coordinate scale and size in such a way that miniatures, for example, are seen from a distance. This rule soon leads to absurdities, especially in the case of frescoes. More probably Leonardo here was the victim of his need to base scales, like everything else, on absolute agreements.

approach it : Of the vanishing point of two parallel lines, the horizon.

approach it : Since there is no reason why an object in the foreground should be of a "simple color " rather than whitish or grayish, Leonardo here requires an " arrangement " of things to achieve the most beautiful " brilliance " of his theory.

reflections : Whenever Leonardo has written "shadow" in this passage, the word has been rendered as "reflection." The substitution would be permissible in Leonardo's eyes.

Page 168

perspective : At the time this passage was written (ca. 1492) it had not yet occurred to Leonardo that there could be any system of perspective other than the one generally taught.

form : As though seen from directly in front.

perspective : Through the foreshortening of the parts of the wall farthest away.

Page 169

columns : This critical analysis of flat perspective was written before Leonardo had found any replacement for it other than a kind of anamorphosis in which the central point of view is still retained. He here recognizes a new limit of the " science of the visible " due to the fact that the conditions of perspective vision and the conditions under which a painting is seen do not coincide. His solution is a double compromise : 1. to act as if all the parts of the representation were seen from straight in front, that is, to correct the flat perspective where it distorts objects too much, such as at the edges. 2. to choose a point of view that is far enough away so that the distortions due to the inadequate system of perspective become negligible. But Leonardo realizes and proves by the example of the colonnade, that these corrections do not guarantee the spectator total freedom of movement.

Page 170

shadow : Here Leonardo takes a definite stand : the errors made by the retina should not be copied.

distance : The first illusion occurs because in normal binocular vision we automatically rectify the diminution in perspective theoretically perceived ; but this does not occur when we look at a painting because there is no automatic accommodation of the eye as it moves from the foreground to the background. As to the second, the answer is that painted objects seen close up appear to be enlarged because they are entirely on one plane as though they had turned their receding sides forward. Optical corrections are possible but Leonardo does not say whether he expects them or whether he prefers the absolute precision of the theoretical construction. The passage that follows presents the same kind of problem.

us : This well-known optical illusion results from the conflict between the color perspective (falsified by the mist) and the linear perspective. The object is believed to be larger than it is because it appears farther away.

Page 171

do : The tiny opening concentrates the daylight on a small work area.

work : Here Leonardo obviously is referring to the artist's regular work, and especially when the model is in the studio.

abcd : On the right in the drawing on p. 172.

bench : On the left in the drawing on p. 172 the panel or canvas (marked with a cross) is held at the appropriate height by means of a system of pulleys. The picture is slid into a flat box *(abcd* in the drawing on the right) which goes through the floor and continues along the wall into the room below (see drawing on the left). A man in the studio may sit on the upper part of this flat box. The handles of the pulley system hang suspended.

Page 173

stone : Some scholars consider Leonardo the inventor of pastels.

negative : In the manuscript Leonardo has printed a leaf in this manner. The instructions appear a little farther along, which suggests that Leonardo got them from oral traditions which he perhaps worked out and improved.

Page 174

choose : The reading *aloe cavallino* for *aole camelino* in the manuscript is generally accepted and the only correct meaning. Aloe caballine or the 3rd aloe is the residue of the distilled tree.

yellow : The directions here and in the next two passages are for the preparation of panels that were not only used for painting in tempera but also for a long time for oil painting.

bend : The original text is not clear. The interpretation follows McMahon (no. 984).

Page 178

transparent : By greasing it.

body : The text reads : " the above-mentioned body," referring to the preceding entry (McMahon, no 667; CU 223r-v).

smaller : The text reads : " that the larger angle mentioned above is double the smaller, " (McMahon, *loc. cit.).*

color : The powdered colors, which indicates that they were mixed before they were prepared with tempera or oil.

grain : The lighting of the sides of a polyhedron is, of course, a function of the angles the different sides make with the incident light. Leonardo's solution to this problem corresponds to his bend for " mechanical " or " practical " solutions though it is a little naïve. In fact, he was not really certain that the color scale thus obtained corresponded to the proportions of the colors as they were mixed (see no. 299).

Page 182

badly : These remarks on sketching find their conclusion in the discovery of the *non finito* (the unfinished) and the fascination it exercises which is the subject of the last chapter of the Treatise.

demonstrations : On painting as mathematics, see the Introduction, pp. 32-35 and nos. 15-18.

Page 185

changeable : By extension, and in order to show that the spectator is at the same level as the figures in the foreground, the horizon usually has been put at approximately their eye level. Leonardo follows this rule in the *St. Jerome, The Last*

Supper, The Madonna and Child with St. Anne, and *The Mona Lisa.* For a more thorough discussion see no. 136.

criticism : That the spectator has to stand at the place the composition assigns to him is one of the results of plane perspective and one of its weaknesses that Leonardo frequently condemns. As a consequence frescoes on the upper parts of walls unavoidably have to be painted *di sotto in sù* (i. e. as seen from below). Later, in 1573, this question is the subject of a famous discussion that centered on the relief for the tympanum of one of the side portals of the Cathedral of Milan. It is not certain, however, that Leonardo here had in mind the supposed necessity of having precisely the same point of view for the real spectator and the imaginary one of the work of art that is placed high up. The systematic application of such a principle results in only too obvious difficulties which, for example, Leonardo had not cared to take on in *The Last Supper,* although it is relatively high up on the wall. More likely, this passage should be interpreted as a statement against the distortion of perspective that occurs in all painting seen from below. A figure with normal proportions painted on a frieze just below the ceiling appears foreshortened and squashed. Therefore, the reason the artist should place himself lower than his model is not to draw it in the perspective appropriate to its being seen from below but to take into consideration the amount of flattening that occurs and compensate for it by a counter distortion. This is a classic rule, already attributed to the masters of antiquity — and rightly so — and one not unfamiliar to Renaissance thought.

point of view : The ideal one being a hole in a screen, as it is for anamorphosis.

praiseworthy : In compositions in perspective that make use of great distances the apparent diminution of the objects is reduced. Therefore, the spectator's moving about does not create such detrimental conflicts in the illusion, particularly if he remains within the painting's main axis. The rest of the passage explains rather lengthily that this conflict always comes from the speed with which the size of the objects is reduced in depth. A spectator who is too far away from the painting will feel that they decrease too quickly in the painting, while one who is too close to it will think the opposite. In *The Last Supper* a part of this problem is avoided because all the figures are in the foreground.

Page 186

supporting them : Possano (retained by McMahon) is here amended to read *posano.*

Page 192

hypocrites : See note to page 200.

things : Seventeenth century painters took this advice literally and painted fantastic walls or made use of the veins in marble (J. Baltrusaitis, *Aberrations. Quatre essais sur la légende des formes,* "Pierres imaginées," Paris, 1957).

fullness : E. Gombrich, "Conseils de Léonard sur les esquisses de tableaux," *Études d'Art* (L'Art et la pensée de Léonard de Vinci), Algiers, nos. 3-10, 1953-54.

subjective : J. Gantner, "Formen des Unvollendeten in der neueren Kunst," *Schicksale des Menschenbildes,* Bern, 1958, pp. 105-136; and *Leonardos Visionen von der Sintflut und vom Untergang der Welt,* Bern, 1958.

Page 195

ourselves : Literally, "that the soul which rules and governs the body is that which makes our judgment before it is actually our judgment." Thus "our actual judgment" merely ratifies what the soul submits to it. The whole passage is clearly inspired by the type of Platonic thought standard in the intellectual atmosphere of Florence in which Leonardo was educated. But as usual with Leonardo, this tradition is here accompanied by observation and consequently enriched and modified : This passage describes in a positive manner, is suported by an incontrovertible fact, and summarily analyzes the intervention of the unconscious in the painter's activity.

mistaken : In other words, because the soul has fashioned in flesh the body it inhabits, according to its leanings, it is natural that later, obeying the same leanings, it will give a similar appearance to the imaginary figures it fashions on the canvas.

Page 196

art : Leonardo did not stop with this program but drew up several others. This one, however, is the most original and the most characteristic for two reasons : first, because he begins with a theoretical study, something no one thought of doing before the age of the academies ; second, because of the sequence. The usual course of study could be reduced to three clearly distinct steps : copying drawings and paintings, drawing from plaster casts and reliefs, drawing from nature. The apprentice was taught by first being permitted to help the master in the most inferior tasks and only gradually with more important work. In contrast, Leonardo proposes theory and practice, study after nature and after the masters, that is, elements that balanced and complemented each other before the artist had reached maturity and independence.

shadow : This note, which seems to bait an argument against official Florentine and Roman taste, poses two problems that were of fundamental importance at the end of the fifteenth century. Although there are a good number of drawings by Leonardo that are derived from antique models (especially profiles taken from coins and equestrian statues), no studies from reliefs comparable to those of Ghirlandaio or Filippino Lippi are known. In respect to the conflict of outline and form, the artist's whole development and effort is involved in it.

Page 197

proportions : On these methods see also nos. 307 and 309.

order : For the beginning of this passage see no. 230.

works : To aim at a large production alone was enough to disqualify the opponent.

nature : Which would permit him to paint everything *di maniera* without the use of a model.

Page 198

blue : The extensive use of gold and blue pigments, the two most expensive materials, was very much to the taste of Gothic art and inappropriate to working from a model. Furthermore, it was a typical concession to the pretentions of ignorant clients. Cf. the anecdote Vasari relates in his Life of Cosimo Roselli about the prize Sixtus IV had promised to award to the best work in the Sistine Chapel (1482). Cosimo Roselli, aware of his shortcomings, made profuse use of gold and blue, and the Pope was very pleased though the others painters laughed at him.

things : A mirror could also be used for this purpose, see nos. 71 and 72.

Page 199

weakness : The copyist of the Codex Urbinas wrote *materia* for which the translation " you show of what stuff you are made " has been suggested. It is more likely, however, that the word should be *miseria*, " a fault to be hidden, " or " a shameful weakness, " and the two words look very much alike in Leonardo's handwriting.

Page 200

more : Leonardo here seems to be railing against the *piagnone*, the members of the extreme religious movement to which Savonarola belonged, who were also called " hypocrites " by their opponents. They must have denounced his working on Sundays and holidays. He replies with great haughtiness that the true spirit of religion is that of the artist.

Page 203

strength : This passage takes up again the theme of no. 338 and completes it.

same : This optical trick, so typical of Leonardo, may have been thought up for a feast.

Page 204

facility : This discussion once again shows how closely Leonardo pays attention to " obscure perceptions. " Moreover, he deduces a strict, ascetic rule from them that is to make each stage of his work conscious. The last sentence sums up his underlying principle.

memory : This exercise is based on the selective value of memory and complements the warning against the mechanization of memory, see no. 335.

Page 205

difficulty : The exactness of memory is a function of a previously acquired framework. This observation and the final entry help one to see the value of the physiognomic studies that are often called caricatures.

imagine : There is a certain similarity to some precepts of Chinese painting (Sung Dynasty, eleventh century) in urging the artist to daydream. It is to be understood in relation to the *componimento inculto* (the informed sketch), which is the subject of the following passage. The accusation that Botticelli left his landscapes in the state of mere stains on walls (no. 88) once more emphasizes that disorder had no right to exist except as an aspect of the perfect clarity that everything should approach.

effects : This concept can best be illustrated by Leonardo's own cartoons, particularly the one for *The Madonna and Child with St. Anne.* The purpose of such an informal composition is to leave the painter completely free to vary the forms. It is the final blow to pure outline. And from this point of view it constitutes a revolution in Florentine painting, and in Italian art in general. Finally, as is well known, the " stain " (interpreted as universal vision) takes a central position in modern art theories, such as those of Benedetto Croce and Julius von Schlosser.

Printed Editions of Leonardo's Writings

All of the more than fifty manuscript copies of the Treatise on Painting *ultimately derive from the Codex Urbinas (Vat., lat. 1270), but none is as complete and many are avowedly simplified. Several manuscripts were compiled in the seventeenth century for Cassiano del Pozzo who wanted to have the Treatise published; one of these versions based on the Codex Urbinas was in part revised on the basis of original texts. The most outstanding manuscript in this group is Ms. H 228 in the Biblioteca Ambrosiana and seems to have been the one used by Raphael Du Fresne for his edition (Paris, 1561) which appeared in a French translation by Paul Fréart de Chambray the same year. This edition took the place of the manuscript tradition and gave rise to a number of later editions that do no more than repeat it: In Italian: Pavia, 1670; Naples, 1723; Naples, 1733; Florence, 1792 (with drawings copied by St. della Bella); Milan, 1804; Perugia, 1805. In French: Paris, 1716. In English: London, 1721, London, 1802. In German: Nuremberg, 1724. In Spanish: Madrid, 1784.*

Guglielmo Manzi's rediscovery of the Codex Urbinas, published in 1817, changed the situation completely. The few editions published thereafter were based on it. Then, in 1882, H. Ludwig published an annotated edition accompanied by a German translation (Leonardo da Vinci: Das Buch von der Malerei, *(Quellenschriften für Kunstgeschichte, vols. XV-XVIII, Vienna, 1882). A French adaptation of it was put out by Péladan in two volumes,* Traité de la Peinture, *and* Traité du Paysage, *Paris, 1910. A facsimile copy of the Codex Urbinas,* Treatise on Painting by Leonardo Da Vinci, *with an English translation by A. Philip McMahon and an introduction by Ludwig H. Heydenreich, was published by Princeton University Press in two volumes, 1956.*

A systematic classification of known manuscripts and printed editions, with a discussion of their interrelation and a list of lost collections known from sources, was compiled by Kate Trauman Steinitz, Leonardo da Vinci's Trattato della Pittura, a Bibliography, *Copenhagen, 1958.*

An important collection of Leonardo's writings, not limited to Melzi's Treatise, has been published by J. P. Richter, The Literary Works of Leonardo da Vinci, *2 vols. 2nd ed. London and New York, 1939. It consists of critical introductions, an annotated Italian text and an English translation. Another English translation is E. MacCurdy,* The Notebooks of Leonardo da Vinci, *London, 1939, New York, 1958. Italian editions include G. Fumagalli,* Leonardo uomo senza lettere, *Florence, 1st. ed. 1938, 2nd ed. 1952; A. M. Brizio,* Scritti scelti di Leonardo da Vinci, *Turin, 1952.*

The best works of a more general nature for convenient consultation are L. H. Heydenreich, Leonardo da Vinci, *Basel & New York, 1954; K. Clark,* Leonardo da Vinci, An Account of his Development as an Artist, *Cambridge, 1939, reprinted 1952. For more extensive Bibliographies see McMahon,* op. cit, *and A. Chastel,* Art et humanisme à Florence au temps de Laurent le Magnifique, *Paris, 1959.*

Table of Manuscripts

Abbreviation	*Name*	*Place*	*Date*
CU	Codex Urbinas, lat. 1270	Rome, The Vatican	16th century copy
CA	Codex Atlanticus	Milan, Biblioteca Ambrosiana	1483-1518
BN 2038	Ashburnham I	Paris, Institut de France	1492
W	(Drawings)	Windsor Castle, Royal Library	
An. A	Anatomical notebook A	Windsor Castle, Royal Library	
An. B	Anatomical notebook B	Windsor Castle, Royal Library	1489-1516
Qu. An.	Anatomical notebook Qu. An.	Windsor Castle, Royal Library	
A	Ms. A	Paris, Institut de France	ca. 1492
B	Ms. B	Paris, Institut de France	ca. 1488-1489
C	Ms. C	Paris, Institut de France	ca. 1490
D	Ms. D	Paris, Institut de France	1508
E	Ms. E	Paris, Institut de France	1513-1514
F	Ms. F	Paris, Institut de France	1508-1509
G	Ms. G	Paris, Institut de France	ca. 1510-1516
H^{1-3}	Ms. H^{1-3}	Paris, Institut de France	1493-1494
I^{1-2}	Ms. I^{1-2}	Paris, Institut de France	1497-1499
L	Ms. L	Paris, Institut de France	1497, 1502-1503
M	Ms. M	Paris, Institut de France	before 1500
VA I^2	Forster Bequest, Ms. I^2	London, Victoria and Albert Museum	ca. 1489
VA II^{1-2}	Forster Bequest Ms. II^{1-2}	London, Victoria and Albert Museum	1495-1497
VA III	Forster Bequest Ms. III	London, Victoria and Albert Museum	1490-1493
Leic.		Holkham Hall, Earl of Leicester	1505-1506
Ar.	Ms. Arundel, no. 263	London, British Museum	1504, 1508, and after 1516
Triv.	Codex Trivulziano	Milan, Castello Sforzesco	1487-1490
Ven.		Venice, Accademia di Belle Arti	1511 and others

Table of Paintings

No.	Date	Work	Documented and known	Documented but lost; no certain copy known	Documented but lost; copies known	Not known whether executed	Attributed; not documented but generally accepted	Attributed; not documented and uncertain
1.	ca. 1470	Rotella (painted shield).		*				
2.	1473-1475	Angel on the left in the *Baptism of Christ* by Verrochio, Florence, Uffizi.	*					
3.	1473-1475	*Annunciation,* Florence, Uffizi.					*	
4.	1473-1475	*Madonna with the Vase,* Munich, Ältere Pinakothek.					*	
5.	1473-1475	*Madonna with the Pomegranate,* Washington, National Gallery, Kress Collection.						*
6.	1475-1478	*Annunciation,* predella panel, Paris, Louvre.					*	
7.	1478	*Madonna Benois,* Leningrad, Hermitage.					*	
8.	ca. 1478	Altarpiece for the Chapel of St. Bernard, Florence, Palazzo Vecchio.				*		
9.	ca. 1478	*Madonna with the Cat,* known from drawings.				*		
10.	1478-1480	*Portrait of Ginevra de' Benci,* Vaduz, Liechtenstein Collection.	*					
11.	ca. 1480	*St. Jerome,* Rome, Vatican Galleries.					*	
12.	ca. 1480	*Adam and Eve,* Cartoon for a tapestry.				*		
13.	ca. 1480	*Madonna della Caraffa,* Collection of Pope Clement VII.		*				
14.	ca. 1480	*Head of Medusa,* Collection of the Dukes of Tuscany.		*				
15.	1481-1482	*Adoration of the Magi,* Florence, Uffizi.	*					

			Documented and known	Documented but lost; no certain copy known	Documented but lost; copies known	Not known whether executed	Attributed; not documented but generally accepted	Attributed; not documented and uncertain
16.	ca. 1483	*Madonna of the Rocks* (1st version), Paris, Louvre.	*					
17.	ca. 1483	*Madonna Litta,* Leningrad, Hermitage.					*	
18.	ca. 1483	*Cecilia Gallerani (Lady with the Ermine),* Krakow.	*				*	
19.	ca. 1485	*Madonna,* for Matthias Corvinus.				*		
20.	1485-1490	*Nativity,* for the Emperor Maximilian.				*		
21.	1485-1490	*La Belle Ferronnière,* Paris, Louvre.						*
22.	1485-1490	*Portrait of a Musician,* Milan, Biblioteca Ambrosiana.					*	
23.	1485-1490	*Portrait of a Lady in Profile,* Milan, Biblioteca Ambrosiana.						*
24.	1494-1498	24 scenes from Roman history, for a room in the Castello Sforzesco, Milan.				*		
25.	1495-1497	*Portrait of Lucrezia Crivelli.*		*				
26.	1495-1497	*Last Supper,* Milan, Refectory of Santa Maria delle Grazie.	*					
27.	ca. 1497	Altarpiece for a church in Brescia.				*		
28.	ca. 1497	*Christ Carrying the Cross,* known from a drawing, Venice, Academy.				*		
29.	ca. 1497	Decoration for the Sala delle Asse, Milan, Castello Sforzesco.	*					

No.	Date	Work	Documented and known	Documented but lost; no certain copy known	Documented but lost; copies known	Not known whether executed	Attributed; not documented but generally accepted	Attributed; not documented and uncertain
30.	1499	*Portrait of Isabella d'Este*, Cartoon, Paris, Louvre.	*				*	
31.	1500-1507	*Virgin and Child with St. Anne*, Paris, Louvre.	*					
32.	ca. 1501	*Madonna with the Yarn-reel.*			*			
33.	1503-1506	*Battle of Anghiari.*			*			
34.	ca. 1504	*Christ Child.*			*			
35.	ca. 1504	*Salvator Mundi*, known from drawings.				*		
36.	ca. 1504	*Mona Lisa*, Paris, Louvre.	*					
37.	1504-1506	*Leda.*			*			
38.	1506-1508	*Angel of the Annunciation.*			*			
39.	1506-1508	*Madonna of the Rocks* (2nd version), London, National Gallery.	*					
40-41.	1506-1510	Two Madonnas for Louis XII.		*				
42.	1506-1510	*Christ Child.*		*				
43.	after 1506	*Bacchus*, Paris, Louvre.		*				*
44.	after 1506	Painting for Pope Leo X.				*		
45.	after 1506	*Portrait of Costanza d'Avalos.*		*				
46.	after 1506	*Flora and Pomona*, Melzi Collection.		*				
47.	ca. 1515	*St. John the Baptist*, Paris, Louvre.	*					

It has been possible to identify tentatively several works documented by early writers with existing paintings. These appear under two headings (see nos. 18, 30, and 43).

Chronological Table

	LEONARDO'S LIFE	HIS WORKS	HIS PERIOD	THE RENAISSANCE
1452	Birth of Leonardo, at Vinci, near Florence.			
1453			Fall of Constantinople.	
1456				Argyropoulos begins to teach Greek in Florence.
1459				The Platonic Academy formed in Florence.
1464			Death of Cosimo Il Vecchio de'Medici.	
1467				Birth of Erasmus of Rotterdam.
1469	Leonardo an apprentice in Verrocchio's workshop.		Lorenzo Il Magnifico comes to power in Florence.	Birth of Macchiavelli. Ferrarese school : frescoes in the Palazzo Schifanoia.
1472	Leonardo inscribed in the Corporation of St. Luke as an independent master.	Paints an angel in Verrocchio's *Baptism of Christ.*		
1473		Drawing of a landscape, dated August 5.		
1475				Birth of Michelangelo.
1476	Two anonymous denunciations accusing Leonardo of sodomy.			Antonella da Messina in Venice ; influences Giovanni Bellini.

	LEONARDO'S LIFE	HIS WORKS	HIS PERIOD	THE RENAISSANCE
1478		Commission for an altarpiece for the Chapel of St. Bernard in the Palazzo Vecchio.	The Pazzi Conspiracy. Lorenzo de' Medici subjugates the families opposing him.	Botticelli paints his *Primavera.*
1481		Commission for the *Adoration of the Magi*, Florence, Uffizi.		Landino writes his commentary on Dante's *Divine Comedy.* Several Florentine painters called to Rome to decorate the Sistine Chapel.
1482	Leonardo offers his services to Lodovico Il Moro ; leaves for Milan (exact date unknown).			Verrocchio in Venice for the casting of the statue of *Colleone.*
1483		Contract for the *Madonna of the Rocks* with the Confraternity of the Immaculate Conception, Milan, April 25.		
1484				Marsilio Ficino's Latin translation of Plato published.
1490	Directs feasts and pageants at court. First sketches out plan for the *Treatise.*	Scale model for the equestrian statue of Francesco Sforza ; work begins.		Pollaiuolo called to Rome.
1492			Death of Lorenzo Il Magnifico, April 9. Alexander VI, a Borgia, elected Pope, August 11. Columbus's departure on his first trip, August 12.	Ficino's translation of Plotinus published.
1493		Full-scale model of the horse for the equestrian statue of Francesco Sforza put on view in the Castello Sforzesco.	Maximilian I becomes Holy Roman Emperor.	

	LEONARDO'S LIFE	HIS WORKS	HIS PERIOD	THE RENAISSANCE
1494		The model of the statue completed.	Charles VIII of France campaigns in Italy. Fall of the Medici ; Savonarola rules Florence.	
1495-97		Paints the *Last Supper.*		Dürer in Italy.
1498		Plans the publication of his notebooks.	Louis XII becomes King of France. Savonarola burned ; Florence under a republican government.	
1499	Leaves Milan for Mantua.		Lodovico Il Moro deposed ; French rule in Milan. Cesare Borgia made Duke of Romagna.	Signorelli paints the frescoes in the Cathedral of Orvieto.
1500	Short visit to Venice. Returns to Florence.			Bramante arrives in Rome.
1501		Cartoon for the *Madonna and Child with St. Anne* exhibited in Florence.		Michelangelo in Rome ; makes the *Pietà.*
1502	Plans to go to Turkey. In the service of Cesare Borgia as military engineer.			
1503	Returns to Florence.	Commission for the *Battle of Anghiari.*	Death of Alexander VI ; fall of Cesare Borgia. Julius II elected to the Papacy. France suffers defeats in Italy.	Titian in Venice.

	LEONARDO'S LIFE	HIS WORKS	HIS PERIOD	THE RENAISSANCE
1504	Serves on the committee to determine the best place for Michelangelo's *David* (January).	Probable date of the *Mona Lisa.*		Raphael arrives in Florence. Michelangelo finishes the David. Giorgione in Venice.
1505				Michelangelo goes to Rome (March).
1506	Summoned to Milan in June by Charles d'Amboise, Governor of the city.	Stops work on the *Battle of Anghiari.*		Dürer's second trip to Italy. Bramante commissioned to rebuild the Vatican and St. Peters's; Michelangelo commissioned to make the tomb of Julius II. Discovery of the *Laocoön.*
1507	Brief stay in Florence.	Plans to publish his notebooks.		Michelangelo's statue of Julius II, Bologna.
1508	Return to Milan.		The League of Cambrai is formed.	Michelangelo begins work on the Sistine Ceiling.
1509			The French defeat the Venetians at Agnadello. Henry VIII becomes king of England.	Raphael commissioned to decorate the Vatican *Stanze.*
1510				Erasmus writes *Praise of Folly.* Death of Giorgione.
1511			The Holy League is formed.	Raphael finishes the *Camera della Segnatura.*
1512			French victory at Ravenna. The Medici return to rule in Florence.	Michelangelo finishes the Sistine Ceiling.

	LEONARDO'S LIFE	HIS WORKS	HIS PERIOD	THE RENAISSANCE
1513	Arrives in Rome August 24, accompanied by Melzi, Salai, and two servants ; in the service of Giuliano de' Medici, brother of Leo X ; has accomodations in the Belvedere.		Death of Julius II. Leo X, a Medici, elected to the Papacy. The French leave Italy.	Machiavelli writes *The Prince* and works on his *Discourses*.
1514				Raphael begins work on the *Farnesina*. Death of Bramante.
1515			Giuliano de' Medici dies in January. Francis I becomes King of France ; is victorious in the Marignano campaign ; new conquests by the Milanese.	
1516	Leaves for Florence in the fall.		Charles V becomes king of Spain.	Ariosto publishes *Orlando Furioso*. Sir Thomas More's *Utopia* published. Erasmus translates the *New Testament*.
1517	In Amboise in April ; at the manor de Cloux in May. Visited by Cardinal Luigi d'Aragona, October 10.		Luther nails his 95 theses against indulgences on the church door.	
1519	Writes his will, April 23 ; dies, May 2, at Cloux.		Charles V crowned emperor. Cortez lands in Mexico.	
1520			Luther burns the Papal bull excommunicating him (Christmas).	Dürer in the Netherlands.
1521			Death of Leo X.	

List of Illustrations

Page 22. *Studies for the Dome of the Cathedral of Milan.* Milan, Biblioteca Ambrosiana, CA 22r. (René-Jacques).

Page 24. *War Machines.* Turin, Biblioteca Reale. (René-Jacques).

Page 25. Boltraffio, *Portrait of Francesco Melzi,* Milan, Biblioteca Ambrosiana. (Anderson-Giraudon).

Page 28. *Sheet of Technical Designs.* Milan, Biblioteca Ambrosiana, CA 358v. (Biblioteca Ambrosiana).
Two sketches cut out of this sheet. Windsor Castle, Royal Library, top : no. 12461; bottom : no. 12720.

Page 29. *Studies for Interlace Ornament.* Milan, Biblioteca Ambrosiana, CA 68v. (René-Jacques).

Page 39. *Musical Instrument,* in the shape of a fantastic animal. Paris, Institut de France, BN 2037, fol. c. (René-Jacques).

Page 40. *Cross-sections of a Head.* Windsor Castle, Royal Library, no. 12603r.

Page 41. *Portrait of a Musician.* Milan, Biblioteca Ambrosiana. (Anderson-Giraudon).

Page 44. *Study of the Veins of the Leg.* Windsor Castle, Royal Library, Qu. An. V 3v.

Page 45. *The Human Heart.* Windsor Castle, Royal Library, Qu. An. II 3v, 4r.

Page 51. *Storm Over an Alpine Valley.* Windsor Castle, Royal Library, no. 12409.

Page 52. *Flood,* from the series on *The End of the World.* Windsor Castle, Royal Library, no. 12382.

Page 53. *Knives,* derived from animal forms. Paris, Institut de France, BN 2037, f. d. (René-Jacques).
Mask and Imaginary Animal. Windsor Castle, Royal Library, no. 12367.

Page 54. *Studies of Cats and a Dragon,* Windsor Castle, Royal Library, no. 12363.

Page 55. *Studies in Comparative Anatomy.* Windsor Castle, Royal Library, no. 12625.

Page 59. *Description of Mount Taurus,* text and sketches. Milan, Biblioteca Ambrosiana, CA 145v a and b. (René-Jacques).

Page 64. *Studies for Battle Scenes.* Venice, Accademia di Belle Arti, no. 215. (René-Jacques).

Page 66. Drawing from the series on *The End of the World.* Windsor Castle, Royal Library, no. 12377.

Page 69. *Study for The Last Supper.* Windsor Castle, Royal Library, no. 12542. (René-Jacques).

Page 71. *Studies for The Last Supper : Head of Judas.* Windsor Castle, Royal Library, no. 12547 ; *Head of St. Philip,* Windsor Castle, Royal Library, no. 12551. (René-Jacques).

Page 72. *Mona Lisa,* detail, the hands. Paris, Louvre. (Giraudon).

Page 77. *The Annunciation,* detail, landscape. Florence, Uffizi. (Alinari-Viollet).

Page 78. Pollaiuolo, *Martyrdom of St. Sebastian,* London, National Gallery. (Anderson-Giraudon).
Botticelli, *The Annunciation.* Florence, Uffizi. (Alinari-Giraudon).

Page 80. Botticelli, *The Annunciation,* detail, landscape. Florence, Uffixi. (Alinari-Brogi-Giraudon).

Page 83. Italian School, fourteenth century, *Madonna and Child.* Florence, Uffizi. (Alinari-Giraudon).

Page 86. Verrocchio, *Study of a Head.* London, British Museum. (Anderson-Giraudon).

Page 87. Francesco di Simone, two pages of sketches. Paris, Louvre, Cabinet des dessins. (Giraudon).

Page 90. *Binocular Vision,* illustrations to the text. Paris, Institut de France, BN 2038 10r.

Page 91. *Mechanics of Vision,* text and illustrations. Paris, Institut de France, D 3r. (René-Jacques).

Page 94. *Madonna of the Rocks.* Paris, Louvre. (Giraudon).

Page 95. *Study of the Lighting of a Profile.* Windsor Castle, Royal Library, no. 12604r.
Study of the Length of Shadows. Paris, Institut de France, BN 2038 13v. (René-Jacques).

Page 97. Diagram accompanying no. 119. Rome, Vatican, CU 2r. (From McMahon).

Page 98. *Light and Shadow,* text and sketches. Paris, Institut de France, BN 2038 11r. (René-Jacques).

Page 103. *Perspective Study for the Adoration of the Magi.* Florence, Uffizi. (Anderson-Giraudon).

Page 104. *Diagram of the Position of the Horizon.* Rome, Vatican, CU 283v. (From McMahon).

Page 105. *Diagram of the Position of the Horizon.* Rome, Vatican, CU 284r. (From McMahon).
Diagram on Linear Perspective. Paris, Institut de France, E 16v. (From Pedretti).

Page 106. *"Accidental" Perspective.* Rome, Vatican, CU 139r. (From McMahon).

Page 107. *Anamorphosis : Head of a Child.* Milan, Biblioteca Ambrosiana, CA 35v. (From Pedretti).
Anamorphosis : The Eye. Milan, Biblioteca Ambrosiana, CA 35v. (From Pedretti).
Diagram of "Accidental" Perspective. London, British Museum, Ar. 62r. (From Pedretti).

Page 109. *Towers,* marginal sketch in a passage on aerial perspective. Paris, Institut de France, A 38r. (René-Jacques).

Page 110. *Chain of the Alps.* Windsor Castle, Royal Library, no. 1241 0.

Page 115. *Sketch of Trees,* Paris, Institut de France, E 18v.
Sketch of Trees. Paris, Institut de France, E 192.

Page 117. *Study for Trees.* Windsor Castle, Royal Library, no. 12431r.

Page 118. *Study of a Tree,* gone over by Cesare da Sesto. Windsor Castle, Royal Library, no. 12417. (René-Jacques).

Page 121. *Studies of Plants.* Windsor Castle, Royal Library, nos. 12427, 12422. (René-Jacques).

Page 124. *Anatomical Study,* text and sketches on movement. Windsor Castle, Royal Library, An. A 2r.

Page 127. *Comparisons of Lengths of Different Members.* Windsor Castle, Royal Library, no. 19133.
Geometric Scheme of the Proportions of the Head. Venice, Accademia di Belle Arti (Anderson-Viollet).

Page 128. *Virgin and Child with St. Anne,* detail, St. Anne's feet. Paris, Louvre. (Giraudon).

Page 131. *Study of Human Proportions.* Windsor Castle, Royal Library, no. 19132. (René-Jacques).

Page 132. *Proportions of the Human Figure,* after Vitruvius, Venice, Accademia di Belle Arti. (René-Jacques).
Proportions of the Face. Windsor Castle, Royal Library, no. 12606.

Page 133. *Studies of Noses.* Rome, Vatican, CU 108v. (From McMahon).

Page 134. *Studies of Shoulder Movements.* Windsor Castle, Royal Library, no. 12640.

Page 135. *Study of the Muscles.* Windsor Castle, Royal Library, no. 19014v.

Page 136. *Sketches Showing Balance and Movement.* Rome, Vatican, CU 105v. (From McMahon).

Studies of Movements. Windsor Castle, Royal Library, no. 12644r.

Page 137. *Sketches Showing Balance and Movement.* Rome, Vatican, CU 106r. (From McMahon).

Page 138. *Study of Facial Expressions.* Windsor Castle, Royal Library, no. 12495.

After Leonardo, *Study of a Mimic.* London, British Museum. (Anderson-Giraudon).

Page 139. *Grotesque Heads.* Windsor Castle, Royal Library, no. 12499.

Page 141. *Studies of Movements, Currents, and Eddies,* sketches and text. Paris, Institut de France, A 5 and 7. (Giraudon).

Page 143. *Chained Beggar,* costume study. Windsor Castle, Royal Library, no. 12573r.

Page 145. *Study of a Man of Importance.* Windsor Castle, Royal Library, no. 12582.

Page 146. *Costume Study.* Windsor Castle, Royal Library, no. 12576.

Page 149. *Comparative Study of Plant and Animal Forms.* Paris, Institut de France, I, 24v and 25r. (Giraudon).

Page 150. *Studies for Leda.* Windsor Castle, Royal Library, no. 12516.

Page 151. *Currents and Eddies in Water,* Windsor Castle, Royal Library, no. 12660v. *Currents and Eddies in the Blood Stream.* Windsor Castle, Royal Library, no. 19083v.

Page 152. *Studies of the Growth of Trees.* Paris, Institut de France, I[1] 12v. (René-Jacques).

Page 153. *War Machines and Shields.* Paris, École des Beaux-Arts. (René-Jacques).

Page 154. *Studies of Plants.* Windsor Castle, Royal Library, no. 12424. (René-Jacques).

Page 155. *Madonna of the Rocks,* detail, the Virgin's head. Paris, Louvre. (Giraudon).

Page 156. *St. Jerome.* Rome, Pinacoteca Vaticana. (Anderson-Giraudon).

Page 157. Botticelli, *Entombment,* detail. Milan, Museo Poldi-Pezzoli. (Anderson-Giraudon).

Page 158. Copy of a lost *Leda.* Rome, Galleria Borghese. (Anderson-Giraudon). *Study for the Leda,* drawing. Rotterdam, Boymans Museum. (Document Larousse).

Page 159. *Allegory,* probably for Cesare Borgia. Windsor Castle, Royal Library, no. 12406.

Page 160. *Rebus.* Windsor Castle, Royal Library, no. 12692r.

Page 163. *Interlaces,* detail, ceiling fresco. Milan, Castello Sforzesco, Sala delle Asse. (Alinari-Giraudon).

Page 166. *Study for the Angel in the Madonna of the Rocks.* Paris, Louvre. (Anderson-Giraudon).

Page 168. *Sketch of a Colonnade,* shown in anamorphosis with a fixed central point of view close up. Paris, Institut de France, A 41r. (René-Jacques).

Page 170. *Madonna of the Rocks,* detail, the Infant Jesus supported by the Angel. Paris, Louvre. (Giraudon).

Page 171. *Diagram showing lighting.* Paris, Institut de France, A 2r. (From Richter).

Page 172. *The Painter's Studio,* text and illustrations to no. 293. Paris, Institut de France, BN 2038, 10r. (René-Jacques).

Page 173. *Imprint of a Leaf.* Milan, Biblioteca Ambrosiana, CA 72v. (René-Jacques).

Page 175. *Portrait of Ginevra de' Benci.* Vaduz, Liechtenstein Collection.

Page 178. *Diagram Showing Foreshortenting of a Figure on a Curved Surface.* Paris, Institut de France, A 38v. *Lighting of a Many-Sided Figure.* Rome, Vatican, CU 223v. (From McMahon). *Spoons for Measuring Pigments.* Rome, Vatican, CU 224r. (From McMahon).

Page 179. *Mona Lisa,* detail, x-ray of the head. (Document Laboratoire du Louvre). *Mona Lisa.* Paris, Louvre. (Giraudon).

Credits : Plate facing page 142 by Draeger reproduced by permission of Gallimard, Galerie de la Pléiade ; plates facing 34, 114, 170, by Giraudon. Unless otherwise stated, the drawings at Windsor Castle are reproduced by the gracious permission of Her Majesty Queen Elizabeth II.

References to Entries

For the abbreviations referring to manuscripts, see p. 229.

The Projects

NOTATIONS CONCERNING THE TREATISES

1. On the 2nd of April, 1489 . . . W *19059r*
2. On the 23rd of April, 1490 . . . C *15v*
3. On the 1st of August, 1499 . . . CA *104r*
4. Begun by me . . . VA I *3r*
5. Begun, in Florence . . . Ar *1r*
6. This winter of 1510 . . . W *19016*
7. The "Treatise on Mechanics". . . W *19070v*
8. My Treatise on Voice . . . CA *287r*
9. Completed, the 7th of July, 1514 . . . CA *90v*
10. It seems to me that it must be my destiny . . . CA *66v*

AGAINST ABBREVIATORS

11. To criticize the supreme certainty . . . W *19084r*

REPLIES MADE TO FORESTALL CRITICS

12. If I do not quote . . . AC *117r*
13. Many believe they have the right . . .

The Paragone or Comparison of the Arts

Painting and Science

Painting, Music, and Poetry

Painting and Sculpture

Experience and Drawing

The Universal Program

The Principles

THE PAINTER QUESTIONS NATURE

THE SOVEREIGN SPIRIT: ATTENTION AND IMAGINATION

THE INFINITE SCOPE OF THE TASK

49. That everywhere there is something to learn. BN 2038 *31v*
50. That the painter is not praiseworthy unless he is versatile. BN 2038 *25v*
51. Of the variety of figures. G *5v*
52. *The infinite variety within a species.* CU *157r–v*
53. Variety among the people in narrative paintings. CU *59v–60r*
54. Ways of becoming versatile. G *5v*

The Great Themes: Man and Nature

TALES

55. *The frightful giant of Libya.* CA *311r*
56. The black face at first seems most horrible . . . CA *96v*
57. *The journey to the East.* CA *145r–v*
58. The Divisions of the Book. CA *169v*
59. The shape of Mount Taurus. CA *145v*
60. Structure and dimensions of Mount Taurus. CA *145v*

SCENES AND VISIONS

61. *The Island of Venus.* W *12591rv*
62. *Fossil of a sea monster.* AR *156r*
63. How to represent a battle. BN 2038 *31r–v*
64. Description of the Flood. W *12665r*
65. The Flood and its representation in painting. W *12665v*

NOTES ON HIS OWN PAINTINGS

66. *The Last Supper.* VA II *62v–63r*, VA II *3r*, VA II *6r*
67. *The Anghiari Battle.* CA *74r–v*

The Problems of the Painter

Leonardo as Critic

HOW TO JUDGE PAINTING

68. *The application of rules.* CA *221v*
69. *Criteria.* G *19r*
70. *All styles should be used.* CU *46v*
71. Why does one see a painting better . . . ? BN 2038 *31v*
72. *Judge with a mirror.* BN 2038 *24v*
73. *Painting and its elements.* CU *45v*
74. *The principal divisions of painting.* CU *50r*

NEEDS AND PREFERENCES

75. *Shadow versus drawing.* CU *133v*
76. *Shadow versus colors.* CU *72v*
77. *Multiplicity of beauty.* CU *51v*
78. Of not ornamenting figures . . . CU *60v*
79. How narrative pictures should not be . . . BN 2038 *8v*
80. Of judges of different beauties . . . CU *51v*
81. *Be natural.* CU *130v–131r*
82. *Against tours de force.* CU *59v*
83. Avoid profiles or sharp edges for objects. CU *46r–v*
84. *Of gracefulness.* BN 2038 *33v*

THE OPPOSING FACTIONS OF PAINTERS

85. *Personality in painters.* CU *32v–33r–v*
86. *Pros and cons of reflections.* CU *56r*

124. There is no difference... CA *204v*
125. *Visual pyramids and cones of light.* C *7r*
126. *Visual pyramids and cones of shadow.* CA *241v*

Applications of These Analogies :

127. *The projection of a shadow and perspective vision.* A *42v*
128. *Pyramids of light and visual pyramids.* BN 2038 *11r*

LINEAR PERSPECTIVE

The Elements :

129. *The basic science of light.* CA *203r*
130. Of the three kinds of perspective. BN 2038 *18r*
131. *Agreement between the three perspectives.* CU *238v*
132. *Definition of linear perspective.* A *3r*
133. The wall of glass. A *1v*
134. *How to determine the apex of the pyramid.* A *37v*
135. Why an object close to the eye has indistinct outlines. BN 2038 *23v*
136. What is the true location of the horizon. CU *283r-284r*

Diminution :

137. *Note taken from Euclid.* A *8v*
138. The degrees of diminution. A *8v*

The Systems :

139. *Spherical and flat perspective.* G *13v*
140. *The inconsistency of plane perspective.* E *16v*
141. *Classification of the perspectives.* E *16v*
142. *Against perspective with a fixed point of view.* E *16r*
143. *The three kinds of linear perspective.* Ar. *62r*
144. *Anamorphosis.* A *38r*

AERIAL PERSPECTIVE

Light and Forms :

145. *The diminishing visibility of objects.* G *53v*
146. *The law of diminishing visibility.* BN 2038 *12v*
147. *Aerial perspective of luminous bodies.* CA *126v*
148. *An illusion of aerial perspective.* L *77v*
149. *Proof that luminous bodies...* A *64v*
150. *The body and its background : contrast in light.* CA *126r*
151. *Contrast flattens.* C *23r*

Color Vision :

152. *The blue of distant views.* BN 2038 *25v*
153. At what distance from the eye... CU *63v*
154. Of the color of the atmosphere. Leic. *4r*
155. *Lighting and color.* CU *154r*
156. *Blue shadows.* F *75r*
157. *Colored lighting.* CU *192r*
158. Of the nature and of the crossing... W *19152r*
159. *Color and apparent size.* I^1 *17v*

Reflection :

160. *Reflections in water.* H^2 *76v*
161. *Splendor, luster, and color.* BN 2038 *32v*
162. *Luster.* H^2 *90v*
163. Of where there can be no luminous reflection. BN 2038 *14v*
164. *Colored reflections.* BN 2038 *33v*
165. *Optics as a general theory of reflections.* CU *191v-192r*

166. *Qualitative laws.* CU *58r*
167. *Quantitative laws.* CU *227v-228r*

Color :

168. *How to make a systematic table of colors.* CU *75v-76r*
169. *Harmony of colors.* CU *75v*
170. *Lighting favorable to each color.* CU *67r*
171. *Transparency.* CU *62v*
172. *Shades and values.* CU *67r*

LANDSCAPE AND PAINTING OUT-OF-DOORS

173. In what way one should paint a landscape. G *19v*
174. How to paint distant views. BN 2038 *18r*
175. Of the color of mountains. CU *77r-v*
176. *Landscapes at nightfall.* CU *151v*
177. *Trees.* Ar. *114r*
178. The smoke of the cities. G *22v*
179. The variations in the color of trees. G *24r*
180. Of opaque leaves . . . G *10v*
181. *Trees seen from below.* G *2v*
182. *Trees in the wind.* Ar. *277v*
183. *Study of mists.* CU *144r*
184. *An optical illusion caused by mists.* CU *147v*
185. *Clouds.* W *12388*
186. *Landscapes at dawn.* Ar. *169r*
187. Of meadows . . . G *20v*
188. *Vegetation in the mountains.* CU *236v-237v*
189. *Distribution of leaves.* G *33r*
190. *A botanical analysis for painters.* G *28r*
191. Trees. L *87v*

APPENDIX : THE RAINBOW

192. *Colored light and colored material.* W *19076r*
193. *The rainbow is not an objective phenomenon.* W *19150r*
194. *The rainbow is not a subjective phenomenon . . .* W *19150r*
195. *An optic phenomenon related . . .* E O'
196. *The conditions of the phenomena.* CU *286r*
197. *Iridescence.* W *19150r*

Man and the Emotions

MEASUREMENTS

The Anatomist at Work :

198. *The drawing as the digest . . .* QU. AN. I *13r*
199. O investigator of this machine . . . QU. AN. II *5v*
200. O man, thou who through my endeavor . . . AN. A *2r*
201. *Program for observation.* E *19v-20r*

The Canon :

202. *Canon of beauty and average stature.* CA *160r*
203. *Proportions of the face.* Ven. frame *33*
204. *Proportions of the foot.* W *19133v*
205. *Corresponding measurements in the human body.* W *19129r*
206. *Body measurements when kneeling or sitting.* W *19132r*
207. *The central axis of man when standing.* W *19136-9*
208. *Vitruvian man.* Ven. frame *29*

The Types :

209. *The law of consistency of type.* E *6v*
210. *The muscular type.* CU *116r*

Tricks, Techniques, and Processes

Advice on Working Methods

The Painter's Activity

All Painters Paint Themselves

Learning and Practice

Of the Painter's Ethics

Memory and Attention